# Pure Mathematics 3

CAMBRIDGE Advanced Level Mathematics

# Pure Mathematics 3

**Hugh Neill and
Douglas Quadling**

**Series editor** Hugh Neill

CAMBRIDGE
UNIVERSITY PRESS

PUBLISHED BY THE PRESS SYNDICATE OF THE UNIVERSITY OF CAMBRIDGE
The Pitt Building, Trumpington Street, Cambridge, United Kingdom

CAMBRIDGE UNIVERSITY PRESS
The Edinburgh Building, Cambridge CB2 2RU, UK
40 West 20th Street, New York, NY 10011-4211, USA
477 Williamstown Road, Port Melbourne, VIC 3207, Australia
Ruiz de Alarcón 13, 28014 Madrid, Spain
Dock House, The Waterfront, Cape Town 8001, South Africa

http://www.cambridge.org

First published 2000
Fifth printing 2003

Printed in the United Kingdom at the University Press, Cambridge

*Typefaces* Times, Helvetica        *Systems* Microsoft® Word, MathType™

*A catalogue record for this book is available from the British Library*

ISBN 0 521 78370 4  paperback

Cover image: Images Colour Library

# Contents

# Introduction

*Cambridge Advanced Level Mathematics* has been written especially for the OCR modular examination. It consists of one book or half-book corresponding to each module. This book is the third Pure Mathematics module, P3.

The books are divided into chapters roughly corresponding to syllabus headings. Occasionally a section includes an important result that is difficult to prove or outside the syllabus. These sections are marked with an asterisk (*) in the section heading, and there is usually a sentence early on explaining precisely what it is that the student needs to know.

Occasionally within the text paragraphs appear in *this type style*. These paragraphs are usually outside the main stream of the mathematical argument, but may help to give insight, or suggest extra work or different approaches.

References are made throughout the text to previous work in modules P1 and P2. It is expected that students still have access to these books in the classroom, even if they do not have a copy for their personal use.

Numerical work is presented in a form intended to discourage premature approximation. In ongoing calculations inexact numbers appear in decimal form like 3.456..., signifying that the number is held in a calculator to more places than are given. Numbers are not rounded at this stage; the full display could be either 3.456 123 or 3.456 789. Final answers are then stated with some indication that they are approximate, for example '1.23 correct to 3 significant figures'.

There are plenty of exercises, and each chapter contains a Miscellaneous exercise which includes some questions of examination standard. Some questions which go beyond examination requirements are marked by an asterisk. In the middle and at the end of the book there is a set of Revision exercises and there are two practice examination papers. The authors thank Lawrence Jarrett, Jean Matthews and Charles Parker, the OCR examiners who contributed to these exercises, and also Peter Thomas, who read the book very carefully and made many extremely useful and constructive comments.

The authors thank OCR and Cambridge University Press for their help in producing this book. However, the responsibility for the text, and for any errors, remains with the authors.

# 1 Trigonometry

This chapter takes further the ideas about trigonometry in module P1. When you have completed it, you should

- know the definitions, properties and graphs of secant, cosecant and cotangent, including the associated Pythagorean identities
- know the addition and double angle formulae for sine, cosine and tangent, and be able to use these results for calculations, solving equations and proving identities
- know how to express $a\sin\theta + b\cos\theta$ in the forms $R\sin(\theta\pm\alpha)$ and $R\cos(\theta\pm\alpha)$
- be able to use the notation for inverse functions, and know their domains and ranges, and their graphs.

## 1.1 Radians or degrees

All through your work in mathematics, you have probably thought of degrees as the natural unit for angle, but in P2 Chapter 15 a new unit, the radian, was introduced. This unit is important in differentiating and integrating trigonometric functions. For this reason, a new convention about angle will be adopted in this book.

If no units are given for trigonometric functions, you should assume that the units are radians, or that it doesn't matter whether the units are radians or degrees.

For example, if you see the equation $\sin x = 0.5$, then $x$ is in radians. If you are asked for the smallest positive solution of the equation, you should give $x = \frac{1}{6}\pi$. Remember,

$$\pi \,\text{rad} = 180°.$$

Identities such as $\cos^2 A + \sin^2 A \equiv 1$ and $\dfrac{\sin\theta}{\cos\theta} \equiv \tan\theta$, or the cosine formula $a^2 = b^2 + c^2 - 2bc\cos A$, are true whatever the units of angle. Formulae such as these, for which it doesn't matter whether the unit is degrees or radians, will be shown without units for angles.

If, however, it is important that degrees are being used, then notation such as $\cos A°$ and $\sin\theta°$ will be used. Thus one solution of the equation $\cos\theta° = -0.5$ is $\theta = 120$.

This may seem complicated, but the context will usually make things clear.

## 1.2 Secant, cosecant and cotangent

It is occasionally useful to be able to write the functions $\dfrac{1}{\cos x}$, $\dfrac{1}{\sin x}$ and $\dfrac{1}{\tan x}$ in shorter forms. These functions, called respectively the secant, cosecant and cotangent (written and pronounced 'sec', 'cosec' and 'cot') are not defined when the denominators are zero, so their domains contain holes.

The definitions of **secant** and **cosecant** are

$$\sec x = \frac{1}{\cos x}, \qquad \text{provided that } \cos x \neq 0,$$

$$\operatorname{cosec} x = \frac{1}{\sin x}, \qquad \text{provided that } \sin x \neq 0.$$

It is a little more complicated to define the cotangent in this way, since there are values of $x$ for which $\tan x$ is undefined. But you can use the fact that $\tan x = \dfrac{\sin x}{\cos x}$, so $\dfrac{1}{\tan x} = \dfrac{\cos x}{\sin x}$, except where the denominators are zero. This can be used as the definition of $\cot x$.

The **cotangent** is defined by

$$\cot x = \frac{\cos x}{\sin x}, \qquad \text{provided that } \sin x \neq 0.$$

Note that $\cot x = \dfrac{1}{\tan x}$ except where $\tan x = 0$ or is undefined.

You won't find sec, cosec or cot keys on your calculator, so to find their values you have to use the sin, cos and tan keys, followed by the reciprocal key.

The graphs of $y = \sec x$, $y = \operatorname{cosec} x$ and $y = \cot x$ are shown in Figs. 1.1, 1.2 and 1.3. The functions $\sec x$ and $\operatorname{cosec} x$ have period $2\pi$, and the period of $\cot x$ is $\pi$.

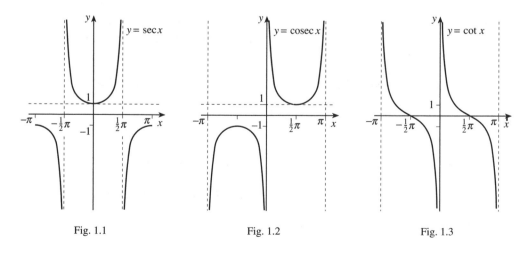

Fig. 1.1                          Fig. 1.2                          Fig. 1.3

**Example 1.2.1**

Find the exact values of    (a) $\sec \frac{2}{3}\pi$,    (b) $\operatorname{cosec} \frac{5}{6}\pi$,    (c) $\cot\left(-\frac{2}{3}\pi\right)$.

You need to find the values of $\cos \frac{2}{3}\pi$, $\sin \frac{5}{6}\pi$ and $\tan\left(-\frac{2}{3}\pi\right)$, using the symmetry properties in P1 Section 11.4 (substituting $\pi$ radians for $180°$ where necessary) together with the exact values in Section 11.3.

(a) $\cos\frac{2}{3}\pi = -\cos\left(\pi - \frac{2}{3}\pi\right) = -\cos\frac{1}{3}\pi = -\frac{1}{2}$, so $\sec\frac{2}{3}\pi = -2$.

(b) $\sin\frac{5}{6}\pi = \sin\left(\pi - \frac{5}{6}\pi\right) = \sin\frac{1}{6}\pi = \frac{1}{2}$, so $\operatorname{cosec}\frac{5}{6}\pi = 2$.

(c) $\tan\left(-\frac{2}{3}\pi\right) = -\tan\frac{2}{3}\pi = -\left(-\tan\frac{1}{3}\pi\right) = \sqrt{3}$, so $\cot\left(-\frac{2}{3}\pi\right) = \frac{1}{\sqrt{3}} = \frac{1}{3}\sqrt{3}$.

There are new forms of Pythagoras' theorem in trigonometry using these new trigonometric functions. For example, if you divide every term in the identity $\cos^2\theta + \sin^2\theta \equiv 1$ by $\cos^2\theta$, you get

$$\frac{\cos^2\theta}{\cos^2\theta} + \frac{\sin^2\theta}{\cos^2\theta} \equiv \frac{1}{\cos^2\theta}, \qquad \text{that is,} \quad 1 + \tan^2\theta \equiv \sec^2\theta. \qquad\qquad \text{Equation 1}$$

Similarly, if you divide every term of $\cos^2\theta + \sin^2\theta \equiv 1$ by $\sin^2\theta$, you get

$$\frac{\cos^2\theta}{\sin^2\theta} + \frac{\sin^2\theta}{\sin^2\theta} \equiv \frac{1}{\sin^2\theta}, \qquad \text{or} \quad 1 + \cot^2\theta \equiv \operatorname{cosec}^2\theta.$$

Summarising,

$$1 + \tan^2\theta \equiv \sec^2\theta,$$
$$1 + \cot^2\theta \equiv \operatorname{cosec}^2\theta.$$

**Example 1.2.2**

Prove the identity $\dfrac{1}{\sec\theta - \tan\theta} \equiv \sec\theta + \tan\theta$, provided that $\sec\theta - \tan\theta \neq 0$.

*There are four ways to approach proving identities: you can start with the left side and work towards the right; you can start with the right side and work towards the left; you can subtract one side from the other and try to show that the result is $0$; or you can divide one side by the other and try to show that the result is $1$. Generally you should start with the more complicated side.*

Use the fourth method, and consider the right side divided by the left side.

You need to show that $(\sec\theta + \tan\theta) \div \dfrac{1}{\sec\theta - \tan\theta}$ is equal to 1.

$$(\sec\theta + \tan\theta) \div \frac{1}{\sec\theta - \tan\theta} \equiv (\sec\theta + \tan\theta)(\sec\theta - \tan\theta)$$
$$\equiv \sec^2\theta - \tan^2\theta \equiv 1 \qquad \text{from Equation 1.}$$

Therefore $\dfrac{1}{\sec\theta - \tan\theta} \equiv \sec\theta + \tan\theta$.

Note that the condition $\sec\theta - \tan\theta \neq 0$ is necessary, because if $\sec\theta - \tan\theta = 0$ the left side is not defined, and therefore the identity has no meaning.

## Exercise 1A

**1** Find, giving your answers to 3 decimal places,

    (a)   $\cot 304°$,          (b)   $\sec(-48)°$,          (c)   $\operatorname{cosec} 62°$.

**2** Simplify the following.

    (a)   $\sec\left(\frac{1}{2}\pi - x\right)$      (b)   $\dfrac{\cos x}{\sin x}$          (c)   $\sec(-x)$

    (d)   $1 + \tan^2 x$         (e)   $\cot(\pi + x)$      (f)   $\operatorname{cosec}(\pi + x)$

**3** Find the exact values of

    (a)   $\sec\frac{1}{4}\pi$,         (b)   $\operatorname{cosec}\frac{1}{2}\pi$,       (c)   $\cot\frac{5}{6}\pi$,        (d)   $\operatorname{cosec}\left(-\frac{3}{4}\pi\right)$,

    (e)   $\cot\left(-\frac{1}{3}\pi\right)$,       (f)   $\sec\frac{13}{6}\pi$,        (g)   $\cot\left(-\frac{11}{2}\pi\right)$,      (h)   $\sec\frac{7}{6}\pi$.

**4** Using a calculator where necessary, find the values of the following, giving any non-exact answers correct to 3 significant figures.

    (a)   $\sin\frac{2}{5}\pi$          (b)   $\sec\frac{1}{10}\pi$        (c)   $\cot\frac{1}{12}\pi$        (d)   $\operatorname{cosec}\frac{17}{6}\pi$

    (e)   $\cos\frac{7}{8}\pi$         (f)   $\tan\frac{5}{12}\pi$        (g)   $\sec\left(-\frac{11}{12}\pi\right)$     (h)   $\cot\left(-\frac{1}{6}\pi\right)$

**5** Given that $\sin A = \frac{3}{5}$, where $A$ is acute, and $\cos B = -\frac{1}{2}$, where $B$ is obtuse, find the exact values of

    (a)   $\sec A$,          (b)   $\cot A$,          (c)   $\cot B$,          (d)   $\operatorname{cosec} B$.

**6** Given that $\operatorname{cosec} C = 7$, $\sin^2 D = \frac{1}{2}$ and $\tan^2 E = 4$, find the possible values of $\cot C$, $\sec D$ and $\operatorname{cosec} E$, giving your answers in exact form.

**7** Simplify the following.

    (a)   $\sqrt{\sec^2\phi - 1}$      (b)   $\dfrac{\tan\phi}{1 + \tan^2\phi}$      (c)   $\dfrac{\tan\phi}{\sec^2\phi - 1}$

    (d)   $\dfrac{1}{\sqrt{1 + \cot^2\phi}}$     (e)   $\dfrac{1}{\sqrt{\operatorname{cosec}^2\phi - 1}}$     (f)   $(\operatorname{cosec}\phi - 1)(\operatorname{cosec}\phi + 1)$

**8** (a) Express $3\tan^2\phi - \sec\phi$ in terms of $\sec\phi$.

    (b) Solve the equation $3\tan^2\phi - \sec\phi = 1$ for $0 \leqslant \phi \leqslant 2\pi$.

**9** Use an algebraic method to find the solution for $0 \leqslant \phi \leqslant 2\pi$ of the equation $5\cot\phi + 2\operatorname{cosec}^2\phi = 5$.

**10** Find, in exact form, all the roots of the equation $2\sin^2\phi + \operatorname{cosec}^2\phi = 3$ which lie between $0$ and $2\pi$.

**11** Prove that $\operatorname{cosec} A + \cot A \equiv \dfrac{1}{\operatorname{cosec} A - \cot A}$ provided that $\operatorname{cosec} A \neq \cot A$.

**12** Prove that $\dfrac{\sec\theta - 1}{\tan\theta} \equiv \dfrac{\tan\theta}{\sec\theta + 1}$ provided that $\tan\theta \neq 0$.

## 1.3 The addition formulae for sine and cosine

Suppose that you know the values of $\sin A$, $\cos A$, $\sin B$ and $\cos B$. How could you calculate the values of $\sin(A+B)$, $\sin(A-B)$, $\cos(A+B)$ and $\cos(A-B)$ without using a calculator to find the angles, which, of course, would only give approximations?

One way is to find a general formula which applies to all values of $A$ and $B$ by starting with the formula for $\cos(A-B)$. However, you may wish to skip the proofs, and start reading from the next set of results in the shaded box on page 6.

In Fig. 1.4, angles $A$ and $B$ are drawn from the $x$-axis. The points $P$ and $Q$ then have coordinates $(\cos A, \sin A)$ and $(\cos B, \sin B)$ respectively.

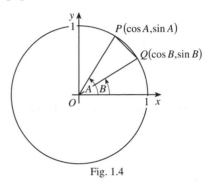

Fig. 1.4

You can now write down the distance $PQ$, or rather an expression for $PQ^2$, in two ways: by using the distance formula in coordinate geometry (see P1 Section 1.1) and by using the cosine formula for the triangle $OPQ$.

Then $PQ^2 = (\cos B - \cos A)^2 + (\sin B - \sin A)^2 = 1^2 + 1^2 - 2 \times 1 \times 1 \times \cos(A-B)$,

so $\cos^2 B - 2\cos B\cos A + \cos^2 A + \sin^2 B - 2\sin B\sin A + \sin^2 A = 2 - 2\cos(A-B)$.

Rearrange the left side to get

$$\left(\cos^2 B + \sin^2 B\right) + \left(\cos^2 A + \sin^2 A\right) - 2\cos B\cos A - 2\sin B\sin A = 2 - 2\cos(A-B).$$

But, from Pythagoras' theorem in trigonometry, $\cos^2 B + \sin^2 B = 1$ and $\cos^2 A + \sin^2 A = 1$. Then, cancelling and rearranging,

$$\cos(A-B) = \cos A\cos B + \sin A\sin B.$$

Although Fig. 1.4 is drawn with angles $A$ and $B$ acute and $A > B$, the proof in fact holds for angles $A$ and $B$ of any size.

### Example 1.3.1
Verify the formula for $\cos(A-B)$ in the cases (a) $B=A$, (b) $A=\frac{1}{2}\pi$, $B=\frac{1}{6}\pi$.

(a) Put $B=A$.

Then $\cos(A-A) = \cos^2 A + \sin^2 A$ and, as $\cos 0 = 1$, you get Pythagoras' theorem, $\cos^2 A + \sin^2 A = 1$.

(b) Put $A=\frac{1}{2}\pi$ and $B=\frac{1}{6}\pi$.

Then $\cos A = 0$, $\sin A = 1$, $\cos B = \frac{1}{2}\sqrt{3}$ and $\sin B = \frac{1}{2}$. The formula then gives $\cos A\cos B + \sin A\sin B = 0 \times \frac{1}{2}\sqrt{3} + 1 \times \frac{1}{2} = \frac{1}{2}$ which is consistent with $\cos(A-B) = \cos\left(\frac{1}{2}\pi - \frac{1}{6}\pi\right) = \cos\frac{1}{3}\pi = \frac{1}{2}$.

If you replace $B$ by $(-B)$ in the formula for $\cos(A-B)$ you get

$$\cos(A-(-B)) = \cos A \cos(-B) + \sin A \sin(-B).$$

Recall that cosine is an even function (P1 Section 11.4), so $\cos(-B) = \cos B$, and that sine is an odd function, so $\sin(-B) = -\sin B$. Writing $\cos(A-(-B))$ as $\cos(A+B)$,

$$\cos(A+B) = \cos A \cos(-B) + \sin A \sin(-B)$$
$$= \cos A \cos B - \sin A \sin B.$$

To find a formulae for $\sin(A+B)$, first recall that $\cos\left(\frac{1}{2}\pi - \theta\right) = \sin\theta$ (see P1 Section 11.4). Using this with $\theta = A+B$,

$$\sin(A+B) = \cos\left(\frac{1}{2}\pi - (A+B)\right) = \cos\left(\left(\frac{1}{2}\pi - A\right) - B\right)$$
$$= \cos\left(\frac{1}{2}\pi - A\right)\cos B + \sin\left(\frac{1}{2}\pi - A\right)\sin B$$
$$= \sin A \cos B + \cos A \sin B.$$

You can obtain the formula for $\sin(A-B)$ in a similar way. (This is Question 6 in Exercise 1B.) The four formulae are true for all angles $A$ and $B$, so they are identities.

> For all angles $A$ and $B$,
>
> $$\sin(A+B) \equiv \sin A \cos B + \cos A \sin B,$$
> $$\sin(A-B) \equiv \sin A \cos B - \cos A \sin B,$$
> $$\cos(A+B) \equiv \cos A \cos B - \sin A \sin B,$$
> $$\cos(A-B) \equiv \cos A \cos B + \sin A \sin B.$$

These formulae are called the **addition formulae**. They are important and you should learn them, but you need not learn how to prove them.

Notice that now you have these formulae, you have a quick method of simplifying expressions such as $\cos\left(\frac{3}{2}\pi - \theta\right)$:

$$\cos\left(\frac{3}{2}\pi - \theta\right) = \cos\left(\frac{3}{2}\pi\right)\cos\theta + \sin\left(\frac{3}{2}\pi\right)\sin\theta$$
$$= 0 \times \cos\theta + (-1) \times \sin\theta = -\sin\theta.$$

**Example 1.3.2**

Use the formulae for $\cos(A \pm B)$ to find exact values of $\cos 75°$ and $\cos 15°$.

$$\cos 75° = \cos(45+30)° = \cos 45° \cos 30° - \sin 45° \sin 30°$$
$$= \tfrac{1}{2}\sqrt{2} \times \tfrac{1}{2}\sqrt{3} - \tfrac{1}{2}\sqrt{2} \times \tfrac{1}{2} = \tfrac{1}{4}\left(\sqrt{6} - \sqrt{2}\right).$$
$$\cos 15° = \cos(45-30)° = \cos 45° \cos 30° + \sin 45° \sin 30°$$
$$= \tfrac{1}{2}\sqrt{2} \times \tfrac{1}{2}\sqrt{3} + \tfrac{1}{2}\sqrt{2} \times \tfrac{1}{2} = \tfrac{1}{4}\left(\sqrt{6} + \sqrt{2}\right).$$

*Check these results for yourself with a calculator.*

**Example 1.3.3**
You are given that $\sin A = \frac{8}{17}$, that $\sin B = \frac{12}{13}$, and that $0 < B < \frac{1}{2}\pi < A < \pi$. Find the exact value of $\tan(A + B)$.

From the Pythagoras identity, $\cos^2 A + \left(\frac{8}{17}\right)^2 = 1$, $\cos^2 A = 1 - \frac{64}{289} = \frac{225}{289}$, so $\cos A = \pm\frac{15}{17}$. As $\frac{1}{2}\pi < A < \pi$, $\cos A$ is negative, so $\cos A = -\frac{15}{17}$.

Similarly, $\cos^2 B + \left(\frac{12}{13}\right)^2 = 1$, so $\cos B = \pm\frac{5}{13}$. As $0 < B < \frac{1}{2}\pi$, $\cos B$ is positive, so $\cos B = \frac{5}{13}$. Then

$$\sin(A + B) = \frac{8}{17} \times \frac{5}{13} + \left(-\frac{15}{17}\right) \times \frac{12}{13} = \frac{40 - 180}{17 \times 13} = \frac{-140}{17 \times 13}$$

and $\quad \cos(A + B) = \left(-\frac{15}{17}\right) \times \frac{5}{13} - \frac{8}{17} \times \frac{12}{13} = \frac{-75 - 96}{17 \times 13} = \frac{-171}{17 \times 13}$,

so $\quad \tan(A + B) = \dfrac{\sin(A + B)}{\cos(A + B)} = \dfrac{-140/17 \times 13}{-171/17 \times 13} = \dfrac{140}{171}$.

**Example 1.3.4**
Prove that $\sin(A + B) + \sin(A - B) \equiv 2 \sin A \cos B$.

Starting from the left side, and 'expanding' both terms,

$$\sin(A + B) + \sin(A - B) \equiv (\sin A \cos B + \cos A \sin B) + (\sin A \cos B - \cos A \sin B)$$
$$\equiv \sin A \cos B + \cos A \sin B + \sin A \cos B - \cos A \sin B$$
$$\equiv 2 \sin A \cos B.$$

Hence $\sin(A + B) + \sin(A - B) \equiv 2 \sin A \cos B$.

**Example 1.3.5**
Find the value of $\tan x°$, given that $\sin(x + 30)° = 2\cos(x - 30)°$.

Use the addition formulae to write the equation as

$$\sin x° \cos 30° + \cos x° \sin 30° = 2 \cos x° \cos 30° + 2 \sin x° \sin 30°.$$

Collect the terms involving $\sin x°$ on the left, and those involving $\cos x°$ on the right, substituting the values of $\sin 30°$ and $\cos 30°$:

$$\sin x° \times \frac{1}{2}\sqrt{3} - 2 \sin x° \times \frac{1}{2} = 2 \cos x° \times \frac{1}{2}\sqrt{3} - \cos x° \times \frac{1}{2},$$

which can be rearranged as

$$\left(\frac{1}{2}\sqrt{3} - 1\right) \sin x° = \left(\sqrt{3} - \frac{1}{2}\right) \cos x°.$$

Hence $\tan x° = \dfrac{\sin x°}{\cos x°} = \dfrac{\sqrt{3} - \frac{1}{2}}{\frac{1}{2}\sqrt{3} - 1} = \dfrac{2\sqrt{3} - 1}{\sqrt{3} - 2}$.

## 1.4 The addition formulae for tangents

To find a formula for $\tan(A+B)$, use $\tan(A+B) = \dfrac{\sin(A+B)}{\cos(A+B)}$ together with the identities for $\cos(A+B)$ and $\sin(A+B)$. Thus

$$\tan(A+B) \equiv \frac{\sin(A+B)}{\cos(A+B)} \equiv \frac{\sin A \cos B + \cos A \sin B}{\cos A \cos B - \sin A \sin B}.$$

You can get a neater formula by dividing the top and the bottom of the fraction on the right by $\cos A \cos B$. The numerator then becomes

$$\frac{\sin A \cos B + \cos A \sin B}{\cos A \cos B} = \frac{\sin A \cos B}{\cos A \cos B} + \frac{\cos A \sin B}{\cos A \cos B} = \tan A + \tan B,$$

and the denominator becomes

$$\frac{\cos A \cos B - \sin A \sin B}{\cos A \cos B} = \frac{\cos A \cos B}{\cos A \cos B} - \frac{\sin A \sin B}{\cos A \cos B} = 1 - \tan A \tan B.$$

Therefore, putting the fraction together, $\tan(A+B) \equiv \dfrac{\tan A + \tan B}{1 - \tan A \tan B}$.

A similar derivation, or the fact that $\tan(-B) = -\tan(B)$, yields a formula for $\tan(A-B)$.

$$\tan(A+B) \equiv \frac{\tan A + \tan B}{1 - \tan A \tan B}, \quad \tan(A-B) \equiv \frac{\tan A - \tan B}{1 + \tan A \tan B}.$$

Note that these identities have no meaning if $\tan A$ or $\tan B$ is undefined, of if either denominator is zero.

### Example 1.4.1

Given that $\tan(x+y) = 1$ and that $\tan x = \frac{1}{2}$, find $\tan y$.

$$\tan y = \tan\big((x+y) - x\big) = \frac{\tan(x+y) - \tan x}{1 + \tan(x+y)\tan x} = \frac{1 - \frac{1}{2}}{1 + 1 \times \frac{1}{2}} = \frac{\frac{1}{2}}{\frac{3}{2}} = \frac{1}{3}.$$

### Example 1.4.2

Find the tangent of the angle between the lines $7y = x + 2$ and $x + y = 3$.

The gradients of the lines are $\frac{1}{7}$ and $-1$, so if they make angles $A$ and $B$ with the $x$-axis respectively, $\tan A = \frac{1}{7}$ and $\tan B = -1$. Then

$$\tan(A-B) = \frac{\tan A - \tan B}{1 + \tan A \tan B} = \frac{\frac{1}{7} - (-1)}{1 + \frac{1}{7} \times (-1)} = \frac{\frac{8}{7}}{\frac{6}{7}} = \frac{4}{3}.$$

**Exercise 1B**

1 By writing $75$ as $30 + 45$, find the exact values of $\sin 75°$ and $\tan 75°$.

2 Find the exact values of
(a) $\cos 105°$, (b) $\sin 105°$, (c) $\tan 105°$.

3 Express $\cos\left(x + \frac{1}{3}\pi\right)$ in terms of $\cos x$ and $\sin x$.

4 Use the expansions for $\sin(A + B)$ and $\cos(A + B)$ to simplify $\sin\left(\frac{3}{2}\pi + \phi\right)$ and $\cos\left(\frac{1}{2}\pi + \phi\right)$.

5 Express $\tan\left(\frac{1}{3}\pi + x\right)$ and $\tan\left(\frac{5}{6}\pi - x\right)$ in terms of $\tan x$.

6 Use $\sin(A - B) \equiv \cos\left(\frac{1}{2}\pi - (A - B)\right) \equiv \cos\left(\left(\frac{1}{2}\pi - A\right) + B\right)$ to derive the formula for $\sin(A - B)$.

7 Given that $\cos A = \frac{3}{5}$ and $\cos B = \frac{24}{25}$, where $A$ and $B$ are acute, find the exact values of
(a) $\tan A$, (b) $\sin B$, (c) $\cos(A - B)$, (d) $\tan(A + B)$.

8 Given that $\sin A = \frac{3}{5}$ and $\cos B = \frac{12}{13}$, where $A$ is obtuse and $B$ is acute, find the exact values of $\cos(A + B)$ and $\cot(A - B)$.

9 Prove that $\cos(A + B) - \cos(A - B) \equiv -2\sin A \sin B$.

## 1.5 Double angle formulae

If you put $A = B$ in the addition formulae, you obtain identities for the sine, cosine and tangent of $2A$. The first comes from $\sin(A + B) = \sin A \cos B + \cos A \sin B$, which gives

$$\sin(A + A) = \sin A \cos A + \cos A \sin A \quad \text{or} \quad \sin 2A = 2\sin A \cos A.$$

From $\cos(A + B) = \cos A \cos B - \sin A \sin B$ you get $\cos 2A = \cos^2 A - \sin^2 A$. There are two other useful forms for this which come from replacing $\cos^2 A$ by $1 - \sin^2 A$, giving

$$\cos 2A = \cos^2 A - \sin^2 A = \left(1 - \sin^2 A\right) - \sin^2 A = 1 - 2\sin^2 A,$$

or from replacing $\sin^2 A$ by $1 - \cos^2 A$, giving

$$\cos 2A = \cos^2 A - \sin^2 A = \cos^2 A - \left(1 - \cos^2 A\right) = 2\cos^2 A - 1.$$

Finally, the formula $\tan(A + B) = \dfrac{\tan A + \tan B}{1 - \tan A \tan B}$ becomes $\tan 2A = \dfrac{2\tan A}{1 - \tan^2 A}$.

These formulae are called the **double angle formulae**.

$$\sin 2A \equiv 2\sin A \cos A,$$
$$\cos 2A \equiv \cos^2 A - \sin^2 A = 1 - 2\sin^2 A = 2\cos^2 A - 1,$$
$$\tan 2A \equiv \frac{2\tan A}{1 - \tan^2 A}.$$

**Example 1.5.1**

Given that $\cos A = \frac{1}{3}$, find the exact value of $\cos 2A$.

$$\cos 2A = 2\cos^2 A - 1 = 2 \times \left(\tfrac{1}{3}\right)^2 - 1 = 2 \times \tfrac{1}{9} - 1 = -\tfrac{7}{9}.$$

**Example 1.5.2**

Given that $\cos A = \frac{1}{3}$, find the possible values of $\cos \frac{1}{2} A$.

Using $\cos 2A \equiv 2\cos^2 A - 1$, with $\frac{1}{2} A$ written in place of $A$, gives

$\cos A \equiv 2\cos^2 \frac{1}{2} A - 1$. In this case, $\frac{1}{3} = 2\cos^2 \frac{1}{2} A - 1$, giving $2\cos^2 \frac{1}{2} A = \frac{4}{3}$.

This simplifies to $\cos^2 \frac{1}{2} A = \frac{2}{3}$, so $\cos \frac{1}{2} A = \pm\sqrt{\frac{2}{3}} = \pm\frac{1}{3}\sqrt{6}$.

**Example 1.5.3**

Solve the equation $2\sin 2\theta° = \sin \theta°$, giving values of $\theta$ such that $0 \leqslant \theta \leqslant 360$ correct to one decimal place.

Using the identity $\sin 2\theta° \equiv 2\sin \theta° \cos \theta°$,

$$2 \times 2\sin \theta° \cos \theta° = \sin \theta°, \text{ so } \sin \theta°(4\cos \theta° - 1) = 0.$$

At least one of these factors must be 0. Therefore either

$$\sin \theta° = 0, \quad \text{giving} \quad \theta = 0, 180, 360$$

or $\quad 4\cos \theta° - 1 = 0, \quad \text{giving} \quad \cos \theta° = 0.25$, so $\theta = 75.52\ldots$ or $284.47\ldots$.

Therefore the required roots are $\theta = 0, 75.5, 180, 284.5, 360$ correct to one decimal place.

**Example 1.5.4**

Prove the identity $\cot A - \tan A \equiv 2\cot 2A$.

    **Method 1**     Put everything in terms of $\tan A$. Starting with the left side,

$$\cot A - \tan A \equiv \frac{1}{\tan A} - \tan A \equiv \frac{1 - \tan^2 A}{\tan A}$$

$$\equiv 2 \times \left(\frac{1 - \tan^2 A}{2\tan A}\right) \equiv 2 \times \frac{1}{\tan 2A} \equiv 2\cot 2A.$$

    **Method 2**     Put everything in terms of $\sin A$ and $\cos A$. Starting with the left side,

$$\cot A - \tan A \equiv \frac{\cos A}{\sin A} - \frac{\sin A}{\cos A} \equiv \frac{\cos^2 A - \sin^2 A}{\sin A \cos A} \equiv \frac{\cos 2A}{\frac{1}{2}\sin 2A} \equiv 2\cot 2A.$$

**Example 1.5.5**

Prove that $\csc x + \cot x \equiv \cot \frac{1}{2} x$.

Starting with the left side, and putting everything in terms of sines and cosines,

$$\csc x + \cot x \equiv \frac{1}{\sin x} + \frac{\cos x}{\sin x} \equiv \frac{1 + \cos x}{\sin x}$$

$$\equiv \frac{1 + \left(2\cos^2 \frac{1}{2} x - 1\right)}{2\sin \frac{1}{2} x \cos \frac{1}{2} x} \equiv \frac{2\cos^2 \frac{1}{2} x}{2\sin \frac{1}{2} x \cos \frac{1}{2} x}$$

$$\equiv \frac{\cos \frac{1}{2} x}{\sin \frac{1}{2} x} \equiv \cot \frac{1}{2} x.$$

## Exercise 1C

1   If $\sin A = \frac{2}{3}$ and $A$ is obtuse, find the exact values of $\cos A$, $\sin 2A$ and $\tan 2A$.

2   If $\cos B = \frac{3}{4}$, find the exact values of $\cos 2B$ and $\cos \frac{1}{2} B$.

3   By expressing $\sin 3A$ as $\sin(2A + A)$, find an expression for $\sin 3A$ in terms of $\sin A$.

4   Express $\cos 3A$ in terms of $\cos A$.

5   By writing $\cos x$ in terms of $\frac{1}{2} x$, find an alternative expression for $\dfrac{1 - \cos x}{1 + \cos x}$.

6   Prove that $4\sin\left(x + \frac{1}{6}\pi\right)\sin\left(x - \frac{1}{6}\pi\right) \equiv 3 - 4\cos^2 x$.

7   If $\cos 2A = \frac{7}{18}$, find the possible values of $\cos A$ and $\sin A$.

8   If $\tan 2A = \frac{12}{5}$, find the possible values of $\tan A$.

9   If $\tan 2A = 1$, find the possible values of $\tan A$. Hence state the exact value of $\tan 22\frac{1}{2}°$.

10   Solve these equations for values of $A$ between $0$ and $2\pi$ inclusive. In each case use trigonometric identities and then check your results using a graphic calculator and its 'intersect' facility.

    (a)   $\cos 2A + 3 + 4\cos A = 0$          (b)   $2\cos 2A + 1 + \sin A = 0$

    (c)   $\tan 2A + 5\tan A = 0$

## 1.6   The form $a\sin x + b\cos x$

Draw the graphs of $y = 3\sin x + 2\cos x$ and $y = \sin x - 4\cos x$ on your calculator, using a window of either $2\pi$ or $360°$, depending on whether you are in radian or degree mode. What you see may surprise you: it shows that both these graphs are either cosine or sine graphs, first translated in the positive $x$-direction, and then enlarged in the $y$-direction.

This suggests that you can write $y = 3\sin x + 2\cos x$ in the form $y = R\sin(x + \alpha)$, where the graph $y = \cos x$ has been translated by $\alpha$ in the negative $x$-direction, and then enlarged in the $y$-direction by the factor $R$, where $R > 0$. The question is how to find the values of $R$ and $\alpha$.

If you equate the two expressions $y = 3\sin x + 2\cos x$ and $y = R\sin(x+\alpha)$, you find that

$$3\sin x + 2\cos x \equiv R\sin x \cos\alpha + R\cos x \sin\alpha.$$

Since these are to be identical, they certainly agree for $x = \frac{1}{2}\pi$ and $x = 0$. Substituting gives

$$3 = R\cos\alpha \quad \text{and} \quad 2 = R\sin\alpha.$$

You can find $R$ and $\alpha$ from these equations. Imagine a right-angled triangle, which you might think of as a set square, with adjacent sides 2 units and 3 units, and hypotenuse $R$ units. Then $\alpha$ is the angle shown in Fig. 1.5.

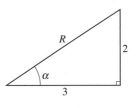

Therefore $\tan\alpha = \frac{2}{3}$, and $R = \sqrt{2^2 + 3^2} = \sqrt{13}$. It is important to remember that $R > 0$. The equations $2 = R\sin\alpha$ and $3 = R\cos\alpha$ then show that $\cos\alpha$ and $\sin\alpha$ are positive, so that the angle $\alpha$ is acute; in radians $\alpha = 0.58\ldots$. Then

Fig. 1.5

$$3\sin x + 2\cos x \equiv \left(\sqrt{13}\cos 0.58\ldots\right)\sin x + \left(\sqrt{13}\sin 0.58\ldots\right)\cos x$$

$$\equiv \sqrt{13}\sin x \cos 0.58\ldots + \sqrt{13}\cos x \sin 0.58\ldots$$

$$\equiv \sqrt{13}\sin(x + 0.58\ldots).$$

The form $\sqrt{13}\sin(x+0.58\ldots)$, while it may look less friendly than $3\sin x + 2\cos x$, is in many ways more convenient. Example 1.6.1 shows two applications.

## Example 1.6.1

(a) Find the maximum and minimum values of $3\sin x + 2\cos x$, and find in radians to two decimal places the smallest positive values of $x$ at which they occur.

(b) Solve the equation $3\sin x + 2\cos x = 1$, for $-\pi \leqslant x \leqslant \pi$, to two decimal places.

(a) Since $3\sin x + 2\cos x \equiv \sqrt{13}\sin(x+0.58\ldots)$, and the maximum and minimum values of the sine function are 1 and $-1$, the maximum and minimum values of $3\sin x + 2\cos x$ are $\sqrt{13}$ and $-\sqrt{13}$. And since the maximum and minimum values of the sine function occur at $\frac{1}{2}\pi$ and $\frac{3}{2}\pi$, the relevant values of $x$ are given by $x + 0.58\ldots = \frac{1}{2}\pi$ and $x + 0.58\ldots = \frac{3}{2}\pi$. Therefore the maximum $\sqrt{13}$ occurs when $x = \frac{1}{2}\pi - 0.58\ldots = 0.98$, and the minimum $-\sqrt{13}$ occurs when $x = \frac{3}{2}\pi - 0.58\ldots = 4.12$, correct to two decimal places.

(b) $3\sin x + 2\cos x = 1 \iff \sqrt{13}\sin(x+0.58\ldots) = 1 \iff \sin(x+0.58\ldots) = \dfrac{1}{\sqrt{13}}$.

Using the methods of P1 Section 11.5, the solutions (between $-\pi$ and $\pi$) are

$$x + 0.58\ldots = 0.28\ldots \quad \text{or} \quad x + 0.58\ldots = 2.86\ldots,$$

so $x = -0.31$ or $2.27$, correct to two decimal places.

In the general case, you can write $a\sin x + b\cos x$ in the form $R\sin(x+\alpha)$ where $R = \sqrt{a^2 + b^2}$ and $\alpha$ is given by the equations $R\cos\alpha = a$ and $R\sin\alpha = b$.

There is nothing special about using the form $R\sin(x+\alpha)$. It is often more convenient to use $R\cos(x+\alpha)$, $R\sin(x-\alpha)$ or $R\cos(x-\alpha)$. Thus, with the values of $R$ and $\alpha$ in Example 1.6.1,

$$3\cos x + 2\sin x \equiv (R\cos\alpha)\cos x + (R\sin\alpha)\sin x \equiv R\cos(x-\alpha).$$

Always try to choose the form which produces the terms in the right order with the correct sign. For example, write $3\cos x - 2\sin x$ in the form $R\cos(x+\alpha)$, and $3\sin x - 2\cos x$ in the form $R\sin(x-\alpha)$.

Summarising all this:

> If $a$ and $b$ are positive,
>
> $\qquad a\sin x \pm b\cos x$ can be written in the form $R\sin(x\pm\alpha)$,
>
> $\qquad a\cos x \pm b\sin x$ can be written in the form $R\cos(x\mp\alpha)$,
>
> where $R=\sqrt{a^2+b^2}$ and $R\cos\alpha=a$, $R\sin\alpha=b$, with $0<\alpha<\frac{1}{2}\pi$.

*It is better not to learn the detail of the result in the shaded box except for $R=\sqrt{a^2+b^2}$.*
*Learn how to find $\alpha$ and work it out each time you come to it.*

### Example 1.6.2
Express $\sin\theta - 4\cos\theta$ in the form $R\sin(\theta-\alpha)$ giving the values of $R$ and $\alpha$. Explain why the equation $\sin\theta - 4\cos\theta = 5$ has no solutions.

Identifying $\sin\theta - 4\cos\theta$ with $R\sin(\theta-\alpha)$ gives

$$\sin\theta - 4\cos\theta \equiv R\sin\theta\cos\alpha - R\cos\theta\sin\alpha\,,$$

so $\qquad R\cos\alpha = 1 \quad$ and $\quad R\sin\alpha = 4$.

Therefore $R=\sqrt{1^2+4^2}=\sqrt{17}$, with $\cos\alpha = \dfrac{1}{\sqrt{17}}$ and $\sin\alpha = \dfrac{4}{\sqrt{17}}$, giving $\tan\alpha = 4$ and $\alpha = 1.32\ldots$.

Then $\sin\theta - 4\cos\theta \equiv \sqrt{17}\sin(\theta-\alpha)$, where $\alpha = 1.32\ldots$.

The equation $\sin\theta - 4\cos\theta = 5$ has no solution since

$$\sin\theta - 4\cos\theta = 5 \;\Rightarrow\; \sqrt{17}\sin(\theta-\alpha)=5 \;\Rightarrow\; \sin(\theta-\alpha)=\frac{5}{\sqrt{17}}>1.$$

As there are no values of $x$ for which the sine function is greater than 1, there is no solution to the equation $\sin(\theta-\alpha)=\dfrac{5}{\sqrt{17}}$, and therefore no solution to the equation $\sin\theta - 4\cos\theta = 5$.

### Exercise 1D

1   Find the value of $\alpha$ between 0 and 90 for which $3\sin x° + 2\cos x° \equiv \sqrt{13}\sin(x+\alpha)°$

2   Find the value of $\phi$ between 0 and 90 for which $3\cos x° - 4\sin x° \equiv 5\cos(x+\phi)°$.

3   Find the value of $R$, such that, if $\tan\beta = \frac{3}{5}$ then $5\sin\theta + 3\cos\theta \equiv R\sin(\theta+\beta)$.

4   Find the value of $R$ and the value of $\beta$ between 0 and $\frac{1}{2}\pi$ correct to 3 decimal places such that $6\cos x + \sin x \equiv R\cos(x-\beta)$.

5   Find the value of $R$ and the value of $\alpha$ between 0 and $\frac{1}{2}\pi$ in each of the following cases, where the given expression is written in the given form.

   (a)  $\sin x + 2\cos x$;   $R\sin(x+\alpha)$      (b)  $\sin x + 2\cos x$;   $R\cos(x-\alpha)$

   (c)  $\sin x - 2\cos x$;   $R\sin(x-\alpha)$      (d)  $2\cos x - \sin x$;   $R\cos(x+\alpha)$

6   Express $5\cos\theta + 6\sin\theta$ in the form $R\cos(\theta-\beta)$ where $R > 0$ and $0 < \beta < \frac{1}{2}\pi$. State

   (a)  the maximum value of $5\cos\theta + 6\sin\theta$ and the least positive value of $\theta$ which gives this maximum,

   (b)  the minimum value of $5\cos\theta + 6\sin\theta$ and the least positive value of $\theta$ which gives this minimum.

7   Describe fully a combination of two single transformations that will transform the graph of $y = \cos x$ to the graph of $y = 6\cos\left(x - \frac{1}{3}\pi\right)$.

8   By expressing $6\cos x - 4\sin x$ in the form $R\cos(x+\beta)$ where $R > 0$ and $0 < \beta < \frac{1}{2}\pi$, describe a combination of two single transformations that will transform the graph of $y = \cos x$ to the graph of $y = 6\cos x - 4\sin x$.

9   Express $8\sin x° + 6\cos x°$ in the form $R\sin(x+\phi)°$, where $R > 0$ and $0 < \phi < 90$. Deduce the number of roots for $0 < x < 180$ of the following equations.

   (a)  $8\sin x° + 6\cos x° = 5$          (b)  $8\sin x° + 6\cos x° = 12$

10  Solve $3\sin x - 2\cos x = 1$ for values of $x$ between 0 and $2\pi$ by

   (a)  expressing $3\sin x - 2\cos x$ in the form $R\sin(x-\beta)$,

   (b)  using a graphical method.

## 1.7  Inverse trigonometric functions

You have already met the notation $\sin^{-1}$, $\cos^{-1}$ and $\tan^{-1}$ a number of times. It is now time to give a more precise definition of the inverse trigonometric functions.

The functions $\cos x$, $\sin x$ and $\tan x$ are not one-one, as you can see from P1 Chapter 11. They therefore do not have inverses unless you restrict their domains of definition (as in P2 Section 2.5). The definitions here are given assuming that you are working in radians.

Fig. 1.6 shows how the domain of the cosine function is restricted to $0 \leqslant x \leqslant \pi$ to define the function $\cos^{-1}$.

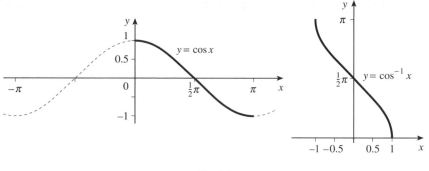

Fig. 1.6

Recall from P2 Section 2.7 that if the graph of a function and its inverse are plotted on the same axes, then one is the reflection of the other in $y = x$. You can see that if the two graphs in Fig. 1.6 were superimposed, then the thicker part of the graph of $y = \cos x$ would be the reflection of $y = \cos^{-1} x$ in $y = x$, and vice versa.

Similarly Fig. 1.7 shows how the domain of the sine function is restricted to $-\frac{1}{2}\pi \leqslant x \leqslant \frac{1}{2}\pi$ to define the function $\sin^{-1}$.

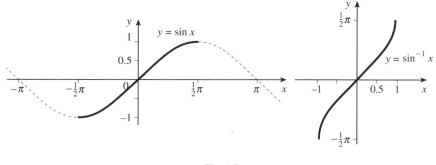

Fig. 1.7

Once again, the thicker part of the graph of $y = \sin x$ is the reflection of $y = \sin^{-1} x$ in the line $y = x$, and vice versa.

Fig. 1.8 shows the graph of the function $\tan^{-1}$, obtained by restricting the domain of the tangent function to $-\frac{1}{2}\pi < x < \frac{1}{2}\pi$.

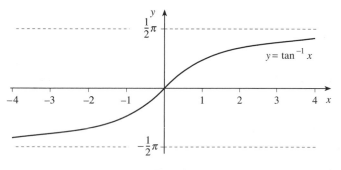

Fig. 1.8

## Exercise 1E

Do not use a calculator in Questions 1 to 5.

**1** Find

(a) $\cos^{-1}\frac{1}{2}\sqrt{3}$,      (b) $\tan^{-1}1$,      (c) $\cos^{-1}0$,      (d) $\sin^{-1}\frac{1}{2}\sqrt{3}$,

(e) $\tan^{-1}\left(-\sqrt{3}\right)$,      (f) $\sin^{-1}(-1)$,      (g) $\cot^{-1}0$,      (h) $\sec^{-1}(-1)$.

**2** Find

(a) $\cos^{-1}\dfrac{1}{\sqrt{2}}$,      (b) $\sin^{-1}(-0.5)$,      (c) $\cos^{-1}(-0.5)$,      (d) $\tan^{-1}\left(\dfrac{1}{\sqrt{3}}\right)$.

**3** Find

(a) $\sin\left(\sin^{-1}0.5\right)$,      (b) $\cos\left(\cos^{-1}(-1)\right)$,      (c) $\tan\left(\tan^{-1}\sqrt{3}\right)$,      (d) $\cos\left(\cos^{-1}0\right)$.

**4** Find

(a) $\cos^{-1}\left(\cos\frac{3}{2}\pi\right)$,      (b) $\sin^{-1}\left(\sin\frac{13}{6}\pi\right)$,      (c) $\tan^{-1}\left(\tan\frac{1}{6}\pi\right)$,      (d) $\cos^{-1}(\cos 2\pi)$.

**5** Find

(a) $\sin\left(\cos^{-1}\frac{1}{2}\sqrt{3}\right)$      (b) $\cot\left(\tan^{-1}2\right)$      (c) $\cos\left(\sin^{-1}(-0.5)\right)$    (d) $\tan\left(\sec^{-1}\sqrt{2}\right)$

**6** Use a graphical method to solve, correct to 3 decimal places, the equation $\cos x = \cos^{-1}x$. What simpler equation has this as its only root?

## Miscellaneous exercise 1

**1** (a) Starting from the identity $\sin^2\phi + \cos^2\phi \equiv 1$, prove that $\sec^2\phi \equiv 1 + \tan^2\phi$.

     (b) Given that $180 < \phi < 270$ and that $\tan\phi^\circ = \frac{7}{24}$, find the exact value of $\sec\phi^\circ$.    (OCR)

**2** Solve the equation $\tan x^\circ = 3\cot x^\circ$, giving all solutions between 0 and 360.      (OCR)

**3** (a) State the value of $\sec^2 x - \tan^2 x$.

     (b) The angle $A$ is such that $\sec A + \tan A = 2$. Show that $\sec A - \tan A = \frac{1}{2}$, and hence find the exact value of $\cos A$.      (OCR)

**4** Let $f(A) = \dfrac{\cos A^\circ}{1 + \sin A^\circ} + \dfrac{1 + \sin A^\circ}{\cos A^\circ}$.

     (a) Prove that $f(A) = 2\sec A^\circ$.

     (b) Solve the equation $f(A) = 4$, giving your answers for $A$, in degrees, in the interval $0 < A < 360$.      (OCR)

**5** You are given that $\cos 30^\circ = \dfrac{\sqrt{3}}{2}$ and $\cos 45^\circ = \dfrac{1}{\sqrt{2}}$. Determine the exact value of $\cos 75^\circ$.      (OCR)

**6** Prove that $\sin\left(\theta + \frac{1}{2}\pi\right) \equiv \cos\theta$.      (OCR)

**7** The angle $\alpha$ is obtuse, and $\sin\alpha = \frac{3}{5}$.

     (a) Find the value of $\cos\alpha$.

     (b) Find the values of $\sin 2\alpha$ and $\cos 2\alpha$, giving your answers as fractions in their lowest terms.      (OCR, adapted)

8  Given that $\sin\theta° = 4\sin(\theta - 60)°$, show that $2\sqrt{3}\cos\theta° = \sin\theta°$. Hence find the value of $\theta$ such that $0 < \theta < 180$. (OCR)

9  Solve the equation $\sin 2\theta° - \cos^2\theta° = 0$, giving values of $\theta$ in the interval $0 < \theta < 360$. (OCR, adapted)

10 (a) Prove the identity $\cot\frac{1}{2}A - \tan\frac{1}{2}A \equiv 2\cot A$.

   (b) By choosing a suitable numerical value for $A$, show that $\tan 15°$ is a root of the quadratic equation $t^2 + 2\sqrt{3}t - 1 = 0$. (OCR)

11 (a) By using the substitution $t = \tan\frac{1}{2}x$, prove that $\csc x - \cot x = \tan\frac{1}{2}x$.

   (b) Use this result to show that $\tan 15° = 2 - \sqrt{3}$. (OCR)

12 Express $\sin\theta° + \sqrt{3}\cos\theta°$ in the form $R\sin(\theta + \alpha)°$, where $R > 0$ and $0 < \alpha < 90$.

   Hence find all values of $\theta$, for $0 < \theta < 360$, which satisfy the equation $\sin\theta° + \sqrt{3}\cos\theta° = 1$. (OCR)

13 The function f is defined for all real $x$ by $f(x) = \cos x° - \sqrt{3}\sin x°$.

   (a) Express $f(x)$ in the form $R\cos(x + \phi)°$, where $R > 0$ and $0 < \phi < 90$.

   (b) Solve the equation $|f(x)| = 1$, giving your answers in the interval $0 \leqslant x \leqslant 360$. (OCR)

14 (a) Express $12\cos x + 9\sin x$ in the form $R\cos(x - \theta)$, where $R > 0$ and $0 < \theta < \frac{1}{2}\pi$.

   (b) Use the method of part (a) to find the smallest positive root $\alpha$ of the equation $12\cos x + 9\sin x = 14$, giving your answer correct to three decimal places. (OCR)

15 Express $2\cos x° + \sin x°$ in the form $R\cos(x - \alpha)°$, where $R > 0$ and $0 < \alpha < 90$. Hence

   (a) solve the equation $2\cos x° + \sin x° = 1$, giving all solutions between 0 and 360,

   (b) find the exact range of values of the constant $k$ for which the equation $2\cos x° + \sin x° = k$ has real solutions for $x$. (OCR)

16 (a) Express $5\sin x° + 12\cos x°$ in the form $R\sin(x + \theta)°$ where $R > 0$, and $0 < \theta < 90$.

   (b) Hence, or otherwise, find the maximum and minimum values of $f(x)$ where
   $$f(x) = \frac{30}{5\sin x° + 12\cos x° + 17}.$$ State also the values of $x$, in the range $0 < x < 360$, at which they occur. (OCR)

17 Express $3\cos x° - 4\sin x°$ in the form $R\cos(x + \alpha)°$ where $R > 0$, and $0 < \alpha < 90$. Hence

   (a) solve the equation $3\cos x° - 4\sin x° = 2$, giving all solutions between 0 and 360,

   (b) find the greatest and least values, as $x$ varies, of the expression $\dfrac{1}{3\cos x° - 4\sin x° + 8}$. (OCR)

18 (a) Find the value of $\tan^{-1}\sqrt{3} + \tan^{-1}\left(-\dfrac{1}{\sqrt{3}}\right)$.

   (b) If $A = \tan^{-1}x$ and $B = \tan^{-1}y$, find $\tan(A + B)$ in terms of $x$ and $y$.

**19** If $\cos^{-1}(3x+2) = \frac{1}{3}\pi$, find the value of $x$.

**20** If $A = \sin^{-1} x$, where $x > 0$,

(a) show that $\cos A = \sqrt{1-x^2}$,

(b) find expressions in terms of $x$ for $\operatorname{cosec} A$ and $\cos 2A$.

**21** (a) Find the equation of the straight line joining the points $A(0,1.5)$ and $B(3,0)$.

(b) Express $\sin\theta° + 2\cos\theta°$ in the form $r\sin(\theta+\alpha)°$, where $r$ is a positive number and $\theta°$ is an acute angle.

(c) The figure shows a map of a moor-land. The units of the coordinates are kilometres, and the $y$-axis points due north. A walker leaves her car somewhere on the straight road between $A$ and $B$. She walks in a straight line for a distance of 2 km to a monument at the origin $O$. While she is looking at it the fog comes down, so that she cannot see the way back to her car. She needs to work out the bearing on which she should walk.

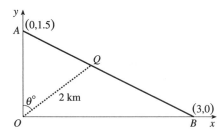

Write down the coordinates of a point $Q$ which is 2 km from $O$ on a bearing of $\theta°$. Show that, for $Q$ to be on the road between $A$ and $B$, $\theta$ must satisfy the equation $2\sin\theta° + 4\cos\theta° = 3$. Calculate the value of $\theta$ between 0 and 90 which satisfies this equation.                                                   (OCR)

**22** The figure shows the graphs

$\{1\}$ $y = 5\cos 2x° + 2$ and $\{2\}$ $y = \cos x°$

for $0 \leqslant x \leqslant 180$.

(a) Find the coordinates of the points $A$ and $B$ where the graph $\{1\}$ meets the $x$-axis.

(b) By solving a suitable trigonometric equation, find the $x$-coordinates of the two points $P$ and $Q$ where the

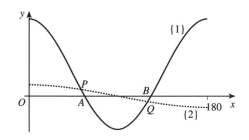

graphs $\{1\}$ and $\{2\}$ intersect. Hence find the coordinates of the points $P$ and $Q$.

(OCR)

**23** Let $a$ and $b$ be the straight lines with equations $y = m_1 x + c_1$ and $y = m_2 x + c_2$ where $m_1 m_2 \neq 0$. Use appropriate trigonometric formulae to prove that $a$ and $b$ are perpendicular if and only if $m_1 m_2 = -1$.

# 2 Differentiating trigonometric functions

This chapter shows how to differentiate the functions $\sin x$ and $\cos x$. When you have completed it, you should

- be familiar with a number of inequalities and limits involving trigonometric functions, and their geometrical interpretations
- know the derivatives and indefinite integrals of $\sin x$ and $\cos x$
- be able to differentiate a variety of trigonometric functions using the chain rule
- be able to integrate a variety of trigonometric functions, using identities where necessary.

## 2.1 Some inequalities and limits

Fig. 2.1 shows a sector $OAB$ of a circle with radius $r$ units and angle $\theta$ radians $\left(<\frac{1}{2}\pi\right)$. The tangent at $B$ meets $OA$ extended at $D$. Comparing areas,

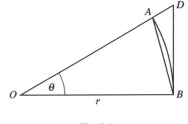

$$\text{triangle } OAB < \text{sector } OAB < \text{triangle } ODB$$

or $\qquad \frac{1}{2}r^2 \sin\theta < \frac{1}{2}r^2\theta < \frac{1}{2}r \times r\tan\theta .$

Fig. 2.1

Dividing by $\frac{1}{2}r^2$, it follows that, for $0 < \theta < \frac{1}{2}\pi$,

$$\sin\theta < \theta < \tan\theta .$$

If $\theta$ is small, Fig. 2.1 suggests that the three numbers $\sin\theta$, $\theta$ and $\tan\theta$ will be very close to each other.

*Try setting $\theta = 0.1$ on your calculator. Remember to put it into radian mode.*

So you can also write, if $\theta$ is small,

$$\sin\theta \approx \theta \quad \text{and} \quad \tan\theta \approx \theta .$$

One useful form of the inequality can be found by taking the left and right parts separately. First, since $\theta > 0$, you can divide the inequality $\sin\theta < \theta$ by $\theta$ to obtain

$$\frac{\sin\theta}{\theta} < 1 .$$

Secondly, you can write $\theta < \tan\theta$ as $\theta < \dfrac{\sin\theta}{\cos\theta}$. Multiplying this by $\cos\theta$ and dividing by $\theta$, both of which are positive since $0 < \theta < \frac{1}{2}\pi$,

$$\cos\theta < \frac{\sin\theta}{\theta} .$$

Putting these new inequalities together again gives, for $0 < \theta < \frac{1}{2}\pi$,

$$\cos\theta < \frac{\sin\theta}{\theta} < 1 .$$

This is illustrated in Fig. 2.2. Notice that the graphs have been extended to cover the interval $-\frac{1}{2}\pi < \theta < \frac{1}{2}\pi$.

Since $\cos(-\theta) = \cos\theta$

and $\dfrac{\sin(-\theta)}{(-\theta)} = \dfrac{-\sin\theta}{-\theta} = \dfrac{\sin\theta}{\theta}$, both

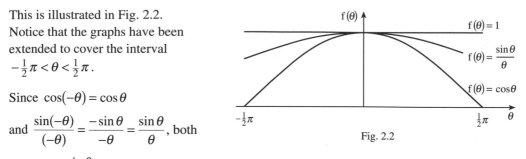

Fig. 2.2

$\cos\theta$ and $\dfrac{\sin\theta}{\theta}$ are even functions. This shows that the inequality holds also for $-\frac{1}{2}\pi < \theta < 0$.

However, Fig. 2.2 obscures an important point, that $\dfrac{\sin\theta}{\theta}$ is not defined when $\theta = 0$, since the fraction then becomes the meaningless $\dfrac{0}{0}$. But the graph does show that $\dfrac{\sin\theta}{\theta}$ approaches the limit 1 as $\theta \to 0$.

> If $0 < \theta < \frac{1}{2}\pi$, $\sin\theta < \theta < \tan\theta$.
>
> As $\theta \to 0$, $\dfrac{\sin\theta}{\theta} \to 1$.

**Example 2.1.1**

Show that the graph of $y = \sin x$, shown in Fig. 2.3, has gradient 1 at the origin.

Let the point $P$ on the graph have coordinates $(\theta, \sin\theta)$, so that $\dfrac{\sin\theta}{\theta}$ is the gradient of the chord $OP$. As $\theta \to 0$, this tends to the gradient of the tangent at the origin. But as $\theta \to 0$, $\dfrac{\sin\theta}{\theta} \to 1$, so the sine graph has gradient 1 at the origin.

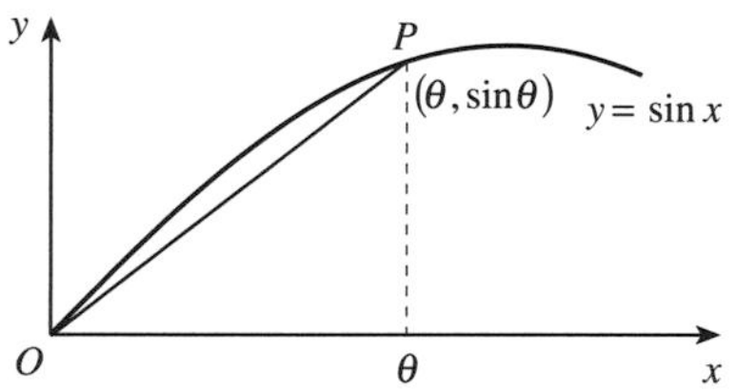

Fig. 2.3

The inequality $\sin\theta < \theta < \tan\theta$ also has an interpretation in terms of lengths. In Fig. 2.4, the sector in Fig. 2.1 has been reflected in the radius $OB$; $C$ and $E$ are the reflections of $A$ and $D$. Then $AC = 2r\sin\theta$, arc $ABC = r(2\theta) = 2r\theta$, and $DE = 2r\tan\theta$. So the inequality states that

$$\text{chord } AC < \text{arc } ABC < \text{tangent } DE.$$

Note also that, in Fig. 2.4,

$$\frac{\text{chord } AC}{\text{arc } ABC} = \frac{2r\sin\theta}{2r\theta} = \frac{\sin\theta}{\theta},$$

so that the ratio of the chord to the arc tends to 1 as $\theta$ tends to 0. This result will be needed in the next section.

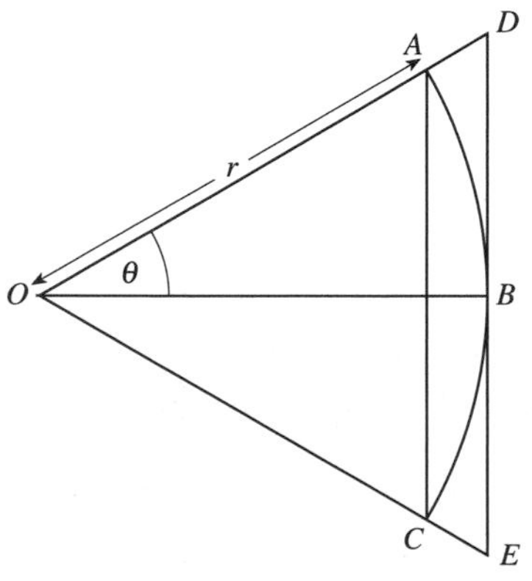

Fig. 2.4

> In a circular sector, as the angle at the centre tends to 0,
> the ratio of the chord to the arc tends to 1.

## 2.2* Derivatives of sine and cosine functions

This section shows how the limits established in Section 2.1 can be used to differentiate
sines and cosines. You can if you like skip this for a first reading, and pick up the chapter at
Section 2.3.

The proof is based on the definitions of $\cos\theta$ and $\sin\theta$ (given in P1 Sections 11.1 and 11.2)
as the $x$- and $y$-coordinates of a point on a circle of radius 1 unit.

*In P1 $\cos\theta$ and $\sin\theta$ were defined with $\theta$ in degrees, but the definitions work just as well
with $\theta$ in radians.*

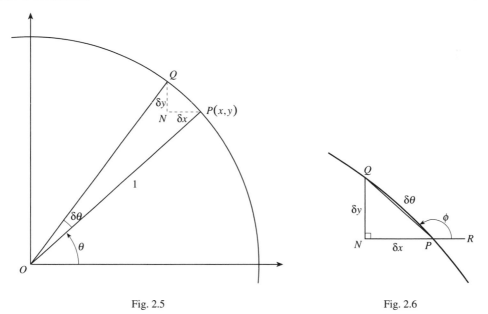

Fig. 2.5                                                    Fig. 2.6

In Fig. 2.5, the point $P$ has coordinates $x = \cos\theta$ and $y = \sin\theta$. If the angle is
increased by $\delta\theta$, $x$ increases by $\delta x$ (actually a negative increase if $\theta$ is an acute angle,
as shown here) and $y$ by $\delta y$. The increases in $x$ and $y$ are represented in the figure by
the displacements $PN$ and $NQ$.

Fig. 2.6 is an enlargement of the part of Fig. 2.5 around $PNQ$. Because the circle has
unit radius, the arc $PQ$ has length $\delta\theta$. Extend the line $NP$ to $R$, parallel to the $x$-axis,
and let $\phi$ be the angle $RPQ$. Then

$$\delta x = PQ\cos\phi \quad \text{and} \quad \delta y = PQ\sin\phi.$$

*Note that, since $\phi$ is an obtuse angle, these equations make $\delta x$ negative and $\delta y$ positive,
as you would expect from the diagrams. If $P$ were located in another quadrant of the circle,
the signs would be different, but the equations for $\delta x$ and $\delta y$ would still be correct.*

The objective is to find $\dfrac{dx}{d\theta}$ and $\dfrac{dy}{d\theta}$, which are defined as

$$\lim_{\delta\theta\to 0}\frac{\delta x}{\delta\theta} \quad \text{and} \quad \lim_{\delta\theta\to 0}\frac{\delta y}{\delta\theta}.$$

Now $\quad \dfrac{\delta x}{\delta\theta} = \dfrac{PQ}{\delta\theta}\times\cos\phi = \cos\phi\times\dfrac{\text{chord } PQ}{\text{arc } PQ},$

and $\quad \dfrac{\delta y}{\delta\theta} = \dfrac{PQ}{\delta\theta}\times\sin\phi = \sin\phi\times\dfrac{\text{chord } PQ}{\text{arc } PQ}.$

The proof can be completed by considering the limits of the two parts of these expressions separately. As $\delta\theta\to 0$, the chord $PQ$ becomes the tangent to the circle at $P$, and Fig. 2.7 shows that the angle $\phi$ tends to $\theta+\frac{1}{2}\pi$. Also it was shown in the last section that $\dfrac{\text{chord } PQ}{\text{arc } PQ}$ tends to 1.

Fig. 2.7

Assuming (as is true) that the limit of the product is equal to the product of the two limits, it follows that

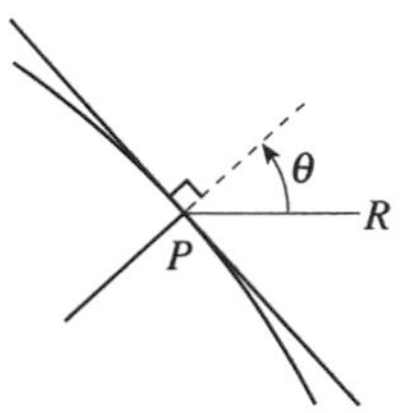

$$\frac{dx}{d\theta} = \cos\left(\theta+\tfrac{1}{2}\pi\right)\times 1 \quad \text{and} \quad \frac{dy}{d\theta} = \sin\left(\theta+\tfrac{1}{2}\pi\right)\times 1.$$

That is, $\quad \dfrac{dx}{d\theta} = -\sin\theta \quad \text{and} \quad \dfrac{dy}{d\theta} = \cos\theta.$

*The relation $\phi = \theta+\frac{1}{2}\pi$ applies whichever quadrant $\theta$ is in, so these results hold for all values of $\theta\in\mathbb{R}$.*

## 2.3 Working with trigonometric derivatives

You have seen the emphasis in trigonometry shift from calculations about triangles to properties of the sine and cosine as functions with domain the real numbers and range the interval $-1\leqslant y\leqslant 1$. This trend is given a further boost by finding the derivatives, so you can now treat trigonometric functions much like other functions in the mathematical store-cupboard, such as polynomials, power functions, exponential functions and logarithms.

Putting the results of the last section into the usual notation, replacing $\theta$ by $x$:

$$\frac{d}{dx}\cos x = -\sin x, \quad \frac{d}{dx}\sin x = \cos x.$$

Fig. 2.8 shows the graph of $f(x) = \sin x$ for $0 < x < 2\pi$ and, below it, the graphs of $f'(x) = \cos x$ and $f''(x) = -\sin x$. You can see from these how the graph of $f(x)$ is increasing when $f'(x)$ is positive and decreasing when $f'(x)$ is negative. There is a maximum at $\frac{1}{2}\pi$ where $\cos x$ is zero, and $f''\left(\frac{1}{2}\pi\right) = -\sin\left(\frac{1}{2}\pi\right) = -1 < 0$. Also, the graph of $f(x)$ is bending downwards between $0$ and $\pi$, where $f''(x) = -\sin x$ is negative. What is different in this example from other similar diagrams is that the three graphs are simply translations of each other parallel to the $x$-axis.

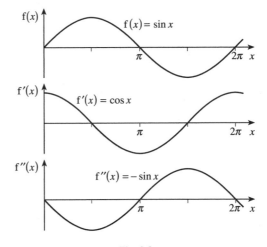

Fig. 2.8

Once you know the derivatives of $\sin x$ and $\cos x$, you can use the chain rule to find the derivatives of many other trigonometric functions.

**Example 2.3.1**

Differentiate with respect to $x$

(a) $\sin\left(3x - \frac{1}{4}\pi\right)$,  (b) $\cos^4 x$,  (c) $\sec x$,  (d) $\ln(\sec x)$.

(a) $\dfrac{d}{dx}\sin\left(3x - \frac{1}{4}\pi\right) = \cos\left(3x - \frac{1}{4}\pi\right) \times 3 = 3\cos\left(3x - \frac{1}{4}\pi\right)$.

(b) Remember that $\cos^4 x$ is the conventional way of writing $(\cos x)^4$.

$$\frac{d}{dx}\cos^4 x = 4\cos^3 x \times (-\sin x) = -4\cos^3 x \sin x.$$

(c) $\dfrac{d}{dx}\sec x = \dfrac{d}{dx}\left(\dfrac{1}{\cos x}\right) = -\dfrac{1}{\cos^2 x} \times (-\sin x) = \dfrac{\sin x}{\cos^2 x}$.

(d) $\dfrac{d}{dx}\ln\sec x = \dfrac{1}{\sec x} \times \sec x \tan x$     using the result of part (c)

$= \tan x$.

There are several ways of writing the answer to part (c). For example,

$$\frac{\sin x}{\cos^2 x} = \frac{\sin x / \cos x}{\cos x} = \frac{\tan x}{\cos x}$$

or   $\dfrac{\sin x}{\cos^2 x} = \sin x \times \left(\dfrac{1}{\cos^2 x}\right) = \sin x \sec^2 x$

or   $\dfrac{\sin x}{\cos^2 x} = \left(\dfrac{1}{\cos x}\right) \times \left(\dfrac{\sin x}{\cos x}\right) = \sec x \tan x$.

The most usual form is the last one, and it is a result worth remembering.

$$\frac{d}{dx}\sec x = \sec x \tan x.$$

For most users of mathematics, the independent variable for the sine and cosine functions usually represents time rather than angle. Just as $e^x$ is the natural function for describing exponential growth and decay, so sine and cosine are the natural functions for describing periodic phenomena. They can be applied to situations as different as the trade cycle, variation in insect populations, seasonal variation in sea temperature, rise and fall of tides (as in P1 Example 11.1.2), motion of a piston in a car cylinder and propagation of radio waves.

**Example 2.3.2**
The height in metres of the water in a harbour is given approximately by the formula $h = 6 + 3\cos\left(\frac{1}{6}\pi t\right)$ where $t$ is the time measured in hours from noon. Find an expression for the rate at which the water is rising at time $t$. When is it rising fastest?

Using the chain rule, the rate at which the tide is rising is

$$\frac{dh}{dt} = \left(-3\sin\tfrac{1}{6}\pi t\right) \times \tfrac{1}{6}\pi = -\tfrac{1}{2}\pi\sin\left(\tfrac{1}{6}\pi t\right).$$

The tide rises fastest when $\sin\left(\frac{1}{6}\pi t\right) = -1$, that is when $\frac{1}{6}\pi t = \frac{3}{2}\pi, \frac{7}{2}\pi, \frac{11}{2}\pi\dots$, or at 9 p.m. and again at 9 a.m. (This is exactly half way between low and high tide.)

**Example 2.3.3**
Find the minima and maxima of $f(x) = 4\cos x + \cos 2x$.

*Although the domain is $\mathbb{R}$, you only need to consider the interval $0 \leqslant x < 2\pi$. Since the period of $\cos x$ is $2\pi$, and the period of $\cos 2x$ is $\pi$ (its graph is obtained from the graph of $\cos x$ by a squash of scale factor $\frac{1}{2}$), the graph of $f(x)$ repeats itself after each interval of length $2\pi$.*

$f'(x) = -4\sin x - 2\sin 2x = -4\sin x - 4\sin x \cos x = -4\sin x(1 + \cos x)$, so
$f'(x) = 0$ when $\sin x = 0$ or $\cos x = -1$, that is when $x = 0$ or $\pi$.

$f''(x) = -4\cos x - 4\cos 2x$, so $f''(0) = -4 - 4 = -8$ and $f''(\pi) = 4 - 4 = 0$. There is therefore a maximum at $x = 0$, but the $f''(x)$ method does not work at $x = \pi$. You must therefore consider the sign of $f'(x)$ below and above $\pi$.

The factor $1 + \cos x$ is always positive except at $x = \pi$, where it is $0$; the factor $\sin x$ is positive for $0 < x < \pi$ and negative for $\pi < x < 2\pi$. So $f'(x) = -4\sin x(1 + \cos x)$ is negative for $0 < x < \pi$ and positive for $\pi < x < 2\pi$. There is therefore a minimum of $f(x)$ at $\pi$.

Over the whole domain there are maxima at $0, \pm 2\pi, \pm 4\pi, \dots$; the maximum value is $4 + 1 = 5$. There are minima at $\pm\pi, \pm 3\pi, \pm 5\pi, \dots$, with minimum value $-4 + 1 = -3$. You can check these results with a graphic calculator.

*Notice that, although periodic, the graph is not a simple transformation of a sine graph.*

## Exercise 2A

1   Use the inequalities $\sin\theta < \theta < \tan\theta$ for a suitable value of $\theta$ to show that $\pi$ lies between 3 and $2\sqrt{3}$.

2   Differentiate the following with respect to $x$.

(a)  $-\sin x$
(b)  $-\cos x$
(c)  $\sin 4x$
(d)  $2\cos 3x$

(e)  $\sin\frac{1}{2}\pi x$
(f)  $\cos 3\pi x$
(g)  $\cos(2x-1)$
(h)  $5\sin\left(3x+\frac{1}{4}\pi\right)$

(i)  $\cos\left(\frac{1}{2}\pi - 5x\right)$
(j)  $-\sin\left(\frac{1}{4}\pi - 2x\right)$
(k)  $-\cos\left(\frac{1}{2}\pi + 2x\right)$
(l)  $\sin\frac{1}{2}\pi(1+2x)$

3   Differentiate the following with respect to $x$.

(a)  $\sin^2 x$
(b)  $\cos^2 x$
(c)  $\cos^3 x$
(d)  $5\sin^2\frac{1}{2}x$

(e)  $\cos^4 2x$
(f)  $\sin x^2$
(g)  $7\cos 2x^3$
(h)  $\sin^2\left(\frac{1}{2}x - \frac{1}{3}\pi\right)$

(i)  $\cos^3 2\pi x$
(j)  $\sin^3 x^2$
(k)  $\sin^2 x^2 + \cos^2 x^2$
(l)  $\cos^2\frac{1}{2}x$

4   Show that $\dfrac{d}{dx}\operatorname{cosec} x = -\operatorname{cosec} x \cot x$. Use this result, together with $\dfrac{d}{dx}\sec x = \sec x \tan x$, to differentiate the following with respect to $x$.

(a)  $\sec 2x$
(b)  $\operatorname{cosec} 3x$
(c)  $\operatorname{cosec}\left(3x + \frac{1}{5}\pi\right)$
(d)  $\sec\left(x - \frac{1}{3}\pi\right)$

(e)  $4\sec^2 x$
(f)  $\operatorname{cosec}^3 x$
(g)  $\operatorname{cosec}^4 3x$
(h)  $\sec^2\left(5x - \frac{1}{4}\pi\right)$

5   Show that $\dfrac{d}{dx}\ln\operatorname{cosec} x = -\cot x$, $\dfrac{d}{dx}\ln\cos x = -\tan x$. Use these and other similar results to differentiate the following with respect to $x$.

(a)  $\ln\sin 2x$
(b)  $\ln\cos 3x$
(c)  $\ln\operatorname{cosec}(x - \pi)$

(d)  $\ln\sec 4x$
(e)  $\ln\sin^2 x$
(f)  $\ln\cos^3 2x$

6   Differentiate the following with respect to $x$.

(a)  $e^{\sin x}$
(b)  $e^{\cos 3x}$
(c)  $5e^{\sin^2 x}$

7   Show that the inequality $\sin\theta < \theta$ holds for all values of $\theta$ greater than $0$. By writing $\cos\theta$ as $\cos 2\left(\frac{1}{2}\theta\right)$, prove that $\cos\theta > 1 - \frac{1}{2}\theta^2$ for all values of $\theta$ except $0$. Use a graphic calculator to display graphs illustrating the inequalities $1 - \frac{1}{2}\theta^2 < \cos\theta < 1$.

8   (a)  Find the equation of the tangent where $x = \frac{1}{3}\pi$ on the curve $y = \sin x$.

(b)  Find the equation of the normal where $x = \frac{1}{4}\pi$ on the curve $y = \cos 3x$.

(c)  Find the equation of the normal where $x = \frac{1}{4}\pi$ on the curve $y = \sec x$.

(d)  Find the equation of the tangent where $x = \frac{1}{4}\pi$ on the curve $y = \ln\sec x$.

(e)  Find the equation of the tangent where $x = \frac{1}{2}\pi$ on the curve $y = 3\sin^2 2x$.

9   Find any stationary points in the interval $0 \leqslant x < 2\pi$ on each of the following curves, and find out whether they are maxima, minima or neither.

(a)  $y = \sin x + \cos x$
(b)  $y = x + \sin x$
(c)  $y = \sin^2 x + 2\cos x$

(d)  $y = \cos 2x + x$
(e)  $y = \sec x + \operatorname{cosec} x$
(f)  $y = \cos 2x - 2\sin x$

10  Find $\dfrac{d}{dx}\sin(a+x)$, first by using the chain rule, and secondly, by using the addition formula to expand $\sin(a+x)$ before differentiating. Verify that you get the same answer by both methods.

11  Find $\dfrac{d}{dx}\cos\left(\tfrac{3}{2}\pi-x\right)$. Check your answer by simplifying $\cos\left(\tfrac{3}{2}\pi-x\right)$ before you differentiate, and $\sin\left(\tfrac{3}{2}\pi-x\right)$ after you differentiate.

12  Show that $\dfrac{d}{dx}\left(2\cos^2 x\right)$, $\dfrac{d}{dx}\left(-2\sin^2 x\right)$ and $\dfrac{d}{dx}\cos 2x$ are all the same. Explain why.

13  Find $\dfrac{d}{dx}\sin^2\left(x+\tfrac{1}{4}\pi\right)$, and write your answer in its simplest form.

14  Find whether the tangent to $y=\cos x$ at $x=\tfrac{5}{6}\pi$ cuts the $y$-axis above or below the origin.

15  Sketch the graphs with the following equations, and find expressions for $\dfrac{dy}{dx}$.

    (a)  $y=\sin\sqrt{x}$                   (b)  $y=\sqrt{\cos x}$                  (c)  $y=\sin\dfrac{1}{x}$

16  Show that, if $y=\sin nx$, where $n$ is constant, then $\dfrac{d^2 y}{dx^2}=-n^2 y$. What can you deduce about the shape of the graph of $y=\sin nx$. Give a more general equation which has the same property.

17  Show that $\dfrac{d}{dx}\dfrac{1}{\cos x}$ can be written as $\dfrac{1}{\operatorname{cosec} x-\sin x}$. Hence find an expression for $\dfrac{d^2}{dx^2}\sec x$, and write your answer in as simple a form as possible.

18  By writing $\tan x$ as $\dfrac{\sin x}{\cos x}$, show that $\dfrac{d}{dx}\ln\tan x=2\operatorname{cosec} 2x$.

19  The gross national product (GNP) of a country, $P$ billion dollars, is given by the formula $P=1+0.02t+0.05\sin 0.6t$, where $t$ is the time in years after the year 2000. At what rate is the GNP changing
    (a)  in the year 2000,           (b)  in the year 2005?

20  A tuning fork sounding A above middle C oscillates 439 times a second. The displacement of the tip of the tuning fork is given by $0.02\cos(2\pi\times 439t)$ millimetres, where $t$ is the time in seconds after it is activated. Find
    (a)  the greatest speed,          (b) the greatest acceleration of the tip as it oscillates.
    (For the calculation of speed and acceleration, see M1 Chapter 11.)

## 2.4   Integrating trigonometric functions

The results $\dfrac{d}{dx}\sin x = \cos x$ and $\dfrac{d}{dx}\cos x = -\sin x$ give you two indefinite integrals:

$$\int \cos x \, dx = \sin x + k, \quad \int \sin x \, dx = -\cos x + k,$$

where $x$ is in radians.

*You have to be very careful to get the signs correct when differentiating or integrating sines and cosines. Notice that the minus sign appears when you differentiate* $\cos x$*, and when you integrate* $\sin x$*. If you forget which way round the signs go, draw for yourself sketches of the* $\sin x$ *and* $\cos x$ *graphs from* $0$ *to* $\frac{1}{2}\pi$*. You can easily see that it is the* $\cos x$ *graph which has the negative gradient.*

### Example 2.4.1
Find the area under the graph of $y = \sin\left(2x + \frac{1}{3}\pi\right)$ from $x = 0$ as far as the first point at which the graph cuts the positive $x$-axis.

$\sin\left(2x + \frac{1}{3}\pi\right) = 0$ when $2x + \frac{1}{3}\pi = 0, \pi, 2\pi, \dots$. The first positive root is $x = \frac{1}{3}\pi$.

$$\int_0^{\frac{1}{3}\pi} \sin\left(2x + \tfrac{1}{3}\pi\right) dx = \left[\tfrac{1}{2} \times \left(-\cos\left(2x + \tfrac{1}{3}\pi\right)\right)\right]_0^{\frac{1}{3}\pi}$$

$$= \tfrac{1}{2} \times \left(-\cos\pi - \left(-\cos\tfrac{1}{3}\pi\right)\right)$$

$$= \tfrac{1}{2} \times \left(1 + \tfrac{1}{2}\right) = \tfrac{3}{4}.$$

So the area is $\frac{3}{4}$.

The range of trigonometric functions that you can integrate can be increased by adapting the addition and double angle formulae found in Chapter 1. The most useful results are:

$$2\sin A \cos A = \sin 2A.$$

$$2\cos^2 A = 1 + \cos 2A, \quad 2\sin^2 A = 1 - \cos 2A.$$

Other results which are sometimes useful are

$$2\sin A \cos B = \sin(A + B) + \sin(A - B),$$

$$2\cos A \cos B = \cos(A - B) + \cos(A + B),$$

$$2\sin A \sin B = \cos(A - B) - \cos(A + B).$$

It is easy to prove all of these product formulae by starting on the right side and using the formulae in the shaded boxes in Sections 1.3 and 1.5.

**Example 2.4.2**

Let $R$ be the region under the graph of $y = \sin^2 x$ over the interval $0 \leqslant x \leqslant \pi$. Find
(a) the area of $R$,　　(b) the volume of revolution formed by rotating $R$ about the $x$-axis.

(a)　The area is given by

$$\int_0^\pi \sin^2 x \, dx = \int_0^\pi \tfrac{1}{2}(1 - \cos 2x) \, dx = \left[ \tfrac{1}{2}\left(x - \tfrac{1}{2}\sin 2x\right) \right]_0^\pi$$

$$= \left(\tfrac{1}{2}\pi - 0\right) - (0 - 0) = \tfrac{1}{2}\pi.$$

(b)　The volume of revolution is given by $\displaystyle\int_0^\pi \pi\left(\sin^2 x\right)^2 dx.$

Now　$\left(\sin^2 x\right)^2 = \left(\tfrac{1}{2}(1 - \cos 2x)\right)^2 = \tfrac{1}{4}\left(1 - 2\cos 2x + \cos^2 2x\right)$

$$= \tfrac{1}{4}\left(1 - 2\cos 2x + \tfrac{1}{2}(1 + \cos 4x)\right) \quad \text{using } \cos^2 2A \text{ with } 2x \text{ instead of } A$$

$$= \tfrac{3}{8} - \tfrac{1}{2}\cos 2x + \tfrac{1}{8}\cos 4x.$$

So　$\displaystyle\int_0^\pi \pi\left(\sin^2 x\right)^2 dx = \left[\pi\left(\tfrac{3}{8}x - \tfrac{1}{4}\sin 2x + \tfrac{1}{32}\sin 4x\right)\right]_0^\pi = \tfrac{3}{8}\pi^2.$

The area is $\tfrac{1}{2}\pi$ and the volume is $\tfrac{3}{8}\pi^2$.

**Example 2.4.3\***

Find　(a) $\displaystyle\int \sin 2x \cos 3x \, dx,$　　(b) $\displaystyle\int \cos^3 x \, dx.$

(a)　Writing $A = 2x$ and $B = 3x$ in the formula for $2 \sin A \cos B$,

$$2 \sin 2x \cos 3x = \sin(2x - 3x) + \sin(2x + 3x) = \sin(-x) + \sin 5x$$

$$= -\sin x + \sin 5x.$$

So　$\displaystyle\int \sin 2x \cos 3x \, dx = \tfrac{1}{2}\left(\cos x - \tfrac{1}{5}\cos 5x\right) + k = \tfrac{1}{2}\cos x - \tfrac{1}{10}\cos 5x + k.$

(b)　None of the formulae given above can be used directly, but $\cos^3 x$ can be written in other forms which can be integrated.

**Method 1**　$\cos^3 x = \cos^2 x \cos x = \tfrac{1}{2}(1 + \cos 2x)\cos x$

$$= \tfrac{1}{2}\cos x + \tfrac{1}{2}\cos 2x \cos x$$

$$= \tfrac{1}{2}\cos x + \tfrac{1}{4}(\cos x + \cos 3x)$$

$$= \tfrac{3}{4}\cos x + \tfrac{1}{4}\cos 3x.$$

Therefore $\displaystyle\int \cos^3 x \, dx = \tfrac{3}{4}\sin x + \tfrac{1}{12}\sin 3x + k.$

**Method 2** $\quad \cos^3 x = \cos^2 x \cos x = \left(1 - \sin^2 x\right)\cos x$

$$= \cos x - \sin^2 x \cos x.$$

You can integrate the first term directly. To see how to integrate $\sin^2 x \cos x$, look back to Example 2.3.1(b). When $\cos^4 x$ was differentiated using the chain rule, a factor $\dfrac{d}{dx}\cos x = -\sin x$ appeared in the answer. In a similar way,

$$\frac{d}{dx}\sin^3 x = 3\sin^2 x \times \cos x = 3\sin^2 x \cos x.$$

Therefore $\displaystyle\int \cos^3 x\,dx = \int \left(\cos x - \sin^2 x \cos x\right)dx$

$$= \sin x - \tfrac{1}{3}\sin^3 x + k.$$

In (b) it is not obvious that the two methods give the same answer, but if you work out some values, or use a calculator to draw the graphs, you will find that they are in agreement. The reason for this is that

$$\sin 3x = \sin(2x + x) = \sin 2x \cos x + \cos 2x \sin x$$

$$= (2\sin x \cos x)\cos x + \left(1 - 2\sin^2 x\right)\sin x$$

$$= 2\sin x\left(1 - \sin^2 x\right) + \left(1 - 2\sin^2 x\right)\sin x = 3\sin x - 4\sin^3 x.$$

Therefore, $\quad \tfrac{3}{4}\sin x + \tfrac{1}{12}\sin 3x = \tfrac{3}{4}\sin x + \tfrac{1}{4}\sin x - \tfrac{1}{3}\sin^3 x = \sin x - \tfrac{1}{3}\sin^3 x.$

### Exercise 2B

**1** Integrate the following with respect to $x$.

(a) $\cos 2x$

(b) $\sin 3x$

(c) $\cos(2x + 1)$

(d) $\sin(3x - 1)$

(e) $\sin(1 - x)$

(f) $\cos\left(4 - \tfrac{1}{2}x\right)$

(g) $\sin\left(\tfrac{1}{2}x + \tfrac{1}{3}\pi\right)$

(h) $\cos\left(3x - \tfrac{1}{4}\pi\right)$

(i) $-\sin\tfrac{1}{2}x$

**2** Evaluate the following.

(a) $\displaystyle\int_0^{\frac{1}{2}\pi} \sin x\,dx$

(b) $\displaystyle\int_0^{\frac{1}{4}\pi} \cos x\,dx$

(c) $\displaystyle\int_0^{\frac{1}{4}\pi} \sin 2x\,dx$

(d) $\displaystyle\int_{\frac{1}{4}\pi}^{\frac{1}{3}\pi} \cos 3x\,dx$

(e) $\displaystyle\int_{\frac{1}{6}\pi}^{\frac{1}{3}\pi} \sin\left(3x + \tfrac{1}{6}\pi\right)dx$

(f) $\displaystyle\int_0^{\frac{1}{2}\pi} \sin\left(\tfrac{1}{4}\pi - x\right)dx$

(g) $\displaystyle\int_0^1 \cos(1 - x)\,dx$

(h) $\displaystyle\int_0^{\frac{1}{2}} \sin\left(\tfrac{1}{2}x + 1\right)dx$

(i) $\displaystyle\int_0^{2\pi} \sin\tfrac{1}{2}x\,dx$

**3** Integrate the following with respect to $x$.

(a) $\tan 2x$

(b) $\cot 5x$

(c) $\sec 3x \tan 3x$

(d) $\operatorname{cosec} 4x \cot 4x$

(e) $\tan\left(\tfrac{1}{4}\pi - x\right)$

(f) $\cot\left(\tfrac{1}{3}\pi - 2x\right)$

(g) $\sec\left(\tfrac{1}{2}x + 1\right)\tan\left(\tfrac{1}{2}x + 1\right)$

(h) $\operatorname{cosec}(1 - 2x)\cot(1 - 2x)$

(i) $\dfrac{\sin 2x}{\cos^2 2x}$

**4** Evaluate the following.

(a) $\displaystyle\int_0^{\frac{1}{4}\pi} \tan x \, dx$

(b) $\displaystyle\int_0^{\frac{1}{12}\pi} \tan 3x \, dx$

(c) $\displaystyle\int_{\frac{1}{6}\pi}^{\frac{1}{4}\pi} \operatorname{cosec} 3x \cot 3x \, dx$

(d) $\displaystyle\int_{\frac{1}{3}\pi}^{\frac{1}{2}\pi} \cot \tfrac{1}{2} x \, dx$

(e) $\displaystyle\int_{\frac{1}{4}}^{\frac{1}{2}} \operatorname{cosec} 2x \cot 2x \, dx$

(f) $\displaystyle\int_{0.1}^{0.3} \sec \tfrac{1}{4} x \tan \tfrac{1}{4} x \, dx$

**5** Integrate the following with respect to $x$.

(a) $\cos^2 x$

(b) $\cos^2 \tfrac{1}{2} x$

(c) $\sin^2 2x$

(d) $\sin^3 x \cos x$

(e) $\sec^3 x \tan x$ (write as $\sec^2 x (\sec x \tan x)$)

(f) $\operatorname{cosec}^5 2x \cot 2x$

(g) $\sin 3x \cos 4x$

(h) $\sin^3 x$ (write as $(1 - \cos^2 x) \sin x$)

(i) $\sin^5 x$ (write as $(1 - \cos^2 x)^2 \sin x$)

(j) $\sin 2x \sin 6x$

**6** (a) Find $\dfrac{d}{dx} \sec^2 x$. Use $\sec^2 x \equiv 1 + \tan^2 x$ to show that $\dfrac{d}{dx} \tan^2 x = 2 \tan x \sec^2 x$.

(b) Explain why $\dfrac{d}{dx} \tan^2 x$ is equal to $2 \tan x \times \dfrac{d}{dx} \tan x$. Deduce $\dfrac{d}{dx} \tan x$.

(c) Write down $\displaystyle\int \sec^2 x \, dx$, and hence find $\displaystyle\int \tan^2 x \, dx$.

(d) Use a similar method to find $\displaystyle\int \operatorname{cosec}^2 x \, dx$ and $\displaystyle\int \cot^2 x \, dx$.

**7** Find the area of the region between the curve $y = \cos x$ and the $x$-axis from $x = 0$ to $x = \tfrac{1}{2}\pi$.

Find also the volume generated when this area is rotated about the $x$-axis.

**8** Find the area of the region bounded by the curve $y = 1 + \sin x$, the $x$-axis and the lines $x = 0$ and $x = \pi$.

Find also the volume generated when this area is rotated about the $x$-axis.

**9** The curves $y = \sin x$, $y = \cos x$ and the $x$-axis enclose a region shown shaded in the sketch.

(a) Find the area of the shaded region.

(b) Find the volume generated when this region is rotated about the $x$-axis.

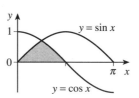

**10** In the interval $0 \leqslant x \leqslant \pi$ the curve $y = \sin x + \cos x$ meets the $y$-axis at $P$ and the $x$-axis at $Q$. Find the coordinates of $P$ and $Q$.

Calculate the area of the region enclosed between the curve and the axes bounded by $P$ and $Q$.

Calculate also the volume generated when this area is rotated about the $x$-axis.

## Miscellaneous exercise 2

1 (a) Differentiate $\ln \sin 2x$ with respect to $x$, simplifying your answer.

   (b) Find $\int \sin \frac{3}{2} x \cos \frac{1}{2} x \, dx$.

   (c) Given that $y = \cos^2 x$, find $\dfrac{dy}{dx}$.

   (d) Differentiate $\sin\left(t^3 + 4\right)$ with respect to $t$.

   (e) Find $\int \cos^2 3x \, dx$.

   (f) Differentiate $\cos \sqrt{x}$ with respect to $x$.

   (g) Find $\int \sin^2 \frac{1}{3} x \, dx$.

2 (a) Express $\sin^2 x$ in terms of $\cos 2x$.

   (b) The region $R$ is bounded by the part of the curve $y = \sin x$ between $x = 0$ and $x = \pi$ and the $x$-axis. Show that the volume of the solid formed when $R$ is rotated completely about the $x$-axis is $\frac{1}{2} \pi^2$. (OCR)

3 (a) Use the addition formulae to find expressions involving surds for $\sin \frac{1}{12} \pi$ and $\tan \frac{1}{12} \pi$.

   (b) Use the fact that $\left(\sqrt{3} + 1\right)\left(\sqrt{3} - 1\right) = 2$ to show that $\tan \frac{1}{12} \pi = 2 - \sqrt{3}$.

   (c) Show that $\pi$ lies between $3\sqrt{2}\left(\sqrt{3} - 1\right)$ and $12\left(2 - \sqrt{3}\right)$. Use a calculator to evaluate these expressions correct to 3 decimal places.

4 Show that, if $0 < x < \frac{1}{2} \pi$, $\tan x = +\sqrt{\sec^2 x - 1}$. Use the chain rule to find $\dfrac{d}{dx} \sqrt{\sec^2 x - 1}$,

   and hence find $\dfrac{d}{dx} \tan x$ for $0 < x < \frac{1}{2} \pi$ in as simple a form as possible.

   Use a similar method to find $\dfrac{d}{dx} \tan x$ for $\frac{1}{2} \pi < x < \pi$.

   (You will meet a much simpler way of finding $\dfrac{d}{dx} \tan x$ in Section 8.3.)

5 $P$, $Q$ and $R$ are the points on the graph of $y = \cos x$ for which $x = 0$, $x = \frac{1}{4} \pi$ and $x = \frac{1}{2} \pi$ respectively. Find the point $S$ where the normal at $Q$ meets the $y$-axis. Compare the distances $SP$, $SQ$ and $SR$. Use your answers to draw a sketch showing how the curve $y = \cos x$ over the interval $-\frac{1}{2} \pi < x < \frac{1}{2} \pi$ is related to the circle with centre $S$ and radius $SQ$.

6 By writing $\cos \theta$ as $\cos 2\left(\frac{1}{2} \theta\right)$, and using the approximation $\sin \theta \approx \theta$ when $\theta$ is small, show that $\cos \theta \approx 1 - \frac{1}{2} \theta^2$ when $\theta$ is small.

   Since sine is an odd function, it is suggested that a better approximation for sine might have the form $\sin \theta \approx \theta - k\theta^3$ when $\theta$ is small. By writing $\sin \theta$ as $\sin 2\left(\frac{1}{2} \theta\right)$, using the approximation $\cos \theta \approx 1 - \frac{1}{2} \theta^2$ and equating the coefficients of $\theta$, find an appropriate numerical value for $k$.

   Investigate whether this approximation is in fact better, by evaluating $\theta$ and $\theta - k\theta^3$ numerically when $\theta = \frac{1}{6} \pi$.

7  Show graphically that there is a number $\alpha$ between $\pi$ and $\frac{3}{2}\pi$ such that the tangent to $y = \sin x$ at $(\alpha, \sin \alpha)$ passes through the origin. Show that $\alpha$ is the smallest positive root of the equation $x = \tan x$.

Use a numerical method to find an approximate value for $\alpha$, correct to 4 decimal places.

8  The motion of an electric train on the straight stretch of track between two stations is given by $x = 11\left(t - \frac{45}{\pi}\sin\left(\frac{\pi}{45}t\right)\right)$, where $x$ metres is the distance covered $t$ seconds after leaving the first station. The train stops at these two stations and nowhere between them.

(a) Find the velocity, $v$ m s$^{-1}$ in terms of $t$. Hence find the time taken for the journey between the two stations.

(b) Calculate the distance between the two stations. Hence find the average velocity of the train.

(c) Find the acceleration of the train 30 seconds after leaving the first station.　　(OCR)

(For the calculation of velocity and acceleration, see M1 Chapter 11.)

9  A mobile consists of a bird with flapping wings suspended from the ceiling by two elastic strings. A small weight $A$ hangs below it. $A$ is pulled down and then released. After $t$ seconds, the distance, $y$ cm, of $A$ below its equilibrium position is modelled by the periodic function $y = 5\cos 2t + 10\sin t$.

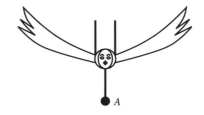

(a) Verify that the $(t, y)$ graph has a stationary point where $t = \frac{1}{6}\pi$.

(b) Show that all the stationary points of the graph correspond to solutions of the equation $\cos t(2\sin t - 1) = 0$. Find the other two solutions in the interval $0 \leqslant t \leqslant \pi$.

(c) State one limitation of the model. Explain why $y = e^{-kt}(5\cos 2t + 10\sin t)$, where $k$ is a small constant, might give a better model.　　(OCR)

10 (a) By first expressing $\cos 4x$ in terms of $\cos 2x$, show that
$$\cos 4x = 8\cos^4 x - 8\cos^2 x + 1,$$
and hence show that
$$8\cos^4 x = \cos 4x + 4\cos 2x + 3.$$

(b) The region $R$, shown shaded in the diagram, is bounded by the part of the curve $y = \cos^2 x$ between $x = 0$ and $x = \frac{1}{2}\pi$ and by the $x$- and $y$-axes. Show that the volume of the solid formed when $R$ is rotated completely about the $x$-axis is $\frac{3}{16}\pi^2$.　　(OCR)

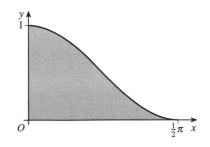

11  The diagram shows a sketch, not to scale, of part of
    the graph of $y = f(x)$, where $f(x) = \sin x + \sin 2x$
    and where $x$ is measured in radians.

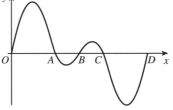

    (a) Find, in terms of $\pi$, the $x$-coordinates of the
        points $A$, $B$, $C$ and $D$, shown in the diagram,
        where the graph of f meets the positive $x$-axis.

    (b) Show that $f(\pi - \theta)$ may be expressed as
        $\sin \theta - \sin 2\theta$, and show also that $f(\pi - \theta) + f(\pi + \theta) = 0$ for all values of $\theta$.

    (c) Differentiate $f(x)$, and hence show that the greatest value of $f(x)$, for $0 \leqslant x \leqslant 2\pi$,
        occurs when

    $$\cos x = \frac{-1 + \sqrt{33}}{8}.$$ 

    (OCR)

12  In this question $f(x) = \sin \frac{1}{2} x + \cos \frac{1}{3} x$.

    (a) Find $f'(x)$.

    (b) Find the values of $f(0)$ and $f'(0)$.

    (c) State the periods of $\sin \frac{1}{2} x$ and $\cos \frac{1}{3} x$.

    (d) Write down another value of $x$ (not $0$) for which $f(x) = f(0)$ and $f'(x) = f'(0)$.

    (OCR)

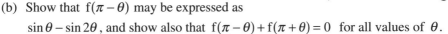

# 3 Circles

This chapter is about circles and their equations. When you have completed it, you should

- be able to write down the equation of a circle with centre $(p, q)$ and radius $r$
- be able to use the equation of a circle in the form $x^2 + y^2 + 2gx + 2fy + c = 0$
- be able to use algebraic methods to solve problems involving lines and circles.

## 3.1 The equation of a circle

You have seen in Chapters 1 and 2 that there is a close connection between sine and cosine functions and the circle. This chapter shows how you can explore the geometry of the circle using coordinate methods.

The equation of a curve is the rule satisfied by the coordinates $(x, y)$ of any point which lies on it, and not by any points which do not lie on it.

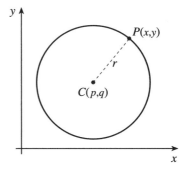

Let $P$ with coordinates $(x, y)$ be a point on the circumference of a circle with centre $C(p, q)$ and radius $r$, where, of course, $r > 0$. Then, for all possible positions of $P$ on the circle, the distance $CP = r$.

But, from the distance formula in P1 Section 1.1, the distance $CP$ is $\sqrt{(x-p)^2 + (y-q)^2}$, so the equation of the circle is

Fig. 3.1

$$\sqrt{(x-p)^2 + (y-q)^2} = r, \quad \text{or} \quad (x-p)^2 + (y-q)^2 = r^2.$$

> The equation of a circle with centre $(p, q)$ and radius $r$ is
>
> $$(x-p)^2 + (y-q)^2 = r^2.$$
>
> When the centre is $(0, 0)$, the equation is $x^2 + y^2 = r^2$.

### Example 3.1.1
Find the equation of the circle with centre $(1, 2)$ and radius 3.

Using the formula, the equation is $(x-1)^2 + (y-2)^2 = 9$.

You can also multiply out the brackets to get

$$x^2 - 2x + 1 + y^2 - 4y + 4 = 9, \quad \text{or} \quad x^2 + y^2 - 2x - 4y - 4 = 0.$$

*Either of the forms $(x-1)^2 + (y-2)^2 = 9$ and $x^2 + y^2 - 2x - 4y - 4 = 0$ is usually acceptable.*

Notice that if you multiply out the brackets in the equation $(x-p)^2 + (y-q)^2 = r^2$ you get the equation

$$x^2 + y^2 - 2px - 2qy + \left(p^2 + q^2 - r^2\right) = 0.$$

Look at the left side of this equation. It looks rather like a polynomial, but there are two variables $x$ and $y$; in fact it is called **a polynomial in two variables**. Extending the definitions which you met in P2 Section 1.1 for polynomials in a single variable $x$,

$\left(p^2 + q^2 - r^2\right)$ is called the 'constant term';

$-2px$ and $-2qy$ are terms 'of degree 1';

$x^2$ and $y^2$ are terms 'of degree 2'.

The most general polynomial of the first degree in two variables is

$$ax + by + c = 0$$

where $a$ and $b$ are not both zero. You know from P1 Section 1.7 that this is the equation of a straight line.

The most general polynomial of the second degree in two variables is

$$ax^2 + 2hxy + by^2 + 2gx + 2fy + c = 0,$$

where $a$, $h$ and $b$ are not all zero. (Don't worry for the moment about the curious conventional choice of letters or the insertion of the 2s.) You can see that there are three characteristics which enable you to recognise the equation of a circle.

- the left side is a polynomial of the second degree in $x$ and $y$
- the coefficients of $x^2$ and $y^2$ are equal to 1
- there is no term in $xy$.

For example, $x^2 + y^2 - 4x + 6y - 36 = 0$ is an equation with the three properties. You can rewrite it in the form

$$x^2 - 4x \quad + y^2 + 6y \quad = 36,$$

where the $x$-terms and the $y$-terms have been separated on the left, and temporary gaps have been left. These gaps will be filled by completing the square (see P1 Section 4.2) and making the right side of the equation fit. Thus

$$\left(x^2 - 4x + 4\right) + \left(y^2 + 6y + 9\right) = 36 + 4 + 9,$$

where, as 4 and 9 were added to the left side of the equation, they are also added to the right side. Thus

$$(x-2)^2 + (y+3)^2 = 49.$$

Comparing with the equation in the shaded box, this is the equation of a circle with centre $(2, -3)$ and radius 7.

**Example 3.1.2**

Find the centre and radius of the circle $x^2 + y^2 - 2x + 4y - 7 = 0$.

Writing the equation as $(x^2 - 2x) + (y^2 + 4y) = 7$, completing the squares inside the brackets and compensating the right side gives

$$(x^2 - 2x + 1) + (y^2 + 4y + 4) = 7 + 1 + 4,$$

that is,

$$(x - 1)^2 + (y + 2)^2 = 12.$$

The circle has centre $(1, -2)$ and radius $\sqrt{12}$.

More generally, consider the equation $x^2 + y^2 + 2gx + 2fy + c = 0$, which has the properties outlined above. Then, carrying through the same process,

$$x^2 + 2gx \qquad + y^2 + 2fy \qquad = -c,$$
$$x^2 + 2gx + g^2 + y^2 + 2fy + f^2 = g^2 + f^2 - c,$$
$$(x + g)^2 + (y + f)^2 = g^2 + f^2 - c.$$

Comparing with the equation in the shaded box at the start of the section, it follows that:

> The equation $x^2 + y^2 + 2gx + 2fy + c = 0$ represents a circle, centre $(-g, -f)$
>
> and radius $\sqrt{g^2 + f^2 - c}$, provided that $g^2 + f^2 - c > 0$.

If $g^2 + f^2 - c = 0$, the equation $(x + g)^2 + (y + f)^2 = g^2 + f^2 - c$ becomes

$$(x + g)^2 + (y + f)^2 = 0.$$

Since the sum of two squares is only 0 if both the squares are themselves 0, both $x + g = 0$ and $y + f = 0$, so $x = -g$ and $y = -f$. Thus the point $(-g, -f)$ is the only point satisfying the equation $x^2 + y^2 + 2gx + 2fy + c = 0$. This is sometimes called a 'point circle'.

If $g^2 + f^2 - c < 0$, the equation is not satisfied by any values of $x$ and $y$, so there is no curve corresponding to the equation $x^2 + y^2 + 2gx + 2fy + c = 0$.

Sometimes, to avoid fractions, it is more convenient to choose the coefficients of $x^2$ and $y^2$ to be equal, but not equal to 1. You can always get back to the standard form of the equation by dividing through by the coefficient. This is illustrated in the next example.

**Example 3.1.3**

Find the centre and radius of the circle $2x^2 + 2y^2 - 6x + 2y - 3 = 0$.

Dividing by 2, you find $x^2 + y^2 - 3x + y - \frac{3}{2} = 0$.

For this equation $g = -\frac{3}{2}$, $f = \frac{1}{2}$ and $c = -\frac{3}{2}$, so the centre is $\left(\frac{3}{2}, -\frac{1}{2}\right)$

and the radius is $\sqrt{\left(-\frac{3}{2}\right)^2 + \left(\frac{1}{2}\right)^2 - \left(-\frac{3}{2}\right)} = \sqrt{\frac{9}{4} + \frac{1}{4} + \frac{3}{2}} = 2$.

## 3.2 Lines and circles

To find the equation of a tangent to a circle, you need to know its gradient. You can't find this by differentiating in the usual way, because its equation is not of the form $y = f(x)$, but you can use the fact that the tangent to a circle is perpendicular to the radius at the point of contact, and that the radius is normal to the circle.

**Example 3.2.1**
Find the equation of the tangent to $x^2 + y^2 - 8x - 2y + 12 = 0$ at the point $(6, 2)$.

The curve is a circle, centre $(4, 1)$.

The gradient of the radius joining $(4, 1)$ to $(6, 2)$ is $\frac{2-1}{6-4} = \frac{1}{2}$. The tangent is perpendicular to this radius, so the gradient of the tangent is $-\frac{1}{1/2} = -2$. The equation of the tangent is therefore $y - 2 = -2(x - 6)$, that is $y + 2x = 14$.

*Notice that in this last example, the magnitude of the radius is never used, nor even found. In fact, it has been taken for granted that $(6, 2)$ is a point on the circle, and this really ought to be checked. If in place of $(6, 2)$ you took a point on the radius inside the circle, then the method would give you the equation of a line perpendicular to the radius; that is, the line segment (or chord) having that point as its mid-point. Draw a figure for yourself to illustrate this.*

**Example 3.2.2**
A map shows a circular lake and a road which passes close to it. On the ground the road has equation $4x + 3y = 12$, and the lake occupies the interior of the circle $x^2 + y^2 - 10x - 8y + 32 = 0$, the units being kilometres. What is the distance of the lake from the road at its closest point?

The centre of the circle is $(5, 4)$, and its radius is $\sqrt{25 + 16 - 32} = 3$.

You can find the nearest point of the road from the centre of the lake, by finding where the line from the centre of the lake perpendicular to the road meets the road.

The gradient of the road is $-\frac{4}{3}$, so the gradient of the line perpendicular to it is $\frac{3}{4}$. The equation of the perpendicular to the road through $(5, 4)$ is $y - 4 = \frac{3}{4}(x - 5)$, which simplifies to $3x - 4y = -1$.

Solving this equation simultaneously with $4x + 3y = 12$ gives the point $\left(\frac{9}{5}, \frac{8}{5}\right)$.

The distance of this point from $(5, 4)$ is $\sqrt{\left(5 - \frac{9}{5}\right)^2 + \left(4 - \frac{8}{5}\right)^2} = \sqrt{\left(\frac{16}{5}\right)^2 + \left(\frac{12}{5}\right)^2} = 4$.

So the nearest point of the lake is 4 km from the road.

**Example 3.2.3**
The line with equation $x + y = k$ is a tangent to the circle $x^2 + y^2 + 4x - 6y + 11 = 0$. Find the possible values of $k$.

*Two methods are given. Method 2 is more general than Method 1 and can be used with curves other than circles.*

**Method 1**    The circle has centre $(-2,3)$. The tangent line has gradient $-1$, so the radius has gradient 1, and, as it passes through the centre $(-2,3)$, its equation is $y = x + 5$. To find where this line meets the circle, solve $y = x + 5$ simultaneously with $x^2 + y^2 + 4x - 6y + 11 = 0$.

$$x^2 + (x+5)^2 + 4x - 6(x+5) + 11 = 0,$$
$$x^2 + \left(x^2 + 10x + 25\right) + 4x - 6x - 30 + 11 = 0,$$
$$2x^2 + 8x + 6 = 0,$$
$$x^2 + 4x + 3 = 0,$$
$$(x+1)(x+3) = 0,$$
$$x = -1 \text{ or } -3.$$

The $y$-coordinates are 4 and 2, so the points where the radius meets the circle are $(-1,4)$ and $(-3,2)$. The line $x + y = k$ must pass through one or other of these points so the value of $k$ is $-1 + 4 = 3$ or $-3 + 2 = -1$. Therefore $k = 3$ or $-1$.

**Method 2**    Start by apparently finding the points of intersection of the line with the circle, by substituting $y = k - x$ into the equation of the circle.

$$x^2 + (k-x)^2 + 4x - 6(k-x) + 11 = 0,$$
$$x^2 + \left(k^2 - 2kx + x^2\right) + 4x - 6k + 6x + 11 = 0,$$
$$2x^2 + (-2k+10)x + \left(k^2 - 6k + 11\right) = 0.$$

If the line is a tangent to the circle, this equation has a repeated root, so the discriminant '$b^2 - 4ac$' of the equation must be 0. Therefore

$$(-2k+10)^2 - 4 \times 2 \times \left(k^2 - 6k + 11\right) = 0,$$
$$\left(4k^2 - 40k + 100\right) - 8k^2 + 48k - 88 = 0,$$
$$-4k^2 + 8k + 12 = 0,$$
$$k^2 - 2k - 3 = 0,$$
$$(k-3)(k+1) = 0,$$
$$k = 3 \text{ or } -1.$$

**Example 3.2.4**

Find the equation of the circle which has the line joining $(1,3)$ to $(-2,5)$ as its diameter.

**Method 1**    The centre of the circle is the mid-point, and the radius is half the distance between the points. So the centre is $\left(-\frac{1}{2},4\right)$, and the radius is $\frac{1}{2}\sqrt{(-3)^2 + 2^2} = \frac{1}{2}\sqrt{13}$.

So the equation of the circle is $\left(x - \left(-\frac{1}{2}\right)\right)^2 + (y-4)^2 = \frac{13}{4}$, which, after multiplying out the brackets, reduces to

$$x^2 + y^2 + x - 8y + 13 = 0.$$

**Method 2**  Let $A$ and $B$ be the two points at opposite ends of the diameter, and let $P$, with coordinates $(x, y)$, be a point on the circle, as shown in Fig. 3.2.

This method relies on the fact that $P$ lies on the circle if, and only if, $AP$ is perpendicular to $BP$.

*This is the 'angle in a semicircle is a right angle' property of a circle.*

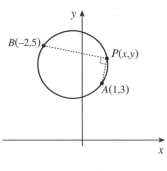

Fig. 3.2

The gradients of $AP$ and $BP$ are respectively $\dfrac{y-3}{x-1}$ and $\dfrac{y-5}{x-(-2)}$, and these are perpendicular if, and only if, $\dfrac{y-3}{x-1} \times \dfrac{y-5}{x-(-2)} = -1$, which is the same as

$$(x-1)(x+2) + (y-3)(y-5) = 0.$$

On multiplying out the brackets, you get $x^2 + y^2 + x - 8y + 13 = 0$, as before.

This result generalises to:

> The circle which has $(a, b)$ and $(c, d)$ as the ends of a diameter is
>
> $$(x-a)(x-c) + (y-b)(y-d) = 0.$$

## Exercise 3

**1** Write down the equation of a circle with

    (a) centre $(0, 0)$ and radius 3,

    (b) centre $(2, 0)$ and radius 5,

    (c) centre $(1, 4)$ and radius 2,

    (d) centre $(-5, 7)$ and radius 1,

    (e) centre $(6, -2)$ and radius 10,

    (f) centre $(-7, -3)$ and radius 10.

**2** Determine the centre and radius of the following circles.

    (a) $(x-3)^2 + (y-2)^2 = 25$

    (b) $(x+4)^2 + (y+1)^2 = 9$

    (c) $(x-6)^2 + y^2 = 20$

    (d) $x^2 + y^2 - 4x - 10y - 20 = 0$

    (e) $x^2 + y^2 + 8x - 2y - 1 = 0$

    (f) $x^2 + y^2 - 2x + y + 1 = 0$

**3** A circle has centre $(2, 5)$ and passes through the point $(4, 1)$. Find its equation.

**4** A circle has centre $(5, 5)$ and passes through the origin. Find its equation.

**5** Find the equation of the normal to the circle $x^2 + y^2 = 40$ at the point $(6, 2)$.

**6** Find the equation of the normal to the circle $x^2 + y^2 - 4x - 30 = 0$ at the point $(7, 3)$.

**7**　Find the equation of the tangent to the circle $x^2 + y^2 = 10$ at the point $(-3,1)$.

**8**　Find the equation of the tangent to the circle $x^2 + (y+3)^2 = 18$ at the point $(3,0)$.

**9**　Find the equation of the tangent to the circle $x^2 + y^2 - 8x + 2y = 0$ at the origin.

**10**　Find the equation of the tangent to the circle $x^2 + y^2 + 10x + 2y + 13 = 0$ at the point $(-3,2)$.

**11**　Of the following equations, three represent circles and three do not. Determine which represent circles and, for each of these, find the centre and radius.

  (a)　$(x+7)^2 + (y-4)^2 + 25 = 0$　　　　　　(b)　$x^2 + y^2 + 5x - 3y - 16 = 0$

  (c)　$9x^2 + 12x + 9y^2 - 24y + 4 = 0$　　　　(d)　$x^2 + 2xy + 3y^2 + 4x + 5y + 6 = 0$

  (e)　$x^2 + y^2 + 14x - 10y + 78 = 0$　　　　　(f)　$(x+y)^2 + (x-y)^2 + 4(x+y) = 2044$

**12**　Find the coordinates of the points where the straight line $y = 1$ meets the circle $x^2 + y^2 - 14x + 2y + 45 = 0$.

**13**　Find the coordinates of the points where the straight line $x + 10 = 0$ meets the circle $(x+3)^2 + (y+8)^2 = 625$.

**14**　Find the coordinates of the points where the straight line $y = 3x + 6$ meets the circle $x^2 + y^2 - 8x + 4y - 30 = 0$.

**15**　Find the coordinates of the points where the straight line $y = 4 - x$ meets the circle $(x-1)^2 + (y+3)^2 = 20$.

**16**　Show that the straight line $x + 2y - 3 = 0$ does not meet the circle $x^2 + y^2 + 3x + 2y - 5 = 0$.

**17**　Show that the straight line $y = x - 8$ is a tangent to the circle $x^2 + y^2 - 6x + 2y + 2 = 0$ and find the coordinates of the point of contact.

**18**　Find the length of the chord formed when the line $x - 2y + 4 = 0$ intersects the circle $(x-2)^2 + (y+7)^2 = 85$, giving your answer in the form $k\sqrt{5}$.

**19**　The equation $x^2 + y^2 - 4\sqrt{2}x + 8\sqrt{3}y + c = 0$ represents a circle. Show that $c < 56$.

**20**　The equation of a circle is $x^2 + y^2 - 8ax + 6ay + 21a^2 = 0$, where $a$ is a positive constant. Find, in terms of $a$,

  (a)　the shortest distance between the circle and the origin,

  (b)　the shortest distance between the circle and the $y$-axis,

  (c)　the equation of the tangent to the circle at the point $(4a, -a)$.

**21**　The straight line with equation $y = -3x + c$ is a tangent to the circle $x^2 + y^2 - 4x - 2y - 5 = 0$. Find the possible values of $c$.

**22**　The straight line with equation $y = kx$ is a tangent to the circle $x^2 + y^2 - 4x - 4y + 7 = 0$. Find the possible values of $k$, giving your answers in the form $a + b\sqrt{7}$.

## Miscellaneous exercise 3

1 Find the centre and radius of the circle with equation $x^2 + y^2 - 7x + y + 8 = 0$.

2 The circle with equation $x^2 + y^2 + 8x - 22y + c = 0$ has radius $7$. Find the value of $c$.

3 The circle $C$ has equation $x^2 + y^2 + 12x - 4y + 11 = 0$. Determine whether the following points lie inside, on or outside $C$.

$P(-4,7)$     $Q(-5,-3)$     $R(-2,6)$     $S(-1,4)$     $T(-9,6)$

4 Find the centre and radius of the circle with equation $3x^2 + 3y^2 - 9x + 15y + 23 = 0$.

5 Points $A$ and $B$ have coordinates $(-3,-6)$ and $(9,2)$ respectively. Find the equation of the circle which has $AB$ as diameter.

6 Find the centre and radius of the circle with equation $x^2 + y^2 - 6y = 0$. Find also the coordinates of the points of intersection of the line $x - 2y + 3 = 0$ and this circle.     (OCR)

7 Find the equation of the tangent to the circle $x^2 + y^2 + 8x + 4y + 7 = 0$ at the point $(-1,0)$.

8 It is given that the circle $x^2 + y^2 - 14x - 10y + c = 0$ lies wholly in the first quadrant. Show that $49 < c < 74$.

9 Three points are $P(-2,7)$, $Q(2,3)$ and $R(4,5)$. Show that $PQ$ is perpendicular to $QR$. Find the equation of the circle which passes through the points $P$, $Q$ and $R$.

10 Prove that each of the circles $x^2 + y^2 - 4x = 0$ and $x^2 + y^2 - 12x - 8y + 43 = 0$ lies completely outside the other.     (OCR)

11 The straight line $y = 20 - 3x$ meets the circle $x^2 + y^2 - 2x - 14y = 0$ at the points $A$ and $B$. Calculate the exact length of the chord $AB$.     (OCR)

12 Prove that the equation $x^2 + y^2 - 8x + 4ky + 3k^2 = 0$ represents a circle for all values of $k$.

13 Circle $C_1$ has equation $x^2 + y^2 + 4x - 6y - 12 = 0$ and circle $C_2$ has equation $x^2 + y^2 - 20x + 12y + 100 = 0$. Point $P$ lies on $C_1$ and point $Q$ lies on $C_2$. The distance between $P$ and $Q$ is denoted by $d$. Show that $4 \leqslant d \leqslant 26$.

14 A circle passes through the point $(9,-1)$ and is such that the straight lines $x = -7$ and $x = 13$ are tangents to the circle. Find the equation of each of the circles which satisfy these conditions.

15 (a) Determine the translation which transforms the circle with equation
$x^2 + y^2 + 4x - 8y = 0$ to the circle with equation $x^2 + y^2 + 10x - 10y + 30 = 0$.

(b) The circle with equation $x^2 + y^2 - 7x - y - 3 = 0$ is translated $5$ units in the positive $x$-direction and $2$ units in the negative $y$-direction. Find the equation of the resulting circle.

(c) The circle with equation $x^2 + y^2 + 10x - 2y + 10 = 0$ is reflected in the $x$-axis and then translated by $4$ units in the positive $x$-direction. Find the equation of the resulting circle.

**16** Verify that the circle with equation $x^2 + y^2 - 2rx - 2ry + r^2 = 0$ touches both the coordinate axes. Find the radii of the two circles which pass through the point $(16, 2)$ and touch both the coordinate axes.      (OCR)

**17** The line $y = -3x + k$ is a tangent to the circle $x^2 + y^2 = 10$. Find the possible values of $k$.

**18** The straight line $y = 2x + k$ meets the circle $x^2 + y^2 - 2x + 4y = 0$ at two points. Find the set of possible values of $k$.

**19** The circles $C_1$, $C_2$ and $C_3$ touch as shown and have centres which lie on a straight line parallel to the $x$-axis. The radii are in the ratio $4:2:1$. Given that the equation of $C_1$ is $x^2 + y^2 + 10x - 8y - 23 = 0$, find the equation of $C_3$.

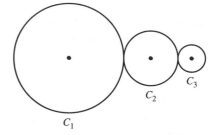

**20** Find the equation of the tangent to the circle $9x^2 + 9y^2 - 24x + 30y + 16 = 0$ at the point $\left(\frac{1}{3}, -3\right)$.

**21** The vertex $A$ of a square $ABCD$, lettered in the anticlockwise sense, has coordinates $(-1, -3)$. The diagonal $BD$ lies along the line $x - 2y + 5 = 0$.

  (a) Prove that the coordinates of $C$ are $(-5, 5)$ and find the coordinates of $B$ and $D$.

  (b) Find the equation of the circle which touches all four sides of the square, confirming that the circle passes through the origin.      (OCR)

**22** The equation of a circle is $x^2 + y^2 + 4x - 6y + k = 0$. Prove that $k < 13$.

  (a) Given that the radius of this circle is $6$, find the value of $k$.

  (b) Given instead that $y = 2x + 17$ is a tangent to the circle, find the value of $k$.

**23** Find the equations of the two circles each of which touches both coordinate axes and passes through the point $(9, 2)$. Find

  (a) the coordinates of the second point of intersection of these circles,

  (b) the equation of the common chord of the two circles.      (OCR)

**24** Show that the circles with equations $x^2 + y^2 - 4x - 2y - 20 = 0$ and $x^2 + y^2 - 16x - 18y + 120 = 0$ have the same radius and touch each other at the point $(5, 5)$. Find the equations of the three lines which are common tangents to the two circles.

**25** Find the equation of the circle which passes through the points $(0, -2)$, $(1, -15)$ and $(9, 1)$.

**26** The point $(a, a+1)$ lies inside the circle $x^2 + y^2 + 10x - 8y - 63 = 0$. Find the set of possible values of $a$.

**27** The shaded region in the diagram is bounded by the lines $y = 0$, $x = 2$ and $x = 4$ and by part of the circle $x^2 + y^2 - 6x = 0$. Find the volume of the solid generated when the shaded region is rotated through four right angles about the $x$-axis.

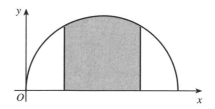

**28** The diagram shows the circle $x^2 + y^2 - 8y + 7 = 0$. The shaded region is bounded by part of this circle and by the line $x = \sqrt{5}$. Find the volume of the solid generated when the shaded region is rotated through four right angles about the $y$-axis.

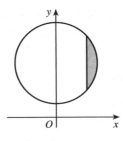

**29** Show that each of the circles $x^2 + y^2 + 4x - 2y - 95 = 0$ and $x^2 + y^2 - 12x - 14y - 15 = 0$ passes through the centre of the other. Show that the line with equation $3x - 4y - 40 = 0$ is a tangent to both circles and find the equation of the other straight line which is a common tangent to the two circles.

**30** Show that the two circles $x^2 + y^2 + 4x - 2y + 3 = 0$ and $x^2 + y^2 + 3x - y - 2 = 0$ have just one point in common. Sketch the graphs of the two circles, showing clearly how the circles are related to each other.

# 4 Parametric equations

This chapter is about a method of describing curves using parameters. When you have completed it, you should

- know how to describe a curve using a parameter
- be able, in simple cases, to convert from a parametric equation of a curve to the cartesian equation of the curve
- be able to use parametric methods to establish properties of curves.

## 4.1 Introduction

Imagine a person $P$ going round on a roundabout, centre the origin $O$ and radius 1 unit, at a constant speed (see Fig. 4.1). Suppose that $P$ starts at the $x$-axis and moves anticlockwise in such a way that the angle at the centre $t$ seconds after starting is $t$ radians.

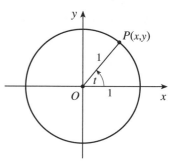

Where is $P$ after $t$ seconds? You can see from Fig. 4.1 that the coordinates of $P$ are given by

$$x = \cos t, \quad y = \sin t.$$

Fig. 4.1

These equations allow you to find the position of $P$ at any time, and they describe the path of $P$ completely.

Fig. 4.2 shows the values of $t$ at various points on the first revolution of the roundabout. Notice that for each value of $t$ there is a unique point on the curve.

During the first revolution, each point on the curve has a $t$-value corresponding to the time that the person is at that point. However, for each further revolution there will be another $t$-value associated with the point.

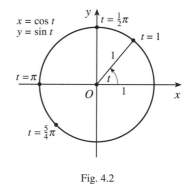

Fig. 4.2

### Example 4.1.1
Find the $t$-value of the starting point, the first time that $P$ returns to it.

> The starting point is $(1,0)$. Since $x = \cos t$, $y = \sin t$, you find that $1 = \cos t$ and $0 = \sin t$. These equations are simultaneously satisfied by $t = 0, \pm 2\pi, \pm 4\pi, \dots$. The smallest positive solution is $t = 2\pi$.

The equations $x = \cos t$, $y = \sin t$ are an example of **parametric equations**, and the variable $t$ is an example of a **parameter**. In this case the variable $t$ represents time, but in other cases it may not, as you will see in Example 4.1.2.

You may be able to draw curves from parametric equations on your graphic calculator. Put your calculator into parametric mode. You then have to enter the parametric equations into the calculator, and you may have to give an interval of values of $t$. For example, if you gave an interval of 0 to $\pi$ for $t$ in Example 4.1.1, you would get only the upper semicircle of the path. If you use the trace key, your calculator will also give you the $t$-value for any point.

*Recall that the curve looks like a circle only if you use the same scale on each axis.*

You could also plot the curve using a spreadsheet with graph-plotting facilities.

Here are other examples of parametric curves.

**Example 4.1.2**
A curve has parametric equations $x = t^2$, $y = 2t$. Sketch the curve for values of $t$ from $-3$ to $3$.

Draw up a table of values, Table 4.3.

| $t$ | $-3$ | $-2$ | $-1$ | $0$ | $1$ | $2$ | $3$ |
|---|---|---|---|---|---|---|---|
| $x$ | 9 | 4 | 1 | 0 | 1 | 4 | 9 |
| $y$ | $-6$ | $-4$ | $-2$ | 0 | 2 | 4 | 6 |

Table 4.3

The points $(9,-6)$, $(4,-4)$, $(1,-2)$, $(0,0)$, $(1,2)$, $(4,4)$ and $(9,6)$ lie on the curve shown in Fig. 4.4. The points which are plotted are labelled with the $t$-values of the parameter.

The idea that a point is defined by the value of its parameter is an important one. Thus, for the curve $x = t^2$, $y = 2t$ you can talk about the point $t = -2$, which means the point $(4,-4)$.

The curve looks like a parabola on its side, and you will, in the next section, be able to prove that it is.

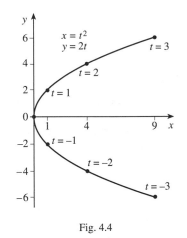

Fig. 4.4

**Example 4.1.3**
A curve has parametric equations $x = \sin t$, $y = \sin 2t$, for values of $t$ from 0 to $2\pi$. Plot the curve, and indicate the points corresponding to values of $t$ which are multiples of $\frac{1}{6}\pi$.

Draw up a table of values, Table 4.5.

| $t$ | 0 | $\frac{1}{6}\pi$ | $\frac{1}{3}\pi$ | $\frac{1}{2}\pi$ | $\frac{2}{3}\pi$ | $\frac{5}{6}\pi$ |
|---|---|---|---|---|---|---|
| $x$ | 0 | 0.5 | 0.866 | 1 | 0.866 | 0.5 |
| $y$ | 0 | 0.866 | 0.866 | 0 | −0.866 | −0.866 |

| $t$ | $\pi$ | $\frac{7}{6}\pi$ | $\frac{4}{3}\pi$ | $\frac{3}{2}\pi$ | $\frac{5}{3}\pi$ | $\frac{11}{6}\pi$ | $2\pi$ |
|---|---|---|---|---|---|---|---|
| $x$ | 0 | −0.5 | −0.866 | −1 | −0.866 | −0.5 | 0 |
| $y$ | 0 | 0.866 | 0.866 | 0 | −0.866 | −0.866 | 0 |

Table 4.5

Fig. 4.6 illustrates this curve, with the points from the table labelled with their $t$-values, except for the origin, which is the point for which $t = 0$, $t = \pi$ and $t = 2\pi$.

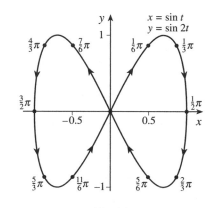

Fig. 4.6

Notice the arrows, which show the way that the values of $t$ are increasing. These are not essential, but you should put them in if you want to show the direction in which the parameter is increasing.

If you use values of $t$ outside the interval from 0 to $2\pi$, the curve will repeat itself.

Finally, you should notice that parametric equations enable you to produce curves whose equations can't be written in the form $y = f(x)$. Neither the circle in Fig. 4.2 nor the curves in Fig. 4.4 or Fig. 4.6 can be drawn using a function equation, because none of them have just one value of $y$ for each value of $x$.

It is time to give a definition of a parameter.

If $x = f(t)$ and $y = g(t)$, where f and g are functions of a variable $t$ defined for some domain of values of $t$, then the equations $x = f(t)$ and $y = g(t)$ are called **parametric equations**, and the variable $t$ is a **parameter**.

## 4.2   From parametric to cartesian equations

Suppose that you have a curve $C$ given parametrically by the equations $x = f(t)$ and $y = g(t)$ where f and g are functions defined for some domain of values of $t$. If you eliminate the parameter $t$ between the two equations, then every point of $C$ lies on the curve with the resulting cartesian equation.

For example, in Example 4.1.2 the curve is given parametrically by $x = t^2$, $y = 2t$. In this case, you can write $t = \frac{1}{2}y$, so that $x = \left(\frac{1}{2}y\right)^2 = \frac{1}{4}y^2$, which you can rewrite as $y^2 = 4x$. The parameter $t$ has been eliminated between the two equations $x = t^2$, $y = 2t$. You can see from Fig. 4.4 that $y^2 = 4x$ is simply $y = \frac{1}{4}x^2$ 'on its side'.

> If $x = f(t)$ and $y = g(t)$ are parametric equations of a curve $C$, and you eliminate the parameter between the two equations, each point of the curve $C$ lies on the curve represented by the resulting cartesian equation.

### Example 4.2.1

A curve is given parametrically by the equations $x = 2t + 1$, $y = 3t - 2$. Show that the 'curve' is a straight line and find its gradient.

From the first equation $t = \frac{1}{2}(x - 1)$, so $y = 3\left(\frac{1}{2}(x - 1)\right) - 2$, that is, $2y = 3x - 7$.

This is the equation of a straight line. Its gradient is $\frac{3}{2}$.

### Example 4.2.2

Let $E$ be the curve given parametrically by $x = a\cos t$, $y = b\sin t$, where $a$ and $b$ are constants and $t$ is a parameter which takes values from $0$ to $2\pi$. Find the cartesian equation of $E$.

Since $x = a\cos t$ and $y = b\sin t$, $\cos t = \dfrac{x}{a}$

and $\sin t = \dfrac{y}{b}$. Then, using $\cos^2 t + \sin^2 t = 1$,

$\left(\dfrac{x}{a}\right)^2 + \left(\dfrac{y}{b}\right)^2 = 1$. This is the equation of the

ellipse shown in Fig. 4.7. If $a$ and $b$ are equal, it is a circle of radius $a$.

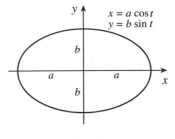

Fig. 4.7

## Exercise 4A

1 Find the coordinates of the point on the curve $x = 5t^2$, $y = 10t$
   (a) when $t = 6$,      (b) when $t = -1$.

2 Find the coordinates of the point on the curve $x = 1 - \dfrac{1}{t}$, $y = 1 + \dfrac{1}{t}$

   (a) when $t = 3$,      (b) when $t = -1$.

3 The parametric equations of a curve are $x = 2\cos t$, $y = 2\sin t$, for $0 \leqslant t < 2\pi$. What is the value of $t$ at the point $(0, 2)$?

4 A curve is given by $x = 5\cos t$, $y = 2\sin t$ for $0 \leqslant t < 2\pi$. Find the value of $t$ at the point $\left(-2\frac{1}{2}, \sqrt{3}\right)$.

**5** Sketch the curve given by $x = t^2$, $y = \dfrac{1}{t}$ for $t > 0$.

**6** Sketch the curve given by $x = 3\cos t$, $y = 2\sin t$ for $0 \leqslant t < 2\pi$.

**7** Sketch the graph of $x = 3t^2$, $y = 6t$ for $-4 \leqslant t \leqslant 4$.

**8** Sketch the locus given by $x = \cos^2 t$, $y = \sin^2 t$ for $0 \leqslant t < 2\pi$.

**9** Find cartesian equations for curves with these parametric equations.

   (a)  $x = t^2$, $y = \dfrac{1}{t}$        (b)  $x = 3t^2$, $y = 6t$        (c)  $x = 2\cos t$, $y = 2\sin t$

**10** Find cartesian equations for curves with these parametric equations.

   (a)  $x = \cos^2 t$, $y = \sin^2 t$             (b)  $x = \cos^3 t$, $y = \sin^3 t$

   (c)  $x = 1 - \dfrac{1}{t}$, $y = 1 + \dfrac{1}{t}$        (d)  $x = 3t^2$, $y = 2t^3$

**11** Show that parametric equations for a circle with centre $(p, q)$ and radius $r$ are
$x = p + r\cos t$, $y = q + r\sin t$. Eliminate the parameter $t$ to obtain the cartesian
equation of the circle in the form $(x - p)^2 + (y - q)^2 = r^2$.

## 4.3 Differentiation and parametric form

Suppose that $C$ is a curve with its equation given parametrically. How can you find the
gradient at a point on the curve without first finding the cartesian equation of the curve?

Consider a point $P$ with parameter $t$ on the curve. The coordinates $(x, y)$ of $P$ are both
functions of $t$, so as $t$ changes, $x$ and $y$ also change. You can use the result in the
shaded box, but if you need to know why the result is true, read the rest of the section.

> If a curve is given parametrically by equations for $x$ and $y$ in terms of
> a parameter $t$, then
>
> $$\frac{dy}{dx} = \frac{dy}{dt} \Big/ \frac{dx}{dt}.$$

To establish the result in the shaded box, increase the value of $t$ by $\delta t$; then there are
corresponding increases of $\delta x$ in $x$ and $\delta y$ in $y$.

Then, provided that $\delta x \neq 0$, $\dfrac{\delta y}{\delta x} = \dfrac{\delta y}{\delta t} \Big/ \dfrac{\delta x}{\delta t}$.

As $\delta t \to 0$, both $\delta x \to 0$ and $\delta y \to 0$, so $\displaystyle\lim_{\delta x \to 0} \frac{\delta y}{\delta x} = \lim_{\delta t \to 0} \frac{\delta y}{\delta x}$.

Therefore, assuming that $\displaystyle\lim_{\delta t \to 0}\left( \frac{\delta y}{\delta t} \Big/ \frac{\delta x}{\delta t} \right) = \left( \lim_{\delta t \to 0} \frac{\delta y}{\delta t} \right) \Big/ \left( \lim_{\delta t \to 0} \frac{\delta x}{\delta t} \right)$,

$$\frac{dy}{dx} = \lim_{\delta x \to 0} \frac{\delta y}{\delta x} = \lim_{\delta t \to 0} \frac{\delta y}{\delta x} = \lim_{\delta t \to 0}\left(\frac{\delta y}{\delta t} \Big/ \frac{\delta x}{\delta t}\right) = \left(\lim_{\delta t \to 0} \frac{\delta y}{\delta t}\right) \Big/ \left(\lim_{\delta t \to 0} \frac{\delta x}{\delta t}\right)$$

$$= \frac{dy}{dt} \Big/ \frac{dx}{dt}.$$

Therefore $\dfrac{dy}{dx} = \dfrac{dy}{dt} \Big/ \dfrac{dx}{dt}.$

*Notice that, just as the chain rule for differentiation is easy to remember because of 'cancelling', so is this rule. However, you should remember that this a helpful feature of the notation, and cancellation has no meaning in this context.*

### Example 4.3.1

Find the gradient at $t = 3$ on the parabola $x = t^2$, $y = 2t$.

$\dfrac{dy}{dt} = 2$ and $\dfrac{dx}{dt} = 2t$, so $\dfrac{dy}{dx} = \dfrac{dy}{dt} \Big/ \dfrac{dx}{dt} = \dfrac{2}{2t} = \dfrac{1}{t}$. When $t = 3$, the gradient is $\frac{1}{3}$.

### Example 4.3.2

Find the equation of the normal at $(-8, 4)$ to the curve which is given parametrically by $x = t^3$, $y = t^2$. Sketch the curve, showing the normal.

For the point $(-8, 4)$, $t^3 = -8$ and $t^2 = 4$. These are both satisfied by $t = -2$.

As $\dfrac{dy}{dt} = 2t$ and $\dfrac{dx}{dt} = 3t^2$, $\dfrac{dy}{dx} = \dfrac{dy}{dt} \Big/ \dfrac{dx}{dt} = \dfrac{2t}{3t^2} = \dfrac{2}{3t}$. When $t = -2$ the gradient is $\dfrac{2}{3 \times (-2)} = -\frac{1}{3}$, so the gradient of the normal is $-\dfrac{1}{-1/3} = 3$.

Therefore the equation of the normal is $y - 4 = 3(x - (-8))$ or $y = 3x + 28$.

Notice with this curve that the gradient is not defined when $t = 0$, because the tangent at the origin is the $y$-axis. The point where $t = 0$ is called a **cusp**.

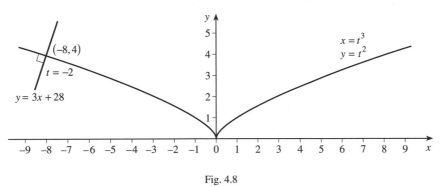

Fig. 4.8

You can now sketch the curve, shown in Fig. 4.8, but recall that the normal will look perpendicular to the curve only if the scales on both axes are the same.

━━━━━━━━ **Exercise 4B** ━━━━━━━━

**1** Find $\dfrac{dy}{dx}$ in terms of $t$ for the following curves.

(a) $x = t^3, y = 2t$

(b) $x = \sin t, y = \cos t$

(c) $x = 2 \cos t, y = 3 \sin t$

(d) $x = t^3 + t, y = t^2 - t$

**2** Find the gradient of the tangent on the following curves, at the specified values of $t$.

(a) $x = 3t^2, y = 6t$ when $t = 0.5$

(b) $x = t^3, y = t^2$ when $t = 2$

(c) $x = 1 - \dfrac{1}{t}, y = 1 + \dfrac{1}{t}$ when $t = 2$

(d) $x = t^2, y = \dfrac{1}{t}$ when $t = 3$

**3** Find the gradient of the normal on the following curves, at the specified values of $t$.

(a) $x = 5t^2, y = 10t$ when $t = 3$

(b) $x = \cos^2 t, y = \sin^2 t$ when $t = \frac{1}{3}\pi$

(c) $x = \cos^3 t, y = \sin^3 t$ when $t = \frac{1}{6}\pi$

(d) $x = t^2 + 2, y = t - 2$ when $t = 4$

**4** Show that the equation of the tangent to the curve $x = 3\cos t, y = 2\sin t$ when $t = \frac{3}{4}\pi$ is $3y = 2x + 6\sqrt{2}$.

**5** (a) Find the gradient of the curve $x = t^3, y = t^2 - t$ at the point $(1, 0)$.

(b) Hence find the equation of the tangent to the curve at this point.

**6** A curve has parametric equations $x = t - \cos t, y = \sin t$. Find the equation of the tangent to the curve when $t = \pi$.

**7** Find the equations of the tangents to these curves at the specified values.

(a) $x = t^2, y = 2t$ when $t = 3$

(b) $x = 5\cos t, y = 3\sin t$ when $t = \frac{11}{6}\pi$

**8** Find the equations of the normals to these curves at the specified values.

(a) $x = 5t^2, y = 10t$ when $t = 3$

(b) $x = \cos t, y = \sin t$ when $t = \frac{2}{3}\pi$

**9** (a) Find the equation of the normal to the hyperbola $x = 4t, y = \dfrac{4}{t}$ at the point $(8, 2)$.

(b) Find the coordinates of the point where this normal crosses the curve again.

**10** (a) Find the equation of the normal to the parabola $x = 3t^2, y = 6t$ at the point where $t = -2$.

(b) Find the coordinates of the point where this normal crosses the curve again.

## 4.4 Proving properties of curves

Parameters are a very powerful tool for proving properties about curves. Here are two examples which show a general method.

**Example 4.4.1**

A parabola is given by $x = at^2$, $y = 2at$. The tangent at a point $P$ on the parabola meets the $x$-axis at $T$. Prove that $PT$ is bisected by the tangent at the vertex of the parabola.

*There is no good reason why this parabola is on its side, but it is conventional to think of the parabola parametrically as $x = at^2$, $y = 2at$ rather than $x = 2at$, $y = at^2$. In this case, the vertex is still the point where the axis of symmetry meets the parabola, which is the origin, and the tangent at the vertex is the $y$-axis.*

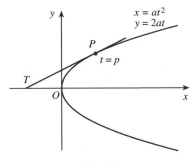

Fig. 4.9

Let $P$ be the point on the parabola, shown in Fig. 4.9. with coordinates $\left(at^2, 2at\right)$. Since

$$\frac{dy}{dx} = \frac{dy}{dt} \Big/ \frac{dx}{dt} = \frac{2a}{2at} = \frac{1}{t}$$

the gradient at $P$ is $\dfrac{1}{t}$. The equation of the tangent at $P$ is therefore

$$y - 2at = \frac{1}{t}\left(x - at^2\right), \text{ which can be simplified to } ty = x + at^2.$$

This tangent meets the $x$-axis at the point where $y = 0$, so $x = -at^2$ and $T$ is the point with coordinates $\left(-at^2, 0\right)$.

The mid-point of $PT$ is $\left(\frac{1}{2}\left(at^2 + \left(-at^2\right)\right), \frac{1}{2}(2at + 0)\right)$ which is $(0, at)$. Since the tangent at the vertex has equation $x = 0$, the point $(0, at)$ lies on it. Therefore $PT$ is bisected by the tangent at the vertex.

**Example 4.4.2**

A curve is given parametrically by $x = a\cos^3 t$, $y = a\sin^3 t$, where $a$ is a positive constant, for $0 \leqslant t < 2\pi$. The tangent at any point $P$ meets the $x$-axis at $A$ and the $y$-axis at $B$. Prove that the length of $AB$ is constant.

Let $P$ be the point on the curve, shown in Fig. 4.10, with parameter $t$. $P$ has coordinates $\left(a\cos^3 t, a\sin^3 t\right)$.

To find the gradient at $P$, calculate

$$\frac{dy}{dx} = \frac{dy}{dt} \Big/ \frac{dx}{dt}$$

$$= \frac{3a\sin^2 t \cos t}{-3a\sin t \cos^2 t} = -\frac{\sin t}{\cos t}.$$

The gradient at $P$ is $-\dfrac{\sin t}{\cos t}$.

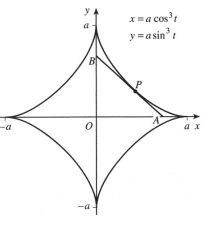

Fig. 4.10

The equation of the tangent at $P$ is $y - a\sin^3 t = -\dfrac{\sin t}{\cos t}\left(x - a\cos^3 t\right)$.

This can be simplified to

$$y\cos t + x\sin t = a\sin^3 t\cos t + a\sin t\cos^3 t$$
$$= a\sin t\cos t\left(\sin^2 t + \cos^2 t\right)$$
$$= a\sin t\cos t.$$

The points $A$ and $B$ have coordinates $(a\cos t, 0)$ and $(0, a\sin t)$. The length $AB$ is

$$\sqrt{(0 - a\cos t)^2 + (a\sin t - 0)^2} = \sqrt{a^2\cos^2 t + a^2\sin^2 t} = a.$$

The length $AB$ is therefore constant.

The curve $x = a\cos^3 t$, $y = a\sin^3 t$ is called an *astroid*. If you think of the tangent as a ladder of length $a$ sliding down the 'wall and floor' made by the $y$-axis and the $x$-axis, then the ladder always touches the astroid.

## Exercise 4C

1   Let $P$ be a point on the curve $x = t^2$, $y = \dfrac{1}{t}$. If the tangent to the curve at $P$ meets the $x$- and $y$-axes at $A$ and $B$ respectively, prove that $PA = 2BP$.

2   A parabola is given parametrically by $x = at^2$, $y = 2at$. If $P$ is any point on the parabola, let $F$ be the foot of the perpendicular from $P$ onto the axis of symmetry. Let $G$ be the point where the normal from $P$ crosses the axis of symmetry.
   Prove that $FG = 2a$.

3   $P$ is a point on the parabola given parametrically by $x = at^2$, $y = 2at$, where $a$ is a constant. Let $S$ be the point $(a, 0)$, $Q$ be the point $(-a, 2at)$ and $T$ be the point where the tangent at $P$ to the parabola crosses the axis of symmetry of the parabola.
   (a)   Show that $SP = PQ = QT = ST = at^2 + a$.
   (b)   Prove that angle $QPT$ is equal to angle $SPT$.
   (c)   If $PM$ is parallel to the axis of the parabola, with $M$ to the right of $P$, and $PN$ is the normal to the parabola at $P$, show that angle $MPN$ is equal to angle $NPS$.

4   $P$, $Q$, $R$ and $S$ are four points on the hyperbola $x = ct$, $y = \dfrac{c}{t}$ with parameters $p$, $q$, $r$ and $s$ respectively. Prove that, if the chord $PQ$ is perpendicular to the chord $RS$, then $pqrs = -1$.

5   Let $P$ be a point on the ellipse with parametric equations $x = 5\cos t$, $y = 3\sin t$ for $0 \le t < 2\pi$, and let $F$ and $G$ be the points $(-4, 0)$ and $(4, 0)$ respectively. Prove that
   (a)   $FP = 5 + 4\cos t$,          (b)   $FP + PG = 10$.
   Let the normal at $P$ make angles $\theta$ and $\phi$ with $FP$ and $GP$ respectively. Prove that
   (c)   $\tan\theta = \frac{4}{3}\sin t$,          (d)   $\theta = \phi$.

6   Let $H$ be the curve with parametric equations $x = t$, $y = \dfrac{1}{t}$, and let $P$ be a point on $H$.

Let the tangent at $P$ meet the $x$-axis at $T$, and let $O$ be the origin. Prove that $OP = PT$.

7   For the curve $H$ in Question 6, let $S$ be the point $\left(\sqrt{2}, \sqrt{2}\right)$. Let $N$ be the point on the tangent to $H$ at $P$ such that $SN$ is perpendicular to $PN$.

(a)   Show that the coordinates of $N$ satisfy the equations $t^2 y + x = 2t$ and $y - t^2 x = \sqrt{2}\left(1 - t^2\right)$.

(b)   If you square and add the equations in part (a), show that you obtain $x^2 + y^2 = 2$. Interpret this result geometrically.

8   Let $P$ and $Q$ be the points with parameters $t$ and $t + \pi$ on the curve, called a *cardioid*, with parametric equations $x = 2\cos t - \cos 2t$, $y = 2\sin t - \sin 2t$. Let $A$ be the point $(1, 0)$. Prove that

(a)   the gradient of $AP$ is $\tan t$,

(b)   $PAQ$ is a straight line,

(c)   the length of the line segment $PQ$ is constant.

<hr>

### Miscellaneous exercise 4

1   The parametric equations of a curve are $x = \cos t$, $y = 2\sin t$ where the parameter $t$ takes all values such that $0 \leqslant t \leqslant \pi$.

(a)   Find the value of $t$ at the point $A$ where the line $y = 2x$ intersects the curve.

(b)   Show that the tangent to the curve at $A$ has gradient $-2$ and find the equation of this tangent in the form $ax + by = c$, where $a$ and $b$ are integers.   (OCR)

2   The parametric equations of a curve are $x = 2\cos t$, $y = 5 + 3\cos 2t$, where $0 < t < \pi$.

Express $\dfrac{dy}{dx}$ in terms of $t$, and hence show that the gradient at any point of the curve is less than $6$.   (OCR)

3   A curve is defined by the parametric equations: $x = t - \dfrac{1}{t}$, $y = t + \dfrac{1}{t}$, $\quad t \neq 0$.

(a)   Use parametric differentiation to determine $\dfrac{dy}{dx}$ as a function of the parameter $t$.

(b)   Show that the equation of the normal to the curve at the point where $t = 2$ may be written as $3y + 5x = 15$.

(c)   Determine the cartesian equation of the curve.   (OCR)

4   A curve is defined parametrically by $x = t^3 + t$, $y = t^2 + 1$.

(a)   Find $\dfrac{dy}{dx}$ in terms of $t$.

(b)   Find the equation of the normal to this curve at the point where $t = 1$.   (OCR)

**5**  A curve is defined by the parametric equations $x = \sin t$, $y = \sqrt{3}\cos t$.

   (a)  Determine $\dfrac{dy}{dx}$ in terms of $t$ for points on the curve where $t$ is not an odd

   multiple of $\frac{1}{2}\pi$.

   (b)  Find an equation for the tangent to the curve at the point where $t = \frac{1}{6}\pi$.

   (c)  Show that all points on the curve satisfy the equation $x^2 + \frac{1}{3}y^2 = 1$.        (OCR)

**6**  The parametric equations of a curve are $x = t + e^{-t}$, $y = 1 - e^{-t}$, where $t$ takes all real

   values. Express $\dfrac{dy}{dx}$ in terms of $t$, and hence find the value of $t$ for which the gradient

   of the curve is 1, giving your answer in logarithmic form.        (OCR)

**7**  A curve is defined by the parametric equations $x = 3\sin t$, $y = 2\cos t$.

   (a)  Show that the cartesian equation of the curve is $4x^2 + 9y^2 = 36$.

   (b)  Determine an equation of the normal to the curve at the point with parameter
        $t = \alpha$ where $\sin \alpha = 0.6$ and $\cos \alpha = 0.8$.

   (c)  Find the cartesian coordinates of the point where the normal in part (b) meets
        the curve again.        (OCR)

**8**  A curve is defined parametrically for $0 \leqslant t \leqslant \pi$ by $x = 2(1 + \cos t)$, $y = 4\sin^2 t$.

   (a)  Determine the equation of the tangent to the curve at the point where $t = \frac{1}{3}\pi$.

   (b)  Obtain the cartesian equation of the curve in simplified form.        (OCR)

**9**  Sketch, with the help of a calculator, curves with the following parametric equations,
   for $0 \leqslant t < 2\pi$. Indicate on your sketches, with arrows, the direction on each curve in
   which $t$ is increasing.

   (a)  $x = \cos t$, $y = \cos 2t$            (b)  $x = \sin t$, $y = \cos 2t$

   (c)  $x = \sin t$, $y = \sin 3t$            (d)  $x = \sin t$, $y = \cos 3t$

   (e)  $x = \cos 2t$, $y = \sin 3t$           (f)  $x = \cos 2t$, $y = \cos 3t$

   (g)  $x = \sin 2t$, $y = \sin 3t$           (h)  $x = \sin 2t$, $y = \cos 3t$

   (These are examples of *Lissajous figures*.)

**10**  A curve is defined parametrically by $x = t^2$, $y = t^2$ where $t$ is real.

   (a)  Describe the curve.

   (b)  Eliminate the parameter to find the cartesian equation of the curve. Describe the
        curve resulting from the cartesian equation.

   (c)  Reconcile what you find with the result in the shaded box in Section 4.2.

# 5 Vectors

This chapter introduces the idea of vectors as a way of doing geometry in two or three dimensions. When you have completed it, you should

- understand the idea of a translation, and how it can be expressed either in column form or in terms of basic unit vectors
- know and be able to use the rules of vector algebra
- understand the idea of displacement and position vectors, and use these to prove geometrical results
- know the form of the vector equation of a line, and use this to solve problems involving intersecting, parallel and skew lines
- appreciate similarities and differences between the geometries of two and three dimensions.

## 5.1 Translations of a plane

In P1 Section 8.5 you saw how to translate a graph through distance $k$ in the $x$- or $y$-direction: $y = f(x)$ becomes respectively $y = f(x - k)$ or $y = f(x) + k$. A practical way of doing this is to draw the graph on a transparent sheet placed over a coordinate grid, and then to move this sheet across or up the grid by $k$ units.

The essential feature of a translation is that the sheet moves over the grid without turning. A more general translation would move the sheet $k$ units across and $l$ units up the grid. This is shown in Fig. 5.1, where several points move in the same direction through the same distance. Such a translation is called a **vector** and is written $\begin{pmatrix} k \\ l \end{pmatrix}$.

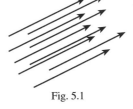

Fig. 5.1

For example, the translations of $y = f(x)$ described above would be performed by the vectors $\begin{pmatrix} k \\ 0 \end{pmatrix}$ and $\begin{pmatrix} 0 \\ k \end{pmatrix}$ respectively.

In practice, drawing several arrows, as in Fig. 5.1, is not a convenient way of representing a vector. It is usual to draw just a single arrow, as in Fig. 5.2. But you must understand that the position of the arrow in the $(x, y)$-plane is of no significance. This arrow is just one of infinitely many that could be drawn to represent the vector.

Fig. 5.2

Later you may meet other uses of vectors. For example, mechanics uses velocity vectors, momentum vectors, force vectors, and so on. When you need to make the distinction, the vectors described here are called **translation vectors**. These are the only vectors used in this module.

## 5.2 Vector algebra

It is often convenient to use a single letter to stand for a vector. In print, bold type is used to distinguish vectors from numbers. For example, in $\mathbf{p} = \begin{pmatrix} k \\ l \end{pmatrix}$, $\mathbf{p}$ is a vector but $k$ and $l$ are numbers, called the **components** of the vector $\mathbf{p}$ in the $x$- and $y$-directions.

*In handwriting vectors are indicated by a wavy line underneath the letter:* $\underset{\sim}{p} = \begin{pmatrix} k \\ l \end{pmatrix}$. *It is*

*important to get into the habit of writing vectors in this way, so that it is quite clear in your work which letters stand for vectors and which for numbers.*

If $s$ is any number and $\mathbf{p}$ is any vector, then $s\mathbf{p}$ is another vector. If $s > 0$, the vector $s\mathbf{p}$ is a translation in the same direction as $\mathbf{p}$ but $s$ times as large; if $s < 0$ it is in the opposite direction and $|s|$ times as large. A number such as $s$ is often called a **scalar**, because it usually changes the scale of the vector.

The similar triangles in Fig. 5.3 show that $s\mathbf{p} = \begin{pmatrix} sk \\ sl \end{pmatrix}$. In particular, $(-1)\mathbf{p} = \begin{pmatrix} -k \\ -l \end{pmatrix}$, which is a translation of the same magnitude as $\mathbf{p}$ but in the opposite direction. It is denoted by $-\mathbf{p}$.

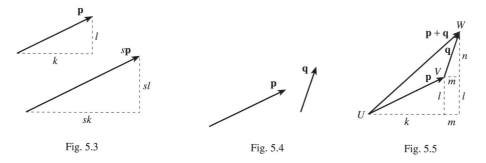

Fig. 5.3                    Fig. 5.4                    Fig. 5.5

Vectors are added by performing one translation after another. In Fig. 5.4, $\mathbf{p}$ and $\mathbf{q}$ are two vectors. To form their sum, you want to represent them as a pair of arrows by which you can trace the path of a particular point of the moving sheet. In Fig. 5.5, $\mathbf{p}$ is shown by an arrow from $U$ to $V$, and $\mathbf{q}$ by an arrow from $V$ to $W$. Then when the translations are combined, the point of the sheet which was originally at $U$ would move first to $V$ and then to $W$. So the sum $\mathbf{p} + \mathbf{q}$ is represented by an arrow from $U$ to $W$.

Fig. 5.5 also shows that:

> If $\mathbf{p} = \begin{pmatrix} k \\ l \end{pmatrix}$ and $\mathbf{q} = \begin{pmatrix} m \\ n \end{pmatrix}$, then $\mathbf{p} + \mathbf{q} = \begin{pmatrix} k+m \\ l+n \end{pmatrix}$.

To form the sum $\mathbf{q} + \mathbf{p}$ the translations are performed in the reverse order. In Fig. 5.6, $\mathbf{q}$ is now represented by the arrow from $U$ to $Z$; and since $UVWZ$ is a parallelogram $\mathbf{p}$ is represented by the arrow from $Z$ to $W$. This shows that

$\mathbf{p} + \mathbf{q} = \mathbf{q} + \mathbf{p}$.

This is called the **commutative rule for addition of vectors.**

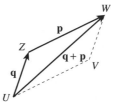

Fig. 5.6

**Example 5.2.1**

If $\mathbf{p} = \begin{pmatrix} 2 \\ -3 \end{pmatrix}$, $\mathbf{q} = \begin{pmatrix} 1 \\ 2 \end{pmatrix}$ and $\mathbf{r} = \begin{pmatrix} 5 \\ 3 \end{pmatrix}$, show that there is a number $s$ such that $\mathbf{p} + s\mathbf{q} = \mathbf{r}$.

You can write $\mathbf{p} + s\mathbf{q}$ in column vector form as

$$\begin{pmatrix} 2 \\ -3 \end{pmatrix} + s\begin{pmatrix} 1 \\ 2 \end{pmatrix} = \begin{pmatrix} 2 \\ -3 \end{pmatrix} + \begin{pmatrix} s \\ 2s \end{pmatrix} = \begin{pmatrix} 2+s \\ -3+2s \end{pmatrix}.$$

If this is equal to $\mathbf{r}$, then both the $x$- and $y$-components of the two vectors must be equal. This gives the two equations

$$2 + s = 5 \quad \text{and} \quad -3 + 2s = 3.$$

Both these equations are satisfied by $s = 3$, so it follows that $\mathbf{p} + 3\mathbf{q} = \mathbf{r}$. You can check this for yourself using squared paper or a screen display, showing arrows representing $\mathbf{p}$, $\mathbf{q}$, $\mathbf{p} + 3\mathbf{q}$ and $\mathbf{r}$.

The idea of addition can be extended to three or more vectors. But when you write $\mathbf{p} + \mathbf{q} + \mathbf{r}$ it is not clear whether you first add $\mathbf{p}$ and $\mathbf{q}$ and then add $\mathbf{r}$ to the result, or whether you add $\mathbf{p}$ to the result of adding $\mathbf{q}$ and $\mathbf{r}$. Fig. 5.7 shows that it doesn't matter, since the outcome is the same either way. That is,

$$(\mathbf{p} + \mathbf{q}) + \mathbf{r} = \mathbf{p} + (\mathbf{q} + \mathbf{r}).$$

This is called the **associative rule for addition of vectors**.

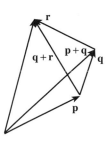

Fig. 5.7

To complete the algebra of vector addition, the symbol $\mathbf{0}$ is needed for the **zero vector**, the 'stay-still' translation, which has the properties that, for any vector $\mathbf{p}$,

$$0\mathbf{p} = \mathbf{0}, \quad \mathbf{p} + \mathbf{0} = \mathbf{p}, \quad \text{and} \quad \mathbf{p} + (-\mathbf{p}) = \mathbf{0}.$$

Vector addition and multiplication by a scalar can be combined according to the two **distributive** rules for vectors:

$$s(\mathbf{p} + \mathbf{q}) = s\mathbf{p} + s\mathbf{q} \qquad \text{(from the similar triangles in Fig. 5.8)}$$

and $\quad (s + t)\mathbf{p} = s\mathbf{p} + t\mathbf{p} \qquad$ (see Fig. 5.9)

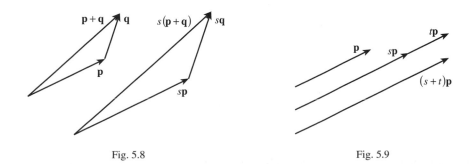

Fig. 5.8                                                Fig. 5.9

Subtraction of vectors is defined by

$$\mathbf{p} + \mathbf{x} = \mathbf{q} \quad \Leftrightarrow \quad \mathbf{x} = \mathbf{q} - \mathbf{p}.$$

This is illustrated in Fig. 5.10. Notice that to show $\mathbf{q} - \mathbf{p}$ you represent $\mathbf{p}$ and $\mathbf{q}$ by arrows which both start at the same point; this is different from addition, where the arrow representing $\mathbf{q}$ starts where the $\mathbf{p}$ arrow ends. Comparing Fig. 5.10 with Fig. 5.11 shows that

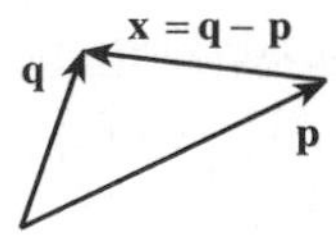

Fig. 5.10

$$\mathbf{q} - \mathbf{p} = \mathbf{q} + (-\mathbf{p}).$$

In summary, the rules of vector addition, subtraction and multiplication by scalars look very similar to the rules of number addition, subtraction and multiplication. But the diagrams show that the rules for vectors are interpreted differently from the rules for numbers.

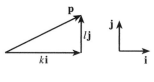

Fig. 5.11

## 5.3 Basic unit vectors

If you apply the rules of vector algebra to a vector in column form, you can see that

$$\mathbf{p} = \begin{pmatrix} k \\ l \end{pmatrix} = \begin{pmatrix} k+0 \\ 0+l \end{pmatrix} = \begin{pmatrix} k \\ 0 \end{pmatrix} + \begin{pmatrix} 0 \\ l \end{pmatrix} = k\begin{pmatrix} 1 \\ 0 \end{pmatrix} + l\begin{pmatrix} 0 \\ 1 \end{pmatrix}.$$

The vectors $\begin{pmatrix} 1 \\ 0 \end{pmatrix}$ and $\begin{pmatrix} 0 \\ 1 \end{pmatrix}$ which appear in this last expression are called **basic unit vectors** in the $x$- and $y$-directions. They are denoted by the letters $\mathbf{i}$ and $\mathbf{j}$, so

$$\mathbf{p} = k\mathbf{i} + l\mathbf{j}.$$

This is illustrated by Fig. 5.12. The equation shows that any vector in the plane can be constructed as the sum of multiples of the two basic vectors $\mathbf{i}$ and $\mathbf{j}$.

The vectors $k\mathbf{i}$ and $l\mathbf{j}$ are called the **component vectors** of $\mathbf{p}$ in the $x$- and $y$-directions.

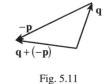

Fig. 5.12

You now have two alternative notations for doing algebra with vectors. For example, if you want to find $3\mathbf{p} - 2\mathbf{q}$, where $\mathbf{p}$ is $\begin{pmatrix} 2 \\ 5 \end{pmatrix}$ and $\mathbf{q}$ is $\begin{pmatrix} 1 \\ -3 \end{pmatrix}$, you can write either

$$3\begin{pmatrix} 2 \\ 5 \end{pmatrix} - 2\begin{pmatrix} 1 \\ -3 \end{pmatrix} = \begin{pmatrix} 6 \\ 15 \end{pmatrix} - \begin{pmatrix} 2 \\ -6 \end{pmatrix} = \begin{pmatrix} 6-2 \\ 15-(-6) \end{pmatrix} = \begin{pmatrix} 4 \\ 21 \end{pmatrix}$$

or     $3(2\mathbf{i} + 5\mathbf{j}) - 2(\mathbf{i} - 3\mathbf{j}) = (6\mathbf{i} + 15\mathbf{j}) - (2\mathbf{i} - 6\mathbf{j}) = 6\mathbf{i} + 15\mathbf{j} - 2\mathbf{i} + 6\mathbf{j} = 4\mathbf{i} + 21\mathbf{j}.$

You will find that sometimes one of these forms is more convenient than the other, but more often it makes no difference which you use.

When you are asked to illustrate a vector equation geometrically, you should show vectors as arrows on a grid of squares, either on paper or on screen.

1  Illustrate the following equations geometrically.

(a) $\begin{pmatrix} 4 \\ 1 \end{pmatrix} + \begin{pmatrix} -3 \\ 2 \end{pmatrix} = \begin{pmatrix} 1 \\ 3 \end{pmatrix}$

(b) $3\begin{pmatrix} 1 \\ -2 \end{pmatrix} = \begin{pmatrix} 3 \\ -6 \end{pmatrix}$

(c) $\begin{pmatrix} 0 \\ 4 \end{pmatrix} + 2\begin{pmatrix} 1 \\ -2 \end{pmatrix} = \begin{pmatrix} 2 \\ 0 \end{pmatrix}$

(d) $\begin{pmatrix} 3 \\ 1 \end{pmatrix} - \begin{pmatrix} 5 \\ 1 \end{pmatrix} = \begin{pmatrix} -2 \\ 0 \end{pmatrix}$

(e) $3\begin{pmatrix} -1 \\ 2 \end{pmatrix} - \begin{pmatrix} -4 \\ 3 \end{pmatrix} = \begin{pmatrix} 1 \\ 3 \end{pmatrix}$

(f) $4\begin{pmatrix} 2 \\ 3 \end{pmatrix} - 3\begin{pmatrix} 3 \\ 2 \end{pmatrix} = \begin{pmatrix} -1 \\ 6 \end{pmatrix}$

(g) $\begin{pmatrix} 2 \\ -3 \end{pmatrix} + \begin{pmatrix} 4 \\ 5 \end{pmatrix} + \begin{pmatrix} -6 \\ -2 \end{pmatrix} = \begin{pmatrix} 0 \\ 0 \end{pmatrix}$

(h) $2\begin{pmatrix} 3 \\ -1 \end{pmatrix} + 3\begin{pmatrix} -2 \\ 3 \end{pmatrix} + \begin{pmatrix} 0 \\ -7 \end{pmatrix} = \begin{pmatrix} 0 \\ 0 \end{pmatrix}$

2  Rewrite each of the equations in Question 1 using unit vector notation.

3  Express each of the following vectors as column vectors, and illustrate your answers geometrically.

(a) $\mathbf{i} + 2\mathbf{j}$        (b) $3\mathbf{i}$        (c) $\mathbf{j} - \mathbf{i}$        (d) $4\mathbf{i} - 3\mathbf{j}$

4  Show that there is a number $s$ such that $s\begin{pmatrix} 1 \\ 2 \end{pmatrix} + \begin{pmatrix} -3 \\ 1 \end{pmatrix} = \begin{pmatrix} -1 \\ 5 \end{pmatrix}$. Illustrate your answer geometrically.

5  If $\mathbf{p} = 5\mathbf{i} - 3\mathbf{j}$, $\mathbf{q} = 2\mathbf{j} - \mathbf{i}$ and $\mathbf{r} = \mathbf{i} + 5\mathbf{j}$, show that there is a number $s$ such that $\mathbf{p} + s\mathbf{q} = \mathbf{r}$. Illustrate your answer geometrically.

   Rearrange this equation so as to express $\mathbf{q}$ in terms of $\mathbf{p}$ and $\mathbf{r}$. Illustrate the rearranged equation geometrically.

6  Find numbers $s$ and $t$ such that $s\begin{pmatrix} 5 \\ 4 \end{pmatrix} + t\begin{pmatrix} -3 \\ -2 \end{pmatrix} = \begin{pmatrix} 1 \\ 2 \end{pmatrix}$. Illustrate your answer geometrically.

7  If $\mathbf{p} = 4\mathbf{i} + \mathbf{j}$, $\mathbf{q} = 6\mathbf{i} - 5\mathbf{j}$ and $\mathbf{r} = 3\mathbf{i} + 4\mathbf{j}$, find numbers $s$ and $t$ such that $s\mathbf{p} + t\mathbf{q} = \mathbf{r}$. Illustrate your answer geometrically.

8  Show that it isn't possible to find numbers $s$ and $t$ such that $\begin{pmatrix} 4 \\ -2 \end{pmatrix} + s\begin{pmatrix} 3 \\ 1 \end{pmatrix} = \begin{pmatrix} -6 \\ 3 \end{pmatrix}$ and $\begin{pmatrix} 3 \\ 4 \end{pmatrix} + t\begin{pmatrix} -1 \\ 2 \end{pmatrix} = \begin{pmatrix} 1 \\ 1 \end{pmatrix}$. Give geometrical reasons.

9  If $\mathbf{p} = 2\mathbf{i} + 3\mathbf{j}$, $\mathbf{q} = 4\mathbf{i} - 5\mathbf{j}$ and $\mathbf{r} = \mathbf{i} - 4\mathbf{j}$, find a set of numbers $f$, $g$ and $h$ such that $f\mathbf{p} + g\mathbf{q} + h\mathbf{r} = \mathbf{0}$. Illustrate your answer geometrically. Give a reason why there is more than one possible answer to this question.

10  If $\mathbf{p} = 3\mathbf{i} - \mathbf{j}$, $\mathbf{q} = 4\mathbf{i} + 5\mathbf{j}$ and $\mathbf{r} = 2\mathbf{j} - 6\mathbf{i}$,

   (a) can you find numbers $s$ and $t$ such that $\mathbf{q} = s\mathbf{p} + t\mathbf{r}$,

   (b) can you find numbers $u$ and $v$ such that $\mathbf{r} = u\mathbf{p} + v\mathbf{q}$?

   Give a geometrical reason for your answers.

## 5.4 Position vectors

If $E$ and $F$ are two points on a grid, there is a unique translation which takes you from $E$ to $F$. This translation can be represented by the arrow which starts at $E$ and ends at $F$, and it is denoted by the symbol $\overrightarrow{EF}$.

(Some books use **EF** in bold type rather than $\overrightarrow{EF}$ to emphasise that it is a vector.)

However, although this translation is unique, its name is not. If $G$ and $H$ are two other points on the grid such that the lines $EF$ and $GH$ are parallel and equal in length (so that $EFHG$ is a parallelogram, see Fig. 5.13), then the translation $\overrightarrow{EF}$ also takes you from $G$ to $H$, so that it could also be denoted by $\overrightarrow{GH}$. In a vector equation $\overrightarrow{EF}$ could be replaced by $\overrightarrow{GH}$ without affecting the truth of the statement.

Vectors written like this are sometimes called **displacement vectors**. But they are not a different kind of vector, just translation vectors written in a different way.

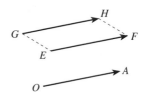

There is, however, one displacement vector which is especially important. This is the translation that starts at the origin $O$ and ends at a point $A$ where (in Fig. 5.13) $\overrightarrow{OA} = \overrightarrow{EF} = \overrightarrow{GH}$. The translation which takes you from $O$ to $A$ is called the **position vector** of $A$.

Fig. 5.13

There is a close link between the coordinates of $A$ and the component form of its position vector. If $A$ has coordinates $(u, v)$, then to get from $O$ to $A$ you must move $u$ units in the $x$-direction and $v$ units in the $y$-direction, so that the vector $\overrightarrow{OA}$ has components $u$ and $v$.

> The position vector of the point $A$ with coordinates $(u, v)$ is
>
> $$\overrightarrow{OA} = \begin{pmatrix} u \\ v \end{pmatrix} = u\mathbf{i} + v\mathbf{j}.$$

A useful convention is to use the same letter for a point and its position vector. For example, the position vector of the point $A$ can be denoted by $\mathbf{a}$. This 'alphabet convention' will be used wherever possible in this book. It has the advantages that it economises on letters of the alphabet and avoids the need for repetitive definitions.

## 5.5 Algebra with position vectors

Multiplication by a scalar has a simple interpretation in terms of position vectors. If the vector $s\mathbf{a}$ is the position vector of a point $D$, then:

- If $s > 0$, $D$ lies on the directed line $OA$ (produced if necessary) such that $OD = sOA$
- If $s < 0$, $D$ lies on the directed line $AO$ produced such that $OD = |s|OA$.

Fig. 5.14

This is shown in Fig. 5.14 for $s = \frac{3}{2}$ and $s = -\frac{1}{2}$.

To identify the point with position vector $\mathbf{a} + \mathbf{b}$ is not quite so easy, because the arrows from $O$ to $A$ and from $O$ to $B$ are not related in the way needed for addition (see Fig. 5.5). It is therefore necessary to complete the parallelogram $OACB$, as in Fig. 5.15.

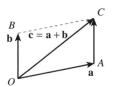

Fig. 5.15

Then

$$\mathbf{a} + \mathbf{b} = \overrightarrow{OA} + \overrightarrow{OB} = \overrightarrow{OA} + \overrightarrow{AC} = \overrightarrow{OC}.$$

This is called the **parallelogram rule of addition** for position vectors.

Subtraction can be shown in either of two ways. If you compare Fig. 5.16 with Fig. 5.10, you will see that $\mathbf{b} - \mathbf{a}$ is the displacement vector $\overrightarrow{AB}$. To interpret this as a position vector, draw a line $OE$ equal and parallel to $AB$, so that $\overrightarrow{OE} = \overrightarrow{AB}$. Then $E$ is the point with position vector $\mathbf{b} - \mathbf{a}$.

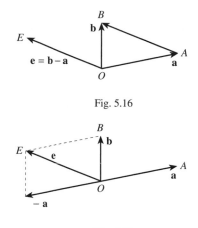

Fig. 5.16

Alternatively, you can write $\mathbf{b} - \mathbf{a}$ as $\mathbf{b} + (-\mathbf{a})$, and then apply the parallelogram rule of addition to the points with position vectors $\mathbf{b}$ and $-\mathbf{a}$. By comparing Figs. 5.16 and 5.17 you can see that this leads to the same point $E$.

Fig. 5.17

### Example 5.5.1
Points $A$ and $B$ have position vectors $\mathbf{a}$ and $\mathbf{b}$. Find the position vectors of
(a) the mid-point $M$ of $AB$,
(b) the point of trisection $T$ such that $AT = \frac{2}{3} AB$.

(a) **Method 1**   The displacement vector $\overrightarrow{AB} = \mathbf{b} - \mathbf{a}$, so $\overrightarrow{AM} = \frac{1}{2}(\mathbf{b} - \mathbf{a})$. Therefore $\mathbf{m} = \overrightarrow{OM} = \overrightarrow{OA} + \overrightarrow{AM} = \mathbf{a} + \frac{1}{2}(\mathbf{b} - \mathbf{a}) = \frac{1}{2}\mathbf{a} + \frac{1}{2}\mathbf{b}$.

**Method 2**   If the parallelogram $OACB$ is completed (see Fig. 5.15) then $\mathbf{c} = \mathbf{a} + \mathbf{b}$. Since the diagonals of $OACB$ bisect each other, the mid-point $M$ of $AB$ is also the midpoint of $OC$. Therefore

$$\mathbf{m} = \tfrac{1}{2}\mathbf{c} = \tfrac{1}{2}(\mathbf{a} + \mathbf{b}) = \tfrac{1}{2}\mathbf{a} + \tfrac{1}{2}\mathbf{b}.$$

(b) The first method of (a) can be modified. $\overrightarrow{AT} = \frac{2}{3}\overrightarrow{AB} = \frac{2}{3}(\mathbf{b} - \mathbf{a})$, so

$$\mathbf{t} = \mathbf{a} + \tfrac{2}{3}(\mathbf{b} - \mathbf{a}) = \tfrac{1}{3}\mathbf{a} + \tfrac{2}{3}\mathbf{b}.$$

The results of this example can be used to prove an important theorem about triangles.

**Example 5.5.2**

In triangle $ABC$ the mid-points of $BC$, $CA$ and $AB$ are $D$, $E$ and $F$. Prove that the lines $AD$, $BE$ and $CF$ (called the **medians**) meet at a point $G$, which is a point of trisection of each of the medians (see Fig. 5.18).

From Example 5.5.1, $\mathbf{d} = \frac{1}{2}\mathbf{b} + \frac{1}{2}\mathbf{c}$, and the point of trisection on the median $AD$ closer to $D$ has position vector

$$\frac{1}{3}\mathbf{a} + \frac{2}{3}\mathbf{d} = \frac{1}{3}\mathbf{a} + \frac{2}{3}\left(\frac{1}{2}\mathbf{b} + \frac{1}{2}\mathbf{c}\right)$$
$$= \frac{1}{3}\mathbf{a} + \frac{1}{3}\mathbf{b} + \frac{1}{3}\mathbf{c}.$$

This last expression is symmetrical in $\mathbf{a}$, $\mathbf{b}$ and $\mathbf{c}$. It therefore also represents the point of trisection on the median $BE$ closer to $E$, and the point of trisection on $CF$ closer to $F$.

Therefore the three medians meet each other at a point $G$, with position vector $\mathbf{g} = \frac{1}{3}(\mathbf{a} + \mathbf{b} + \mathbf{c})$. This point is called the **centroid** of the triangle.

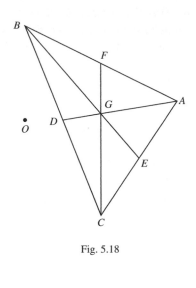

Fig. 5.18

## Exercise 5B

In this exercise the alphabet convention is used, that $\mathbf{a}$ stands for the position vector of the point $A$, and so on.

1   The points $A$ and $B$ have coordinates $(3,1)$ and $(1,2)$. Plot on squared paper the points $C$, $D$, ..., $H$ defined by the following vector equations, and state their coordinates.

(a)   $\mathbf{c} = 3\mathbf{a}$          (b)   $\mathbf{d} = -\mathbf{b}$          (c)   $\mathbf{e} = \mathbf{a} - \mathbf{b}$

(d)   $\mathbf{f} = \mathbf{b} - 3\mathbf{a}$          (e)   $\mathbf{g} = \mathbf{b} + 3\mathbf{a}$          (f)   $\mathbf{h} = \frac{1}{2}(\mathbf{b} + 3\mathbf{a})$

2   Points $A$ and $B$ have coordinates $(2,7)$ and $(-3,-3)$ respectively. Use a vector method to find the coordinates of $C$ and $D$, where

(a)   $C$ is the point such that $\overrightarrow{AC} = 3\overrightarrow{AB}$,          (b)   $D$ is the point such that $\overrightarrow{AD} = \frac{3}{5}\overrightarrow{AB}$.

3   $C$ is the point on $AB$ produced such that $\overrightarrow{AB} = \overrightarrow{BC}$. Express $C$ in terms of $\mathbf{a}$ and $\mathbf{b}$. Check your answer by using the result of Example 5.5.1(a) to find the position vector of the mid-point of $AC$.

4   $C$ is the point on $AB$ such that $AC:CB = 4:3$. Express $\mathbf{c}$ in terms of $\mathbf{a}$ and $\mathbf{b}$.

5   If $C$ is the point on $AB$ such that $\overrightarrow{AC} = t\,\overrightarrow{AB}$, prove that $\mathbf{c} = t\mathbf{b} + (1-t)\mathbf{a}$.

6   Write a vector equation connecting $\mathbf{a}$, $\mathbf{b}$, $\mathbf{c}$ and $\mathbf{d}$ to express the fact that $\overrightarrow{AB} = \overrightarrow{DC}$. Deduce from your equation that

(a)   $\overrightarrow{DA} = \overrightarrow{CB}$,

(b)   if $E$ is the point such that $OAEC$ is a parallelogram, then $OBED$ is a parallelogram.

7   $ABC$ is a triangle. $D$ is the mid-point of $BC$, $E$ is the mid-point of $AC$, $F$ is the mid-point of $AB$ and $G$ is the mid-point of $EF$. Express the displacement vectors $\overrightarrow{AD}$ and $\overrightarrow{AG}$ in terms of $\mathbf{a}$, $\mathbf{b}$ and $\mathbf{c}$. What can you deduce about the points $A$, $D$ and $G$?

8   $OABC$ is a parallelogram, $M$ is the mid-point of $BC$, and $P$ is the point of trisection of $AC$ closer to $C$. Express $\mathbf{b}$, $\mathbf{m}$ and $\mathbf{p}$ in terms of $\mathbf{a}$ and $\mathbf{c}$. Deduce that $\mathbf{p} = \frac{2}{3}\mathbf{m}$, and interpret this equation geometrically.

9   $ABC$ is a triangle. $D$ is the mid-point of $BC$, $E$ is the mid-point of $AD$ and $F$ is the point of trisection of $AC$ closer to $A$. $G$ is the point on $FB$ such that $\overrightarrow{FG} = \frac{1}{4}\overrightarrow{FB}$. Express $\mathbf{d}$, $\mathbf{e}$, $\mathbf{f}$ and $\mathbf{g}$ in terms of $\mathbf{a}$, $\mathbf{b}$ and $\mathbf{c}$, and deduce that $G$ is the same point as $E$. Draw a figure to illustrate this result.

10  $OAB$ is a triangle, $Q$ is the point of trisection of $AB$ closer to $B$ and $P$ is the point on $OQ$ such that $\overrightarrow{OP} = \frac{2}{5}\overrightarrow{OQ}$. $AP$ produced meets $OB$ at $R$. Express $\overrightarrow{AP}$ in terms of $\mathbf{a}$ and $\mathbf{b}$, and hence find the number $k$ such that $\overrightarrow{OA} + k\,\overrightarrow{AP}$ does not depend on $\mathbf{a}$. Use your answer to express $\mathbf{r}$ in terms of $\mathbf{b}$, and interpret this geometrically.

Use a similar method to identify the point $S$ where $BP$ produced meets $OA$.

## 5.6   The vector equation of a line

Fig. 5.19 shows a line through a point $A$ in the direction of a non-zero vector $\mathbf{p}$. If $R$ is any point on the line, the displacement vector $\overrightarrow{AR}$ is a multiple of $\mathbf{p}$, so that

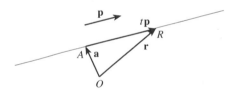

$$\mathbf{r} = \overrightarrow{OR} = \overrightarrow{OA} + \overrightarrow{AR} = \mathbf{a} + t\mathbf{p},$$

Fig. 5.19

where $t$ is a scalar. The value of $t$ measures the ratio of the displacement $\overrightarrow{AR}$ to $\mathbf{p}$, and so takes a different value for each point $R$ on the line.

Points on a line through $A$ in the direction of $\mathbf{p}$ have position vectors $\mathbf{r} = \mathbf{a} + t\mathbf{p}$, where $t$ is a variable scalar. This is called the **vector equation** of the line.

The following examples show how vector equations can be used as an alternative to the cartesian equations with which you are familiar.

To illustrate alternative techniques the first will be solved by using vectors in column form, and the second by using the basic unit vectors.

**Example 5.6.1**

Find a vector equation for the line through $(2, -1)$ with gradient $\frac{3}{4}$, and deduce its cartesian equation.

This question will be solved using vectors in column form.

The position vector of the point $(2, -1)$ is $\begin{pmatrix} 2 \\ -1 \end{pmatrix}$. There are many vectors with gradient $\frac{3}{4}$, but the simplest is the vector which goes $4$ units across the grid and $3$ units up, that is, $\begin{pmatrix} 4 \\ 3 \end{pmatrix}$. So the equation of the line is

$$\mathbf{r} = \begin{pmatrix} 2 \\ -1 \end{pmatrix} + t \begin{pmatrix} 4 \\ 3 \end{pmatrix}.$$

If $R$ has coordinates $(x, y)$, the position vector $\mathbf{r}$ is $\begin{pmatrix} x \\ y \end{pmatrix}$, so this can be written

$$\begin{pmatrix} x \\ y \end{pmatrix} = \begin{pmatrix} 2 + 4t \\ -1 + 3t \end{pmatrix}.$$

This is equivalent to the two equations

$$x = 2 + 4t, \quad y = -1 + 3t,$$

which you will recognise as parametric equations for the line.

The cartesian equation is found by eliminating $t$:

$$3x - 4y = 3(2 + 4t) - 4(-1 + 3t) = 10.$$

You can check that $3x - 4y = 10$ has gradient $\frac{3}{4}$ and contains the point $(2, -1)$.

**Example 5.6.2**

Find a vector equation for the line through $(3, 1)$ parallel to the $y$-axis, and deduce its cartesian equation.

This question will be solved using the basic unit vectors.

A vector parallel to the $y$-axis is $\mathbf{j}$, and the position vector of $(3, 1)$ is $3\mathbf{i} + \mathbf{j}$, so the vector equation of the line is

$$\mathbf{r} = (3\mathbf{i} + \mathbf{j}) + t\mathbf{j}.$$

Writing $\mathbf{r}$ as $x\mathbf{i} + y\mathbf{j}$, this is

$$x\mathbf{i} + y\mathbf{j} = (3\mathbf{i} + \mathbf{j}) + t\mathbf{j}.$$

This is equivalent to the two equations $x = 3$, $y = 1 + t$.

No elimination is necessary this time: the first equation does not involve $t$, so the cartesian equation is just $x = 3$.

### Example 5.6.3

Find the points common to the pairs of lines

(a) $\mathbf{r} = \begin{pmatrix} 1 \\ 2 \end{pmatrix} + s\begin{pmatrix} 1 \\ 1 \end{pmatrix}$ and $\mathbf{r} = \begin{pmatrix} 3 \\ -2 \end{pmatrix} + t\begin{pmatrix} 1 \\ 4 \end{pmatrix}$,   (b) $\mathbf{r} = \begin{pmatrix} 3 \\ 1 \end{pmatrix} + s\begin{pmatrix} 4 \\ -2 \end{pmatrix}$ and $\mathbf{r} = \begin{pmatrix} 1 \\ 2 \end{pmatrix} + t\begin{pmatrix} -6 \\ 3 \end{pmatrix}$.

*Notice that different letters are used for the variable scalars on the two lines.*

(a) Position vectors of points on the two lines can be written as

$$\mathbf{r} = \begin{pmatrix} 1+s \\ 2+s \end{pmatrix} \quad \text{and} \quad \mathbf{r} = \begin{pmatrix} 3+t \\ -2+4t \end{pmatrix}.$$

If these are the same point,

$$1+s = 3+t \quad \text{and} \quad 2+s = -2+4t,$$

that is $\quad s-t = 2 \quad$ and $\quad s-4t = -4.$

This is a pair of simultaneous equations for $s$ and $t$, with solution $s = 4$, $t = 2$. Substituting these values into the equation of one of the lines gives $\mathbf{r} = \begin{pmatrix} 5 \\ 6 \end{pmatrix}$. So the point common to the two lines has coordinates $(5,6)$.

(b) You can check for yourself that the procedure used in (a) leads to the equations

$$3+4s = 1-6t \quad \text{and} \quad 1-2s = 2+3t,$$

that is $\quad 2s+3t = -1 \quad$ and $\quad 2s+3t = -1.$

The two equations are the same! So there is really only one equation to solve, and this has infinitely many solutions in $s$ and $t$. If you take any value for $s$, say $s = 7$, and calculate the corresponding value $t = -5$, then you have a solution of both vector equations. You can easily check that $s = 7$, $t = -5$ gives the position vector $\begin{pmatrix} 31 \\ -13 \end{pmatrix}$ in both lines. (Try some other pairs of values for yourself.)

The reason for this is that the direction vectors of the two lines are $\begin{pmatrix} 4 \\ -2 \end{pmatrix} = 2\begin{pmatrix} 2 \\ -1 \end{pmatrix}$ and $\begin{pmatrix} -6 \\ 3 \end{pmatrix} = -3\begin{pmatrix} 2 \\ -1 \end{pmatrix}$. This means that the lines have the same direction, so they are either parallel or the same line. Also the position vectors of the given points on the two lines are $\begin{pmatrix} 3 \\ 1 \end{pmatrix}$ and $\begin{pmatrix} 1 \\ 2 \end{pmatrix}$, and $\begin{pmatrix} 3 \\ 1 \end{pmatrix} - \begin{pmatrix} 1 \\ 2 \end{pmatrix} = \begin{pmatrix} 2 \\ -1 \end{pmatrix}$; so the line joining these points is also in the same direction. The lines are therefore identical. This is illustrated in Fig. 5.20.

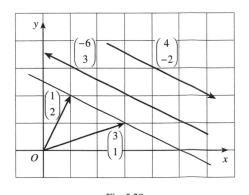

Fig. 5.20

The general result demonstrated in Example 5.6.3(b) is:

> The lines with vector equations $\mathbf{r} = \mathbf{a} + s\mathbf{p}$ and $\mathbf{r} = \mathbf{b} + s\mathbf{q}$ have the same direction if $\mathbf{p}$ is a multiple of $\mathbf{q}$. If in addition $\mathbf{b} - \mathbf{a}$ is a multiple of $\mathbf{q}$, the lines are the same; otherwise the lines are parallel.

This also shows that lines do not have unique vector equations. Two equations may represent the same line even though the vectors $\mathbf{a}$ and $\mathbf{b}$, and the vectors $\mathbf{p}$ and $\mathbf{q}$, are different.

### Example 5.6.4

Show that the lines with vector equations $\mathbf{r} = 2\mathbf{i} - 3\mathbf{j} + s(-\mathbf{i} + 3\mathbf{j})$ and $\mathbf{r} = 4\mathbf{i} + t(2\mathbf{i} - 6\mathbf{j})$ are parallel, and find a vector equation for the parallel line through $(1,1)$.

The direction vectors of the two lines are $-\mathbf{i} + 3\mathbf{j}$ and $2\mathbf{i} - 6\mathbf{j}$.

As $2\mathbf{i} - 6\mathbf{j} = -2(-\mathbf{i} + 3\mathbf{j})$, $2\mathbf{i} - 6\mathbf{j}$ is a scalar multiple of $-\mathbf{i} + 3\mathbf{j}$, so the lines are in the same or, in this case, opposite directions. The lines are therefore parallel.

The position vector of $(1,1)$ is $\mathbf{i} + \mathbf{j}$, so an equation for the parallel line through $(1,1)$ is $\mathbf{r} = \mathbf{i} + \mathbf{j} + s(-\mathbf{i} + 3\mathbf{j})$. Or, alternatively, you could use $\mathbf{r} = \mathbf{i} + \mathbf{j} + t(2\mathbf{i} - 6\mathbf{j})$.

### Example 5.6.5

Find a vector equation for the line with cartesian equation $2x + 5y = 1$.

The gradient of the line is $-\frac{2}{5}$, so the direction vector could be taken as $\begin{pmatrix} 5 \\ -2 \end{pmatrix}$. A point on the line is $(-2,1)$, with position vector $\begin{pmatrix} -2 \\ 1 \end{pmatrix}$. So a possible vector equation is $\mathbf{r} = \begin{pmatrix} -2 \\ 1 \end{pmatrix} + t\begin{pmatrix} 5 \\ -2 \end{pmatrix}$.

But in this example the direction vector could have been taken as $\begin{pmatrix} 10 \\ -4 \end{pmatrix}$ and the point on the line as $(3,-1)$, giving $\mathbf{r} = \begin{pmatrix} 3 \\ -1 \end{pmatrix} + t\begin{pmatrix} 10 \\ -4 \end{pmatrix}$. It is not obvious from these two equations that they represent the same line.

## Exercise 5C

1   Write down vector equations for the line through the given point in the specified direction. Then eliminate $t$ to obtain the cartesian equation.

(a)   $(2,-3)$, $\begin{pmatrix} 1 \\ 2 \end{pmatrix}$

(b)   $(4,1)$, $\begin{pmatrix} -3 \\ 2 \end{pmatrix}$

(c)   $(5,7)$, parallel to the $x$-axis

(d)   $(0,0)$, $\begin{pmatrix} 2 \\ -1 \end{pmatrix}$

(e)   $(a,b)$, $\begin{pmatrix} 0 \\ 1 \end{pmatrix}$

(f)   $(\cos\alpha, \sin\alpha)$, $\begin{pmatrix} -\sin\alpha \\ \cos\alpha \end{pmatrix}$

2   Find vector equations for lines with the following cartesian equations.

(a)   $x = 2$

(b)   $x + 3y = 7$

(c)   $2x - 5y = 3$

**3** Find the coordinates of the points common to the following pairs of lines, if any.

(a) $\mathbf{r} = \begin{pmatrix} 2 \\ 0 \end{pmatrix} + s\begin{pmatrix} 5 \\ 3 \end{pmatrix}$, $\mathbf{r} = \begin{pmatrix} 3 \\ -1 \end{pmatrix} + t\begin{pmatrix} 1 \\ 1 \end{pmatrix}$    (b) $\mathbf{r} = \begin{pmatrix} 5 \\ 1 \end{pmatrix} + s\begin{pmatrix} -1 \\ 2 \end{pmatrix}$, $\mathbf{r} = \begin{pmatrix} 3 \\ -5 \end{pmatrix} + t\begin{pmatrix} 1 \\ 0 \end{pmatrix}$

(c) $\mathbf{r} = \begin{pmatrix} 2 \\ -1 \end{pmatrix} + s\begin{pmatrix} 1 \\ -3 \end{pmatrix}$, $\mathbf{r} = \begin{pmatrix} 4 \\ 0 \end{pmatrix} + t\begin{pmatrix} -2 \\ 6 \end{pmatrix}$    (d) $\mathbf{r} = \begin{pmatrix} -1 \\ -4 \end{pmatrix} + s\begin{pmatrix} 3 \\ 4 \end{pmatrix}$, $\mathbf{r} = \begin{pmatrix} 11 \\ -1 \end{pmatrix} + t\begin{pmatrix} -4 \\ 3 \end{pmatrix}$

(e) $\mathbf{r} = \begin{pmatrix} 7 \\ 1 \end{pmatrix} + s\begin{pmatrix} 6 \\ -4 \end{pmatrix}$, $\mathbf{r} = \begin{pmatrix} 10 \\ -1 \end{pmatrix} + t\begin{pmatrix} -9 \\ 6 \end{pmatrix}$    (f) $\mathbf{r} = \begin{pmatrix} 2 \\ 1 \end{pmatrix} + s\begin{pmatrix} 3 \\ 0 \end{pmatrix}$, $\mathbf{r} = \begin{pmatrix} -1 \\ 3 \end{pmatrix} + t\begin{pmatrix} 0 \\ -2 \end{pmatrix}$

**4** Write down in parametric form the coordinates of any point on the line through $(2, -1)$ in the direction $\begin{pmatrix} 1 \\ 3 \end{pmatrix}$. Use these to find the point where this line intersects the line $5y - 6x = 1$.

**5** Find the coordinates of the point where the line with vector equation $\mathbf{r} = \begin{pmatrix} -3 \\ 4 \end{pmatrix} + t\begin{pmatrix} 2 \\ -1 \end{pmatrix}$ intersects the line with cartesian equation $2x + y = 7$.

**6** Which of the following points lie on the line joining $(2, 0)$ to $(4, 3)$?

(a) $(8, 9)$    (b) $(12, 13)$    (c) $(-4, -1)$    (d) $(-6, -12)$    (e) $\left(3\tfrac{1}{3}, 2\right)$

**7** Find vector equations for the lines joining the following pairs of points.

(a) $(3, 7)$, $(5, 4)$    (b) $(2, 3)$, $(2, 8)$    (c) $(-1, 2)$, $(5, -1)$

(d) $(-3, -4)$, $(5, 8)$    (e) $(-2, 7)$, $(4, 7)$    (f) $(1, 3)$, $(-4, -2)$

**8** A quadrilateral $ABCD$ has vertices $A(4, -1)$, $B(-3, 2)$, $C(-8, -5)$ and $D(4, -5)$.

(a) Find vector equations for the diagonals $AC$, $BD$ and find their point of intersection.

(b) Find the points of intersection of $BA$ produced and $CD$ produced, and of $CB$ produced and $DA$ produced.

**9** Show that the vectors $\begin{pmatrix} a \\ b \end{pmatrix}$ and $\begin{pmatrix} -b \\ a \end{pmatrix}$ are perpendicular to each other. Is this still true

(a) if $a$ is zero but $b$ is not,    (b) if $b$ is zero but $a$ is not,

(c) if both $a$ and $b$ are zero?

Find a vector equation for the line through $(1, 2)$ perpendicular to the line with vector equation $\mathbf{r} = \begin{pmatrix} 7 \\ 2 \end{pmatrix} + t\begin{pmatrix} 3 \\ 4 \end{pmatrix}$.

**10** Find a vector in the direction of the line $l$ with cartesian equation $3x - y = 8$. Write down a vector equation for the line through $P(1, 5)$ which is perpendicular to $l$. Hence find the coordinates of the foot of the perpendicular from $P$ to $l$.

**11** Use the method of Question 10 to find the coordinates of the foot of the perpendicular from $(-3, -2)$ to $5x + 2y = 10$.

**12** Find a vector equation for the line joining the points $(-1, 1)$ and $(4, 11)$. Use this to write parametric equations for any point on the line. Hence find the coordinates of the points where the line meets the parabola $y = x^2$.

**13** Find the coordinates of the points where the line through $(-5, -1)$ in the direction $\begin{pmatrix} 2 \\ 3 \end{pmatrix}$ meets the circle $x^2 + y^2 = 65$.

## 5.7 Vectors in three dimensions

The power of vector methods is best appreciated when they are used to do geometry in three dimensions. This requires setting up axes in three directions, as in Fig. 5.21. The usual convention is to take $x$- and $y$-axes in a horizontal plane (shown shaded), and to add a $z$-axis pointing vertically upwards.

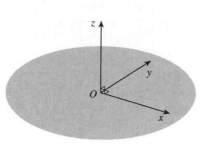

Fig. 5.21

These axes are said to be 'right-handed': if the outstretched index finger of your right hand points in the $x$-direction, and you bend your middle finger to point in the $y$-direction, then your thumb can naturally point up in the $z$-direction.

A vector $\mathbf{p}$ in three dimensions is a translation of the whole of space relative to a fixed coordinate framework. (You could imagine Fig. 5.1 as a blizzard, with the arrows showing the translations of the individual snowflakes.)

It is written as $\begin{pmatrix} l \\ m \\ n \end{pmatrix}$, which is a translation of $l$, $m$ and $n$ units in the $x$-, $y$- and $z$-directions. It can also be written in the form $l\mathbf{i} + m\mathbf{j} + n\mathbf{k}$, where $\mathbf{i} = \begin{pmatrix} 1 \\ 0 \\ 0 \end{pmatrix}$, $\mathbf{j} = \begin{pmatrix} 0 \\ 1 \\ 0 \end{pmatrix}$, $\mathbf{k} = \begin{pmatrix} 0 \\ 0 \\ 1 \end{pmatrix}$ are basic unit vectors in the $x$-, $y$- and $z$-directions.

Almost everything that you know about coordinates in two dimensions carries over into three dimensions in an obvious way, but you need to notice a few differences:

- The axes can be taken in pairs to define coordinate planes. For example, the $x$- and $y$-axes define the horizontal plane, called the $xy$-plane. All points in this plane have $z$-coordinate zero, so the equation of the plane is $z = 0$. Similarly the $xz$-plane and the $yz$-plane have equations $y = 0$ and $x = 0$; these are both vertical planes.
- The idea of the gradient of a line does not carry over into three dimensions. However, you can still use a vector to describe the direction of a line. This is one of the main reasons why vectors are especially useful in three dimensions.
- In three dimensions lines which are not parallel may or may not meet. (Think of a railway crossing a road. They may either intersect, at a level crossing, or not intersect, with a viaduct.) Non-parallel lines which do not meet are said to be **skew**.

### Example 5.7.1

Points $A$ and $B$ have coordinates $(-5, 3, 4)$ and $(-2, 9, 1)$. The line $AB$ meets the $xy$-plane at $C$. Find the coordinates of $C$.

The displacement vector $\overrightarrow{AB}$ is

$$\mathbf{b} - \mathbf{a} = \begin{pmatrix} -2 \\ 9 \\ 1 \end{pmatrix} - \begin{pmatrix} -5 \\ 3 \\ 4 \end{pmatrix} = \begin{pmatrix} 3 \\ 6 \\ -3 \end{pmatrix} = 3 \begin{pmatrix} 1 \\ 2 \\ -1 \end{pmatrix}.$$

So $\begin{pmatrix} 1 \\ 2 \\ -1 \end{pmatrix}$ can be taken as a direction vector for the line. A vector equation for the

line is therefore

$$\mathbf{r} = \begin{pmatrix} -5 \\ 3 \\ 4 \end{pmatrix} + t \begin{pmatrix} 1 \\ 2 \\ -1 \end{pmatrix}, \quad \text{or} \quad \mathbf{r} = \begin{pmatrix} -5+t \\ 3+2t \\ 4-t \end{pmatrix}.$$

$C$ is the point on the line at which $z = 0$, so that $4 - t = 0$, $t = 4$. It therefore has

position vector $\mathbf{c} = \begin{pmatrix} -1 \\ 11 \\ 0 \end{pmatrix}$ and coordinates $(-1, 11, 0)$.

### Example 5.7.2
Find the value of $u$ for which the lines $\mathbf{r} = (\mathbf{j} - \mathbf{k}) + s(\mathbf{i} + 2\mathbf{j} + \mathbf{k})$ and
$\mathbf{r} = (\mathbf{i} + 7\mathbf{j} - 4\mathbf{k}) + t(\mathbf{i} + u\mathbf{k})$ intersect.

Points on the lines can be written as $s\mathbf{i} + (1 + 2s)\mathbf{j} + (-1 + s)\mathbf{k}$ and
$(1 + t)\mathbf{i} + 7\mathbf{j} + (-4 + ut)\mathbf{k}$. If these are the same point, then

$$s = 1 + t, \quad 1 + 2s = 7, \quad \text{and} \quad -1 + s = -4 + ut.$$

The first two equations give $s = 3$ and $t = 2$. Putting these values into the third
equation gives $-1 + 3 = -4 + 2u$, so $u = 3$.

You can easily check that, with these values, both equations give $\mathbf{r} = 3\mathbf{i} + 7\mathbf{j} + 2\mathbf{k}$, so the
point of intersection has coordinates $(3, 7, 2)$.

### Exercise 5D

1 Investigate whether or not it is possible to find numbers $s$ and $t$ which satisfy the
following vector equations.

(a) $s\begin{pmatrix} 3 \\ 4 \\ 1 \end{pmatrix} + t\begin{pmatrix} 2 \\ -1 \\ 0 \end{pmatrix} = \begin{pmatrix} 0 \\ 11 \\ 2 \end{pmatrix}$ (b) $\begin{pmatrix} -1 \\ -2 \\ 3 \end{pmatrix} + s\begin{pmatrix} 1 \\ 2 \\ -1 \end{pmatrix} + t\begin{pmatrix} 3 \\ -1 \\ 1 \end{pmatrix} = \begin{pmatrix} 5 \\ 3 \\ 4 \end{pmatrix}$ (c) $s\begin{pmatrix} 1 \\ 2 \\ -3 \end{pmatrix} + t\begin{pmatrix} 5 \\ 1 \\ 1 \end{pmatrix} = \begin{pmatrix} 1 \\ -7 \\ 11 \end{pmatrix}$

2 If $\mathbf{p} = 2\mathbf{i} - \mathbf{j} + 3\mathbf{k}$, $\mathbf{q} = 5\mathbf{i} + 2\mathbf{j}$ and $\mathbf{r} = 4\mathbf{i} + \mathbf{j} + \mathbf{k}$, find a set of numbers $f$, $g$ and $h$ such
that $f\mathbf{p} + g\mathbf{q} + h\mathbf{r} = \mathbf{0}$. What does this tell you about the translations represented by $\mathbf{p}$, $\mathbf{q}$
and $\mathbf{r}$?

3 $A$ and $B$ are points with coordinates $(2, 1, 4)$ and $(5, -5, -2)$. Find the coordinates of the
point $C$ such that $\overrightarrow{AC} = \frac{2}{3}\overrightarrow{AB}$.

4 Four points $A$, $B$, $C$ and $D$ with position vectors $\mathbf{a}$, $\mathbf{b}$, $\mathbf{c}$ and $\mathbf{d}$ are vertices of a
tetrahedron. The mid-points of $BC$, $CA$, $AB$, $AD$, $BD$, $CD$ are denoted by $P$, $Q$, $R$,
$U$, $V$, $W$. Find the position vectors of the mid-points of $PU$, $QV$ and $RW$.

What do you notice about the answer? State your conclusion as a geometrical theorem.

5  If $E$ and $F$ are two points with position vectors $\mathbf{e}$ and $\mathbf{f}$, find the position vector of the point $H$ such that $\overrightarrow{EH} = \frac{3}{4}\overrightarrow{EF}$.

With the notation of Question 4, express in terms of $\mathbf{a}$, $\mathbf{b}$, $\mathbf{c}$ and $\mathbf{d}$ the position vectors of $G$, the centroid of triangle $ABC$, and of $H$, the point on $DG$ such that $DH:HG = 3:1$.

6  For each of the following sets of points $A$, $B$, $C$ and $D$, determine whether the lines $AB$ and $CD$ are parallel, intersect each other, or are skew.

(a)  $A(3,2,4)$, $B(-3,-7,-8)$, $C(0,1,3)$, $D(-2,5,9)$

(b)  $A(3,1,0)$, $B(-3,1,3)$, $C(5,0,-1)$, $D(1,0,1)$

(c)  $A(-5,-4,-3)$, $B(5,1,2)$, $C(-1,-3,0)$, $D(8,0,6)$

(d)  $A(2,0,3)$, $B(-1,2,1)$, $C(4,-1,5)$, $D(10,-5,1)$

7  Find a vector equation for the line $l$ through $(3,2,6)$ parallel to the line with vector equation $\mathbf{r} = \begin{pmatrix} 4 \\ 0 \\ 5 \end{pmatrix} + t \begin{pmatrix} -3 \\ 1 \\ 2 \end{pmatrix}$. Find also the coordinates of the points where $l$ meets the $xy$-plane and the $xz$-plane.

8  A line cuts the $yz$-plane at the point $(0,4,3)$ and the $xz$-plane at the point $(6,0,5)$. Find the coordinates of the point where it cuts the $xy$-plane.

9  A student displays her birthday cards on strings which she has pinned to opposite walls of her room, whose floor measures 3 metres by 4 metres. Relative to one corner of the room, the coordinates of the ends of the first string are $(0,3.3,2.4)$ and $(3,1.3,1.9)$ in metre units. The coordinates of the ends of the second string are $(0.7,0,2.3)$ and $(1.5,4,1.5)$. Find the difference in the heights of the two strings where one passes over the other.

## Miscellaneous exercise 5

1  Two lines have equations $\mathbf{r} = \begin{pmatrix} 1 \\ 3 \\ 2 \end{pmatrix} + \lambda \begin{pmatrix} 4 \\ -2 \\ 1 \end{pmatrix}$ and $\mathbf{r} = \begin{pmatrix} 3 \\ 8 \\ 7 \end{pmatrix} + \mu \begin{pmatrix} 2 \\ -3 \\ -1 \end{pmatrix}$. Show that the lines intersect, and find the position vector of the point of intersection.   (OCR)

2  (a)  A straight line, $l_1$, has vector equation $\mathbf{r} = \begin{pmatrix} 4 \\ 2 \end{pmatrix} + t \begin{pmatrix} 1 \\ 4 \end{pmatrix}$ where $\mathbf{r} = \begin{pmatrix} x \\ y \end{pmatrix}$. Find the cartesian equation of this line.

(b)  Another straight line, $l_2$, has equation $2x - 3y + 3 = 0$. Find a vector equation for it.

(c)  Find, in either cartesian or vector form, an equation of the line through $(-1,5)$ parallel to $l_2$.   (OCR)

3  Investigate the intersection of the following pairs of lines, one given by a vector equation and the other by a cartesian equation.

(a)  $\mathbf{r} = \begin{pmatrix} 2 \\ 0 \end{pmatrix} + t \begin{pmatrix} 1 \\ -3 \end{pmatrix}$,  $3x + y = 8$

(b)  $\mathbf{r} = \begin{pmatrix} -1 \\ 4 \end{pmatrix} + t \begin{pmatrix} 2 \\ 5 \end{pmatrix}$,  $x - 4y = 1$

(c)  $\mathbf{r} = \begin{pmatrix} 0 \\ 3 \end{pmatrix} + t \begin{pmatrix} 2 \\ -1 \end{pmatrix}$,  $2y + x = 6$

**4** (a) Find a vector equation for the line with cartesian equation $2x + 3y = 7$.

(b) Find the cartesian equation of the line with vector equation $\mathbf{r} = \begin{pmatrix} 3 \\ 4 \end{pmatrix} + t \begin{pmatrix} 1 \\ 3 \end{pmatrix}$.

(c) Find the point of intersection of the two lines

(i) by using both cartesian equations,

(ii) by using both vector equations,

(iii) by using the equations in the forms given in parts (a) and (b).

**5** $ABCD$ is a parallelogram. The coordinates of $A$, $B$, $D$ are $(4, 2, 3)$, $(18, 4, 8)$ and $(-1, 12, 13)$ respectively. The origin of coordinates is $O$.

(a) Find the vectors $\overrightarrow{AB}$ and $\overrightarrow{AD}$. Find the coordinates of $C$.

(b) Show that $\overrightarrow{OA}$ can be expressed in the form $\lambda \overrightarrow{AB} + \mu \overrightarrow{AD}$, stating the values of $\lambda$ and $\mu$. What does this tell you about the plane $ABCD$? (MEI)

**6** A tunnel is to be excavated through a hill. In order to define position, coordinates $(x, y, z)$ are taken relative to an origin $O$ such that $x$ is the distance east from $O$, $y$ is the distance north and $z$ is the vertical distance upwards, with one unit equal to 100 m. The tunnel starts at point $A(2, 3, 5)$ and runs in the direction $\begin{pmatrix} 1 \\ 1 \\ -0.5 \end{pmatrix}$.

(a) Write down the equation of the tunnel in the form $\mathbf{r} = \mathbf{u} + \lambda \mathbf{t}$.

(b) An old tunnel through the hill has equation $\mathbf{r} = \begin{pmatrix} 4 \\ 1 \\ 2 \end{pmatrix} + \mu \begin{pmatrix} 7 \\ 15 \\ 0 \end{pmatrix}$. Show that the point $P$ on the new tunnel where $x = 7\frac{1}{2}$ is directly above a point $Q$ in the old tunnel. Find the vertical separation $PQ$ of the tunnels at this point. (MEI)

**7** A curve is given by parametric equations $x = f(\theta)$, $y = g(\theta)$. Show that the direction of the tangent at the point with parameter $\theta$ is given by $\begin{pmatrix} f'(\theta) \\ g'(\theta) \end{pmatrix}$. Write down a vector equation for the tangent to the curve at this point.

Hence find a vector equation for the tangent at the point with parameter $\theta$ for the curves with the following equations, and deduce the cartesian equation.

(a) $x = \theta^2$, $y = \theta^3$ (b) $x = 3\cos\theta$, $y = 2\sin\theta$

**8** A mathematical market trader packages fruit in three sizes. An Individual bag holds 1 apple and 2 bananas; a Jumbo bag holds 4 apples and 3 bananas; and a King-size bag holds 8 apples and 7 bananas. She draws two vector arrows $\mathbf{a}$ and $\mathbf{b}$ to represent an apple and a banana respectively, and then represents the three sizes of bag by vectors $\mathbf{I} = \mathbf{a} + 2\mathbf{b}$, $\mathbf{J} = 4\mathbf{a} + 3\mathbf{b}$ and $\mathbf{K} = 8\mathbf{a} + 7\mathbf{b}$. Find numbers $s$ and $t$ such that $\mathbf{K} = s\mathbf{I} + t\mathbf{J}$.

By midday she has sold all her King-size bags, but she has plenty of Individual and Jumbo bags left. She decides to make up some more King-size bags by using the contents of the other bags. How can she do this so that she has no loose fruit left over?

**9** Find the intersection of the lines $\mathbf{r} = \begin{pmatrix} -1 \\ 0 \end{pmatrix} + s\begin{pmatrix} \cos\alpha \\ \sin\alpha \end{pmatrix}$ and $\mathbf{r} = \begin{pmatrix} 1 \\ 0 \end{pmatrix} + t\begin{pmatrix} -\sin\alpha \\ \cos\alpha \end{pmatrix}$, giving your answer in a simplified form. Interpret your answer geometrically.

**10** A balloon flying over flat fenland reports its position at 7:40 a.m. as $(7.8, 5.4, 1.2)$, the coordinates being given in kilometres relative to a checkpoint on the ground. By 7:50 a.m. its position has changed to $(9.3, 4.4, 0.7)$. Assuming that it continues to descend at the same speed along the same line, find the coordinates of the point where it would be expected to land, and the time when this would occur.

**11** An airliner climbs so that its position relative to the airport control tower $t$ minutes after take-off is given by the vector $\mathbf{r} = \begin{pmatrix} 1 \\ 2 \\ 0 \end{pmatrix} + t\begin{pmatrix} 4 \\ 5 \\ 0.6 \end{pmatrix}$ the units being kilometres. The $x$- and $y$-axes point towards the east and the north respectively.

(a) Find the position of the airliner when it reaches its cruising height of 9 km.

(b) With reference to $(x, y)$ coordinates on the ground, the coastline has equation $x + 3y = 140$. How high is the aircraft flying as it crosses the coast?

(c) Calculate the speed of the airliner over the ground in kilometres per hour, and the bearing on which it is flying.

(d) Calculate the speed of the airliner through the air, and the angle to the horizontal at which it is climbing.

**12** Two airliners take off simultaneously from different airports. As they climb, their positions relative to an air traffic control centre $t$ minutes later are given by the vectors $\mathbf{r}_1 = \begin{pmatrix} 5 \\ -30 \\ 0 \end{pmatrix} + t\begin{pmatrix} 8 \\ 2 \\ 0.5 \end{pmatrix}$ and $\mathbf{r}_2 = \begin{pmatrix} 13 \\ 26 \\ 0 \end{pmatrix} + t\begin{pmatrix} 6 \\ -3 \\ 0.6 \end{pmatrix}$, the units being kilometres. Find the coordinates of the point on the ground over which both airliners pass. Find also the difference in heights, and the difference in the times, when they pass over that point.

**13** The centre line of an underground railway tunnel follows a line given by $\mathbf{r} = t\begin{pmatrix} 10 \\ 8 \\ -1 \end{pmatrix}$ for $0 \leqslant t \leqslant 40$, the units being metres. The centre line of another tunnel at present stops at the point with position vector $\begin{pmatrix} 200 \\ 100 \\ -25 \end{pmatrix}$ and it is proposed to extend this in a direction $\begin{pmatrix} 5 \\ 7 \\ u \end{pmatrix}$. The constant $u$ has to be chosen so that, at the point where one tunnel passes over the other, there is at least 15 metres difference in depth between the centre lines of the two tunnels. What restriction does this impose on the value of $u$?

Another requirement is that the tunnel must not be inclined at more than $5°$ to the horizontal. What values of $u$ satisfy both requirements?

# 6 The binomial expansion

The binomial theorem tells you how to expand $(1+x)^n$ when $n$ is a positive integer. This chapter extends this to all rational values of $n$. When you have completed it, you should

- be able to expand $(1+x)^n$ in ascending powers of $x$
- know that the expansion is valid for $|x|<1$
- understand how to use expansions to find approximations
- know how to extend the method to expand powers of more general expressions.

## 6.1 Generalising the binomial theorem

You learnt in P2 Chapter 4 how to expand $(x+y)^n$ by the binomial theorem, when $n$ is a positive integer. If you replace $x$ by 1 and $y$ by $x$, this becomes

$$(1+x)^n = 1^n + \frac{n}{1} \times 1^{n-1}x + \frac{n(n-1)}{1\times 2} \times 1^{n-2}x^2 + \frac{n(n-1)(n-2)}{1\times 2\times 3} \times 1^{n-3}x^3 + \dots.$$

You can remove all the powers of 1, and write this more simply as

$$(1+x)^n = 1 + \frac{n}{1}x + \frac{n(n-1)}{1\times 2}x^2 + \frac{n(n-1)(n-2)}{1\times 2\times 3}x^3 + \dots. \qquad \text{Equation A}$$

Notice that in this form the terms are written in ascending powers of $x$ (see P2 Section 1.1).

This chapter tackles the question, 'Can you still use this expansion when $n$ is not a positive integer?'.

Before trying to answer this, you should notice an important point about the terms. If $n$ is a positive integer, then the form of the coefficients ensures that there are no terms with powers higher than $x^n$. For example, if $n=5$ the coefficient of $n^6$ is

$$\frac{5\times 4\times 3\times 2\times 1\times 0}{1\times 2\times 3\times 4\times 5\times 6} = 0,$$

and all the coefficients which follow it are zero. But this only happens when $n$ is a positive integer. For example, if $n = 4\frac{1}{2}$ the coefficients of $x^4$, $x^5$ and $x^6$ are

$$\frac{4\frac{1}{2}\times 3\frac{1}{2}\times 2\frac{1}{2}\times 1\frac{1}{2}}{1\times 2\times 3\times 4}, \qquad \frac{4\frac{1}{2}\times 3\frac{1}{2}\times 2\frac{1}{2}\times 1\frac{1}{2}\times \frac{1}{2}}{1\times 2\times 3\times 4\times 5} \quad \text{and} \quad \frac{4\frac{1}{2}\times 3\frac{1}{2}\times 2\frac{1}{2}\times 1\frac{1}{2}\times \frac{1}{2}\times \left(-\frac{1}{2}\right)}{1\times 2\times 3\times 4\times 5\times 6}.$$

Whichever coefficient you consider, you never get a factor of 0. So, if $n$ is not a positive integer, the expansion never stops.

### The case $n = -1$

You know from P2 Section 10.3 that the sum to infinity of the geometric series

$1 + r + r^2 + r^3 + \dots$ is $\dfrac{1}{1-r}$, provided that $|r|<1$. Replacing $r$ by $-x$ now gives

$$\frac{1}{1-(-x)} = (1+x)^{-1} = 1 - x + x^2 - x^3 + \dots .$$

Now try using Equation A with $n = -1$. This gives

$$(1+x)^{-1} = 1 + \frac{(-1)}{1}x + \frac{(-1)(-2)}{1 \times 2}x^2 + \frac{(-1)(-2)(-3)}{1 \times 2 \times 3}x^3 + \dots ,$$

which simplifies to

$$(1+x)^{-1} = 1 - x + x^2 - x^3 + \dots .$$

So far so good: Equation A works when $n = -1$.

**The case $n = \frac{1}{2}$**

If $(1+x)^{\frac{1}{2}}$ can be expanded in the form $A + Bx + Cx^2 + Dx^3 + \dots$, then you want to find $A, B, C, D, \dots$ so that

$$\left(A + Bx + Cx^2 + Dx^3 + \dots\right)^2 \equiv 1 + x.$$

This needs to be true for $x = 0$, so $A^2 = 1$. Since $(1+x)^{\frac{1}{2}}$ is the positive square root, this means that $A = 1$.

Then

$$\left(1 + Bx + Cx^2 + Dx^3 + \dots\right)^2 \equiv \left(1 + Bx + Cx^2 + Dx^3 + \dots\right)\left(1 + Bx + Cx^2 + Dx^3 + \dots\right)$$
$$\equiv 1 + (B+B)x + \left(C + B^2 + C\right)x^2$$
$$+ (D + BC + CB + D)x^3 + \dots$$
$$\equiv 1 + (2B)x + \left(2C + B^2\right)x^2 + (2D + 2BC)x^3 + \dots .$$

So

$$1 + x \equiv 1 + (2B)x + \left(2C + B^2\right)x^2 + (2D + 2BC)x^3 + \dots .$$

Since that is an identity, you can equate coefficients of each power of $x$ in turn.

$$2B = 1 \qquad \Rightarrow B = \tfrac{1}{2},$$

$$2C + B^2 = 0 \quad \Rightarrow C = -\tfrac{1}{8},$$

$$2D + 2BC = 0 \Rightarrow D = \tfrac{1}{16}.$$

So it appears that $\left(1 + \tfrac{1}{2}x - \tfrac{1}{8}x^2 + \tfrac{1}{16}x^3 + \dots\right)^2 \equiv 1 + x$, and

$$(1+x)^{\frac{1}{2}} = 1 + \tfrac{1}{2}x - \tfrac{1}{8}x^2 + \tfrac{1}{16}x^3 + \dots .$$

Using Equation A with $n = \tfrac{1}{2}$ gives

$$(1+x)^{\frac{1}{2}} = 1 + \frac{\frac{1}{2}}{1}x + \frac{\frac{1}{2}\left(-\frac{1}{2}\right)}{1 \times 2}x^2 + \frac{\frac{1}{2}\left(-\frac{1}{2}\right)\left(-\frac{3}{2}\right)}{1 \times 2 \times 3}x^3 + \ldots$$

$$= 1 + \tfrac{1}{2}x - \tfrac{1}{8}x^2 + \tfrac{1}{16}x^3 + \ldots.$$

So Equation A seems to work when $n = \frac{1}{2}$.

**The general case**

In fact Equation A works for all rational powers of $n$, positive or negative. There is, however, an important restriction. You will remember from P2 Section 10.3, that the series $1 + r + r^2 + r^3 + \ldots$ only converges to $\dfrac{1}{1-r}$ if $|r| < 1$. A similar condition applies to the binomial expansion of $(1+x)^n$ for any value of $n$ which is not a positive integer.

> **The binomial expansion**     When $n$ is rational, but not a positive integer, and $|x| < 1$,
>
> $$(1+x)^n = 1 + \frac{n}{1}x + \frac{n(n-1)}{1 \times 2}x^2 + \frac{n(n-1)(n-2)}{1 \times 2 \times 3}x^3 + \ldots.$$

This is sometimes called the **binomial series**.

**Example 6.1.1**

Find the expansion of $(1+x)^{-2}$ in ascending powers of $x$ up to the term in $x^4$.

Putting $n = -2$ in the formula for $(1+x)^n$,

$$(1+x)^{-2} = 1 + \frac{(-2)}{1}x + \frac{(-2)(-3)}{1 \times 2}x^2 + \frac{(-2)(-3)(-4)}{1 \times 2 \times 3}x^3 + \frac{(-2)(-3)(-4)(-5)}{1 \times 2 \times 3 \times 4}x^4 + \ldots$$

$$= 1 - 2x + 3x^2 - 4x^3 + 5x^4 + \ldots.$$

The required expansion is $1 - 2x + 3x^2 - 4x^3 + 5x^4$.

**Example 6.1.2**

Find the expansion of $(1+3x)^{\frac{3}{2}}$ in ascending powers of $x$ up to and including the term in $x^3$. For what values of $x$ is the expansion valid?

Putting $n = \frac{3}{2}$ in the formula for $(1+x)^n$, and writing $3x$ in place of $x$,

$$(1+3x)^{\frac{3}{2}} = 1 + \frac{\frac{3}{2}}{1}(3x) + \frac{\left(\frac{3}{2}\right)\left(\frac{1}{2}\right)}{1 \times 2}(3x)^2 + \frac{\left(\frac{3}{2}\right)\left(\frac{1}{2}\right)\left(-\frac{1}{2}\right)}{1 \times 2 \times 3}(3x)^3 + \ldots$$

$$= 1 + \tfrac{9}{2}x + \tfrac{27}{8}x^2 - \tfrac{27}{16}x^3 + \ldots.$$

The required expansion is $1 + \frac{9}{2}x + \frac{27}{8}x^2 - \frac{27}{16}x^3$.

The expansion $(1+x)^n$ is valid for $|x| < 1$, so this expansion is valid for $|3x| < 1$: that is, for $|x| < \frac{1}{3}$.

You should notice one other point. When $n$ is a positive integer, the coefficient $\dfrac{n(n-1)\ldots(n-(r-1))}{1 \times 2 \times \ldots \times r}$ can be written more concisely using factorials, as $\dfrac{n!}{r!(n-r)!}$. You can't use this when $n$ is not a positive integer, since $n!$ isn't defined unless $n$ is a positive integer or zero. However, $r$ is always an integer, so you can still if you like write the coefficient as $\dfrac{n(n-1)\ldots(n-(r-1))}{r!}$.

## 6.2 Approximations

One use of binomial expansions is to find numerical approximations to square roots, cube roots and other calculations. If $|x|$ is much smaller than 1, the power $|x^2|$ will be very small, $|x^3|$ will be smaller still, and you soon reach a power which is, to all intents and purposes, negligible. So the sum of the first few terms of the expansion is a very close approximation to $(1+x)^n$.

### Example 6.2.1

Find the expansion of $(1-2x)^{\frac{1}{2}}$ in ascending powers of $x$ up to and including the term in $x^3$. By giving a suitable value to $x$, find an approximation for $\sqrt{2}$.

$$(1-2x)^{\frac{1}{2}} = 1 + \frac{\frac{1}{2}}{1}(-2x) + \frac{\frac{1}{2}\left(-\frac{1}{2}\right)}{1 \times 2}(-2x)^2 + \frac{\frac{1}{2}\left(-\frac{1}{2}\right)\left(-\frac{3}{2}\right)}{1 \times 2 \times 3}(-2x)^3 + \ldots$$

$$= 1 - x - \tfrac{1}{2}x^2 - \tfrac{1}{2}x^3 + \ldots.$$

Choosing a suitable value for $x$ needs a bit of ingenuity. It is no use simply taking $x$ so that $1 - 2x = 2$, which would give $x = -\frac{1}{2}$, since this is nowhere near small enough for the terms in $x^4$, $x^5$, ... to be neglected. The trick is to try to find a value of $x$ so that $1 - 2x$ has the form $2 \times$ a perfect square. A good choice is to take $x = 0.01$, so that $1 - 2 \times 0.01 = 0.98$, which is $2 \times 0.7^2$.

So put $x = 0.01$ in the expansion. This gives

$$0.98^{\frac{1}{2}} = 1 - 0.01 - \tfrac{1}{2} \times 0.01^2 - \tfrac{1}{2} \times 0.01^3 - \ldots,$$

so     $0.7\sqrt{2} \approx 1 - 0.01 - 0.000\,05 - 0.000\,000\,5 = 0.989\,949\,5.$

Therefore $\frac{7}{10}\sqrt{2} \approx 0.989\,949\,5$, giving $\sqrt{2} \approx 1.414\,214$.

## 6.3 Expanding other expressions

The binomial series can also be used to expand powers of expressions more complicated than $1 + x$ or $1 + ax$. If you can rewrite an expression as $Y(1+Z)^n$ where $Y$ and $Z$ are expressions involving $x$, then you can expand $(1+Z)^n$ and then substitute the appropriate expressions in the result.

**Example 6.3.1**

Find the binomial expansion of $\left(4-3x^2\right)^{\frac{1}{2}}$ up to and including terms in $x^4$.

$4-3x^2$ is not of the required form, but you can write it as $4\left(1-\frac{3}{4}x^2\right)$. So, using the fraction rule for indices,

$$\left(4-3x^2\right)^{\frac{1}{2}} = 4^{\frac{1}{2}}\left(1-\frac{3}{4}x^2\right)^{\frac{1}{2}} = 2\left(1-\frac{3}{4}x^2\right)^{\frac{1}{2}}.$$

Then $\left(1-\frac{3}{4}x^2\right)^{\frac{1}{2}} = 1+\frac{\frac{1}{2}}{1}\left(-\frac{3}{4}x^2\right)+\frac{\left(\frac{1}{2}\right)\left(-\frac{1}{2}\right)}{1\times 2}\left(-\frac{3}{4}x^2\right)^2 +\ldots.$

Therefore $\left(4-3x^2\right)^{\frac{1}{2}} = 2\left(1-\frac{3}{4}x^2\right)^{\frac{1}{2}} = 2-\frac{3}{4}x^2-\frac{9}{64}x^4 +\ldots$ and the required expansion is $2-\frac{3}{4}x^2-\frac{9}{64}x^4$.

**Example 6.3.2**

Expand $\dfrac{5+x}{2-x+x^2}$ in ascending powers of $x$ up to the term in $x^3$.

Write $\dfrac{5+x}{2-x+x^2} = \dfrac{5+x}{2\left(1-\frac{1}{2}x+\frac{1}{2}x^2\right)} = \frac{1}{2}(5+x)\left(1-\frac{1}{2}\left(x-x^2\right)\right)^{-1}.$

Now $(1-u)^{-1} = 1+\frac{(-1)}{1}(-u)+\frac{(-1)(-2)}{1\times 2}(-u)^2 +\frac{(-1)(-2)(-3)}{1\times 2\times 3}(-u)^3 +\ldots$

$$= 1+u+u^2+u^3+\ldots.$$

Writing $\frac{1}{2}\left(x-x^2\right)$ in place of $u$,

$$\left(1-\frac{1}{2}\left(x-x^2\right)\right)^{-1} = 1+\left(\frac{1}{2}\left(x-x^2\right)\right)+\left(\frac{1}{2}\left(x-x^2\right)\right)^2+\left(\frac{1}{2}\left(x-x^2\right)\right)^3+\ldots.$$

Collecting together the terms on the right, and ignoring any powers higher than $x^3$,

$$\left(1-\frac{1}{2}\left(x-x^2\right)\right)^{-1} = 1+\frac{1}{2}\left(x-x^2\right)+\frac{1}{4}\left(x^2-2x^3\right)+\frac{1}{8}\left(x^3+\ldots\right)+\ldots$$
$$= 1+\frac{1}{2}x-\frac{1}{4}x^2-\frac{3}{8}x^3+\ldots.$$

Therefore, multiplying by $\frac{1}{2}(5+x)$,

$$\frac{5+x}{2-x+x^2} = \frac{1}{2}(5+x)\left(1+\frac{1}{2}x-\frac{1}{4}x^2-\frac{3}{8}x^3+\ldots\right)$$
$$= \frac{1}{2}\left(5+\frac{5}{2}x-\frac{5}{4}x^2-\frac{15}{8}x^3+x+\frac{1}{2}x^2-\frac{1}{4}x^3+\ldots\right)$$
$$= \frac{1}{2}\left(5+\frac{7}{2}x-\frac{3}{4}x^2-\frac{17}{8}x^3+\ldots\right)$$
$$= \frac{5}{2}+\frac{7}{4}x-\frac{3}{8}x^2-\frac{17}{16}x^3+\ldots.$$

The required expansion is $\frac{5}{2}+\frac{7}{4}x-\frac{3}{8}x^2-\frac{17}{16}x^3$.

If an algebraic expression has a denominator which factorises, like

$$\frac{5+x}{2-x-x^2} = \frac{5+x}{(2+x)(1-x)},$$

there is a simpler way of expanding it, using partial fractions. This is explained in the next chapter.

## Exercise 6

**1** Find the expansion of the following in ascending powers of $x$ up to and including the term in $x^2$.

    (a) $(1+x)^{-3}$      (b) $(1+x)^{-5}$      (c) $(1-x)^{-4}$      (d) $(1-x)^{-6}$

**2** Find the expansion of the following in ascending powers of $x$ up to and including the term in $x^2$.

    (a) $(1+4x)^{-1}$      (b) $(1-2x)^{-3}$      (c) $(1-3x)^{-4}$      (d) $\left(1+\frac{1}{2}x\right)^{-2}$

**3** Find the coefficient of $x^3$ in the expansion of the following.

    (a) $(1-x)^{-7}$      (b) $(1+2x)^{-1}$      (c) $(1+3x)^{-3}$      (d) $(1-4x)^{-2}$

    (e) $\left(1-\frac{1}{3}x\right)^{-6}$      (f) $(1+ax)^{-4}$      (g) $(1-bx)^{-4}$      (h) $(1-cx)^{-n}$

**4** Find the expansion of the following in ascending powers of $x$ up to and including the term in $x^2$.

    (a) $(1+x)^{\frac{1}{3}}$      (b) $(1+x)^{\frac{3}{4}}$      (c) $(1-x)^{\frac{2}{3}}$      (d) $(1-x)^{-\frac{1}{2}}$

**5** Find the expansion of the following in ascending powers of $x$ up to and including the term in $x^2$.

    (a) $(1+4x)^{\frac{1}{2}}$      (b) $(1+3x)^{-\frac{1}{3}}$      (c) $(1-6x)^{\frac{4}{3}}$      (d) $\left(1-\frac{1}{2}x\right)^{-\frac{1}{4}}$

**6** Find the coefficient of $x^3$ in the expansion of the following.

    (a) $(1+2x)^{\frac{3}{2}}$      (b) $(1-5x)^{-\frac{1}{2}}$      (c) $\left(1+\frac{3}{2}x\right)^{\frac{1}{3}}$      (d) $(1-4x)^{\frac{3}{4}}$

    (e) $(1-7x)^{-\frac{1}{7}}$      (f) $\left(1+\sqrt{2}x\right)^{\frac{1}{2}}$      (g) $(1+ax)^{\frac{3}{2}}$      (h) $(1-bx)^{-\frac{1}{2}n}$

**7** Show that, for small $x$, $\sqrt{1+\frac{1}{4}x} \approx 1+\frac{1}{8}x-\frac{1}{128}x^2$. Deduce the first three terms in the expansions of the following.

    (a) $\sqrt{1-\frac{1}{4}x}$      (b) $\sqrt{1+\frac{1}{4}x^2}$      (c) $\sqrt{4+x}$      (d) $\sqrt{36+9x}$

**8** Show that $\dfrac{1}{\left(1-\frac{3}{2}x\right)^2} \approx 1+3x+\frac{27}{4}x^2+\frac{27}{2}x^3$ and state the interval of values of $x$ for which the expansion is valid. Deduce the first four terms in the expansions of the following.

    (a) $\dfrac{4}{\left(1-\frac{3}{2}x\right)^2}$      (b) $\dfrac{1}{(2-3x)^2}$

**9** Find the first four terms in the expansion of each of the following in ascending powers of $x$. State the interval of values of $x$ for which each expansion is valid.

(a) $\sqrt{1-6x}$

(b) $\dfrac{1}{1+5x}$

(c) $\dfrac{1}{\sqrt[3]{1+9x}}$

(d) $\dfrac{1}{(1-2x)^4}$

(e) $\sqrt{1+2x^2}$

(f) $\sqrt[3]{8-16x}$

(g) $\dfrac{10}{\left(1+\frac{1}{5}x\right)^2}$

(h) $\dfrac{2}{2-x}$

(i) $\dfrac{1}{(2+x)^3}$

(j) $\dfrac{4x}{\sqrt{4+x^3}}$

(k) $\sqrt[4]{1+8x}$

(l) $\dfrac{12}{\left(\sqrt{3}-x\right)^4}$

**10** Find the expansion of $\sqrt{1+8x}$ in ascending powers of $x$ up to and including the term in $x^3$. By giving a suitable value to $x$, find an approximation for $\sqrt{1.08}$. Deduce approximations for

(a) $\sqrt{108}$,

(b) $\sqrt{3}$.

**11** Find the expansion of $\sqrt[3]{1+4x}$ in ascending powers of $x$ up to and including the term in $x^2$.

(a) By putting $x=0.01$, determine an approximation for $\sqrt[3]{130}$.

(b) By putting $x=-0.000\,25$, determine an approximation for $\sqrt[3]{999}$.

**12** Given that the coefficient of $x^3$ in the expansion of $\dfrac{1}{(1+ax)^3}$ is $-2160$, find the value of $a$.

**13** Find the coefficient of $x^2$ in the expansion of $\dfrac{(1-2x)^2}{(1+x)^2}$.

**14** Find the first three terms in the expansion in ascending powers of $x$ of $\dfrac{\sqrt{1+2x}}{\sqrt{1-4x}}$. State the values of $x$ for which the expansion is valid. By substituting $x=0.01$ in your expansion, find an approximation for $\sqrt{17}$.

**15** Given that terms involving $x^4$ and higher powers may be ignored and that
$$\frac{1}{(1+ax)^3} - \frac{1}{(1+3x)^4} = bx^2 + cx^3,$$ find the values of $a$, $b$ and $c$.

**16** Find the expansion of $\dfrac{1}{1-\left(x+x^2\right)}$ in ascending powers of $x$ up to and including the term in $x^4$. By substitution of a suitable value of $x$, find the approximation, correct to twelve decimal places, of $\dfrac{1}{0.998\,999}$.

**17** Find the first three terms in the expansion in ascending powers of $x$ of

(a) $\dfrac{8}{\left(2+x-x^2\right)^2}$

(b) $\dfrac{1+2x}{\left(1-x+2x^2\right)^3}$

**18** Given that the expansion of $(1+ax)^n$ is $1-2x+\frac{7}{3}x^2+kx^3+\dots$, find the value of $k$.

<hr>

                       **Miscellaneous exercise 6**

**1** Find the series expansion of $(1+2x)^{\frac{5}{2}}$ up to and including the term in $x^3$, simplifying the coefficients. (OCR)

**2** Expand $(1-4x)^{\frac{1}{2}}$ as a series of ascending powers of $x$, where $|x|<\frac{1}{4}$, up to and including the term in $x^3$, expressing the coefficients in their simplest form. (OCR)

**3** Expand $(1+2x)^{-3}$ as a series of ascending powers of $x$, where $|x|<\frac{1}{2}$, up to and including the term in $x^3$, expressing the coefficients in their simplest form. (OCR)

**4** Expand $\dfrac{1}{\left(1+2x^2\right)^2}$ as a series in ascending powers of $x$, up to and including the term in $x^6$, giving the coefficients in their simplest form. (OCR)

**5** Obtain the first three terms in the expansion, in ascending powers of $x$, of $(4+x)^{\frac{1}{2}}$. State the set of values of $x$ for which the expansion is valid. (OCR)

**6** If $x$ is small compared with $a$, expand $\dfrac{a^3}{\left(a^2+x^2\right)^{\frac{3}{2}}}$ in ascending powers of $\dfrac{x}{a}$ up to and including the term in $\dfrac{x^4}{a^4}$. (OCR)

**7** Given that $|x|<1$, expand $\sqrt{1+x}$ as a series of ascending powers of $x$, up to and including the term in $x^2$. Show that, if $x$ is small, then $(2-x)\sqrt{1+x}\approx a+bx^2$, where the values of $a$ and $b$ are to be stated. (OCR)

**8** Expand $(1-x)^{-2}$ as a series of ascending powers of $x$, given that $|x|<1$. Hence express $\dfrac{1+x}{(1-x)^2}$ in the form $1+3x+ax^2+bx^3+\dots$, where the values of $a$ and $b$ are to be stated. (OCR)

**9** Obtain the first three terms in the expansion, in ascending powers of $x$, of $(8+3x)^{\frac{2}{3}}$, stating the set of values of $x$ for which the expansion is valid. (OCR)

**10** Write down the first four terms of the series expansion in ascending powers of $x$ of $(1-x)^{\frac{1}{3}}$, simplifying the coefficients. By taking $x=0.1$, use your answer to show that $\sqrt[3]{900}\approx\dfrac{15\,641}{1620}$. (OCR)

**11** Give the binomial expansion, for small $x$, of $(1+x)^{\frac{1}{4}}$ up to and including the term in $x^2$, and simplify the coefficients. By putting $x=\frac{1}{16}$ in your expression, show that $\sqrt[4]{17}\approx\dfrac{8317}{4096}$. (OCR)

12  Show that $26\left(1-\dfrac{1}{26^2}\right)^{\frac{1}{2}} = n\sqrt{3}$, where $n$ is an integer whose value is to be found. Given

that $|x| < 1$, expand $(1-x)^{\frac{1}{2}}$ as a series of ascending powers of $x$, up to and including the

term in $x^2$, simplifying the coefficients. By using the first *two* terms of the expansion of

$26\left(1-\dfrac{1}{26^2}\right)^{\frac{1}{2}}$, obtain an approximate value for $\sqrt{3}$ in the form $\dfrac{p}{q}$, where $p$ and $q$ are

integers.                                                                 (OCR)

13  Expand $\dfrac{2+\left(1+\frac{1}{2}x\right)^6}{2+3x}$ in ascending powers of $x$ up to and including the term in $x^2$. (OCR)

14  Show that, for small values of $x$, $(1+x)^{\frac{1}{3}} \approx 1 + \frac{1}{3}x - \frac{1}{9}x^2$. Sketch on the same axes (with
the aid of a graphic calculator where necessary) the graphs of $y = (1+x)^{\frac{1}{3}}$, $y = 1 + \frac{1}{3}x$
and $y = 1 + \frac{1}{3}x - \frac{1}{9}x^2$.

Compare the graphs for values of $x$ such that

(a)  $-3 < x < 3$,        (b)  $-1 < x < 1$,        (c)  $-0.2 < x < 0.2$.

15  Show that the expansion of $(1+4x)^{-2}$ in ascending powers of $x$ is $1 - 8x + 48x^2 - \ldots$
nd state the set of values of $x$ for which the expansion is valid. Compare, for suitable
values of $x$, the graphs of $y = (1+4x)^{-2}$, $y = 1 - 8x$ and $y = 1 - 8x + 48x^2$.

16  Given that $1 \equiv (1+x)^2\left(A + Bx + Cx^2 + Dx^3 + \ldots\right)$, equate coefficients of powers of $x$ to
find the values of $A$, $B$, $C$ and $D$. Hence state the first four terms of the expansion in
ascending powers of $x$ of

(a)  $(1+x)^{-2}$,        (b)  $\left(1-x^2\right)^{-2}$,        (c)  $\left(1+2x^2\right)^{-2}$.

17  Given that $1 \equiv \left(1 + x + x^2\right)\left(A + Bx + Cx^2 + Dx^3 + Ex^4 + \ldots\right)$, equate coefficients of powers
of $x$ to find the values of $A$, $B$, $C$, $D$ and $E$. Hence

(a)  find the value of $\dfrac{1}{1.000\,300\,09}$ correct to sixteen decimal places;

(b)  show that $\dfrac{1}{\left(1 + x + x^2\right)\left(1 + 2x + 4x^2\right)} \approx 1 - 3x + 2x^2 + 9x^3 - 27x^4$ for small

values of $x$.

18  Expand $\dfrac{1}{(1-x)^2}$, where $|x| < 1$, in ascending powers of $x$ up to and including the term in

$x^3$. You should simplify the coefficients. By putting $x = 10^{-4}$ in your expansion, find

$\dfrac{1}{0.9999^2}$ correct to twelve decimal places.        (OCR)

19  Expand $(1+x)^{-\frac{1}{4}}$ in ascending powers of $x$ as far as the term in $x^2$, simplifying the

coefficients. Prove that $\dfrac{3}{2}\left(1 + \dfrac{1}{80}\right)^{-\frac{1}{4}} = 5^{\frac{1}{4}}$ and, using your expansion of $(1+x)^{-\frac{1}{4}}$ with

$x = \frac{1}{80}$, find an approximate value for $5^{\frac{1}{4}}$, giving five places of decimals in your answer.

                                                                          (OCR)

**20** Write down and simplify the series expansion of $\dfrac{1}{\sqrt{1+x}}$, where $|x|<1$, up to and i

ncluding the term in $x^3$. Show that using just these terms of the series with $x = 0.4$ gives

a value for $\dfrac{1}{\sqrt{1.4}}$ which differs from the true value by less than 0.7%. By replacing $x$ by

$z^2$ in your series and then integrating, show that $\displaystyle\int_0^{0.2} \dfrac{1}{\sqrt{1+z^2}}\,dz \approx 0.1987$.

(OCR, adapted)

**21\*** Show that the coefficient of $x^n$ in the series expansion of $(1+2x)^{-2}$ is $(-1)^n(n+1)2^n$.

**22\*** Show that the coefficient of $x^n$ in the series expansion of $(1-x)^{-\frac{1}{2}}$ is $\dfrac{(2n)!}{2^{2n}(n!)^2}$.

**23** Find the first three terms in the expansion in ascending powers of $x$ of $\sqrt{\dfrac{1+2x}{1-x}}$. By

putting $x = 0.02$ in your expansion, find an approximation for $\sqrt{13}$.

**24** Find the first five terms in the series expansion of $\dfrac{1}{1+2x}$. Use the expansion to find an

approximation to $\displaystyle\int_{-0.2}^{0.1} \dfrac{1}{1+2x}\,dx$. By also evaluating the integral exactly, find an

approximation for $\ln 2$.

**25** Find the first three terms in the expansion in ascending powers of $x$ of $\dfrac{3+4x+x^2}{\sqrt[3]{1+\frac{1}{2}x}}$.

Hence find an approximation to $\displaystyle\int_{-0.5}^{0.5} \dfrac{3+4x+x^2}{\sqrt[3]{1+\frac{1}{2}x}}\,dx$.

**26** Find the first three terms in the expansion
in ascending powers of $x$ of
$$\dfrac{1}{\left(1-2x^2\right)^2\left(1+3x^2\right)^2}.$$

The diagram shows the graph of
$y = 3 - 52x^2$ and part of the graph of
$$y = \dfrac{1}{\left(1-2x^2\right)^2\left(1+3x^2\right)^2}.$$

Use your expansion to find an
approximation to the area of the region
shaded in the diagram.

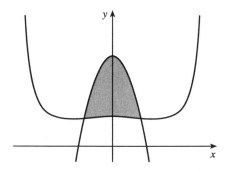

# Revision exercise 1

**1** Use the addition formulae to find an expression for $\cos^2(A+B)+\sin^2(A+B)$. Verify that your expression reduces to 1.

Use a similar method to find an expression for $\cos^2(A+B)-\sin^2(A+B)$. Verify that this reduces to $\cos(2A+2B)$.

**2** In the figure $A$, $B$, $C$ are the points on the graph of $y=\sin x$ for which $x=\alpha-\frac{1}{3}\pi$, $\alpha$, $\alpha+\frac{1}{3}\pi$ respectively. $D$ is the point $(\alpha,0)$.

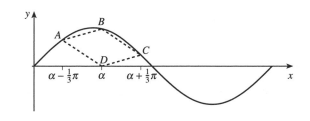

(a) Sketch separate diagrams showing $ABCD$ in the special cases where $\alpha=\frac{1}{3}\pi$, $\alpha=\frac{1}{2}\pi$, $\alpha=\frac{2}{3}\pi$.

(b) Use addition formulae to simplify $\sin\left(\alpha-\frac{1}{3}\pi\right)+\sin\left(\alpha+\frac{1}{3}\pi\right)$.

(c) Write down the coordinates of the mid-point of $AC$.

(d) Show that $ABCD$ is a parallelogram. (OCR)

**3** The angle made by a wasp's wings with the horizontal is given by the equation $\theta=0.4\sin 600t$ radians, where $t$ is the time in seconds. How many times a second do its wings oscillate? Find an expression for $\dfrac{d\theta}{dt}$, the angular velocity, in radians per second.

What is the value of $\theta$ when the angular velocity has

(a) its greatest magnitude,　　　　　　　(b) its smallest magnitude?

**4** A curve has parametric equations $x=2\cos^2\theta$, $y=3\sin 2\theta$. Find the value of $\dfrac{dy}{dx}$ at the point on this curve where $\theta=\frac{1}{8}\pi$. Express $y^2$ as a function of $x$. (OCR)

**5** Write down the first five terms in the expansion of $(1+2x)^{\frac{1}{2}}$. Show that, when differentiated, the result is zero plus the first four terms in the expansion of $(1+2x)^{-\frac{1}{2}}$.

Investigate similarly the effect of differentiation on the terms of $(1+3x)^{\frac{1}{3}}$ and $(1+x)^{-3}$.

**6** The equations of three circles are $x^2+y^2-2x-4y-4=0$, $x^2+y^2-8x+4y+16=0$ and $4x^2+4y^2-48x-16y+135=0$. Find the number of points common to at least two of the circles.

**7** Express $6\cos x-\sin x$ in the form $R\cos(x+\alpha)$, where $R>0$ and $0<\alpha<\frac{1}{2}\pi$.

Hence, or otherwise, solve the equation $6\cos x-\sin x=5$ for $x$ in the interval $-\frac{1}{2}\pi<x<\frac{1}{2}\pi$, giving your answer in radians, correct to 3 decimal places. (OCR)

8   Determine whether or not the point $(1,2,-1)$ lies on the line passing through $(3,1,2)$ and $(5,0,5)$.

9   Find the following integrals.

   (a) $\displaystyle\int \sin\left(2x + \tfrac{1}{6}\pi\right) dx$     (b) $\displaystyle\int \sin^2 3x \, dx$     (c) $\displaystyle\int \sin^2 2x \cos 2x \, dx$

10  Find the vector equation of the line which passes through $(1,4,2)$ and $(-2,3,3)$, and find the coordinates of its point of intersection with the line with vector equation
$$\mathbf{r} = \begin{pmatrix} 1 \\ 0 \\ 2 \end{pmatrix} + t \begin{pmatrix} 3 \\ -1 \\ -1 \end{pmatrix}.$$

11  A curve has parametric equations $x = 3t^2 + 2t$, $y = 2t^2 + 3t$. Find the coordinates of the point where the tangent has gradient $\tfrac{3}{4}$.

12  Sketch the graph of $y = \sec x$ between $x = -\tfrac{1}{2}\pi$ and $x = \tfrac{1}{2}\pi$. The part of the curve between $x = -\tfrac{1}{4}\pi$ and $x = \tfrac{1}{4}\pi$ is rotated about the $x$-axis to form a solid of revolution. Find the volume of this solid, giving your answer as a multiple of $\pi$.

13  Expand $\left(1 - x + x^2\right)^{\tfrac{1}{2}}$ as a series in ascending powers of $x$ up to and including the term in $x^3$.

14  By identifying the series $1 - \dfrac{1}{4} + \dfrac{1 \times 3}{4 \times 8} - \dfrac{1 \times 3 \times 5}{4 \times 8 \times 12} + \dots$ as a binomial series of the form $(1+x)^n$ and finding the values of $x$ and $n$, find the sum to infinity of the series
$$1 - \dfrac{1}{4} + \dfrac{1 \times 3}{4 \times 8} - \dfrac{1 \times 3 \times 5}{4 \times 8 \times 12} + \dots.$$

15  Find the vector equation of the straight line parallel to $\mathbf{r} = \begin{pmatrix} -2 \\ 1 \\ 3 \end{pmatrix} + s \begin{pmatrix} 1 \\ -1 \\ 1 \end{pmatrix}$ through the point $(2,-1,4)$.

16  Show that the circles with equations $x^2 + y^2 - 6x + 4y - 23 = 0$ and $x^2 + y^2 - 22x - 8y + 121 = 0$ touch one another, and find the coordinates of their common point.

17  Solve the equation $3\cos 2x + 4\sin 2x = 2$, for values of $x$ between $0$ and $2\pi$, giving your answers correct to two decimal places.

18  Find the equation of the tangent at the point $P$ with parameter $t$ to the curve with parametric equations $x = ct$, $y = \dfrac{c}{t}$, where $c$ is a constant. Show that, if this tangent meets the $x$- and $y$-axes at $X$ and $Y$, then $P$ is the mid-point of $XY$.

19  A straight line has vector equation $\mathbf{r} = \begin{pmatrix} 1 \\ 2 \end{pmatrix} + t \begin{pmatrix} 3 \\ 4 \end{pmatrix}$. Find its cartesian equation.

**20** $ABC$ is a right-angled triangle as shown in the diagram. A rectangle $AXYZ$ is drawn around the triangle, with angle $XAB = \theta$.

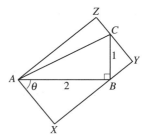

By expressing the perimeter of the rectangle in the form $R\cos(\theta - \alpha)$, find

(a) the maximum perimeter of the rectangle as $\theta$ varies,

(b) the corresponding value of $\theta$, giving your answer to the nearest 0.1. (OCR)

**21** The figure shows part of a circle with centre $O$ and radius $r$. Points $A$, $B$ and $C$ lie on the circle such that $AB$ is a diameter. Angle $BAC = \theta$ radians.

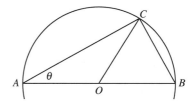

(a) Find angle $AOC$ in terms of $\theta$, and use the cosine rule in triangle $AOC$ to express $AC^2$ in terms of $r$ and $\theta$.

(b) By considering triangle $ABC$, write down the length of $AC$ in terms of $r$ and $\theta$, and deduce that $\cos 2\theta = 2\cos^2 \theta - 1$. (OCR)

**22** $1 + ax + bx^2$ are the first three terms of a binomial expansion for $(1 + cx)^n$. Write two equations involving $n$ and $c$, and hence express $n$ and $c$ in terms of $a$ and $b$.

Prove that the next term of the expansion is $\dfrac{b}{3a}\left(4b - a^2\right)x^3$.

**23** A curve has parametric equations $x = 2 + t$, $y = 1 + mt$, where $m$ is a constant. Find the cartesian equation of the curve. Interpret the geometric meaning of $m$.

**24** By squaring both sides of the expansion $(1 + x)^{-1} = 1 - x + x^2 - x^3 + \ldots$, obtain the expansion of $(1 + x)^{-2}$. Then use $(1 + x)^{-2}(1 + x)^{-1} \equiv (1 + x)^{-3}$ to obtain the expansion of $(1 + x)^{-3}$.

**25** $A$ is the point $(a, b)$. The parametric equations of a straight line $l$ passing through $A$ are $x = a + t\cos\theta$, $y = b + t\sin\theta$, where $\theta$ is fixed and $t$ is a parameter.

(a) Find the gradient of this line, and interpret geometrically the meaning of $t$.

(b) Write down the equation of a circle $C$ whose centre is the origin and whose radius is $R$.

(c) Find a quadratic equation in $t$ for the parameters of the points on $l$ where $l$ meets $C$.

(d) Deduce from your answer to part (c) that the roots are coincident if
$R^2 = (a\sin\theta - b\cos\theta)^2$.

(e) Find the maximum value of $a\sin\theta - b\cos\theta$, and deduce that, for the equation in part (d) to be satisfied, $a^2 + b^2 \geqslant R^2$. Interpret this condition geometrically.

# 7 Rational functions

This chapter is about rational functions, which are algebraic fractions in which the numerator and the denominator are both polynomials. When you have completed the chapter, you should

- be able to simplify algebraic fractions by cancelling
- be able to add, subtract, multiply and divide algebraic fractions
- be able to split simple rational expressions into their partial fractions
- be able to use partial fractions to integrate some rational functions.

## 7.1 Simplifying rational functions

In P2 Chapter 1 you saw that in many ways polynomials behave like integers. Similarly rational functions (algebraic fractions) have many properties in common with ordinary fractions. For example, just as you can cancel a fraction like $\frac{10}{15}$ to get $\frac{2}{3}$, you can cancel a rational function, but it is a little more complicated. Since you cancel $\frac{10}{15}$ in your head, it is worth looking to see what is actually happening:

$$\frac{10}{15} = \frac{2 \times 5}{3 \times 5} = \frac{2}{3}.$$

The first step is to factorise the numerator and denominator. Then you can divide the numerator and denominator by any common factor (in the example this was 5) to get the simplified fraction.

The same process is used to simplify rational functions. However, you need to realise that you cannot cancel common factors of single terms. For example, you can't cancel the 2s which appear in the numerator and denominator of $\frac{x-2}{2x-1}$. A fraction bar has the effect of a bracket, so $\frac{x-2}{2x-1}$ must be thought of as $\frac{(x-2)}{(2x-1)}$. Since $x-2$ and $2x-1$ have no common factor, no cancellation is possible.

### Example 7.1.1

Simplify (a) $\dfrac{x-2}{2x-4}$, (b) $\dfrac{2x-3}{6x^2-x-12}$, (c) $\dfrac{3x^2-8x+4}{6x^2-7x+2}$.

(a) $\dfrac{x-2}{2x-4} = \dfrac{(x-2)}{2(x-2)} = \dfrac{1}{2}.$

(b) $\dfrac{2x-3}{6x^2-x-12} = \dfrac{(2x-3)}{(2x-3)(3x+4)} = \dfrac{1}{3x+4}.$

(c) $\dfrac{3x^2-8x+4}{6x^2-7x+2} = \dfrac{(x-2)(3x-2)}{(2x-1)(3x-2)} = \dfrac{x-2}{2x-1}.$

You cannot cancel the last answer any further. If you have factorised fully, you can only cancel factors if they are exactly the same, or if one is the negative of the other. For example, you could cancel $\dfrac{x-2}{2-x}$ as $\dfrac{-(2-x)}{2-x} = -1$.

*You can check these simplifications by putting $x$ equal to a particular value, say $x = 0$ (provided that the value of $x$ that you choose does not make the denominator equal to 0). In part (a), putting $x = 0$ in the original expression gives $\frac{-2}{-4} = \frac{1}{2}$, which is the same as the simplified version. In part (b), the original becomes $\frac{-3}{-12} = \frac{1}{4}$ and the answer becomes $\frac{1}{4}$. In part (c), the original is $\frac{4}{2} = 2$ and the answer is $\frac{-2}{-1} = 2$.*

## 7.2 Adding and subtracting rational functions

In cancelling and simplifying algebraic fractions, you worked in the same way as in normal arithmetic. To add and subtract algebraic fractions you also follow the same principles as arithmetic, but you need to take special care of signs.

In arithmetic, to calculate $\frac{11}{15} - \frac{7}{20}$ you start by finding the lowest common multiple (LCM) of 15 and 20. You can probably easily see that the LCM is 60. But to calculate it properly, you would factorise the denominators,

$$\frac{11}{15} - \frac{7}{20} = \frac{11}{3 \times 5} - \frac{7}{2 \times 2 \times 5},$$

from which you can work out that the LCM is $2 \times 2 \times 3 \times 5 = 60$. Now

$$\frac{11}{15} - \frac{7}{20} = \frac{11 \times 4}{15 \times 4} - \frac{7 \times 3}{20 \times 3} = \frac{44}{60} - \frac{21}{60} = \frac{44 - 21}{60} = \frac{23}{60}.$$

**Example 7.2.1**

Express as single fractions in their simplest forms (a) $\dfrac{1}{x} - \dfrac{2}{3}$, (b) $\dfrac{3}{x+2} - \dfrac{6}{2x-1}$.

(a) The LCM of $x$ and 3 is $3x$. So $\dfrac{1}{x} - \dfrac{2}{3} = \dfrac{1 \times 3}{3x} - \dfrac{2 \times x}{3x} = \dfrac{3}{3x} - \dfrac{2x}{3x} = \dfrac{3 - 2x}{3x}$.

(b) The LCM of $x+2$ and $2x-1$ is $(x+2)(2x-1)$. Subtracting in the usual way,

$$\frac{3}{x+2} - \frac{6}{2x-1} = \frac{3(2x-1)}{(x+2)(2x-1)} - \frac{6(x+2)}{(x+2)(2x-1)}$$

$$= \frac{6x - 3 - 6x - 12}{(x+2)(2x-1)} = \frac{-15}{(x+2)(2x-1)}.$$

Notice the sign change which gives $-6x - 12$ in the second step of part (b).

*Don't forget to check mentally by putting $x$ as a value which makes the calculations easy. Try $x = 1$ for part (a) and $x = 0$ for part (b).*

**Example 7.2.2**

Express $\dfrac{31x-8}{2x^2+3x-2}-\dfrac{14}{x+2}$ as a single fraction in its lowest terms.

The first step, as before, is to find the LCM. The solution goes:

$$\frac{31x-8}{2x^2+3x-2}-\frac{14}{x+2}=\frac{31x-8}{(2x-1)(x+2)}-\frac{14}{x+2}=\frac{31x-8-14(2x-1)}{(2x-1)(x+2)}$$

$$=\frac{31x-8-28x+14}{(2x-1)(x+2)}=\frac{3x+6}{(2x-1)(x+2)}$$

$$=\frac{3(x+2)}{(2x-1)(x+2)}=\frac{3}{2x-1}.$$

## 7.3 Multiplying and dividing rational functions

Normal arithmetic methods also apply to multiplication and division of rational functions. The meaning of, and the method for, division may need some revision.

Division is defined as the reverse of multiplication in the sense that

$$a\times k=b \iff b\div k=a \text{ (provided that } k\neq 0).$$

Thus $\dfrac{4}{15}\div\dfrac{3}{20}$ is the number (or fraction) $x$, such that $\dfrac{3}{20}x=\dfrac{4}{15}$.

Multiply both sides of the equation by the inverse (reciprocal) of $\dfrac{3}{20}$, which is $\dfrac{20}{3}$:

$$\frac{20}{3}\times\left(\frac{3}{20}x\right)=\frac{20}{3}\times\frac{4}{15} \iff \left(\frac{20}{3}\times\frac{3}{20}\right)x=\frac{20}{3}\times\frac{4}{15} \iff 1x=\frac{20}{3}\times\frac{4}{15}$$

$$\iff x=\frac{20}{3}\times\frac{4}{15}.$$

This justifies the method for dividing by fractions in arithmetic ('turn it upside down and multiply'), which you may have used before. Then

$$x=\frac{20}{3}\times\frac{4}{15}=\frac{2\times2\times5}{3}\times\frac{2\times2}{3\times5}=\frac{16}{9}.$$

In general, if $a$, $b$, $c$ and $d$ are integers, and $x=\dfrac{c}{d}\div\dfrac{a}{b}$, then $\dfrac{a}{b}x=\dfrac{c}{d}$.

Multiplying by the inverse of $\dfrac{a}{b}$, which is $\dfrac{b}{a}$, gives $\dfrac{b}{a}\times\dfrac{a}{b}x=\dfrac{b}{a}\times\dfrac{c}{d} \iff x=\dfrac{b}{a}\times\dfrac{c}{d}$.

**Example 7.3.1**

Simplify the fractions (a) $\dfrac{2}{x}\times\dfrac{x^2-2x}{x-2}$,   (b) $\dfrac{x-2}{x^2-4x+3}\div\dfrac{x}{2x^2-7x+3}$.

(a)   $\dfrac{2}{x}\times\dfrac{x^2-2x}{x-2}=\dfrac{2}{x}\times\dfrac{x(x-2)}{x-2}=\dfrac{2x(x-2)}{x(x-2)}=2.$

(b) $\dfrac{x-2}{x^2-4x+3} \div \dfrac{x}{2x^2-7x+3} = \dfrac{x-2}{x^2-4x+3} \times \dfrac{2x^2-7x+3}{x}$

$$= \dfrac{x-2}{(x-1)(x-3)} \times \dfrac{(2x-1)(x-3)}{x}$$

$$= \dfrac{(x-2)(2x-1)}{x(x-1)}.$$

## Exercise 7A

**1** Simplify

(a) $\dfrac{4x-8}{2}$,

(b) $\dfrac{9x+6}{3}$,

(c) $\dfrac{2x^2-6x+12}{2}$,

(d) $\dfrac{6}{18x+12}$,

(e) $\dfrac{(2x+6)(2x-4)}{4}$,

(f) $\dfrac{x}{x^3+x^2+x}$.

**2** Simplify

(a) $\dfrac{5x+15}{x+3}$,

(b) $\dfrac{x+1}{4x+4}$,

(c) $\dfrac{2x+5}{5+2x}$,

(d) $\dfrac{3x-7}{7-3x}$,

(e) $\dfrac{(2x+8)(3x+6)}{(2x+4)(3x+12)}$,

(f) $\dfrac{2x^2-6x+10}{3x^2-9x+15}$.

**3** Simplify

(a) $\dfrac{x^2+5x+4}{x+1}$,

(b) $\dfrac{x-2}{x^2+5x-14}$,

(c) $\dfrac{6x^2+4x}{4x^2+2x}$,

(d) $\dfrac{x^2+5x-6}{x^2-4x+3}$,

(e) $\dfrac{2x^2+5x-12}{2x^2-11x+12}$,

(f) $\dfrac{8x^2-6x-20}{2+5x-3x^2}$.

**4** Simplify

(a) $\dfrac{2x}{3}-\dfrac{x}{4}$,

(b) $\dfrac{5x}{2}+\dfrac{x}{3}-\dfrac{3x}{4}$,

(c) $\dfrac{x+2}{3}+\dfrac{x+1}{4}$,

(d) $\dfrac{2x+1}{5}-\dfrac{x+2}{3}$,

(e) $\dfrac{(x+1)(x+3)}{2}-\dfrac{(x+2)^2}{4}$,

(f) $3x+4-\dfrac{2(x+3)}{5}$.

**5** Simplify

(a) $\dfrac{2}{x}+\dfrac{3}{4}$,

(b) $\dfrac{1}{2x}+\dfrac{2}{x}$,

(c) $\dfrac{5}{4x}-\dfrac{2}{3x}$,

(d) $\dfrac{x+3}{2x}+\dfrac{x-4}{x}$,

(e) $\dfrac{3x-1}{x}-\dfrac{x+1}{2}$,

(f) $\dfrac{x+1}{x}+\dfrac{x+1}{x^2}$.

**6** Simplify

(a) $\dfrac{2}{x+1}+\dfrac{4}{x+3}$,

(b) $\dfrac{5}{x-2}+\dfrac{3}{2x+1}$,

(c) $\dfrac{4}{x+3}-\dfrac{2}{x+4}$,

(d) $\dfrac{7}{x-3}-\dfrac{2}{x+1}$,

(e) $\dfrac{4}{2x+3}+\dfrac{5}{3x+1}$,

(f) $\dfrac{6}{2x+1}-\dfrac{2}{5x-3}$.

**7** Simplify

(a) $\dfrac{5}{3x-1}-\dfrac{2}{2x+1}$,

(b) $\dfrac{6}{4x+1}-\dfrac{3}{2x}$,

(c) $\dfrac{3x}{x+2}+\dfrac{5x}{x+1}$,

(d) $\dfrac{8x}{2x-1}-\dfrac{x}{x+2}$,

(e) $\dfrac{x+1}{x+2}+\dfrac{x+2}{x+1}$,

(f) $\dfrac{2x+1}{x+4}-\dfrac{x-5}{x-2}$.

**8** Simplify

(a) $\dfrac{2x+3}{(x+1)(x+3)}+\dfrac{2}{x+3}$,

(b) $\dfrac{5x}{x^2+x-2}+\dfrac{1}{x+2}$,

(c) $\dfrac{5}{x-3}+\dfrac{x+2}{x^2-3x}$,

(d) $\dfrac{8}{x^2-4}-\dfrac{4}{x-2}$,

(e) $\dfrac{13-3x}{x^2-2x-3}+\dfrac{4}{x+1}$,

(f) $\dfrac{11x+27}{2x^2+11x-6}-\dfrac{3}{x+6}$.

**9** Simplify

(a) $\dfrac{4x+6}{x-4}\times\dfrac{3x-12}{2x+3}$,

(b) $\dfrac{x^2-4}{x+2}\times\dfrac{3x}{x-2}$,

(c) $\dfrac{x^2+9x+20}{x+3}\times\dfrac{3}{x+4}$,

(d) $\dfrac{x^2+3x+2}{x^2+4x+4}\times\dfrac{x^2+5x+6}{x^2+2x+1}$,

(e) $\dfrac{4x+12}{2x+2}\times\dfrac{x^2+2x+1}{x^2+6x+9}$,

(f) $\dfrac{4x^2-9}{9x^2-4}\times\dfrac{9x^2-12x+4}{4x^2-12x+9}$.

**10** Simplify

(a) $\dfrac{x+2}{2x+3}\div\dfrac{2x+4}{8x+12}$,

(b) $\dfrac{x}{5-2x}\div\dfrac{3x}{2x-5}$,

(c) $\dfrac{1}{x^2+6x+6}\div\dfrac{1}{x^2+8x+16}$,

(d) $\dfrac{5x-1}{2x^2+x-3}\div\dfrac{1}{2x^2+7x+6}$,

(e) $\dfrac{x^2+5x-6}{x^2-5x+4}\div\dfrac{x^2+9x+18}{x^2-x-12}$,

(f) $\dfrac{-2x^2+7x-6}{8x^2-10x-3}\div\dfrac{7x-x^2-10}{5+19x-4x^2}$.

**11** Given that $\dfrac{a}{x-2}+\dfrac{b}{x+c}\equiv\dfrac{15x}{x^2+2x-8}$, find the values of the constants $a$, $b$ and $c$.

**12** Given that $\dfrac{(x+2)\mathrm{f}(x)}{(x+3)\left(x^2-x-6\right)}\equiv 1$, find $\mathrm{f}(x)$ in its simplest form.

**13** Given that $\mathrm{P}(x)\equiv\dfrac{5}{x+4}$ and $\mathrm{Q}(x)\equiv\dfrac{2}{x-3}$,

(a) find $2\mathrm{P}(x)+3\mathrm{Q}(x)$ in simplified form,

(b) find $\mathrm{R}(x)$, where $\mathrm{R}(x)+4\mathrm{Q}(x)\equiv 3\mathrm{P}(x)$.

**14** Simplify

(a) $\dfrac{2}{x^3-3x^2+2x}+\dfrac{1}{x^3-6x^2+11x-6}$,

(b) $\dfrac{5}{2x+1}-\dfrac{4}{3x-1}-\dfrac{7x-10}{6x^2+x-1}$.

## 7.4  Partial fractions with simple denominators

Sometimes you need to reverse the process of adding or subtracting rational functions. For example, instead of adding $\dfrac{3}{2x-1}$ and $\dfrac{2}{x-2}$ to get $\dfrac{7x-8}{(2x-1)(x-2)}$, you might need to find the fractions which, when added together, give $\dfrac{7x-8}{(2x-1)(x-2)}$.

This useful process is called **splitting into partial fractions**. Suppose you needed to calculate

$$\int \frac{7x-8}{(2x-1)(x-2)}\,dx$$

You cannot do this as it stands. However, if you rewrite the integrand using partial fractions, you can integrate it, as follows:

$$\int \frac{7x-8}{(2x-1)(x-2)}\,dx = \int \left( \frac{3}{2x-1} + \frac{2}{x-2} \right) dx = \int \frac{3}{2x-1}\,dx + \int \frac{2}{x-2}\,dx$$

$$= \tfrac{3}{2}\ln|2x-1| + 2\ln|x-2| + k.$$

*You may need to refresh your memory from P2 Section 12.5.*

In this case, splitting into partial fractions starts by supposing that you can write $\dfrac{7x-8}{(2x-1)(x-2)}$ in the form

$$\frac{7x-8}{(2x-1)(x-2)} \equiv \frac{A}{2x-1} + \frac{B}{x-2},$$

where the identity sign $\equiv$ means that the two sides are equal for all values of $x$ for which they are defined: here, all values except $x = \tfrac{1}{2}$ and $x = 2$, where the denominators become 0.

There are two methods you can use.

**Method 1**    Expressing the right side as a single fraction,

$$\frac{7x-8}{(2x-1)(x-2)} \equiv \frac{A(x-2)+B(2x-1)}{(2x-1)(x-2)}.$$

Multiplying both sides of the identity by $(2x-1)(x-2)$,

$$7x-8 \equiv A(x-2) + B(2x-1).$$

You can now find $A$ and $B$ by the method of equating coefficients (P2 Section 1.3).

Equating coefficients of $x^1$ :   $7 = A + 2B.$
Equating coefficients of $x^0$ :   $-8 = -2A - B.$

Solving these two equations simultaneously gives $A = 3$, $B = 2$.

**Method 2**    To find $A$, multiply both sides of the identity

$$\frac{7x-8}{(2x-1)(x-2)} \equiv \frac{A}{2x-1} + \frac{B}{x-2} \text{ by } 2x-1 \text{ to obtain}$$

$$\frac{7x-8}{x-2} \equiv A + B\frac{2x-1}{x-2}.$$

Putting $x = \frac{1}{2}$ gives $A = \dfrac{\frac{7}{2}-8}{\frac{1}{2}-2} = \dfrac{-\frac{9}{2}}{-\frac{3}{2}} = 3.$

Similarly, to find $B$, multiply the identity by $x-2$ to get $\dfrac{7x-8}{2x-1} \equiv A\dfrac{x-2}{2x-1} + B.$

Putting $x = 2$ gives $B = \dfrac{7 \times 2 - 8}{2 \times 2 - 1} = \dfrac{6}{3} = 2.$

By either method $\dfrac{7x-8}{(2x-1)(x-2)} \equiv \dfrac{3}{2x-1} + \dfrac{2}{x-2}.$

There are three important points to make about these solutions.

- Always check by giving $x$ a simple value. For example, putting $x = 0$ gives $-4$ for the left side, and $-3 - 1 = -4$ for the right.
- In Method 2, the values $x = \frac{1}{2}$ and $x = 2$ are chosen because they give simple equations for $A$ and $B$. You could have chosen other values for $x$, but the equations for $A$ and $B$ would have been more complicated. Try it and see!
- You may be worried that, at the beginning of the example, the values $x = \frac{1}{2}$ and $x = 2$ were excluded, but were then used in Method 2. The fact is that $\dfrac{7x-8}{x-2} \equiv 3 + 2\dfrac{2x-1}{x-2}$ is true for all $x$ except $x = 2$, including $x = \frac{1}{2}$. So it is all right to use $x = \frac{1}{2}$ to find $A$, since there is no need to exclude $x = \frac{1}{2}$ in the identity $\dfrac{7x-8}{x-2} \equiv A + B\dfrac{2x-1}{x-2}$. But the partial fraction form $\dfrac{A}{2x-1} + \dfrac{B}{x-2} \equiv \dfrac{7x-8}{(2x-1)(x-2)}$ has no meaning when $x = \frac{1}{2}$ (or when $x = 2$).

Method 1 always works, but you might have some awkward equations to solve. Method 2 doesn't always work straight away but you can always modify it to make it work (see pages 95 and 96).

An expression of the form $\dfrac{ax+b}{(px+q)(rx+s)}$ can be split into partial fractions of the form $\dfrac{A}{px+q} + \dfrac{B}{rx+s}.$

**Example 7.4.1**

Split $\dfrac{13x-6}{3x^2-2x}$ into partial fractions.

Rewrite $\dfrac{13x-6}{3x^2-2x}$ in the form $\dfrac{13x-6}{x(3x-2)}$, and then put $\dfrac{13x-6}{x(3x-2)} \equiv \dfrac{A}{x} + \dfrac{B}{3x-2}$.

Using Method 1, $\dfrac{13x-6}{x(3x-2)} \equiv \dfrac{A(3x-2)+Bx}{x(3x-2)}$, so $A(3x-2)+Bx \equiv 13x-6$.

Equating coefficients of $x^1$ :    $3A + B = 13$.
Equating coefficients of $x^0$ :  $-2A$      $= -6$.

Solving these two equations simultaneously gives $A = 3$, $B = 4$.

Therefore $\dfrac{13x-6}{x(3x-2)} \equiv \dfrac{3}{x} + \dfrac{4}{3x-2}$.

**Example 7.4.2**

Split $\dfrac{12x}{(x+1)(2x+3)(x-3)}$ into partial fractions.

Put $\dfrac{12x}{(x+1)(2x+3)(x-3)} \equiv \dfrac{A}{x+1} + \dfrac{B}{2x+3} + \dfrac{C}{x-3}$.

Use Method 2: multiplying by $x+1$ gives

$$\dfrac{12x}{(2x+3)(x-3)} \equiv A + B\dfrac{x+1}{2x+3} + C\dfrac{x+1}{x-3}.$$

Putting $x = -1$, $A = \dfrac{12 \times (-1)}{(2\times(-1)+3)((-1)-3)} = \dfrac{-12}{1\times(-4)} = 3$.

Similarly, after multiplying by $2x+3$ and putting $x = -\frac{3}{2}$, you get $B = -8$; multiplying by $x-3$ and putting $x = 3$ gives $C = 1$.

Therefore $\dfrac{12x}{(x+1)(2x+3)(x-3)} \equiv \dfrac{3}{x+1} - \dfrac{8}{2x+3} + \dfrac{1}{x-3}$.

If you try to use Method 1 in this example, you get three simultaneous equations, with three unknowns, to solve. In this case, Method 2 is easier.

**Example 7.4.3**

Calculate the value of $\displaystyle\int_1^4 \dfrac{1}{x(x-5)}\,dx$.

Write $\dfrac{1}{x(x-5)}$ in partial fraction form, as $\dfrac{1}{x(x-5)} \equiv \dfrac{A}{x} + \dfrac{B}{x-5}$.

Then either method gives $A = -\frac{1}{5}$ and $B = \frac{1}{5}$, so $\dfrac{1}{x(x-5)} \equiv \dfrac{-\frac{1}{5}}{x} + \dfrac{\frac{1}{5}}{x-5}$.

Therefore $\displaystyle\int_1^4 \frac{1}{x(x-5)}\,dx = \int_1^4 \left( -\frac{\frac{1}{5}}{x} + \frac{\frac{1}{5}}{x-5} \right) dx.$

Remembering that $x-5$ is negative over the interval of integration, rewrite this integral as $\displaystyle\int_1^4 \left( -\frac{\frac{1}{5}}{x} - \frac{\frac{1}{5}}{5-x} \right) dx$. Then

$$\int_1^4 \left( -\frac{\frac{1}{5}}{x} - \frac{\frac{1}{5}}{5-x} \right) dx = \left[ -\tfrac{1}{5}\ln x + \tfrac{1}{5}\ln(5-x) \right]_1^4$$

$$= \left( -\tfrac{1}{5}\ln 4 + \tfrac{1}{5}\ln 1 \right) - \left( -\tfrac{1}{5}\ln 1 + \tfrac{1}{5}\ln 4 \right)$$

$$= -\tfrac{1}{5}\ln 4 + \tfrac{1}{5}\ln 1 + \tfrac{1}{5}\ln 1 - \tfrac{1}{5}\ln 4$$

$$= \tfrac{2}{5}\ln 1 - \tfrac{2}{5}\ln 4 = -\tfrac{2}{5}\ln 4.$$

*You may find it helpful to look up P2 Section 12.5 on definite integrals involving logarithms.*

## Exercise 7B

**1** Split the following into partial fractions.

(a) $\dfrac{2x+8}{(x+5)(x+3)}$ 　　　　　　　　　　(b) $\dfrac{10x+8}{(x-1)(x+5)}$

(c) $\dfrac{x}{(x-4)(x-5)}$ 　　　　　　　　　　(d) $\dfrac{28}{(2x-1)(x+3)}$

**2** Split the following into partial fractions.

(a) $\dfrac{8x+1}{x^2+x-2}$ 　　　　　　　　　　(b) $\dfrac{25}{x^2-3x-4}$

(c) $\dfrac{10x-6}{x^2-9}$ 　　　　　　　　　　(d) $\dfrac{3}{2x^2+x}$

**3** Split into partial fractions

(a) $\dfrac{35-5x}{(x+2)(x-1)(x-3)}$, 　　(b) $\dfrac{8x^2}{(x+1)(x-1)(x+3)}$, 　　(c) $\dfrac{15x^2-28x-72}{x^3-2x^2-24x}$.

**4** Find

(a) $\displaystyle\int \frac{7x-1}{(x-1)(x-3)}\,dx,$ 　　　　　　(b) $\displaystyle\int \frac{4}{x^2-4}\,dx,$

(c) $\displaystyle\int \frac{15x+35}{2x^2+5x}\,dx,$ 　　　　　　(d) $\displaystyle\int \frac{x-8}{6x^2-x-1}\,dx.$

**5** Evaluate the following, expressing each answer in a form involving a single logarithm.

(a) $\displaystyle\int_2^{10} \frac{2x+5}{(x-1)(x+6)}\,dx$

(b) $\displaystyle\int_0^3 \frac{3x+5}{(x+1)(x+2)}\,dx$

(c) $\displaystyle\int_4^5 \frac{6x}{x^2-9}\,dx$

(d) $\displaystyle\int_1^{\frac{3}{2}} \frac{4x-18}{4x^2+4x-3}\,dx$

**6** Split $\dfrac{2-x}{(1+x)(1-2x)}$ into partial fractions and hence find the binomial expansion of

$\dfrac{2-x}{(1+x)(1-2x)}$ up to and including the term in $x^3$.

**7** Split $\dfrac{3}{8x^2+6x+1}$ into partial fractions and hence find the binomial expansion of

$\dfrac{3}{8x^2+6x+1}$ up to and including the term in $x^3$. State the values of $x$ for which the

expansion is valid.

**8** Split $\dfrac{4ax-a^2}{x^2+ax-2a^2}$ into partial fractions.

**9** Find the exact value of $\displaystyle\int_{2\sqrt5}^{3\sqrt5} \frac{4\sqrt5}{x^2-5}\,dx$.

## 7.5 Partial fractions with a repeated factor

You will have noticed in the examples of the last section that when the denominator has
two factors there are two partial fractions, with unknowns $A$ and $B$. When the
denominator has three factors, there are three fractions, with unknowns $A$, $B$ and $C$.
Method 1 shows why, since you can find two unknowns by equating coefficients of $x^0$
and $x^1$, and three unknowns by equating coefficients of $x^0$, $x^1$ and $x^2$.

So you would expect $\dfrac{3x^2+6x+2}{(2x+3)(x+1)^2}$ to split into three fractions. Two of these must be

$\dfrac{A}{2x+3}$ and $\dfrac{B}{(x+1)^2}$. The third fraction is $\dfrac{C}{x+1}$. So write

$$\frac{3x^2+6x+2}{(2x+3)(x+1)^2} \equiv \frac{A}{2x+3}+\frac{B}{(x+1)^2}+\frac{C}{x+1}.$$

Then (using Method 2) multiplying the identity by $2x+3$ gives

$$\frac{3x^2+6x+2}{(x+1)^2} \equiv A+\frac{B(2x+3)}{(x+1)^2}+\frac{C(2x+3)}{x+1}.$$

Putting $x=-\tfrac{3}{2}$ gives $A=\dfrac{3\times\left(-\frac{3}{2}\right)^2+6\times\left(-\frac{3}{2}\right)+2}{\left(-\frac{3}{2}+1\right)^2}=\dfrac{\frac{27}{4}-9+2}{\left(-\frac{1}{2}\right)^2}=\dfrac{-\frac{1}{4}}{\frac{1}{4}}=-1.$

You might next try multiplying the identity by $x+1$, which gives

$$\frac{3x^2+6x+2}{(2x+3)(x+1)} \equiv \frac{A(x+1)}{2x+3} + \frac{B}{(x+1)} + C.$$

But you cannot put $x=-1$ because neither side of the identity is defined for $x=-1$.

However, you can multiply the original identity by $(x+1)^2$ to get

$$\frac{3x^2+6x+2}{(2x+3)} \equiv \frac{A(x+1)^2}{2x+3} + B + C(x+1).$$

Putting $x=-1$ now gives $B = \dfrac{3\times(-1)^2+6\times(-1)+2}{(2\times(-1)+3)} = \dfrac{3-6+2}{1} = -1.$

Thus $\dfrac{3x^2+6x+2}{(2x+3)(x+1)^2} \equiv \dfrac{-1}{2x+3} + \dfrac{-1}{(x+1)^2} + \dfrac{C}{x+1}.$

Here are two ways to find $C$. The first uses substitution, and will be called the substitution method; the second uses algebra, and will be called the algebraic method.

**Substitution method**     There is no other especially convenient value to give $x$, but putting $x=0$ in the original identity gives $\dfrac{3\times(0)^2+6\times0+2}{(2\times0+3)(0+1)^2} = \dfrac{A}{2\times0+3} + \dfrac{B}{(0+1)^2} + \dfrac{C}{0+1}$, or $\frac{2}{3} = \frac{1}{3}A+B+C$. Using the values $A=-1$ and $B=-1$, which you know, leads to $C=2$.

Thus $\dfrac{3x^2+6x+2}{(2x+3)(x+1)^2} \equiv \dfrac{-1}{2x+3} + \dfrac{-1}{(x+1)^2} + \dfrac{2}{x+1}.$

**Algebraic method**     Write $\dfrac{3x^2+6x+2}{(2x+3)(x+1)^2} \equiv \dfrac{-1}{2x+3} + \dfrac{-1}{(x+1)^2} + \dfrac{C}{x+1}$ as

$$\frac{C}{x+1} \equiv \frac{3x^2+6x+2}{(2x+3)(x+1)^2} + \frac{1}{2x+3} + \frac{1}{(x+1)^2}$$

$$\equiv \frac{3x^2+6x+2+(x+1)^2+2x+3}{(2x+3)(x+1)^2}$$

$$\equiv \frac{3x^2+6x+2+x^2+2x+1+2x+3}{(2x+3)(x+1)^2}$$

$$\equiv \frac{4x^2+10x+6}{(2x+3)(x+1)^2} \equiv \frac{2(2x+3)(x+1)}{(2x+3)(x+1)^2} \equiv \frac{2}{x+1}.$$

Therefore $C=2$, as before, and $\dfrac{3x^2+6x+2}{(2x+3)(x+1)^2} \equiv \dfrac{-1}{2x+3} + \dfrac{-1}{(x+1)^2} + \dfrac{2}{x+1}.$

The key to finding partial fractions is to start with the correct form involving $A$, $B$ and $C$. If you do not have that form, you will not be able to find the partial fractions.

> An expression of the form $\dfrac{ax^2 + bx + c}{(px+q)(rx+s)^2}$ can be split into partial
>
> fractions of the form $\dfrac{A}{px+q} + \dfrac{B}{(rx+s)^2} + \dfrac{C}{rx+s}$.

**Example 7.5.1**

Express $\dfrac{x^2 - 7x - 6}{x^2(x-3)}$ in partial fractions.

Write $\dfrac{x^2 - 7x - 6}{x^2(x-3)}$ in the form $\dfrac{x^2 - 7x - 6}{x^2(x-3)} \equiv \dfrac{A}{x^2} + \dfrac{B}{x} + \dfrac{C}{x-3}$.

Multiplying by $x^2$ gives $\dfrac{x^2 - 7x - 6}{x-3} \equiv A + Bx + \dfrac{Cx^2}{x-3}$, and putting $x = 0$ leads to $A = 2$.

Multiplying by $x - 3$ gives $\dfrac{x^2 - 7x - 6}{x^2} \equiv \dfrac{A(x-3)}{x^2} + \dfrac{B(x-3)}{x} + C$, and putting $x = 3$ leads to $C = -2$.

Therefore $\dfrac{x^2 - 7x - 6}{x^2(x-3)} \equiv \dfrac{2}{x^2} + \dfrac{B}{x} - \dfrac{2}{x-3}$.

Using the substitution method on page 96, putting $x = 1$ leads to $B = 3$.

Thus $\dfrac{x^2 - 7x - 6}{x^2(x-3)} \equiv \dfrac{2}{x^2} + \dfrac{3}{x} - \dfrac{2}{x-3}$.

**Example 7.5.2**

Express $\dfrac{9 + 4x^2}{(1-2x)^2(2+x)}$ in partial fractions, and hence find the binomial expansion of

$\dfrac{9 + 4x^2}{(1-2x)^2(2+x)}$ up to and including the term in $x^3$. State the values of $x$ for which the

expansion is valid.

$$\dfrac{9 + 4x^2}{(1-2x)^2(2+x)} \equiv \dfrac{A}{(1-2x)^2} + \dfrac{B}{1-2x} + \dfrac{C}{2+x}$$

Multiplying both sides by $(1-2x)^2$ gives $\dfrac{9 + 4x^2}{2+x} \equiv A + B(1-2x) + \dfrac{C(1-2x)^2}{2+x}$.

Putting $x = \frac{1}{2}$ leads to $A = 4$.

Multiplying both sides by $2+x$ gives $\dfrac{9+4x^2}{(1-2x)^2} \equiv \dfrac{A(2+x)}{(1-2x)^2} + \dfrac{B(2+x)}{1-2x} + C$;

putting $x=-2$ leads to $C=1$.

Therefore $\dfrac{9+4x^2}{(1-2x)^2(2+x)} \equiv \dfrac{4}{(1-2x)^2} + \dfrac{B}{1-2x} + \dfrac{1}{2+x}$.

Using the algebraic method on page 96,

$$\frac{B}{1-2x} \equiv \frac{9+4x^2}{(1-2x)^2(2+x)} - \frac{4}{(1-2x)^2} - \frac{1}{2+x}$$

$$\equiv \frac{9+4x^2-4(2+x)-(1-2x)^2}{(1-2x)^2(2+x)}$$

$$\equiv \frac{9+4x^2-8-4x-1+4x-4x^2}{(1-2x)^2(2+x)}$$

$$\equiv \frac{0}{(1-2x)^2(2+x)} \equiv 0.$$

Thus $\dfrac{9+4x^2}{(1-2x)^2(2+x)} \equiv \dfrac{4}{(1-2x)^2} + \dfrac{1}{2+x} \equiv 4(1-2x)^{-2} + (2+x)^{-1}$.

Using the binomial expansion,

$$4(1-2x)^{-2} = 4\left(1 + \frac{(-2)}{1}(-2x) + \frac{(-2)(-3)}{1\times 2}(-2x)^2 + \frac{(-2)(-3)(-4)}{1\times 2\times 3}(-2x)^3 + \ldots\right)$$

$$= 4\left(1+4x+12x^2+32x^3+\ldots\right) = 4+16x+48x^2+128x^3+\ldots,$$

$$(2+x)^{-1} = 2^{-1}\left(1+\tfrac{1}{2}x\right)^{-1} = \tfrac{1}{2}\left(1+\tfrac{1}{2}x\right)^{-1}$$

$$= \tfrac{1}{2}\left(1 + \frac{(-1)}{1}\left(\tfrac{1}{2}x\right) + \frac{(-1)(-2)}{1\times 2}\left(\tfrac{1}{2}x\right)^2 + \frac{(-1)(-2)(-3)}{1\times 2\times 3}\left(\tfrac{1}{2}x\right)^3 + \ldots\right)$$

$$= \tfrac{1}{2}\left(1-\tfrac{1}{2}x+\tfrac{1}{4}x^2-\tfrac{1}{8}x^3+\ldots\right) = \tfrac{1}{2} - \tfrac{1}{4}x + \tfrac{1}{8}x^2 - \tfrac{1}{16}x^3 + \ldots.$$

Therefore

$$4(1-2x)^{-2} + (2+x)^{-1} = 4+16x+48x^2+128x^3+\ldots+\tfrac{1}{2}-\tfrac{1}{4}x+\tfrac{1}{8}x^2-\tfrac{1}{16}x^3+\ldots$$

$$= \tfrac{9}{2} + \tfrac{63}{4}x + \tfrac{385}{8}x^2 + \tfrac{2047}{16}x^3 + \ldots,$$

so the required expansion is $\tfrac{9}{2} + \tfrac{63}{4}x + \tfrac{385}{8}x^2 + \tfrac{2047}{16}x^3$.

The expansion of $(1-2x)^{-2}$ is valid when $|2x|<1$, that is, when $|x|<\tfrac{1}{2}$.

The expansion of $\left(1+\tfrac{1}{2}x\right)^{-1}$ is valid when $|\tfrac{1}{2}x|<1$, that is, when $|x|<2$.

For the final result to hold you require both $|x|<\tfrac{1}{2}$ and $|x|<2$, that is, $|x|<\tfrac{1}{2}$.

## Exercise 7C

**1** Split into partial fractions

(a) $\dfrac{4}{(x-1)(x-3)^2}$,

(b) $\dfrac{6x^2+11x-8}{(x+2)^2(x-1)}$,

(c) $\dfrac{6}{x^3-4x^2+4x}$,

(d) $\dfrac{8-7x}{2x^3+3x^2-1}$.

**2** Find

(a) $\displaystyle\int \dfrac{6x^2+27x+25}{(x+2)^2(x+1)}\,dx$,

(b) $\displaystyle\int \dfrac{97x+35}{(2x-3)(5x+2)^2}\,dx$.

**3** Show that $\displaystyle\int_1^6 \dfrac{16}{x^2(x+4)}\,dx = \frac{10}{3} - \ln 3$.

**4** Find the exact value of $\displaystyle\int_2^3 \dfrac{x(x+14)}{2x^3-3x^2+1}\,dx$.

**5** Obtain the series expansion of $\dfrac{1}{(1+2x)^2(1-x)}$ up to and including the term in $x^2$ by

(a) multiplying the expansion of $(1+2x)^{-2}$ by the expansion of $(1-x)^{-1}$,

(b) resolving $\dfrac{1}{(1+2x)^2(1-x)}$ into partial fractions and finding the expansion of each fraction.

## Miscellaneous exercise 7

**1** Express $\dfrac{4}{(x-3)(x+1)}$ in partial fractions. (OCR)

**2** Express $\dfrac{2}{x(x-1)(x+1)}$ in partial fractions. (OCR)

**3** Express $\dfrac{2x^2+1}{x(x-1)^2}$ in partial fractions. (OCR)

**4** Express $\dfrac{x^2-11}{(x+2)^2(3x-1)}$ in partial fractions. (OCR)

**5** Find $\displaystyle\int \dfrac{1}{x(x+1)}\,dx$. (OCR)

**6** Find $\displaystyle\int \dfrac{x}{(x+1)(x+2)}\,dx$. (OCR)

**7** Express $\dfrac{1}{x^2(x-1)}$ in the form $\dfrac{A}{x}+\dfrac{B}{x^2}+\dfrac{C}{x-1}$, where $A$, $B$ and $C$ are constants. Hence

find $\displaystyle\int\dfrac{1}{x^2(x-1)}\,dx$. $\hspace{3cm}$ (OCR)

**8** Simplify $\dfrac{2x^2+x}{x^2-5x+4}\times\dfrac{x^2-4x}{4x^2+6x}$.

**9** Simplify $\sqrt{\dfrac{3x^2+5x-2}{4x-3}\div\dfrac{4x^3+13x^2+4x-12}{2x(x+3)-(2-x)(1+x)}}$.

**10** Simplify $\dfrac{x-21}{x^2-9}-\dfrac{3}{x+3}+\dfrac{4}{x-3}$.

**11** Express $\dfrac{3}{(2x+1)(x-1)}$ in partial fractions. Hence find the exact value of

$\displaystyle\int_2^3\dfrac{3}{(2x+1)(x-1)}\,dx$, giving your answer as a single logarithm. $\hspace{1cm}$ (OCR)

**12** Express $\dfrac{1}{(x+3)(4-x)}$ in partial fractions. Hence find the exact value of

$\displaystyle\int_0^2\dfrac{1}{(x+3)(4-x)}\,dx$, giving your answer as a single logarithm. $\hspace{1cm}$ (OCR)

**13** Express $f(x)\equiv\dfrac{2}{2-3x+x^2}$ in partial fractions and hence, or otherwise, obtain $f(x)$ as a

series of ascending powers of $x$, giving the first four non-zero terms of this expansion.
State the set of values of $x$ for which this expansion is valid. $\hspace{1cm}$ (OCR)

**14** Express $\dfrac{3-x}{(2+x)(1-2x)}$ in partial fractions and hence, or otherwise, obtain the first three

terms in the expansion of this expression in ascending powers of $x$. State the range of
values of $x$ for which the expansion is valid. $\hspace{1cm}$ (OCR)

**15** Given that $\dfrac{18-4x-x^2}{(4-3x)(1+x)^2}\equiv\dfrac{A}{4-3x}+\dfrac{B}{1+x}+\dfrac{C}{(1+x)^2}$, show that $A=2$, and obtain the

values of $B$ and $C$. Hence show that $\displaystyle\int_0^1\dfrac{18-4x-x^2}{(4-3x)(1+x)^2}\,dx=\tfrac{7}{3}\ln 2+\tfrac{3}{2}$. $\hspace{1cm}$ (OCR)

**16** Let $y=\dfrac{4+7x}{(2-x)(1+x)^2}$. Express $y$ in the form $\dfrac{A}{2-x}+\dfrac{B}{1+x}+\dfrac{C}{(1+x)^2}$, where the

numerical values of $A$, $B$ and $C$ are to be found. Hence, or otherwise, expand $y$ in a
series of ascending powers of $x$ up to and including the term in $x^3$, simplifying the

coefficients. Use your result to find the value of $\dfrac{dy}{dx}$ when $x=0$.

**17**  Express $\dfrac{15-13x+4x^2}{(1-x)^2(4-x)}$ in partial fractions. Hence evaluate $\displaystyle\int_2^3 \dfrac{15-13x+4x^2}{(1-x)^2(4-x)}\,dx$ giving the exact value in terms of logarithms.  (OCR)

**18**  Let $\mathrm{f}(x)=\dfrac{x^2+5x}{(1+x)(1-x)^2}$. Express $\mathrm{f}(x)$ in the form $\dfrac{A}{1+x}+\dfrac{B}{1-x}+\dfrac{C}{(1-x)^2}$ where $A$, $B$ and $C$ are constants. The expansion of $\mathrm{f}(x)$, in ascending powers of $x$, is

$$c_0+c_1x+c_2x^2+c_3x^3+\ldots+c_rx^r+\ldots .$$ Find $c_0$, $c_1$, $c_2$ and show that $c_3=11$. Express $c_r$ in terms of $r$.  (OCR)

**19**  It is given that $\mathrm{g}(x)=(2x-1)(x+2)(x-3)$.

(a)  Express $\mathrm{g}(x)$ in the form $Ax^3+Bx^2+Cx+D$, giving the values of the constants $A$, $B$, $C$ and $D$.

(b)  Find the value of the constant $a$, given that $x+3$ is a factor of $\mathrm{g}(x)+ax$.

(c)  Express $\dfrac{x-3}{\mathrm{g}(x)}$ in partial fractions.  (OCR)

**20**  Express $\dfrac{1}{2x}-\dfrac{7}{2(x+2)}+\dfrac{4}{x+4}$ as a single fraction, and hence show that the equation

$\dfrac{1}{2x}-\dfrac{7}{2(x+2)}+\dfrac{4}{x+4}=0$ has no real roots.

**21**  The diagram shows part of the graph of $y=\dfrac{3}{\sqrt{x}(x-3)}$. The shaded region is bounded by the curve and the lines $y=0$, $x=4$ and $x=6$. Find the volume of the solid formed when the shaded region is rotated through four right angles about the $x$-axis.

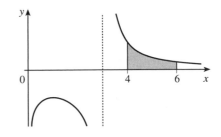

**22**  Resolve $\dfrac{1}{x^4-13x^2+36}$ into partial fractions.

**23**  Express $\dfrac{3x}{(x-1)(x+2)}$ in partial fractions. Show that $\dfrac{dy}{dx}$ is negative at all points on the graph of $y=\dfrac{3x}{(x-1)(x+2)}$. Sketch this graph. By sketching on the same diagram a second graph (the equation of which should be stated), find the number of real roots of the equation $(x-1)(x+2)(x+3)=3x$.  (OCR)

**24**  The sequence $u_1,u_2,u_3,\ldots$ is defined by $u_n=\dfrac{1}{n(n+1)}$. Express $u_n$ in partial fractions and hence show that $u_1+u_2+u_3+\ldots+u_N=\dfrac{N}{N+1}$.

**25**  The sequence $u_1,u_2,u_3,\ldots$ is defined by $u_n=\dfrac{2}{n^3+3n^2+2n}$. Express $\dfrac{2}{n^3+3n^2+2n}$ in partial fractions and hence show that $u_1+u_2+u_3+\ldots+u_N=\dfrac{1}{N+2}-\dfrac{1}{N+1}+\dfrac{1}{2}$.

# 8 Differentiating products

This chapter extends further the range of functions which you can differentiate and integrate. When you have completed it you should

- know and be able to apply the product and quotient rules for differentiation
- know and be able to apply the method of integration by parts.

## 8.1 The sum and product rules

If $f(x) = x^2 + \sin x$, then $f'(x) = 2x + \cos x$. You know this, because it was proved (in P1) that $\dfrac{d}{dx} x^2 = 2x$, and (in Chapter 2) that $\dfrac{d}{dx} \sin x = \cos x$. But the statement also depends on another property of differentiation:

> **The sum rule**   If $u$ and $v$ are functions of $x$, and
>
> $$\text{if } y = u + v, \text{ then } \frac{dy}{dx} = \frac{du}{dx} + \frac{dv}{dx}.$$

This was justified in P1 Chapter 5 by means of an example. For a general proof, it is convenient to use 'delta notation'.

Take a particular value of $x$, and increase $x$ by $\delta x$. There will then be corresponding increases in $u$, $v$ and $y$ of $\delta u$, $\delta v$ and $\delta y$:

$$y = u + v \quad \text{and} \quad y + \delta y = (u + \delta u) + (v + \delta v).$$

Subtracting the first equation from the second gives

$$\delta y = \delta u + \delta v; \text{ and, dividing by } \delta x, \quad \frac{\delta y}{\delta x} = \frac{\delta u}{\delta x} + \frac{\delta v}{\delta x}.$$

To find $\dfrac{dy}{dx}$, you must take the limit as $\delta x \to 0$:

$$\frac{dy}{dx} = \lim_{\delta x \to 0} \frac{\delta y}{\delta x} = \lim_{\delta x \to 0}\left(\frac{\delta u}{\delta x} + \frac{\delta v}{\delta x}\right) = \lim_{\delta x \to 0} \frac{\delta u}{\delta x} + \lim_{\delta x \to 0} \frac{\delta v}{\delta x} = \frac{du}{dx} + \frac{dv}{dx}, \text{ as required.}$$

You might (rightly) object that the crucial assumption of the proof, that the limit of the sum of two terms is the sum of the limits, has never been justified. This can only be an assumption at this stage, because you don't yet have a mathematical definition of what is meant by a limit. But it *can* be justified, and for the time being you may quote the result with confidence. You may also assume the corresponding result for the limit of the product of two terms: this has already been assumed in earlier chapters, when proving the chain rule and the derivatives of $\sin x$ and $\cos x$.

The rule for differentiating the product of two functions is rather more complicated than the rule for sums.

## Example 8.1.1

Show that, if $y = uv$, then in general $\dfrac{dy}{dx}$ does *not* equal $\dfrac{du}{dx} \times \dfrac{dv}{dx}$.

The words 'in general' are put in because there might be special functions for which equality does hold. For example, if $u$ and $v$ are both constant functions, then $y$ is also constant: $\dfrac{du}{dx}, \dfrac{dv}{dx}$ and $\dfrac{dy}{dx}$ are all $0$, so $\dfrac{dy}{dx}$ does equal $\dfrac{du}{dx} \times \dfrac{dv}{dx}$.

To show that this is not always true, it is sufficient to find a counterexample. For example, if $u = x^2$ and $v = x^3$, then $y = x^5$. In this case $\dfrac{dy}{dx} = 5x^4$, but $\dfrac{du}{dx} \times \dfrac{dv}{dx} = 2x \times 3x^2 = 6x^3$. These two expressions are not the same.

To find the correct rule, use the same notation as for the sum rule, but with $y = uv$. Then

$$y = uv \quad \text{and} \quad y + \delta y = (u + \delta u)(v + \delta v) = uv + (\delta u)v + u(\delta v) + (\delta u)(\delta v).$$

Subtracting the first equation from the second,

$$\delta y = (\delta u)v + u(\delta v) + (\delta u)(\delta v); \quad \text{then} \quad \frac{\delta y}{\delta x} = \left(\frac{\delta u}{\delta x}\right)v + u\left(\frac{\delta v}{\delta x}\right) + \left(\frac{\delta u}{\delta x}\right)(\delta v).$$

Taking limits as $\delta x \to 0$, and making the assumptions about limits of sums and products,

$$\frac{dy}{dx} = \lim_{\delta x \to 0}\left(\left(\frac{\delta u}{\delta x}\right)v\right) + \lim_{\delta x \to 0}\left(u\left(\frac{\delta v}{\delta x}\right)\right) + \lim_{\delta x \to 0}\left(\frac{\delta u}{\delta x}\right)\lim_{\delta x \to 0}(\delta v).$$

The last term on the right is $0$ because, as $\delta x \to 0$, $\delta v \to 0$.

Therefore:

**The product rule**    If $u$ and $v$ are functions of $x$, and

if $y = uv$, then $\dfrac{dy}{dx} = \dfrac{du}{dx}v + u\dfrac{dv}{dx}$.

In function notation, if $y = f(x)g(x)$, then $\dfrac{dy}{dx} = f'(x)g(x) + f(x)g'(x)$.

## Example 8.1.2

Verify the product rule when $u = x^2$ and $v = x^3$.

The right side is $2x \times x^3 + x^2 \times 3x^2 = 2x^4 + 3x^4 = 5x^4$, which is the derivative of $y = x^2 \times x^3 = x^5$.

**Example 8.1.3**

Find the derivatives with respect to $x$ of (a) $x^3 \sin x$,   (b) $xe^{3x}$,   (c) $\sin^5 x \cos^3 x$.

(a) $\dfrac{d}{dx}\left(x^3 \sin x\right) = 3x^2 \times \sin x + x^3 \times \cos x = 3x^2 \sin x + x^3 \cos x.$

(b) $\dfrac{d}{dx}\left(xe^{3x}\right) = 1 \times e^{3x} + x \times \left(e^{3x} \times 3\right) = e^{3x} + 3xe^{3x} = (1+3x)e^{3x}.$

(c) $\dfrac{d}{dx}\left(\sin^5 x \cos^3 x\right) = \left(5\sin^4 x \times \cos x\right)\cos^3 x + \sin^5 x\left(3\cos^2 x \times (-\sin x)\right)$

$$= 5\sin^4 x \cos^4 x - 3\sin^6 x \cos^2 x$$

$$= \sin^4 x \cos^2 x\left(5\cos^2 x - 3\sin^2 x\right).$$

Notice that in part (c) the chain rule is used to find $\dfrac{du}{dx}$ and $\dfrac{dv}{dx}$.

**Example 8.1.4**

Find the points on the graph of $y = x \sin x$ at which the tangent passes through the origin.

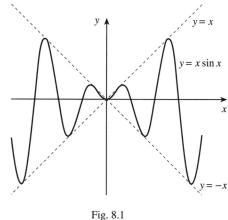

The product rule gives $\dfrac{dy}{dx} = \sin x + x \cos x$, so the tangent at a point $P$

$(p, p\sin p)$ has gradient $\sin p + p\cos p$. This has to equal the gradient of $OP$,

which is $\dfrac{p\sin p}{p} = \sin p$. Therefore

$$\sin p + p\cos p = \sin p,$$

giving $p\cos p = 0$.

This equation is satisfied by $p = 0$ and all odd multiples of $\frac{1}{2}\pi$. These points have coordinates $(0,0)$, $\left(\pm\frac{1}{2}\pi, \frac{1}{2}\pi\right)$, $\left(\pm\frac{3}{2}\pi, -\frac{3}{2}\pi\right)$, $\left(\pm\frac{5}{2}\pi, \frac{5}{2}\pi\right)$, ... .

Fig. 8.1

This is illustrated in Fig. 8.1. The graph oscillates between the lines $y = x$ and $y = -x$, touching $y = x$ when $\sin|x| = 1$, and $y = -x$ when $\sin|x| = -1$.

---

### Exercise 8A

**1** Differentiate the following functions with respect to $x$ by using the product rule. Verify your answers by multiplying out the products and then differentiating.

(a) $(x+1)(x-1)$       (b) $x^2(x+2)$       (c) $\left(x^3+4\right)\left(x^2+3\right)$

(d) $\left(3x^2+5x+2\right)(7x+5)$     (e) $\left(x^2-2x+4\right)(x+2)$     (f) $x^m x^n$

**2** Differentiate the following with respect to $x$.

(a) $xe^x$

(b) $x^2 \ln x$

(c) $x^3 (\sin x + 1)$

(d) $\sin x \cos x$

(e) $x \cos x$

(f) $e^{-x} \sin x$

**3** Find $\dfrac{dy}{dx}$ when

(a) $y = (x^2 + 3)e^x$,

(b) $y = x^2 (\sin x + \cos x)$,

(c) $y = x \sin^2 x$.

**4** Find $f'(x)$ when

(a) $f(x) = x^2 (2 + e^x)$,

(b) $f(x) = x^3 e^{2x}$,

(c) $f(x) = (4 + 3x^2) \ln x$.

**5** Find the value of the gradient of the following curves when $x = 2$. Give your answers in exact form.

(a) $y = xe^{-2x}$

(b) $y = e^x \sin x$

(c) $y = x \ln 3x$

**6** Find the equations of tangents to the following curves at the given points.

(a) $y = x \sin x$ when $x = \pi$

(b) $y = x^3 \ln x$ when $x = 1$

(c) $y = x\sqrt{3x + 1}$ when $x = 5$

(d) $y = x^3 e^{-2x}$ when $x = 0$

**7** Find the coordinates of the turning points of the curve $y = x^2 e^{-x}$.

**8** Differentiate the following with respect to $x$.

(a) $x^2 \sin^3 2x$

(b) $e^x \sqrt{5x^2 + 2}$

(c) $\sin^4 2x \cos^3 5x$

(d) $(4x + 1)^3 \ln 3x$

(e) $\sqrt{x} \ln 2x$

(f) $e^{ax} \cos(bx + \tfrac{1}{2}\pi)$

**9** When $f(x) = x \sin(\tfrac{1}{2}x)$, find the exact value of $f'(4)$.

**10** Find the equation of the normal to the curve $y = x \ln(2x - 1)$ at the point on the curve with $x$-coordinate 1.

**11** Find the coordinates of the stationary point on the curve $y = (x^2 - 4)\sqrt{4x - 1}$, $x \geqslant \tfrac{1}{4}$.

**12** The volume, $V$, of a solid is given by $V = x^2 \sqrt{8 - x}$. Use calculus to find the maximum value of $V$ and the value of $x$ at which it occurs.

**13** Find the $x$-coordinates of the stationary points on the curve $y = x^n e^{-x}$, where $n$ is a positive integer. Determine the nature of these stationary points, distinguishing between the cases when $n$ is odd and when $n$ is even.

**14** Use the product rule to establish the product rule, $\dfrac{d}{dx}uvw = \dfrac{du}{dx}vw + u\dfrac{dv}{dx}w + uv\dfrac{dw}{dx}$, for differentiating a 'triple' product. Use the new rule to find

(a) $\dfrac{d}{dx}xe^x \sin x$,

(b) $\dfrac{d}{dx}x^2 e^{-3x} \cos 4x$.

## 8.2  Integration by parts

The product rule for differentiation extends the range of functions which can be integrated. For example, from

$$\frac{d}{dx}(x\sin x) = \sin x + x\cos x$$

you can deduce that

$$x\sin x = \int \sin x\,dx + \int x\cos x\,dx = -\cos x + k + \int x\cos x\,dx.$$

You can rearrange this to give the new result

$$\int x\cos x\,dx = x\sin x + \cos x - k.$$

But if you were asked to find $\int x\cos x\,dx,$ you would not immediately guess that the answer comes from differentiating $x\sin x$. You can overcome this by applying the same argument to the general product rule.

From $\dfrac{d}{dx}(uv) = \dfrac{du}{dx}v + u\dfrac{dv}{dx}$ you can deduce that

$$uv = \int \frac{du}{dx}v\,dx + \int u\frac{dv}{dx}\,dx.$$

If you can find one of the integrals on the right, this equation tells you the other. It can be rearranged to give the rule:

**Integration by parts**

$$\int u\frac{dv}{dx}\,dx = uv - \int \frac{du}{dx}v\,dx.$$

For example, if you want to integrate $x\cos x$, you write $u = x$ and find a function $v$ such that $\dfrac{dv}{dx} = \cos x$. The simplest function is $v = \sin x$. The rule gives

$$\int x\cos x\,dx = x\sin x - \int 1\times\sin x\,dx$$

$$= x\sin x + \cos x + k.$$

*Notice that the result at the top of the page has a constant $-k$, and the same integral here has a constant $+k$. It is not difficult to see that the two forms are equivalent.*

**Example 8.2.1**

Find $\displaystyle\int xe^{3x}\,dx.$

Take $u = x$ and find $v$ such that $\dfrac{dv}{dx} = e^{3x}$. The simplest function for $v$ is $\frac{1}{3}e^{3x}$. The rule gives

$$\int xe^{3x}\,dx = x \times \tfrac{1}{3}e^{3x} - \int 1 \times \tfrac{1}{3}e^{3x}\,dx$$

$$= \tfrac{1}{3}xe^{3x} - \tfrac{1}{9}e^{3x} + k$$

$$= \tfrac{1}{9}(3x-1)e^{3x} + k.$$

The next example applies the method to a definite integral. The rule then takes the form:

$$\int_a^b u\frac{dv}{dx}\,dx = \left[uv\right]_a^b - \int_a^b \frac{du}{dx}v\,dx.$$

## Example 8.2.2

Find $\displaystyle\int_2^8 x\ln x\,dx$.

If you write $u = x$, you need $v$ to satisfy $\dfrac{dv}{dx} = \ln x$. But although P2 Chapter 12 gave the derivative of $\ln x$, its integral is not yet known. (See Example 8.2.3.)

When this occurs, try writing the product the other way round. Take $u = \ln x$, and find a $v$ such that $\dfrac{dv}{dx} = x$, which is $v = \frac{1}{2}x^2$. The rule then gives

$$\int_2^8 x\ln x\,dx = \left[\ln x \times \tfrac{1}{2}x^2\right]_2^8 - \int_2^8 \frac{1}{x} \times \tfrac{1}{2}x^2\,dx$$

$$= 32\ln 8 - 2\ln 2 - \int_2^8 \tfrac{1}{2}x\,dx$$

$$= 32\ln 2^3 - 2\ln 2 - \left[\tfrac{1}{4}x^2\right]_2^8$$

$$= 32(3\ln 2) - 2\ln 2 - (16 - 1)$$

$$= 94\ln 2 - 15.$$

It is usually best to leave the answer in a simple exact form like this. If you need a numerical value, it is easy enough to calculate one.

## Example 8.2.3

Find $\displaystyle\int \ln x\,dx$.

You wouldn't at first expect to use integration by parts for this, since it doesn't appear to be a product. But taking $u$ as $u = \ln x$ and $\dfrac{dv}{dx} = 1$, so that $v = x$, the rule gives

$$\int \ln x\,dx = \ln x \times x - \int \frac{1}{x} \times x\,dx = x\ln x - \int 1\,dx$$

$$= x\ln x - x + k.$$

The integral of $\ln x$ is an important result. You need not remember the answer, but you should remember how to get it.

The next example concerns two integrals which are used in probability.

### Example 8.2.4

Find $\displaystyle\int_0^\infty xe^{-ax}\,dx$ and $\displaystyle\int_0^\infty x^2 e^{-ax}\,dx,$ , where $a$ is positive.

Begin by finding the integrals from $0$ to $s$, and then consider their limits as $s \to \infty$.

For both integrals take $\dfrac{dv}{dx} = e^{-ax}$, so $v = -\dfrac{1}{a}e^{-ax}$.

$$\int_0^s xe^{-ax}\,dx = \left[x \times \left(-\frac{1}{a}\right)e^{-ax}\right]_0^s - \int_0^s 1 \times \left(-\frac{1}{a}\right)e^{-ax}\,dx$$

$$= -\frac{1}{a}se^{-as} - \left[\left(\frac{1}{a^2}\right)e^{-ax}\right]_0^s$$

$$= -\frac{1}{a}se^{-as} - \frac{1}{a^2}e^{-as} + \frac{1}{a^2}.$$

$$\int_0^s x^2 e^{-ax}\,dx = \left[x^2 \times \left(-\frac{1}{a}\right)e^{-ax}\right]_0^s - \int_0^s 2x \times \left(-\frac{1}{a}\right)e^{-ax}\,dx$$

$$= -\frac{1}{a}s^2 e^{-as} + \frac{2}{a}\int_0^s xe^{-ax}\,dx.$$

The integral in the last line here is the integral that has just been found, so if you wanted to find the value of $\displaystyle\int_0^s x^2 e^{-ax}\,dx,$ you could do this by substitution. But since you want the infinite integral, it is better not to take this step too soon.

For the infinite integral, you need to know the limits of $e^{-as}$, $se^{-as}$ and $s^2 e^{-as}$ as $s \to \infty$. It was proved in P2 Section 12.7 that if $n$ is positive $\dfrac{t^n}{e^t} \to 0$ as $t \to \infty$.

Replacing $t$ with $as$ and removing the constant factor $a^n$ (which does not affect the limit) gives $s^n e^{-as} \to 0$ as $s \to \infty$. (The solution uses this result for $n=1$ and $n=2$.)

It follows that $\displaystyle\int_0^\infty xe^{-ax}\,dx = \frac{1}{a^2},$

and that $\displaystyle\int_0^\infty x^2 e^{-ax}\,dx = \frac{2}{a}\int_0^\infty xe^{-ax}\,dx = \frac{2}{a^3}.$

## Exercise 8B

1   Use integration by parts to integrate the following functions with respect to $x$.

   (a)  $x \sin x$                (b)  $3xe^x$                (c)  $(x+4)e^x$

2   Use integration by parts to integrate the following functions with respect to $x$.

   (a)  $xe^{2x}$                (b)  $x \cos 4x$                (c)  $x \ln 2x$

3   Find

   (a)  $\displaystyle\int x^5 \ln 3x \, dx,$     (b)  $\displaystyle\int xe^{2x+1} \, dx,$     (c)  $\displaystyle\int \ln 2x \, dx.$

4   Find the exact values of

   (a)  $\displaystyle\int_1^e x \ln x \, dx,$     (b)  $\displaystyle\int_0^{\frac{1}{2}\pi} x \sin \tfrac{1}{2} x \, dx,$     (c)  $\displaystyle\int_1^e x^n \ln x \, dx \ \ (n>0).$

5   Find

   (a)  $\displaystyle\int x(1+x)^6 \, dx,$     (b)  $\displaystyle\int x(3x-1)^4 \, dx,$     (c)  $\displaystyle\int x(ax+b)^{12} \, dx.$

6   Prove that $\displaystyle\int x^2 \sin x \, dx = -x^2 \cos x + 2 \int x \cos x \, dx.$ Hence, by using integration by parts a

   second time, find $\displaystyle\int x^2 \sin x \, dx.$ Use a similar method to integrate the following functions

   with respect to $x$.

   (a)  $x^2 e^{2x}$                (b)  $x^2 \cos \tfrac{1}{2} x$

7   Integrate with respect to $x$,

   (a)  $x\sqrt{4x-1},$                (b)  $x\sqrt{2-x},$                (c)  $x\sqrt{2x+3}.$

8   Find the area bounded by the curve $y = xe^{-x}$, the $x$-axis and the lines $x=0$ and $x=2$.
   Find also the volume of the solid of revolution obtained by rotating this region about the
   $x$-axis.

9   Find the area between the $x$-axis and the curve $y = x \sin 3x$ for $0 \leqslant x \leqslant \tfrac{1}{3}\pi$. Leave your
   answer in terms of $\pi$. Find also the volume of the solid of revolution obtained by rotating
   this region about the $x$-axis.

10  Find

   (a)  $\displaystyle\int_0^{\pi} e^x \cos x \, dx,$     (b)  $\displaystyle\int_{-\pi}^{\pi} e^{-4x} \sin 2x \, dx,$     (c)  $\displaystyle\int_0^{2\pi} e^{-ax} \cos bx \, dx.$

11  Find

   (a)  $\displaystyle\int_0^{\infty} e^{-x} \sin x \, dx,$     (b)  $\displaystyle\int_0^1 \frac{x}{\sqrt{1-x}} \, dx.$

   Draw diagrams to illustrate the areas measured by these definite integrals.

## 8.3  Differentiating quotients

Functions of the form $\dfrac{u}{v}$ can often be written in a different form so that they can be differentiated by the product rule.

**Example 8.3.1**

Differentiate with respect to $x$     (a) $f(x) = \dfrac{\sin x}{e^x}$,     (b) $g(x) = \dfrac{e^x}{\sin x}$.

(a)  Since $\dfrac{1}{e^x} = e^{-x}$, you can write $f(x)$ as $e^{-x}\sin x$. Therefore

$$f'(x) = \frac{d}{dx}\left(e^{-x}\sin x\right) = \left(-e^{-x}\right)\sin x + e^{-x}\cos x = e^{-x}(\cos x - \sin x).$$

(b)  **Method 1**    You can write $g(x)$ as $e^x \times \dfrac{1}{\sin x}$, so

$$g'(x) = \frac{d}{dx}e^x \times \frac{1}{\sin x} + e^x \times \frac{d}{dx}\left(\frac{1}{\sin x}\right) = e^x \times \frac{1}{\sin x} + e^x \times \left(\frac{-1}{\sin^2 x} \times \cos x\right),$$

using the product rule and then the chain rule.

You can simplify this to $g'(x) = e^x\left(\dfrac{\sin x - \cos x}{\sin^2 x}\right)$.

**Method 2**    Since $g(x) = \dfrac{1}{f(x)}$, the chain rule gives

$$g'(x) = \left(\frac{-1}{f(x)^2}\right) \times f'(x) = -\frac{f'(x)}{f(x)^2}.$$

Therefore, using the result of (a),

$$g'(x) = -\frac{e^{-x}(\cos x - \sin x)}{\left(\dfrac{\sin x}{e^x}\right)^2} = e^{2x}e^{-x}\left(\frac{\sin x - \cos x}{\sin^2 x}\right)$$

$$= e^x\left(\frac{\sin x - \cos x}{\sin^2 x}\right).$$

However, it is often useful to have a separate formula for differentiating $\dfrac{u}{v}$. This can be found by applying the product rule to $u \times \dfrac{1}{v}$, using the chain rule to differentiate $\dfrac{1}{v}$. This gives

$$\frac{d}{dx}\left(\frac{u}{v}\right) = \frac{d}{dx}\left(u \times \frac{1}{v}\right) = \frac{du}{dx} \times \frac{1}{v} + u \times \left(-\frac{1}{v^2}\right)\frac{dv}{dx}$$

$$= \frac{du}{dx}\frac{1}{v} - \frac{u}{v^2}\frac{dv}{dx}.$$

This can be conveniently written as:

**The quotient rule**    If $u$ and $v$ are functions of $x$, and

$$\text{if } y = \frac{u}{v}, \text{ then } \frac{dy}{dx} = \frac{\dfrac{du}{dx}v - u\dfrac{dv}{dx}}{v^2}.$$

In function notation, if $y = \dfrac{\mathrm{f}(x)}{\mathrm{g}(x)}$, then $\dfrac{dy}{dx} = \dfrac{\mathrm{f}'(x)\mathrm{g}(x) - \mathrm{f}(x)\mathrm{g}'(x)}{\mathrm{g}(x)^2}.$

An important application of this rule is to differentiate $\tan x$. Since $\tan x = \dfrac{\sin x}{\cos x}$, the quotient rule with $u = \sin x$, $v = \cos x$ gives

$$\frac{d}{dx}\tan x = \frac{\cos x \times \cos x - \sin x \times (-\sin x)}{(\cos x)^2} = \frac{\cos^2 x + \sin^2 x}{\cos^2 x} = \frac{1}{\cos^2 x}.$$

Since $\dfrac{1}{\cos x}$ is $\sec x$, you can write this as:

$$\frac{d}{dx}\tan x = \sec^2 x.$$

*You will often need this result, so you should remember it.*

## Example 8.3.2

Find the minimum and maximum values of $\mathrm{f}(x) = \dfrac{x-1}{x^2+3}$.

The denominator is never zero, so $\mathrm{f}(x)$ is defined for all real numbers.

The quotient rule with $u = x-1$ and $v = x^2 + 3$ gives

$$\mathrm{f}'(x) = \frac{1 \times (x^2+3) - (x-1) \times 2x}{(x^2+3)^2} = \frac{-x^2 + 2x + 3}{(x^2+3)^2}$$

$$= \frac{-(x^2 - 2x - 3)}{(x^2+3)^2} = \frac{-(x+1)(x-3)}{(x^2+3)^2}.$$

So $\mathrm{f}'(x) = 0$ when $x = -1$ and $x = 3$.

You could use the quotient rule again to find $\mathrm{f}''(x)$, but in this example it is much easier to note that $\mathrm{f}'(x)$ is positive when $-1 < x < 3$ and negative when $x < -1$ and when $x > 3$. So there is a minimum at $x = -1$ and a maximum at $x = 3$.

The minimum value is $\mathrm{f}(-1) = \frac{-2}{4} = -\frac{1}{2}$, and the maximum value is $\frac{2}{12} = \frac{1}{6}$.

## Exercise 8C

**1** Differentiate with respect to $x$

(a) $\dfrac{x}{1+5x}$,

(b) $\dfrac{x^2}{3x-2}$,

(c) $\dfrac{x^2}{1+2x^2}$,

(d) $\dfrac{e^{3x}}{4x-3}$,

(e) $\dfrac{x}{1+x^3}$,

(f) $\dfrac{e^x}{x^2+1}$.

**2** By writing $\cot x = \dfrac{\cos x}{\sin x}$, differentiate $\cot x$ with respect to $x$.

**3** Differentiate with respect to $x$

(a) $\dfrac{\sin x}{x}$,

(b) $\dfrac{x}{\sin x}$,

(c) $\left(\dfrac{x}{\sin x}\right)^2$.

**4** Differentiate with respect to $x$

(a) $\dfrac{x}{\sqrt{x+1}}$,

(b) $\dfrac{\sqrt{x-5}}{x}$,

(c) $\dfrac{\sqrt{3x+2}}{2x}$.

**5** Find $\dfrac{dy}{dx}$ when

(a) $y = \dfrac{\cos x}{\sqrt{x}}$,

(b) $y = \dfrac{e^x+5x}{e^x-2}$,

(c) $y = \dfrac{\sqrt{1-x}}{\sqrt{1+x}}$.

**6** Find $\dfrac{dy}{dx}$ when

(a) $y = \dfrac{\ln x}{x}$,

(b) $y = \dfrac{\ln\left(x^2+4\right)}{x}$,

(c) $y = \dfrac{\ln(3x+2)}{2x-1}$.

**7** Find the equation of the tangent at the point with coordinates $(1,1)$ to the curve with equation $y = \dfrac{x^2+3}{x+3}$. (OCR)

**8** (a) If $f(x) = \dfrac{e^x}{2x+1}$, find $f'(x)$.

(b) Find the coordinates of the turning point of the curve $y = f(x)$.

**9** Find the equation of the normal to the curve $y = \dfrac{2x-1}{x(x-3)}$ at the point on the curve where $x = 2$.

**10** Find the turning points of the curve $y = \dfrac{x^2+4}{2x-x^2}$.

**11** (a) If $f(x) = \dfrac{x^2-3x}{x+1}$, find $f'(x)$.

(b) Find the values of $x$ for which $f(x)$ is decreasing.

## Miscellaneous exercise 8

1 (a) Differentiate $x^3 \sin x$.

   (b) Differentiate $\dfrac{x}{\sqrt{x+3}}$ simplifying your answer as far as possible. (OCR)

2 Given that $y = xe^{-3x}$, find $\dfrac{dy}{dx}$.

   Hence find the coordinates of the stationary point on the curve $y = xe^{-3x}$. (OCR)

3 A function $f$ is defined by $f(x) = e^x \cos x$ $(0 \leqslant x \leqslant 2\pi)$.

   (a) Find $f'(x)$.

   (b) State the values of $x$ between $0$ and $2\pi$ for which $f'(x) < 0$.

   (c) What does the fact that $f'(x) < 0$ in this interval tell you about the shape of the graph of $y = f(x)$? (OCR)

4 Use appropriate rules of differentiation to find $\dfrac{dy}{dx}$ in each of the following cases.

   (a) $y = \sin 2x \cos 4x$ (b) $y = \dfrac{3x^2}{\ln x}$ for $x > 1$ (c) $y = \left(1 - \dfrac{x}{5}\right)^{10}$ (OCR)

5 Find the gradient of the curve $y = \dfrac{\sin x}{x^2}$ at the point where $x = \pi$, leaving your answer in terms of $\pi$. (OCR)

6 Use differentiation to find the coordinates of the turning point on the curve whose equation is $y = \dfrac{4x+2}{\sqrt{x}}$. (OCR)

7 A curve $C$ has equation $y = \dfrac{\sin x}{x}$, where $x > 0$.

   Find $\dfrac{dy}{dx}$, and hence show that the $x$-coordinate of any stationary point of $C$ satisfies the equation $x = \tan x$. (OCR)

8 A curve has equation $y = \dfrac{x}{\sqrt{2x^2 + 1}}$.

   (a) Show that $\dfrac{dy}{dx} = \left(2x^2 + 1\right)^{-\frac{3}{2}}$.

   (b) Hence show that the curve has no turning points. (OCR)

9 Use integration by parts to find the value of $\displaystyle\int_1^2 x \ln x \, dx$. (OCR)

10 Use integration by parts to determine $\displaystyle\int_0^{\frac{1}{3}} xe^{2x} \, dx$. (OCR)

**11** Evaluate $\displaystyle\int_0^1 xe^{-x}\,dx$, showing all your working.                    (OCR)

**12** Use integration by parts to determine $\displaystyle\int 3x\sqrt{x-1}\,dx$.               (OCR)

**13** Use integration by parts to determine the exact value of $\displaystyle\int_0^{\frac{1}{2}\pi} 3x\sin 2x\,dx$.   (OCR)

**14** Showing your working clearly, use integration by parts to evaluate $\displaystyle\int_0^{\pi} 4x\sin\tfrac{1}{2}x\,dx$.  (OCR)

**15** A sketch of part of the curve $y=\dfrac{x(x+3)}{2x-2}$
is shown in the diagram.

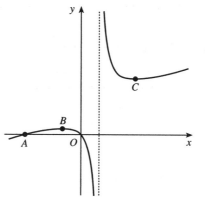

(a) Write down the coordinates of the
point $A$ and state the equation of the
asymptote shown as a broken line
parallel to the $y$-axis.

(b) Find the equation of the tangent to the
curve at $A$.

(c) Show, by using calculus, that the
coordinates of the turning point at $B$
are $(-1,0.5)$ and calculate the
coordinates of the turning point at $C$.

                                              (OCR)

**16** The region $R$, shown shaded in the
diagram, is bounded by the $x$- and $y$-axes,
the line $x=\tfrac{1}{3}\pi$ and the curve $y=\sec\tfrac{1}{2}x$.
Show that the volume of the solid formed
when $R$ is rotated completely about the
$x$-axis is $\dfrac{2\pi}{\sqrt{3}}$.

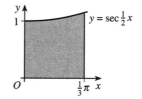

**17** A length of channel of given depth $d$ is to
be made from a rectangular sheet of metal
of width $2a$. The metal is to be bent in
such a way that the cross-section $ABCD$ is
as shown in the figure, with

$AB+BC+CD=2a$ and with $AB$ and $CD$ each inclined to the line $BC$ at an angle $\theta$.
Show that $BC=2(a-d\operatorname{cosec}\theta)$ and that the area of the cross-section $ABCD$ is
$$2ad+d^2(\cot\theta-2\operatorname{cosec}\theta).$$

Show that the maximum value of $2ad+d^2(\cot\theta-2\operatorname{cosec}\theta)$, as $\theta$ varies, is $d(2a-d\sqrt{3})$.

By considering the length of $BC$, show that the cross-sectional area can only be made
equal to this maximum value if $2d\leqslant a\sqrt{3}$.                    (OCR)

# 9 Differential equations

This chapter is about differential equations of the form $\dfrac{dy}{dx} = f(x)$ or $\dfrac{dy}{dx} = f(y)$. When you have completed it, you should

- be able to find general solutions of these equations, or particular solutions satisfying given initial conditions
- know the relation connecting the derivatives $\dfrac{dy}{dx}$ and $\dfrac{dx}{dy}$, and understand its significance
- be able to formulate differential equations as models, and interpret the solutions.

## 9.1 Forming and solving equations

Many applications of mathematics involve two variables, and you want to find a relation between them. Often this relation is expressed in terms of the rate of change of one variable with respect to the other. This then leads to a **differential equation**. Its **solution** will be an algebraic equation connecting the two variables.

### Example 9.1.1

At each point $P$ of a curve for which $x > 0$ the tangent cuts the $y$-axis at $T$, and $N$ is the foot of the perpendicular from $P$ to the $y$-axis (see Fig. 9.1). If $T$ is always 1 unit below $N$, find the equation of the curve.

Since $NP = x$, the gradient of the tangent is $\dfrac{1}{x}$, so that

$$\frac{dy}{dx} = \frac{1}{x}.$$

This can be integrated directly to give

$$y = \ln x + k.$$

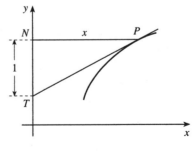

Fig. 9.1

The modulus sign is not needed, since $x > 0$.

The equation $y = \ln x + k$ is called the **general solution** of the differential equation $\dfrac{dy}{dx} = \dfrac{1}{x}$ for $x > 0$. It can be represented by a family of graphs, one for each value of $k$. Fig. 9.2 shows just a few typical graphs, but there are in fact infinitely many graphs with the property described.

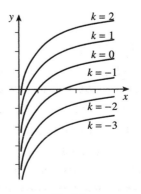

Fig. 9.2

A differential equation often originates from a scientific law, or hypothesis. The equation is then called a **mathematical model** of the real-world situation.

### Example 9.1.2

A rodent has mass $30$ grams at birth. It reaches maturity in $3$ months. The rate of growth is modelled by the differential equation $\dfrac{dm}{dt} = 120(t-3)^2$, where $m$ grams is the mass of the rodent $t$ months after birth. Find the mass of the rodent when fully grown.

The differential equation has general solution

$$m = 40(t-3)^3 + k.$$

However, only one equation from this family of solutions is right for this problem. It is given that, when $t = 0$ (at birth), $m = 30$. So $k$ must satisfy the equation

$$30 = 40(0-3)^3 + k, \text{ giving } 30 = -1080 + k, \text{ so } k = 1110.$$

The mass of the rodent after $t$ months is therefore $m = 40(t-3)^3 + 1110$.

The mass when fully grown is found by putting $t = 3$ in this formula, giving $m = 0 + 1110 = 1110$. So the mass of the rodent at maturity is $1110$ grams.

In this example the variables have to satisfy an **initial condition**, or **boundary condition**, that $m = 30$ when $t = 0$. The equation $m = 40(t-3)^3 + 1110$ is the **particular solution** of the differential equation which satisfies the initial condition.

### Example 9.1.3

A botanist makes a hypothesis that the rate of growth of hothouse plants is proportional to the amount of daylight they receive. If $t$ is the time in years after the shortest day of the year, the length of effective daylight is given by the formula $12 - 4\cos 2\pi t$ hours. On the shortest day in the December of one year the height of one plant is measured to be $123.0$ cm; $55$ days later the height is $128.0$ cm. What will its height be on the longest day of the year in the following June?

If $h$ is the height in centimetres, the rate of growth is given by

$$\frac{dh}{dt} = c(12 - 4\cos 2\pi t),$$

but $c$, the constant of proportionality, is not known. Nor can it be found directly from the data. However, integration gives

$$h = c\left(12t - \frac{2}{\pi}\sin 2\pi t\right) + k.$$

The initial condition is that $h = 123.0$ when $t = 0$, so

$$123.0 = c(0-0) + k, \text{ giving } k = 123.0. \text{ Therefore}$$

$$h = c\left(12t - \frac{2}{\pi}\sin 2\pi t\right) + 123.0.$$

After $55$ days the value of $t$ is $\frac{55}{365} = 0.150\ldots$, and it is given that at this time $h = 128.0$. So

$$128.0 = c\left(12 \times 0.150\ldots - \frac{2}{\pi}\sin(2\pi \times 0.150\ldots)\right) + 123.0$$

$$= c(1.80\ldots - 0.51\ldots) + 123.0, \text{ which gives } c = 3.87\ldots.$$

The longest day occurs when $t = \frac{1}{2}$, and then

$$h = 3.87\ldots(6-0) + 123.0 = 146, \text{ correct to 3 significant figures.}$$

According to the botanist's hypothesis, the height of the plant on the longest day will be $146$ cm.

This last example is typical of many applications of differential equations. Often the form of a hypothetical law is known, but the values of the numerical constants are not. But once the differential equation has been solved, experimental data can be used to find values for the constants.

## Exercise 9A

**1** Find general solutions of the following differential equations.

(a) $\dfrac{dy}{dx} = (3x - 1)(x - 3)$

(b) $\dfrac{dx}{dt} = \sin^2 3t$

(c) $\dfrac{dP}{dt} = 50e^{0.1t}$

(d) $e^{2t}\dfrac{du}{dt} = 100$

(e) $\sqrt{x}\,\dfrac{dy}{dx} = x + 1$, for $x > 0$

(f) $\sin t\,\dfrac{dx}{dt} = \cos t + \sin 2t$, for $0 < t < \pi$

**2** Solve the following differential equations with the given initial conditions. Display graphs to illustrate your answers.

(a) $\dfrac{dx}{dt} = 2e^{0.4t}$, $x = 1$ when $t = 0$

(b) $\dfrac{dv}{dt} = 6(\sin 2t - \cos 3t)$, $v = 0$ when $t = 0$

(c) $(1 - t^2)\dfrac{dy}{dt} = 2t$, $y = 0$ when $t = 0$, for $-1 < t < 1$

**3** Find the solution curves of the following differential equations which pass through the given points. Display graphs to illustrate your answers.

(a) $\dfrac{dy}{dx} = \dfrac{x - 1}{x^2}$, through $(1, 0)$, for $x > 0$

(b) $\dfrac{dy}{dx} = \dfrac{1}{\sqrt{x}}$, through $(4, 0)$, for $x > 0$

(c) $(x + 1)\dfrac{dy}{dx} = x - 1$, through the origin, for $x > -1$

4   In starting from rest, the driver of an electric car depresses the throttle gradually. If the speed of the car after $t$ seconds is $v$ m s$^{-1}$, the acceleration $\dfrac{dv}{dt}$ (in metre–second units) is given by $0.2t$. How long does it take for the car to reach a speed of $20$ m s$^{-1}$?

5   The solution curve for a differential equation of the form $\dfrac{dy}{dx} = x - \dfrac{a}{x^2}$ for $x > 0$, passes through the points $(1,0)$ and $(2,0)$. Find the value of $y$ when $x = 3$.

6   A point moves on the $x$-axis so that its coordinate at time $t$ satisfies the differential equation $\dfrac{dx}{dt} = 5 + a\cos 2t$ for some value of $a$. It is observed that $x = 3$ when $t = 0$, and $x = 0$ when $t = \frac{1}{4}\pi$. Find the value of $a$, and the value of $x$ when $t = \frac{1}{3}\pi$.

7   The normal to a curve at a point $P$ cuts the $y$-axis at $T$, and $N$ is the foot of the perpendicular from $P$ to the $y$-axis. If, for all $P$, $T$ is always 1 unit below $N$, find the equation of the curve.

8   Water is leaking slowly out of a tank. The depth of the water after $t$ hours is $h$ metres, and these variables are related by a differential equation of the form $\dfrac{dh}{dt} = -ae^{-0.1t}$. Initially the depth of water is $6$ metres, and after $2$ hours it has fallen to $5$ metres. At what depth will the level eventually settle down?

Find an expression for $\dfrac{dh}{dt}$ in terms of $h$.

9   Four theories are proposed about the growth of an organism:

  (a)   It grows at a constant rate of $k$ units per year.

  (b)   It only grows when there is enough daylight, so that its rate of growth at time $t$ years is $k\left(1 - \frac{1}{2}\cos 2\pi t\right)$ units per year.

  (c)   Its growth is controlled by the 10-year sunspot cycle, so that its rate of growth at time $t$ years is $k\left(1 + \frac{1}{4}\cos\frac{1}{5}\pi t\right)$ units per year.

  (d)   Both (b) and (c) are true, so that its rate of growth is $k\left(1 - \frac{1}{2}\cos 2\pi t\right)\left(1 + \frac{1}{4}\cos\frac{1}{5}\pi t\right)$ units per year.

     The size of the organism at time $t = 0$ is $A$ units. For each model, find an expression for the size of the organism at time $t$ years. Display graphs to compare the size given by the four models for $0 < t < 10$. Do they all give the same value for the size of the organism after 10 years?

## 9.2   Independent and dependent variables

In many applications there is little doubt which of two variables to regard as the independent variable (often denoted by $x$), and which as the dependent variable ($y$). But when a function is one–one, so that an inverse function exists, there are occasions when you can choose to treat either variable as the independent variable.

For example, you could record the progress of a journey either by noting the distance you have gone at certain fixed intervals of time, or by noting the time when you pass certain fixed landmarks. If $x$ denotes the distance from the start and $t$ the time, then the rate of change would be either $\dfrac{dx}{dt}$ (the speed) or $\dfrac{dt}{dx}$ (which would be measured in a unit such as minutes per mile).

What is the connection between $\dfrac{dy}{dx}$ and $\dfrac{dx}{dy}$? The notation suggests that

$$\frac{dx}{dy} = \frac{1}{\dfrac{dy}{dx}},$$

and this is in fact correct. Fig. 9.3 shows the graph of a relation connecting variables $x$ and $y$, and triangles showing the increases $\delta x$ and $\delta y$ when you move from $P$ to $Q$. If you are thinking of $y$ as a function of $x$, then you would draw the triangle $PNQ$, and the gradient of the chord $PQ$ would be $\dfrac{\delta y}{\delta x}$. For $x$ as a function of $y$, you would draw the triangle $PMQ$, and the gradient of

Fig. 9.3

$PQ$ would be $\dfrac{\delta x}{\delta y}$. The product of the gradients is $\dfrac{\delta y}{\delta x} \times \dfrac{\delta x}{\delta y}$, which clearly equals 1.

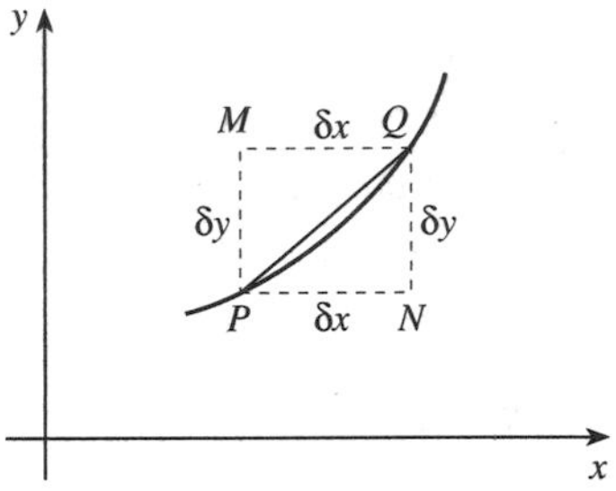

Now let $Q$ tend to $P$, so that both $\delta x$ and $\delta y$ tend to $0$. Then $\dfrac{\delta y}{\delta x}$ tends to $\dfrac{dy}{dx}$ and $\dfrac{\delta x}{\delta y}$ tends to $\dfrac{dx}{dy}$. Assuming (as in Chapter 8) that the limit of a product is the product of the limits,

$$\frac{dy}{dx} \times \frac{dx}{dy} = \lim\left(\frac{\delta y}{\delta x}\right) \times \lim\left(\frac{\delta x}{\delta y}\right) = \lim\left(\frac{\delta y}{\delta x} \times \frac{\delta x}{\delta y}\right) = \lim 1 = 1.$$

**Example 9.2.1**

Verify that $\dfrac{dy}{dx} \times \dfrac{dx}{dy} = 1$ when $y = x^3$.

If $y = x^3$, then $\dfrac{dy}{dx} = 3x^2$. You can also write the relation $y = x^3$ as $x = y^{\frac{1}{3}}$, so

$$\frac{dx}{dy} = \tfrac{1}{3}y^{-\frac{2}{3}} = \tfrac{1}{3}\left(x^3\right)^{-\frac{2}{3}} = \tfrac{1}{3}x^{-2} = \frac{1}{3x^2}.$$

Therefore $\dfrac{dy}{dx} \times \dfrac{dx}{dy} = 3x^2 \times \dfrac{1}{3x^2} = 1.$

## 9.3 Switching variables in differential equations

In all the differential equations in Section 9.1 the derivative was given as a formula involving the independent variable, which was $x$ in Example 9.1.1 and $t$ in Examples 9.1.2 and 9.1.3.

Often, however, the derivative is known in terms of the dependent variable. When this occurs, you can use the relation $\dfrac{dy}{dx} \times \dfrac{dx}{dy} = 1$ to turn the differential equation into a form which you know how to solve. That is,

$$\frac{dy}{dx} = f(y) \quad \Leftrightarrow \quad \frac{dx}{dy} = \frac{1}{f(y)} \quad \Leftrightarrow \quad x = \int \frac{1}{f(y)} \, dy.$$

### Example 9.3.1

A hot-air balloon can reach a maximum height of 1.25 km, and the rate at which it gains height decreases as it climbs, according to the formula

$$\frac{dh}{dt} = 20 - 16h,$$

where $h$ is the height in km and $t$ is the time in hours after lift-off. How long does the balloon take to reach a height of 1 km?

You can invert the differential equation to give

$$\frac{dt}{dh} = \frac{1}{\dfrac{dh}{dt}} = \frac{1}{20 - 16h},$$

so that $t = \displaystyle\int \frac{1}{20 - 16h} \, dh$.

The solution can be completed in either of two ways.

**Method 1**     The indefinite integral is

$$t = \int \frac{1}{20 - 16h} \, dh = -\frac{1}{16} \ln(20 - 16h) + k.$$

(Notice that $20 - 16h$ is always positive when $0 \leqslant h \leqslant 1$.) Since $t$ is measured from the instant of lift-off, $h = 0$ when $t = 0$. The particular solution with this initial condition must therefore satisfy

$$0 = -\tfrac{1}{16} \ln 20 + k, \text{ so } k = \tfrac{1}{16} \ln 20.$$

The equation connecting the variables $h$ and $t$ is therefore

$$t = -\tfrac{1}{16} \ln(20 - 16h) + \tfrac{1}{16} \ln 20 = \tfrac{1}{16} \ln\left(\frac{20}{20 - 16h}\right) = \tfrac{1}{16} \ln\left(\frac{5}{5 - 4h}\right).$$

When $h = 1$, $t = \tfrac{1}{16} \ln\left(\dfrac{5}{5 - 4}\right) = \tfrac{1}{16} \ln 5 \approx 0.10$.

**Method 2**    Since only the time at $h = 1$ is required, you need not find the general equation connecting $h$ and $t$. Instead, you can find the time as a definite integral, from $h = 0$ to $h = 1$:

$$\int_0^1 \frac{1}{20 - 16h}\, dh = \left[ -\tfrac{1}{16} \ln(20 - 16h) \right]_0^1 = -\tfrac{1}{16}(\ln 4 - \ln 20)$$

$$= -\tfrac{1}{16} \ln\!\left(\tfrac{4}{20}\right) = -\tfrac{1}{16} \ln\!\left(\tfrac{1}{5}\right) = \tfrac{1}{16} \ln 5 \approx 0.10.$$

The balloon takes $0.1$ hours, or $6$ minutes, to reach a height of $1$ km.

**Example 9.3.2**
When a ball is dropped from the roof of a tall building, the greatest speed that it can reach (called the terminal speed) is $u$. One model for its speed $v$ when it has fallen a distance $x$ is given by the differential equation

$$\frac{dv}{dx} = c\,\frac{u^2 - v^2}{v}, \text{ where } c \text{ is a positive constant.}$$

Find an expression for $v$ in terms of $x$.

No units are given, but the constants $u$ and $c$ will depend on the units in which $v$ and $x$ are measured.

Since $\dfrac{dv}{dx}$ is given in terms of $v$ rather than $x$, invert the equation to give

$$\frac{dx}{dv} = \frac{1}{c}\,\frac{v}{\left(u^2 - v^2\right)}, \text{ so that } x = \int \frac{1}{c}\,\frac{v}{\left(u^2 - v^2\right)}\, dv.$$

The integral can be found by writing the integrand in partial fractions, as

$$\frac{1}{2c}\left( \frac{1}{u - v} - \frac{1}{u + v} \right).$$

Note that $v$ must be less than $u$, so $u - v > 0$. Integrating,

$$x = \frac{1}{2c}\left( -\ln(u - v) - \ln(u + v) \right) + k.$$

The ball is not moving at the instant when it is dropped, so $v = 0$ when $x = 0$. This initial condition gives an equation for $k$:

$$0 = \frac{1}{2c}\left( -\ln(u) - \ln(u) \right) + k, \text{ so } k = \frac{2\ln u}{2c}.$$

The equation connecting $v$ and $x$ is therefore

$$x = \frac{1}{2c}\left( 2\ln u - \ln(u - v) - \ln(u + v) \right) = \frac{1}{2c} \ln\!\left( \frac{u^2}{u^2 - v^2} \right).$$

*You might have noticed that since, by the chain rule,* $\dfrac{d}{dv}\ln(u^2-v^2)=\dfrac{-2v}{u^2-v^2}$, *the*

*integral could be found directly as* $\displaystyle\int\dfrac{v}{u^2-v^2}\,dv=-\tfrac{1}{2}\ln(u^2-v^2)+k.$

You must now turn this equation round to get $v$ in terms of $x$:

$$2cx=\ln\left(\dfrac{u^2}{u^2-v^2}\right),$$

$$\dfrac{u^2}{u^2-v^2}=e^{2cx},$$

$$u^2=(u^2-v^2)e^{2cx},$$

$$v^2e^{2cx}=u^2(e^{2cx}-1),$$

$$v^2=u^2(1-e^{-2cx}).$$

Therefore, since $v>0$, the required expression is $v=u\sqrt{1-e^{-2cx}}$ .

### Example 9.3.3

A steel ball is heated to a temperature of 700 degrees Celsius and dropped into a drum of powdered ice. The temperature falls to 500 degrees in 30 seconds. Two models are suggested for the temperature, $T$ degrees, after $t$ seconds:

(a)  the rate of cooling is proportional to $T$,
(b)  the rate of cooling is proportional to $T^{1.2}$.

It is found that it takes a further 3 minutes for the temperature to fall from 500 to 100 degrees. Which model fits this information better?

The rate of cooling is measured by $\dfrac{dT}{dt}$, and this is negative.

(a)  This model is described by the differential equation

$$\dfrac{dT}{dt}=-aT,\text{ where } a \text{ is a positive constant.}$$

Inverting, $\dfrac{dt}{dT}=-\dfrac{1}{aT}$, which has solution $t=-\dfrac{1}{a}\ln T+k$.

Since $T=700$ when $t=0$, $0=-\dfrac{1}{a}\ln 700+k$, so $k=\dfrac{1}{a}\ln 700$.

The equation connecting $T$ and $t$ is therefore

$$t=\dfrac{1}{a}(\ln 700-\ln T)=\dfrac{1}{a}\ln\dfrac{700}{T}.$$

The value of $a$ can be found from the fact that $T=500$ when $t=30$:

$$30=\dfrac{1}{a}\ln\dfrac{700}{500},\text{ which gives } a=\dfrac{\ln 1.4}{30}\approx 0.0112.$$

(b) For this model

$$\frac{dT}{dt} = -bT^{1.2}, \text{ so } \frac{dt}{dT} = -\frac{1}{b}T^{-1.2}, \text{ and } t = \frac{1}{0.2b}T^{-0.2} + k.$$

From the initial condition, that $T = 700$ when $t = 0$,

$$0 = \frac{5}{b}700^{-0.2} + k, \text{ so } t = \frac{5}{b}\left(T^{-0.2} - 700^{-0.2}\right).$$

From the other boundary condition, that $T = 500$ when $t = 30$,

$$30 = \frac{5}{b}\left(500^{-0.2} - 700^{-0.2}\right), \text{ so } b = \frac{500^{-0.2} - 700^{-0.2}}{6} \approx 0.00313.$$

Fig. 9.4 shows the two models to be compared, whose equations are

(a) $t = \dfrac{1}{0.0112}\ln\dfrac{700}{T}$, and

(b) $t = \dfrac{5}{0.00313}\left(T^{-0.2} - 700^{-0.2}\right).$

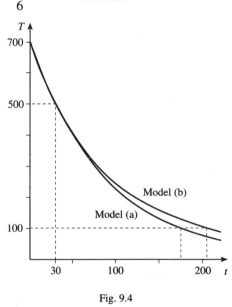

That is, (a) $T = 700e^{-0.0112t}$, and

(b) $T = \dfrac{1}{(0.000\,626t + 0.270)^5}.$

To choose between the models, use the other piece of data, that $T = 100$ after a further 3 minutes, which is when $t = 30 + 180 = 210$. Try putting $T = 100$ in the two equations: model (a) gives $t = 174$, and model (b) gives $t = 205$.

Fig. 9.4

This suggests that (b) is the better model.

## 9.4 The equation for exponential growth

The key feature of exponential growth or decay is that the rate of increase or decrease of a quantity is proportional to its current value. Denoting the quantity by $Q$, this is expressed mathematically by the differential equation $\dfrac{dQ}{dt} = aQ$, where $t$ stands for the time and $a$ is a constant. The sign of $a$ is positive for exponential growth, and negative for exponential decay.

You can solve this equation by writing $\dfrac{dt}{dQ} = \dfrac{1}{aQ}$ and integrating:

$$t = \int \frac{1}{aQ}\,dQ = \frac{1}{a}\ln|Q| + k.$$

Suppose that $Q$ has the value $Q_0$ when $t = 0$. Then $0 = \frac{1}{a} \ln |Q_0| + k$, so that

$$t = \frac{1}{a} \ln |Q| - \frac{1}{a} \ln |Q_0|, \text{ giving } \left| \frac{Q}{Q_0} \right| = e^{at}.$$

Now $Q$ must have the same sign as $Q_0$. In the equation $\frac{dt}{dQ} = \frac{1}{aQ}$ the value $Q = 0$ has to

be excluded, since $\frac{1}{a \times 0}$ has no meaning. So if a solution begins at a value $Q_0 > 0$, $Q$

remains positive; and if a solution begins at a value $Q_0 < 0$, $Q$ remains negative. So $\frac{Q}{Q_0}$

is always positive, and you can replace $\left| \frac{Q}{Q_0} \right|$ in the above equation by $\frac{Q}{Q_0}$

It follows that:

> If $\frac{dQ}{dt} = aQ$, where $a$ is a non-zero constant,
>
> and $Q = Q_0$ when $t = 0$, then $Q = Q_0 e^{at}$.

You will meet this differential equation so often that it is worthwhile learning this result. In a particular application, you can then write down the solution without going through the theory each time.

If $e^a$ is written as $b$, then $b > 0$ whether $a$ is positive or negative. The equation $Q = Q_0 e^{at}$ can then be written as $Q = Q_0 \left( e^a \right)^t = Q_0 b^t$, which has the form of the definition of exponential growth given in P2 Section 10.5.

## Exercise 9B

1   Find general solutions of the following differential equations, expressing the dependent variable as a function of the independent variable. Display graphs of a number of typical solutions.

(a) $\frac{dy}{dx} = y^2$     (b) $\frac{dy}{dx} = \tan y$, for $-\frac{1}{2}\pi < y < \frac{1}{2}\pi$     (c) $\frac{dx}{dt} = 4x$

(d) $\frac{dz}{dt} = \frac{1}{z}$, for $z > 0$   (e) $\frac{dx}{dt} = \operatorname{cosec} x$, for $0 < x < \pi$     (f) $u^2 \frac{du}{dx} = a$, for $u > 0$

2   Solve the following differential equations with the given initial conditions, Display graphs to illustrate your answers.

(a)  $\frac{dx}{dt} = -2x$, $x = 3$ when $t = 0$        (b)  $\frac{du}{dt} = u^3$, $u = 1$ when $t = 0$

**3** Find the solution curves of the following differential equations which pass through the given points. Display graphs to illustrate your answer, and suggest any restrictions which should be placed on the values of $x$.

(a)  $\dfrac{dy}{dx} = y + y^2$, through $(0,1)$

(b)  $\dfrac{dy}{dx} = e^y$, through $(2,0)$

**4** A girl lives 500 metres from school. She sets out walking at $2 \text{ m s}^{-1}$, but when she has walked a distance of $x$ metres her speed has dropped to $\left(2 - \frac{1}{400}x\right) \text{ m s}^{-1}$. How long does she take to get to school?

**5** A boy is eating a 250 gram hamburger. When he has eaten a mass $m$ grams, his rate of consumption is $100 - \frac{1}{900}m^2$ grams per minute. How long does he take to finish his meal?

**6** A sculler is rowing a 2 kilometre course. She starts rowing at $5 \text{ m s}^{-1}$, but gradually tires, so that when she has rowed $x$ metres her speed has dropped to $5e^{-0.0001x} \text{ m s}^{-1}$. How long will she take to complete the course?

**7** A tree is planted as a seedling of negligible height. The rate of increase in its height, in metres per year, is given by the formula $0.2\sqrt{25 - h}$, where $h$ is the height of the tree, in metres, $t$ years after it is planted.

(a) Explain why the height of the tree can never exceed 25 metres.

(b) Write down a differential equation connecting $h$ and $t$, and solve it to find an expression for $t$ as a function of $h$.

(c) How long does it take for the tree to put on

   (i)  its first metre of growth,          (ii) its last metre of growth?

(d) Find an expression for the height of the tree after $t$ years. Over what interval of values of $t$ is this model valid?

**8** Astronomers observe a luminous cloud of stellar gas which appears to be expanding. When it is observed a month later, its radius is estimated to be 5 times the original radius. After a further 3 months, the radius appears to be 5 times as large again.

It is thought that the expansion is described by a differential equation of the form $\dfrac{dr}{dt} = cr^m$

where $c$ and $m$ are constants. There is, however, a difference of opinion about the appropriate value to take for $m$. Two hypotheses are proposed, that $m = \frac{1}{3}$ and $m = \frac{1}{2}$.

Investigate which of these models gives the best fit to the observed data.

## Miscellaneous exercise 9

**1** Find the solution of the differential equation $x\dfrac{dy}{dx} = 2x^2 + 7x + 3$ for which $y = 10$ when $x = 1$.

(OCR)

**2** In a chemical reaction, the amount $z$ grams of a substance after $t$ hours is modelled by the differential equation $\dfrac{dz}{dt} = 0.005(20 - z)^2$. Initially $z = 0$. Find an expression for $t$ in terms of $z$, and show that $t = 15$ when $z = 12$.     (OCR)

**3** The gradient of a curve is given by $\dfrac{dy}{dx} = 3x^2 - 8x + 5$. The curve passes through the point $(0, 3)$. Find the equation of the curve. Find the coordinates of the two stationary points. State, with a reason, the nature of each stationary point.     (MEI)

**4** The area of a circle of radius $r$ metres is $A\ \mathrm{m}^2$.

(a) Find $\dfrac{dA}{dr}$ and write down an expression, in terms of $r$, for $\dfrac{dr}{dA}$.

(b) The area increases with time $t$ seconds in such a way that $\dfrac{dA}{dt} = \dfrac{2}{(t+1)^3}$. Find an expression, in terms of $r$ and $t$, for $\dfrac{dr}{dt}$.

(c) Solve the differential equation $\dfrac{dA}{dt} = \dfrac{2}{(t+1)^3}$ to obtain $A$ in terms of $t$, given that $A = 0$ when $t = 0$.

(d) Show that, when $t = 1$, $\dfrac{dr}{dt} = 0.081$ correct to 2 significant figures.     (OCR)

**5** The rate of destruction of a drug by the kidneys is proportional to the amount of drug present in the body. The constant of proportionality is denoted by $k$. At time $t$ the quantity of drug in the body is $x$. Write down a differential equation relating $x$ and $t$, and show that the general solution is $x = Ae^{-kt}$, where $A$ is an arbitrary constant.

Before $t = 0$ there is no drug in the body, but at $t = 0$ a quantity $Q$ of the drug is administered. When $t = 1$ the amount of drug in the body is $Q\alpha$, where $\alpha$ is a constant such that $0 < \alpha < 1$ Show that $x = Q\alpha^t$.

When $t = 1$ and again when $t = 2$ another dose $Q$ is administered. Show that the amount of drug in the body immediately after $t = 2$ is $Q(1 + \alpha + \alpha^2)$.

If the drug is administered at regular intervals for an indefinite period, and if the greatest amount of the drug that the body can tolerate is $T$, show that $Q$ should not exceed $T(1 - \alpha)$.     (OCR, adapted)

**6** (a) The number of people, $x$, in a queue at a travel centre $t$ minutes after it opens is modelled by the differential equation $\dfrac{dx}{dt} = 1.4t - 4$ for values of $t$ up to 10. Interpret the term '$-4$' on the right side of the equation. Solve the differential equation, given that $x = 8$ when $t = 0$.

(b) An alternative model gives the differential equation $\dfrac{dx}{dt} = 1.4t - 0.5x$ for the same values of $t$. Verify that $x = 13.6e^{-0.5t} + 2.8t - 5.6$ satisfies this differential equation. Verify also that when $t = 0$ this function takes the value 8.     (OCR)

**7** At time $t = 0$ there are 8000 fish in a lake. At time $t$ days the birth-rate of fish is equal to one-fiftieth of the number $N$ of fish present. Fish are taken from the lake at the rate of 100 per day. Modelling $N$ as a continuous variable, show that $50\dfrac{dN}{dt} = N - 5000$.

Solve the differential equation to find $N$ in terms of $t$. Find the time taken for the population of fish in the lake to increase to $11\,000$.

When the population of fish has reached $11\,000$, it is decided to increase the number of fish taken from the lake from 100 per day to $F$ per day. Write down, in terms of $F$, the new differential equation satisfied by $N$. Show that if $F > 220$, then $\dfrac{dN}{dt} < 0$ when $N = 11\,000$. For this range of values of $F$, give a reason why the population of fish in the lake continues to decrease. (OCR)

**8** A metal rod is 60 cm long and is heated at one end. The temperature at a point on the rod at distance $x$ cm from the heated end is denoted by $T$ °C. At a point halfway along the rod, $T = 290$ and $\dfrac{dT}{dx} = -6$.

(a) In a simple model for the temperature of the rod, it is assumed that $\dfrac{dT}{dx}$ has the same value at all points on the rod. For this model, express $T$ in terms of $x$ and hence determine the temperature difference between the ends of the rod.

(b) In a more refined model, the rate of change of $T$ with respect to $x$ is taken to be proportional to $x$. Set up a differential equation for $T$, involving a constant of proportionality $k$. Solve the differential equation and hence show that, in this refined model, the temperature along the rod is predicted to vary from 380 °C to 20 °C. (OCR)

**9** A battery is being charged. The charging rate is modelled by $\dfrac{dq}{dt} = k(Q - q)$, where $q$ is the charge in the battery (measured in ampere–hours) at time $t$ (measured in hours), $Q$ is the maximum charge the battery can store and $k$ is a constant of proportionality. The model is valid for $q \geqslant 0.4Q$.

(a) It is given that $q = \lambda Q$ when $t = 0$, where $\lambda$ is a constant such that $0.4 \leqslant \lambda < 1$. Solve the differential equation to find $q$ in terms of $t$. Sketch the graph of the solution.

(b) It is noticed that the charging rate halves every 40 minutes. Show that $k = \frac{3}{2}\ln 2$.

(c) Charging is always stopped when $q = 0.95Q$. If $T$ is the time until charging is stopped, show that $T = \dfrac{2\ln(20(1 - \lambda))}{3\ln 2}$ for $0.4 \leqslant \lambda \leqslant 0.95$. (MEI)

**10** The rate at which the water level in a cylindrical barrel goes down is modelled by the equation $\dfrac{dh}{dt} = -\sqrt{h}$, where $h$ is the height in metres of the level above the tap and $t$ is the time in minutes. When $t = 0$, $h = 1$. Show by integration that $h = \left(1 - \tfrac{1}{2}t\right)^2$. How long does it take for the water flow to stop?

An alternative model would be to use a sine function, such as $h = 1 - \sin kt$. Find the value of $k$ which gives the same time before the water flow stops as the previous model. Show that this model satisfies the differential equation $\dfrac{dh}{dt} = -k\sqrt{2h - h^2}$.              (OCR, adapted)

**11** A tropical island is being set up as a nature reserve. Initially there are 100 nesting pairs of fancy terns on the island. In the first year this increases by 8. In one theory being tested, the number $N$ of nesting pairs after $t$ years is assumed to satisfy the differential equation $\dfrac{dN}{dt} = \tfrac{1}{5000} N(500 - N)$.

   (a) Show that, according to this model, the rate of increase of $N$ is 8 per year when $N = 100$. Find the rate of increase when $N = 300$ and when $N = 450$. Describe what happens as $N$ approaches 500, and interpret your answer.

   (b) Use your answers to part (a) to sketch the solution curve of the differential equation for which $N = 100$ when $t = 0$.

   (c) Obtain the general solution of the differential equation, and the solution for which $N = 100$ when $t = 0$. Use your answer to predict after how many years the number of pairs of nesting fancy terns on the island will first exceed 300.              (OCR)

**12** A biologist is researching the population of a species. She tries a number of different models for the rate of growth of the population and solves them to compare with observed data. Her first model is $\dfrac{dp}{dt} = kp\left(1 - \dfrac{p}{m}\right)$ where $p$ is the population at time $t$ years, $k$ is a constant and $m$ is the maximum population sustainable by the environment. Find the general solution of the differential equation.

Her observations suggest that $k = 0.2$ and $m = 100\,000$. If the initial population is $30\,000$, estimate the population after 5 years to 2 significant figures.

She decides that the model needs to be refined. She proposes a model $\dfrac{dp}{dt} = kp\left(1 - \left(\dfrac{p}{m}\right)^\alpha\right)$ and investigates suitable values of $\alpha$. Her observations lead her to the conclusion that the maximum growth rate occurs when the population is 70% of its maximum. Show that $(\alpha + 1)0.7^\alpha = 1$, and that an approximate solution of this equation is $\alpha \approx 5$. Express the time that it will take the population to reach $54\,000$ according to this model as a definite integral, and use the trapezium rule to find this time approximately.

              (MEI, adapted)

# 10 Integration by substitution

This chapter is about a method of integration which is derived from the chain rule for differentiation. When you have completed it, you should

- understand and be able to find integrals using both direct and reverse substitution
- be able to find new limits of integration when a definite integral is evaluated by substitution
- recognise the form $\int \dfrac{f'(x)}{f(x)}\, dx$, and be able to write down the integral at sight.

## 10.1 Direct substitution

None of the methods of integration described so far could be used to find

$$\int \frac{1}{x + \sqrt{x}}\, dx .$$

However, by changing the variable $x$ to a new variable, integrals like this can be put into a form which you know how to integrate.

Denote the integral by $I$, so that

$$\frac{dI}{dx} = \frac{1}{x + \sqrt{x}} .$$

The difficulty in solving this differential equation lies in the square root, so write $x = u^2$. Then, by the chain rule,

$$\frac{dI}{du} = \frac{dI}{dx} \times \frac{dx}{du} = \frac{1}{u^2 + u} \times 2u = \frac{2}{u + 1} .$$

This is a differential equation for $I$ in terms of $u$, with solution

$$I = 2 \ln \left| u + 1 \right| + k .$$

The solution to the original equation is then found by replacing $u$ by $\sqrt{x}$, so that

$$I = 2 \ln \left( \sqrt{x} + 1 \right) + k .$$

(You do not need the modulus sign, since $\sqrt{x} + 1$ is always positive.)

You can easily check by differentiation that this integral is correct.

This method is called **integration by substitution**. It is the equivalent for integrals of the chain rule for differentiation.

In general, to find $I = \int f(x)\,dx$, the equation $\dfrac{dI}{dx} = f(x)$ is changed by writing $x$ as some function $s(u)$. Then $\dfrac{dI}{du} = f(x) \times \dfrac{dx}{du} = g(u) \times \dfrac{dx}{du}$, where $g(u) = f(s(u))$. If you can find $\int g(u) \times \dfrac{dx}{du}\,du$, then you can find the original integral by replacing $u$ by $u = s^{-1}(x)$.

So, if $x = s(u)$ and $g(u) = f(s(u))$, then $\int f(x)\,dx$ is equal to

$\int g(u) \times \dfrac{dx}{du}\,du$, with $u$ replaced by $s^{-1}(x)$.

Do not try to remember this as a formal statement; what is important is to learn how to use the method. Notice how the notation helps; although the $dx$ and $du$ in the integrals have no meaning in themselves, the replacement of $dx$ in the first integral by $\dfrac{dx}{du}\,du$ in the second makes the method easy to apply.

## Example 10.1.1

Find $\displaystyle\int \frac{1}{x} \ln x\,dx$.

The difficulty lies in the logarithm factor, so remove it by writing $x = e^u$. Then $\dfrac{dx}{du} = e^u$, and the integral becomes

$$\int \frac{1}{e^u} \ln(e^u) \times e^u\,du = \int u\,du = \tfrac{1}{2}u^2 + k.$$

Replacing $u$ in this expression by $\ln x$, the original integral is

$$\int \frac{1}{x} \ln x\,dx = \tfrac{1}{2}(\ln x)^2 + k.$$

## Example 10.1.2

Find $\displaystyle\int \frac{6x}{\sqrt{2x+1}}\,dx$.

The awkward bit of the integral is the expression $\sqrt{2x+1}$. If $2x+1$ could be written as $u^2$, then $\sqrt{2x+1}$ would equal $u$. So write $2x+1 = u^2$, which is equivalent to $x = \tfrac{1}{2}u^2 - \tfrac{1}{2}$. This gives $\dfrac{dx}{du} = \tfrac{1}{2}(2u) = u$. So $\displaystyle\int \frac{6x}{\sqrt{2x+1}}\,dx$ becomes

$$\int \frac{6\left(\tfrac{1}{2}u^2 - \tfrac{1}{2}\right)}{u} \times u\,du = \int \left(3u^2 - 3\right)du = u^3 - 3u + k.$$

You want this in terms of $x$, so substituting $\sqrt{2x+1}$ for $u$ gives

$$\int \frac{6x}{\sqrt{2x+1}}\,dx = \left(\sqrt{2x+1}\right)^3 - 3\sqrt{2x+1} + k.$$

It is quite acceptable to leave the answer in this form, but it would be neater to note that $\left(\sqrt{2x+1}\right)^3 = (2x+1)\sqrt{2x+1}$, so

$$\int \frac{6x}{\sqrt{2x+1}}\,dx = (2x+1)\sqrt{2x+1} - 3\sqrt{2x+1} + k$$

$$= (2x+1-3)\sqrt{2x+1} + k = 2(x-1)\sqrt{2x+1} + k.$$

Since this is quite a complicated piece of algebra, it is worth checking it by using the product rule to differentiate $2(x-1)\sqrt{2x+1}$, and showing that the result is $\dfrac{6x}{\sqrt{2x+1}}$.

*The method used in this example is sometimes described as 'substituting $u = \sqrt{2x+1}$' and sometimes as 'substituting $x = \frac{1}{2}\left(u^2-1\right)$'. In the course of the calculation you use the relation both ways round, so either description is equally appropriate.*

**Example 10.1.3**

Find $\displaystyle\int \sqrt{4-x^2}\,dx$.

You need to find a substitution for $x$ such that $4-x^2$ simplifies to an exact square. A function with this property is $2\sin u$, since

$$x = 2\sin u \quad \Rightarrow \quad 4-x^2 = 4-4\sin^2 u = 4\left(1-\sin^2 u\right) = 4\cos^2 u.$$

Therefore $\sqrt{4-x^2} = 2\cos u$. Also $\dfrac{dx}{du} = 2\cos u$. The integral then becomes

$$\int 2\cos u \times 2\cos u\,du = \int 4\cos^2 u\,du = \int 2(1+\cos 2u)\,du$$

$$= 2u + \sin 2u + k.$$

To get the original integral, note that $\sin u = \frac{1}{2}x$, so that $2u = 2\sin^{-1}\left(\frac{1}{2}x\right)$. But rather than using this form in the second term, it is simpler to expand $\sin 2u$ as $2\sin u\cos u$, which is $x \times \frac{1}{2}\sqrt{4-x^2}$. Therefore

$$\int \sqrt{4-x^2}\,dx = 2\sin^{-1}\left(\frac{1}{2}x\right) + \frac{1}{2}x\sqrt{4-x^2} + k.$$

Notice one further detail. The reference in the general statement (near the top of page 130) to the inverse function $s^{-1}$ should alert you to the need for the substitution function $s$ to be one–one. This is arranged in the usual way, by restricting the domain of $s$.

In the introductory example on page 129, for $x = u^2$ to have an inverse you can restrict $u$ to be non-negative. This justifies writing $\sqrt{x}$ as $u$ (since by definition $\sqrt{x} \geq 0$) when the variable was changed from $x$ to $u$, and then replacing $u$ by $\sqrt{x}$ (rather than $-\sqrt{x}$) at the final stage.

In Example 10.1.3, the domain of $u$ is restricted to the interval $-\frac{1}{2}\pi \leqslant u \leqslant \frac{1}{2}\pi$, so that the substitution function $x = 2\sin u$ has inverse $u = \sin^{-1}\left(\frac{1}{2}x\right)$, with $\sin^{-1}$ defined as in Section 1.7. Over this interval $\cos u \geqslant 0$, which justifies taking $2\cos u$ to be the positive square root of $4 - x^2$.

## Exercise 10A

**1** Use the given substitutions to find the following integrals.

(a) $\displaystyle\int \frac{1}{x - 2\sqrt{x}}\,\mathrm{d}x \quad x = u^2$

(b) $\displaystyle\int \frac{1}{(3x + 4)^2}\,\mathrm{d}x \quad 3x + 4 = u$

(c) $\displaystyle\int \sin\left(\frac{1}{3}\pi - \frac{1}{2}x\right)\mathrm{d}x \quad \frac{1}{3}\pi - \frac{1}{2}x = u$

(d) $\displaystyle\int x(x - 1)^5\,\mathrm{d}x \quad x = 1 + u$

(e) $\displaystyle\int \frac{e^x}{1 + e^x}\,\mathrm{d}x \quad x = \ln u$

(f) $\displaystyle\int \frac{1}{3\sqrt{x} + 4x}\,\mathrm{d}x \quad x = u^2$

(g) $\displaystyle\int 3x\sqrt{x + 2}\,\mathrm{d}x \quad x = u^2 - 2$

(h) $\displaystyle\int \frac{x}{\sqrt{x - 3}}\,\mathrm{d}x \quad x = 3 + u^2$

(i) $\displaystyle\int \frac{1}{x \ln x}\,\mathrm{d}x \quad x = e^u$

(j) $\displaystyle\int \frac{1}{\sqrt{4 - x^2}}\,\mathrm{d}x \quad x = 2\sin u$

**2** Use suitable substitutions to find the following integrals.

(a) $\displaystyle\int x(2x + 1)^3\,\mathrm{d}x$

(b) $\displaystyle\int (x + 2)(2x - 3)^5\,\mathrm{d}x$

(c) $\displaystyle\int x\sqrt{2x - 1}\,\mathrm{d}x$

(d) $\displaystyle\int \frac{x - 2}{\sqrt{x - 4}}\,\mathrm{d}x$

(e) $\displaystyle\int \frac{x}{(x + 1)^2}\,\mathrm{d}x$

(f) $\displaystyle\int \frac{x}{2x + 3}\,\mathrm{d}x$

(g) $\displaystyle\int \frac{1}{\sqrt{1 - 9x^2}}\,\mathrm{d}x$

(h) $\displaystyle\int \sqrt{16 - 9x^2}\,\mathrm{d}x$

(i) $\displaystyle\int \frac{1}{2 + e^{-x}}\,\mathrm{d}x$

(j) $\displaystyle\int \frac{x}{\sqrt[3]{1 + x}}\,\mathrm{d}x$

(k) $\displaystyle\int \left(1 - x^2\right)^{-\frac{3}{2}}\,\mathrm{d}x$

(l) $\displaystyle\int \frac{1}{2 - \sqrt{x}}\,\mathrm{d}x$

**3** (a) Use the substitution $x = \tan u$ to show that $\displaystyle\int \frac{1}{1 + x^2}\,\mathrm{d}x = \tan^{-1} x + k$.

(b) Use the substitution $x = \ln u$ to find $\displaystyle\int \frac{e^x}{1 + e^{2x}}\,\mathrm{d}x$.

**4** For the following integrals, use a substitution to produce an integrand which is a rational function of $u$, then use partial fractions to complete the integration.

(a) $\displaystyle\int \frac{1}{e^x - e^{-x}}\,\mathrm{d}x$

(b) $\displaystyle\int \frac{1}{x\left(\sqrt{x} + 1\right)}\,\mathrm{d}x$

**5** For the following integrals, use a substitution and then use integration by parts to complete the integration.

(a) $\displaystyle\int \cos^{-1} x\,\mathrm{d}x$

(b) $\displaystyle\int \tan^{-1} x\,\mathrm{d}x$

(c) $\displaystyle\int (\ln x)^2\,\mathrm{d}x$

## 10.2 Definite integrals

The most difficult part in Example 10.1.3 was not the integration, but getting the result back from an expression in $u$ to an expression in $x$. If you have a definite integral to find, this last step is not necessary. Instead you can use the substitution equation to change the interval of integration from values of $x$ to values of $u$.

If $x = s(u)$, then $\displaystyle\int_a^b f(x)\,dx = \int_p^q g(u) \times \frac{dx}{du}\,du$, where $g(u) = f(s(u))$, and
$p = s^{-1}(a)$, $q = s^{-1}(b)$.

Once again, it is more important to be able to use the result than to remember it in this form.

**Example 10.2.1**

Find $\displaystyle\int_0^1 \sqrt{4 - x^2}\,dx$.

Two methods are given. One uses integration by substitution; the other uses the fact that $y = \sqrt{4 - x^2}$ is the equation of a semicircle and evaluates the integral by calculating an area.

**Method 1**  Follow Example 10.1.3 as far as the form of the integral in terms of $u$, but note also that the new limits of integration are $\sin^{-1}\left(\frac{1}{2} \times 0\right) = 0$ and $\sin^{-1}\left(\frac{1}{2} \times 1\right) = \frac{1}{6}\pi$. Therefore

$$\int_0^1 \sqrt{4 - x^2}\,dx = \int_0^{\frac{1}{6}\pi} 4\cos^2 u\,du = [2u + \sin 2u]_0^{\frac{1}{6}\pi}$$

$$= \tfrac{1}{3}\pi + \sin\tfrac{1}{3}\pi = \tfrac{1}{3}\pi + \tfrac{1}{2}\sqrt{3}.$$

**Method 2**  If $y = \sqrt{4 - x^2}$, then
$x^2 + y^2 = 4$, which is the equation of a
circle with radius 2 units. The integral
therefore represents the area of the
region under the upper semicircle from
$x = 0$ to $x = 1$, shown shaded in
Fig. 10.1. This region consists of a sector
with angle $\frac{1}{6}\pi$ and a triangle with base 1
unit and height $\sqrt{3}$ units. The value of the integral is therefore

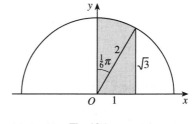

Fig. 10.1

$$\tfrac{1}{2} \times 2^2 \times \left(\tfrac{1}{6}\pi\right) + \tfrac{1}{2} \times 1 \times \sqrt{3} = \tfrac{1}{3}\pi + \tfrac{1}{2}\sqrt{3}.$$

**Example 10.2.2**

Find $\displaystyle\int_0^1 \frac{1}{1+x^2}\,dx$.

The substitution $x = \tan u$ makes $1 + x^2 = 1 + \tan^2 u = \sec^2 u$ (see Section 1.2).

Also $\dfrac{dx}{du} = \sec^2 u$ (see Section 8.3), $\tan^{-1} 0 = 0$ and $\tan^{-1} 1 = \frac{1}{4}\pi$. Therefore

$$\int_0^1 \frac{1}{1+x^2}\,dx = \int_0^{\frac{1}{4}\pi} \frac{1}{\sec^2 u} \times \sec^2 u \, du = \int_0^{\frac{1}{4}\pi} 1\,du = \left[u\right]_0^{\frac{1}{4}\pi} = \frac{1}{4}\pi.$$

## Exercise 10B

**1** Use substitutions to find the following integrals.

(a) $\displaystyle\int_0^1 \frac{e^x}{1+e^x}\,dx$

(b) $\displaystyle\int_9^{16} \frac{1}{x - 2\sqrt{x}}\,dx$

(c) $\displaystyle\int_1^2 x(x-1)^5\,dx$

(d) $\displaystyle\int_1^2 x\sqrt{x-1}\,dx$

(e) $\displaystyle\int_0^1 \frac{1}{\sqrt{4-x^2}}\,dx$

(f) $\displaystyle\int_6^9 \frac{x^2}{\sqrt{x-5}}\,dx$

(g) $\displaystyle\int_{-4}^4 \sqrt{16-x^2}\,dx$

(h) $\displaystyle\int_1^6 \frac{1}{4+x^2}\,dx$

(i) $\displaystyle\int_e^{e^2} \frac{1}{x(\ln x)^2}\,dx$

(j) $\displaystyle\int_0^{\frac{1}{2}} \frac{1}{\left(1-x^2\right)^{\frac{3}{2}}}\,dx$

(k) $\displaystyle\int_1^8 \frac{1}{x\left(1+\sqrt[3]{x}\right)}\,dx$

(l) $\displaystyle\int_0^1 \sin^{-1} x \, dx$

**2** Use the substitution $x = \sin^2 u$ to calculate $\displaystyle\int_0^{\frac{1}{2}} \sqrt{\frac{x}{1-x}}\,dx$.

**3** Use trigonometric substitutions to evaluate the following infinite and improper integrals.

(a) $\displaystyle\int_0^\infty \frac{1}{x^2+4}\,dx$

(b) $\displaystyle\int_0^3 \frac{1}{\sqrt{9-x^2}}\,dx$

(c) $\displaystyle\int_{-\infty}^\infty \frac{1}{9x^2+4}\,dx$

(d) $\displaystyle\int_0^1 \frac{1}{\sqrt{x(1-x)}}\,dx$

(e) $\displaystyle\int_1^\infty \frac{1}{\left(1+x^2\right)^{\frac{3}{2}}}\,dx$

(f) $\displaystyle\int_1^\infty \frac{1}{x\sqrt{x^2-1}}\,dx$

**4** Evaluate the following infinite integrals.

(a) $\displaystyle\int_2^\infty \frac{1}{x(\ln x)^3}\,dx$

(b) $\displaystyle\int_{\ln 2}^\infty \frac{1}{e^x - 1}\,dx$

(c) $\displaystyle\int_1^\infty \frac{1}{x\left(x+\sqrt{x}\right)}\,dx$

(d) $\displaystyle\int_0^\infty x e^{-\frac{1}{2}x^2}\,dx$

**5**  Use a substitution, followed by a change of letter in the integrand, to show that, if $\sigma > 0$,

$$\int_{-\infty}^{\infty} e^{-\frac{x^2}{2\sigma^2}} \, dx = \sigma \int_{-\infty}^{\infty} e^{-\frac{1}{2}x^2} \, dx.$$

**6**  Use the substitution $x = \dfrac{a^2}{u}$, where $a > 0$, to show that

$$\int_0^a \frac{1}{a^2 + x^2} \, dx = \int_a^\infty \frac{1}{a^2 + x^2} \, dx.$$

**7**  Use a substitution to prove that $\displaystyle\int_0^\pi x \sin x \, dx = \int_0^\pi (\pi - x) \sin x \, dx$. Hence show that

$$\int_0^\pi x \sin x \, dx = \tfrac{1}{2} \pi \int_0^\pi \sin x \, dx, \text{ and evaluate this without using integration by parts.}$$

## 10.3 Reverse substitution

If $y = \sqrt{1 + \ln x}$, then the chain rule gives $\dfrac{dy}{dx} = \dfrac{1}{2\sqrt{1 + \ln x}} \times \dfrac{1}{x}$. So, turning this into integral form,

$$\int \frac{1}{\sqrt{1 + \ln x}} \times \frac{1}{x} \, dx = 2\sqrt{1 + \ln x} + k.$$

But how could you find this integral if you didn't know the answer to start with? You can see that the integrand is the product of two factors. The first of these has the form of a composite function of $x$; you could write it as $\dfrac{1}{\sqrt{u}}$, where $u = 1 + \ln x$. The lucky break is that the second factor is the derivative $\dfrac{du}{dx}$. So the integral could be written as

$$\int \frac{1}{\sqrt{u}} \times \frac{du}{dx} \, dx,$$

which can be worked out as

$$\int \frac{1}{\sqrt{u}} \, du = 2\sqrt{u} + k = 2\sqrt{1 + \ln x} + k.$$

This seems to be a different form of integration by substitution, in which you can already see the derivative $\dfrac{du}{dx}$ as part of the integrand. To describe it in general terms, write $\dfrac{1}{\sqrt{1 + \ln x}}$ as $f(x)$, $u = 1 + \ln x$ as $r(x)$ and $\dfrac{1}{\sqrt{u}}$ as $g(u)$, so $f(x) = g(r(x))$ and $\dfrac{du}{dx} = \dfrac{1}{x}$. You then get:

If $u = r(x)$, and if $g(r(x)) = f(x)$, then $\int f(x) \times \dfrac{du}{dx} dx$ is equal to $\int g(u) du$, with $u$ replaced by $r(x)$.

You can check that this statement is in effect the same statement as the one in Section 10.1, with f and g, $x$ and $u$ interchanged, and r written in place of s. But the method of applying it is different, because of the need to begin by identifying the derivative $\dfrac{du}{dx}$ as a factor in the integrand.

As before, it is best not to bother with the general statement, but to learn to use the method by studying some examples.

**Example 10.3.1**

Find $\int x^2 \sqrt{1 + x^3}\, dx$.

Begin by noticing that the derivative of $1 + x^3$ is $3x^2$, so that if the integral is written as

$$\int \tfrac{1}{3} \sqrt{1 + x^3} \times 3x^2\, dx,$$

then it can be changed into the form

$$\int \tfrac{1}{3}\left(1 + x^3\right)^{\frac{1}{2}} \times \dfrac{du}{dx} dx$$

with $u = 1 + x^3$. This is equal to

$$\int \tfrac{1}{3} u^{\frac{1}{2}}\, du = \tfrac{2}{9} u^{\frac{3}{2}} + k,$$

with $u$ replaced by $1 + x^3$. That is,

$$\int x^2 \sqrt{1 + x^3}\, dx = \tfrac{2}{9}\left(1 + x^3\right)^{\frac{3}{2}} + k.$$

**Example 10.3.2**

Find $\displaystyle\int_0^{\frac{1}{2}\pi} \cos^4 x \sin x\, dx$.

If the integrand is written as $-\cos^4 x \times (-\sin x)$, then the second factor is $\dfrac{du}{dx}$ with $u = \cos x$.

$$\int_0^{\frac{1}{2}\pi} \cos^4 x \sin x\, dx = \int_0^{\frac{1}{2}\pi} -\cos^4 x \times \dfrac{du}{dx} dx$$

$$= \int_1^0 -u^4\, du = -\left[\tfrac{1}{5} u^5\right]_1^0 = \tfrac{1}{5}.$$

Notice that the limits of integration change from $0$, $\frac{1}{2}\pi$ to $1$, $0$ at the step where the

integral changes from $\int_0^{\frac{1}{2}\pi} -\cos^4 x \times \frac{du}{dx}\,dx$ to $\int_1^0 -u^4\,du$. Since $\cos x$ is decreasing over

the interval $0 \leqslant x \leqslant \frac{1}{2}\pi$, the limits for $u$ appear in reversed order.

**Example 10.3.3**

Find $\displaystyle\int \frac{\cos x - \sin x}{\sin x + \cos x}\,dx$.

Write this as $\displaystyle\int \frac{1}{\sin x + \cos x} \times (\cos x - \sin x)\,dx$. If $u = \sin x + \cos x$, this is

$\displaystyle\int \frac{1}{\sin x + \cos x} \times \frac{du}{dx}\,dx$, which is $\displaystyle\int \frac{1}{u}\,du = \ln|u| + k$. So

$$\int \frac{\cos x - \sin x}{\sin x + \cos x}\,dx = \ln|\sin x + \cos x| + k.$$

In this last example the integral has the form $\displaystyle\int \frac{f'(x)}{f(x)}\,dx$, where $f(x) = \sin x + \cos x$. This

is a type of integral which arises frequently, and the result is important:

$$\int \frac{f'(x)}{f(x)}\,dx = \ln|f(x)| + k.$$

**Example 10.3.4**

Find $\displaystyle\int_0^1 \frac{e^x - e^{-x}}{e^x + e^{-x}}\,dx$.

The integrand is $\dfrac{f'(x)}{f(x)}$ with $f(x) = e^x + e^{-x}$, so the value of the integral is

$$\left[\ln\left|e^x + e^{-x}\right|\right]_0^1 = \ln\left(e + \frac{1}{e}\right) - \ln 2 = \ln\left(\frac{e^2 + 1}{2e}\right).$$

## Exercise 10C

1   Use the given substitutions to find the following integrals.

(a) $\displaystyle\int 2x\left(x^2 + 1\right)^3 dx$     $u = x^2 + 1$     (b) $\displaystyle\int x\sqrt{4 + x^2}\,dx$     $u = 4 + x^2$

(c) $\displaystyle\int \sin^5 x \cos x\,dx$     $u = \sin x$     (d) $\displaystyle\int \tan^3 x \sec^2 x\,dx$     $u = \tan x$

(e) $\displaystyle\int \frac{2x^3}{\sqrt{1 - x^4}}\,dx$     $u = 1 - x^4$     (f) $\displaystyle\int \cos^3 2x \sin 2x\,dx$     $u = \cos 2x$

**2** Find the following integrals.

(a) $\displaystyle\int x\left(1-x^2\right)^5 dx$

(b) $\displaystyle\int x\sqrt{3-2x^2}\, dx$

(c) $\displaystyle\int x^2\left(5-3x^3\right)^6 dx$

(d) $\displaystyle\int \frac{x^2}{\sqrt{1+x^3}}\, dx$

(e) $\displaystyle\int \sec^4 x \tan x\, dx$

(f) $\displaystyle\int \sin^3 4x \cos 4x\, dx$

**3** Without carrying out a substitution, write down the following indefinite integrals.

(a) $\displaystyle\int \frac{\cos x}{1+\sin x}\, dx$

(b) $\displaystyle\int \frac{x^2}{1+x^3}\, dx$

(c) $\displaystyle\int \cot x\, dx$

(d) $\displaystyle\int \frac{e^x}{4+e^x}\, dx$

(e) $\displaystyle\int \frac{2e^{3x}}{5-e^{3x}}\, dx$

(f) $\displaystyle\int \tan 3x\, dx$

**4** Evaluate each of the following integrals, giving your answer in an exact form.

(a) $\displaystyle\int_0^{\frac{1}{2}\pi} \frac{\cos x}{\sqrt{1+3\sin x}}\, dx$

(b) $\displaystyle\int_0^2 x\left(x^2+1\right)^3 dx$

(c) $\displaystyle\int_0^{\frac{1}{4}\pi} \sin x \cos^2 x\, dx$

(d) $\displaystyle\int_1^2 \frac{e^x}{e^x-1}\, dx$

(e) $\displaystyle\int_1^8 (1+2x)\sqrt{x+x^2}\, dx$

(f) $\displaystyle\int_0^{\frac{1}{3}\pi} \frac{\sin x}{(1+\cos x)^2}\, dx$

(g) $\displaystyle\int_0^3 2x\sqrt{1+x^2}\, dx$

(h) $\displaystyle\int_4^5 \frac{x-2}{x^2-4x+5}\, dx$

(i) $\displaystyle\int_0^{\frac{1}{6}\pi} \frac{\sin 2x}{1+\cos 2x}\, dx$

(j) $\displaystyle\int_0^{\frac{1}{4}\pi} \sec^2 x \tan^2 x\, dx$

(k) $\displaystyle\int_1^e \frac{(\ln x)^n}{x}\, dx$

(l) $\displaystyle\int_0^{\frac{1}{3}\pi} \sec^3 x \tan x\, dx$

**5** Find an expression, in terms of $n$ and $a$, for $\displaystyle\int_0^a \frac{x}{\left(1+x^2\right)^n}\, dx$. For what values of $n$ does

$\displaystyle\int_0^\infty \frac{x}{\left(1+x^2\right)^n}\, dx$ exist? State its value in terms of $n$.

## Miscellaneous exercise 10

**1** By using the substitution $u = 2x-1$, or otherwise, find $\displaystyle\int \frac{2x}{(2x-1)^2}\, dx$.                    (OCR)

**2** Find $\displaystyle\int \frac{1}{4x^2+9}\, dx$.                    (OCR)

**3** By using a suitable substitution, or otherwise, evaluate $\displaystyle\int_0^1 x(1-x)^9\, dx$.                    (OCR)

**4**  Find $\displaystyle\int \frac{1}{e^x + 4e^{-x}}\,dx$, by means of the substitution $u = e^x$, followed by another substitution, or otherwise. (OCR, adapted)

**5**  Find $\displaystyle\int \frac{6x}{1+3x^2}\,dx$. (OCR)

**6**  Calculate the exact value of $\displaystyle\int_0^3 \frac{x}{1+x^2}\,dx$. (OCR)

**7**  By using the substitution $u = \sin x$, or otherwise, find $\displaystyle\int \sin^3 x \sin 2x\,dx$, giving your answer in terms of $x$. (OCR)

**8**  By means of the substitution $u = 1 + \sqrt{x}$, or otherwise, find $\displaystyle\int \frac{1}{1+\sqrt{x}}\,dx$, giving your answer in terms of $x$. (OCR)

**9**  Use the substitution $u = \ln x$ to show that $\displaystyle\int_e^{e^2} \frac{1}{x\sqrt{\ln x}}\,dx = 2\sqrt{2} - 2$. (OCR)

**10**  Use the substitution $u = 4 + x^2$ to show that $\displaystyle\int_0^1 \frac{x^3}{\sqrt{4+x^2}}\,dx = \tfrac{1}{3}\left(16 - 7\sqrt{5}\right)$. (OCR)

**11**  Use the substitution $u = 3x - 1$ to express $\displaystyle\int x(3x-1)^4\,dx$ as an integral in terms of $u$.

Hence, or otherwise, find $\displaystyle\int x(3x-1)^4\,dx$, giving your answer in terms of $x$. (OCR)

**12**  Show, by means of the substitution $x = \tan\theta$, that $\displaystyle\int_0^1 \frac{1}{\left(x^2+1\right)^2}\,dx = \int_0^{\frac{1}{4}\pi} \cos^2\theta\,d\theta$.

Hence find the exact value of $\displaystyle\int_0^1 \frac{1}{\left(x^2+1\right)^2}\,dx$.

**13**  By using the substitution $u = 3x + 1$, or otherwise, show that

$$\int_0^1 \frac{x}{(3x+1)^2}\,dx = \tfrac{2}{9}\ln 2 - \tfrac{1}{12}.$$

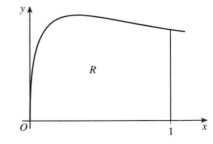

The diagram shows the finite region $R$ in the first quadrant which is bounded by the curve $y = \dfrac{6\sqrt{x}}{3x+1}$, the $x$-axis and the line

$x = 1$. Find the volume of the solid formed when $R$ is rotated completely about the $x$-axis, giving your answer in terms of $\pi$ and $\ln 2$. (OCR)

**14** The diagram (not to scale) shows the
region $R$ bounded by the axes, the curve
$y = \left(x^2 + 1\right)^{-\frac{3}{2}}$ and the line $x = 1$. The
integral

$$\int_0^1 \left(x^2 + 1\right)^{-\frac{3}{2}} \mathrm{d}x$$

is denoted by $I$.

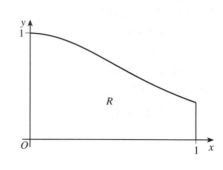

(a) Use the trapezium rule, with ordinates
at $x = 0$, $x = \frac{1}{2}$ and $x = 1$, to estimate
the value of $I$, giving your answer
correct to 2 significant figures.

(b) Use the substitution $x = \tan\theta$ to show that $I = \frac{1}{2}\sqrt{2}$.

(c) By using the trapezium rule, with the same ordinates as in part (a), or otherwise,
estimate the volume of the solid formed when $R$ is rotated completely about the
$x$-axis, giving your answer correct to 3 significant figures.

(d) Find the exact value of the volume in part (c), and compare your answers to
parts (c) and (d).                                                      (OCR, adapted)

**15** Use the trapezium rule with subdivisions at $x = 3$ and $x = 5$ to obtain an approximation to
$$\int_1^7 \frac{x^3}{1 + x^4}\, \mathrm{d}x,$$ giving your answer correct to three places of decimals.

By evaluating the integral exactly, show that the error in the approximation is about 4.1%.

**16** It is given that $\mathrm{f}(x) = \dfrac{1}{\sqrt{1 + \sqrt{x}}}$ and the
integral $\displaystyle\int_0^1 \mathrm{f}(x)\,\mathrm{d}x$ is denoted by $I$.

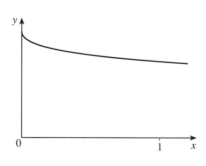

(a) Using the trapezium rule, with four
trapezia of equal width, obtain an
approximation $I_1$ to the value of $I$,
giving three decimal places in your
answer.

(b) A sketch of the graph of $y = \mathrm{f}(x)$ is
given in the diagram. Use this diagram
to justify the inequality $I < I_1$.

(c) Evaluate $I_2$ where $I_2 = \frac{1}{3}\sum_{r=1}^{3} \mathrm{f}\left(\frac{1}{3}r\right)$, giving three decimal places in your answer,
and use the diagram to justify the inequality $I > I_2$.

(d) By means of the substitution $\sqrt{x} = u - 1$, show that the exact value of $I$ is
$\frac{4}{3}\left(2 - \sqrt{2}\right)$.                                      (OCR)

**17\*** The figure shows part of a *cycloid*, given by the parametric equations

$$x = a(t - \sin t), \quad y = a(1 - \cos t)$$

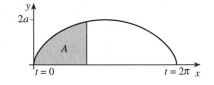

for $0 \leqslant t \leqslant 2\pi$. Show that, if $A$ denotes the region between the cycloid and the $x$-axis as far as the value of $x$ with parameter $t$, then

$\dfrac{\mathrm{d}A}{\mathrm{d}t} = y\dfrac{\mathrm{d}x}{\mathrm{d}t}$. Deduce that the total area of the region enclosed between this arch of the

cycloid and the $x$-axis is $\displaystyle\int_0^{2\pi} y\frac{\mathrm{d}x}{\mathrm{d}t}\,\mathrm{d}t$. Calculate this area in terms of $a$.

Use a similar method to find the volume of the solid of revolution formed when this region is rotated about the $x$-axis.

**18\*** The figure shows part of a *tractrix*, given by parametric equations

$$x = c\ln(\sec t + \tan t) - c\sin t, \quad y = c\cos t$$

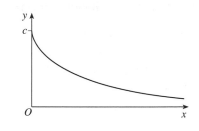

for $0 \leqslant t < \frac{1}{2}\pi$. Find the area of the region between the tractrix and the positive $x$-axis, and the volume of the solid of revolution formed when this region is rotated about the $x$-axis.

**19\*** Show that the area enclosed by the astroid in Example 4.4.2 is given by the integral

$\displaystyle\int_0^{\frac{1}{2}\pi} 12a^2 \sin^4 t \cos^2 t\,\mathrm{d}t$. Use the substitution $t = \frac{1}{2}\pi - u$ to show that the area could also

be calculated as $\displaystyle\int_0^{\frac{1}{2}\pi} 12a^2 \cos^4 t \sin^2 t\,\mathrm{d}t$.

Prove that $\sin^4 t \cos^2 t + \cos^4 t \sin^2 t = \frac{1}{8}(1 - \cos 4t)$, and deduce that the area enclosed by

the astroid is equal to $a^2 \displaystyle\int_0^{\frac{1}{2}\pi} \frac{3}{4}(1 - \cos 4t)\,\mathrm{d}t$. Evaluate this integral.

**20** Let $I = \displaystyle\int_0^{\frac{1}{2}\pi} \sin^2 x\,\mathrm{d}x$ and $J = \displaystyle\int_0^{\frac{1}{2}\pi} \cos^2 x\,\mathrm{d}x$.

(a) Use the substitution $x = \frac{1}{2}\pi - u$ to deduce that $I = J$.

(b) Find the value of $I + J$.

(c) Deduce that $I = J = \frac{1}{4}\pi$.

# 11 Curves defined implicitly

This chapter shows how to find gradients of curves which are described by implicit equations. When you have completed it, you should

- understand the nature of implicit equations, and be able to differentiate them
- be able to integrate differential equations with separable variables.

## 11.1 Equations of curves

In this course you have used coordinates and graphs in two ways: for understanding functions, and for obtaining geometrical results.

The graph of a function provides a visual representation of an equation $y = f(x)$. The variables $x$ and $y$ play different roles: for each $x$ there is a unique $y$, but the reverse need not be true. The graph shows properties of the function such as whether it is increasing or decreasing, and where it has its maximum value. It is usually unnecessary to have equal scales in the $x$- and $y$-directions. Indeed, in applications, the two variables may represent quite different kinds of quantity, measured in different units.

When you use coordinates in geometry, the $x$- and $y$-coordinates have equal status. You must use the same scales in both directions, otherwise circles will not look circular and perpendicular lines will not appear perpendicular. Equations are often written not as $y = f(x)$, but in forms such as $ax + by + c = 0$ or $x^2 + y^2 + 2gx + 2fy + c = 0$, which emphasise that $x$ and $y$ are equal partners. These are **implicit equations** which define the relation between $x$ and $y$.

Sometimes you can put such equations into the $y = f(x)$ form: for example, you can write $3x - 2y + 6 = 0$ as $y = \frac{3}{2}x + 3$.

However, the circle $(x - 2)^2 + (y - 3)^2 = 16$ has two values of $y$ for each $x$ between $-2$ and $6$, given by $y = 3 \pm \sqrt{16 - (x - 2)^2}$. So the equation of the circle cannot be written as an equation of the form $y = f(x)$.

Similarly, the curve in Fig. 11.1, whose equation is

$$x^3 + y^3 + x^2 - y = 0,$$

cannot be put into either of the forms $y = f(x)$ or $x = f(y)$. If you take a particular value for $x$, it gives a cubic equation for $y$, and if you take a particular value for $y$, it gives a cubic equation for $x$. For some values of $y$ there are three values of $x$, and for some values of $x$ there are three values of $y$, so the equation cannot be expressed in function form, as $y = f(x)$ or as $x = f(y)$.

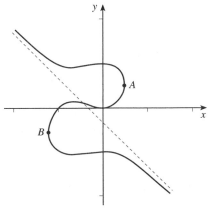

Fig. 11.1

You can easily find a few features of the curve from the equation:

- The equation is satisfied by $x = 0$, $y = 0$, so the curve contains the origin.
- The curve cuts the $x$-axis, $y = 0$, where $x^3 + x^2 = 0$ so $x = 0$ or $-1$.
- The curve cuts the $y$-axis, $x = 0$, where $y^3 - y = 0$ so $y = -1$, 0 or 1.

## 11.2 Finding gradients from implicit equations

When differentiation was first introduced in P1, the method used was to take two points $P$ and $Q$ close together on the graph of $y = f(x)$, and to find the gradient of the chord joining them. Denoting their coordinates by $(x, y)$ and $(x + \delta x, y + \delta y)$, you can write $y = f(x)$ and $y + \delta y = f(x + \delta x)$, so the gradient is

$$\frac{\delta y}{\delta x} = \frac{f(x + \delta x) - f(x)}{\delta x}.$$

Then, letting $Q$ move round the curve towards $P$, you get the limiting value

$$\frac{dy}{dx} = \lim_{\delta x \to 0} \frac{\delta y}{\delta x} = \lim_{\delta x \to 0} \frac{f(x + \delta x) - f(x)}{\delta x}.$$

If you want to find $\dfrac{dy}{dx}$ for a curve like the one in Section 11.1, the same principles apply, but the algebra is different because you don't have an equation in the form $y = f(x)$. The coordinates therefore have to be substituted into the implicit equation, giving (for this example) the two equations

$$x^3 + y^3 + x^2 - y = 0, \qquad\qquad \text{Equation P}$$

and     $(x + \delta x)^3 + (y + \delta y)^3 + (x + \delta x)^2 - (y + \delta y) = 0.$     Equation Q

Using the binomial theorem, the terms of Equation Q can be expanded to give

$$\left( x^3 + 3x^2(\delta x) + 3x(\delta x)^2 + (\delta x)^3 \right) + \left( y^3 + 3y^2(\delta y) + 3y(\delta y)^2 + (\delta y)^3 \right)$$
$$+ \left( x^2 + 2x(\delta x) + (\delta x)^2 \right) - (y + \delta y) = 0.$$

To make this look less complicated, rearrange the terms according to the degree to which $\delta x$ and $\delta y$ appear, as

$$\overbrace{\left( x^3 + y^3 + x^2 - y \right)}^{\text{degree 0}} + \overbrace{\left( 3x^2(\delta x) + 3y^2(\delta y) + 2x(\delta x) - \delta y \right)}^{\text{degree 1}}$$
$$+ \underbrace{\left( 3x(\delta x)^2 + 3y(\delta y)^2 + (\delta x)^2 \right)}_{\text{degree 2}} + \underbrace{\left( (\delta x)^3 + (\delta y)^3 \right)}_{\text{degree 3}} = 0.$$

The first group of terms is just the left side of Equation P, so it is zero. Since you want to find the gradient of the chord, $\dfrac{\delta y}{\delta x}$, rewrite the other groups to show this fraction:

$$(0) + \left(3x^2 + 3y^2 \frac{\delta y}{\delta x} + 2x - \frac{\delta y}{\delta x}\right)\delta x + \left(3x + 3y\left(\frac{\delta y}{\delta x}\right)^2 + 1\right)(\delta x)^2 + \left(1 + \left(\frac{\delta y}{\delta x}\right)^3\right)(\delta x)^3 = 0.$$

There is now a common factor $\delta x$ (which is non-zero), so divide by it to get

$$\left(3x^2 + 3y^2 \frac{\delta y}{\delta x} + 2x - \frac{\delta y}{\delta x}\right) + \left(3x + 3y\left(\frac{\delta y}{\delta x}\right)^2 + 1\right)\delta x + \left(1 + \left(\frac{\delta y}{\delta x}\right)^3\right)(\delta x)^2 = 0.$$

There is one last step, to see what happens as $Q$ approaches $P$, when $\delta x$ tends to $0$. Then $\dfrac{\delta y}{\delta x}$ becomes $\dfrac{dy}{dx}$, so the equation becomes

$$\left(3x^2 + 3y^2 \frac{dy}{dx} + 2x - \frac{dy}{dx}\right) + \left(3x + 3y\left(\frac{dy}{dx}\right)^2 + 1\right) \times 0 + \left(1 + \left(\frac{dy}{dx}\right)^3\right) \times 0^2 = 0,$$

which is simply $3x^2 + 3y^2 \dfrac{dy}{dx} + 2x - \dfrac{dy}{dx} = 0.$

Now compare this with the original equation, Equation P. You can see that each term has been replaced by its derivative with respect to $x$. Thus $x^3$ has become $3x^2$, $x^2$ has become $2x$ and $y$ has become $\dfrac{dy}{dx}$. The only term which calls for comment is the second, which is an application of the chain rule:

$$\frac{d}{dx}\left(y^3\right) = \frac{d}{dy}\left(y^3\right) \times \frac{dy}{dx} = 3y^2 \frac{dy}{dx}.$$

This is an example of a general rule:

> To find $\dfrac{dy}{dx}$ from an implicit equation, differentiate each term with respect to $x$, using the chain rule to differentiate any function $f(y)$ as $f'(y)\dfrac{dy}{dx}$.

For the curve in Fig. 11.1, you can find the gradient by rearranging the differentiated equation as $\left(3x^2 + 2x\right) = \left(1 - 3y^2\right)\dfrac{dy}{dx}$, so

$$\frac{dy}{dx} = \frac{3x^2 + 2x}{1 - 3y^2}.$$

It is interesting to notice that $\dfrac{dy}{dx} = 0$ when $x = 0$ or $x = -\frac{2}{3}$. Fig. 11.1 shows that each of these values of $x$ corresponds to three points on the curve: $x = 0$ at $(0,1)$, $(0,0)$ and $(0,-1)$, and $x = -\frac{2}{3}$ where $y^3 - y = -\frac{4}{27}$. This is a cubic equation whose roots can be found by numerical methods of the kind described in P2 Chapter 14; they are $0.92$, $0.15$ and $-1.07$, correct to 2 decimal places.

Since when using equations in implicit form the $x$- and $y$-coordinates are regarded equally, you might also want to find $\dfrac{dx}{dy}$, which is $1\Big/\dfrac{dy}{dx}$:

$$\frac{dx}{dy} = \frac{1-3y^2}{3x^2+2x}.$$

The tangent to the curve is parallel to the $y$-axis when $\dfrac{dx}{dy} = 0$, which is when $y = \dfrac{1}{\sqrt{3}}$ or $-\dfrac{1}{\sqrt{3}}$. These points are labelled $A$ and $B$ in Fig. 11.1.

If you imagine the curve split into three pieces by making cuts at $A$ and $B$, then each of these pieces defines $y$ as a function of $x$ (since for each $x$ there is a unique $y$). On each piece $\dfrac{dy}{dx}$ can then be defined as the limit of $\dfrac{\delta y}{\delta x}$ in the usual way. If the curve is then stitched up again, you have a definition of $\dfrac{dy}{dx}$ at every point of the curve except at $A$ and $B$, which are the points where the gradient of the tangent is not defined.

This makes it possible to justify the rule in the shaded box. Although the algebraic expression for $y$ in terms of $x$ is not known, the implicit equation defines $y$ in terms of $x$ on each piece of the curve; and when this $y$ is substituted, the equation becomes an identity which is true for all relevant values of $x$. Any identity in $x$ can be differentiated to give another identity. This produces an equation in which each term is differentiated with respect to $x$, as described by the rule.

**Example 11.2.1**
Show that $(1,2)$ is on the circle $x^2 + y^2 - 6x + 2y - 3 = 0$, and find the gradient there.

Substituting $x = 1$, $y = 2$ in the left side of the equation gives $1 + 4 - 6 + 4 - 3$, which is equal to $0$.

**Method 1**    Differentiating term by term with respect to $x$,

$$2x + 2y\frac{dy}{dx} - 6 + 2\frac{dy}{dx} - 0 = 0, \quad \text{that is,} \quad x + y\frac{dy}{dx} - 3 + \frac{dy}{dx} = 0.$$

Setting $x = 1$, $y = 2$ gives $1 + 2\dfrac{dy}{dx} - 3 + \dfrac{dy}{dx} = 0$, so $\dfrac{dy}{dx} = \dfrac{2}{3}$ at this point.

**Method 2**    The centre of the circle is $(3,-1)$, so the gradient of the radius to $(1,2)$ is $\dfrac{2-(-1)}{1-3} = -\dfrac{3}{2}$.

The gradient of the tangent at $(1,2)$ is therefore $-\dfrac{1}{-\frac{3}{2}} = \dfrac{2}{3}$.

**Example 11.2.2**

Find an expression for $\dfrac{dy}{dx}$ on the curve $3x^2 - 2y^3 = 1$.

**Method 1**    Differentiating term by term,

$$6x - 6y^2 \frac{dy}{dx} = 0, \text{ so that } \frac{dy}{dx} = \frac{x}{y^2}.$$

**Method 2**    This equation can be written explicitly as $y = \left(\frac{3}{2}x^2 - \frac{1}{2}\right)^{\frac{1}{3}}$,

and by the chain rule $\dfrac{dy}{dx} = \frac{1}{3}\left(\frac{3}{2}x^2 - \frac{1}{2}\right)^{-\frac{2}{3}} \times 3x = x\left(y^3\right)^{-\frac{2}{3}} = \dfrac{x}{y^2}.$

**Example 11.2.3**

Sketch the graph of $\cos x + \cos y = \frac{1}{2}$, and find the equation of the tangent at the point $\left(\frac{1}{2}\pi, \frac{1}{3}\pi\right)$.

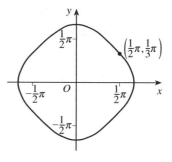

Fig. 11.2 shows the part of the graph for which the values of both of $x$ and $y$ are between $-\pi$ and $\pi$. Since $\cos y \leqslant 1$, $\cos x \geqslant -\frac{1}{2}$, so $-\frac{2}{3}\pi \leqslant x \leqslant \frac{2}{3}\pi$. Similarly $-\frac{2}{3}\pi \leqslant y \leqslant \frac{2}{3}\pi$.

Because $\cos$ is an even function, the graph is symmetrical about both axes; and because the equation is unaltered by interchanging $x$ and $y$, the graph is also symmetrical about $y = x$, and hence about $y = -x$. Also, because the function $\cos$ has period $2\pi$, this shape is repeated over the whole plane at intervals of $2\pi$ in both directions.

Fig. 11.2

Differentiating,

$$-\sin x + \left(-\sin y\right)\frac{dy}{dx} = 0, \quad \text{so} \quad \frac{dy}{dx} = -\frac{\sin x}{\sin y}.$$

At $\left(\frac{1}{2}\pi, \frac{1}{3}\pi\right)$ the gradient is $-\dfrac{1}{\frac{1}{2}\sqrt{3}} = -\dfrac{2}{\sqrt{3}}$, so the equation of the tangent is

$$y - \frac{1}{3}\pi = -\frac{2}{\sqrt{3}}\left(x - \frac{1}{2}\pi\right), \quad \text{or} \quad y + \frac{2}{\sqrt{3}}x = \frac{1}{3}\pi\left(1 + \sqrt{3}\right).$$

## Exercise 11A

1   Each of the following equations represents a circle. Find the gradient of the tangent at the given point (i) by finding the coordinates of the centre as in Method 2 of Example 11.2.1, and (ii) by differentiating the implicit equations.

(a)   $x^2 + y^2 = 25$              $(-3, 4)$              (b)   $x^2 + y^2 + 4x - 6y = 24$    $(4, 2)$

(c)   $x^2 + y^2 - 6x + 8y = 0$    $(6, -8)$              (d)   $x^2 + y^2 - 2x - 4y = 0$    $(0, 0)$

2  Consider the curve with equation $x^2 + 4y^2 = 1$.

   (a)  Find the coordinates of the points where the curve cuts the coordinate axes.

   (b)  Show that the curve is symmetrical about both the $x$- and $y$-axes.

   (c)  Show that the equation of the curve can be written in the form $y = \pm \frac{1}{2}\sqrt{1 - x^2}$ and use the binomial expansion to get approximations for $y$ up to and including the terms in $x^2$.

   (d)  Use your approximations to draw the shape of the curve for small values of $x$ near the points where the curve crosses the $y$-axis.

   (e)  Repeat parts (c) and (d) with the roles of $x$ and $y$ reversed.

   (f)  Join up the pieces and make a sketch of the curve.

3  Repeat Question 2, using the curve with equation $x^2 - y^2 = 1$. If there are parts of the question which have no answer, or are impossible, say why that is so.

4  Consider the curve $y^3 = (x - 1)^2$.

   (a)  Find the coordinates of the points where the curve crosses the axes.

   (b)  Are there any values which either $x$ or $y$ cannot take?

   (c)  Differentiate the equation $y^3 = (x - 1)^2$ to find an expression for the gradient in terms of $x$ and $y$. Find the gradient of the curve where it crosses the $y$-axis.

   (d)  What happens to the gradient as $x$ gets close to 1?

   (e)  By making the substitution $x = 1 + X$, and examining the resulting equation between $y$ and $X$, show that the curve is symmetrical about the line $x = 1$.

   (f)  Make a sketch of the curve, and check your result by using your graphic calculator.

5  Differentiate the implicit equation $y^2 = 4x$ to find the gradient at $(9, -6)$ on the curve.

6  Differentiate the implicit equation of the ellipse $3x^2 + 4y^2 = 16$ to find the equation of the tangent at the point $(2, -1)$.

7  Differentiate the implicit equation of the hyperbola $4x^2 - 3y^2 = 24$ to find the equation of the normal at the point $(3, -2)$. Find the $y$-coordinate of the point where the normal meets the curve again.

8  Use methods similar to those of Question 2 to draw a sketch of the curve $x^4 + y^4 = 1$. On the same diagram, sketch the curve $x^2 + y^2 = 1$.

9  (a)  Show that the origin lies on the curve $e^x + e^y = 2$.

   (b)  Differentiate the equation with respect to $x$, and explain why the gradient is always negative.

   (c)  Find any restrictions that you can on the values of $x$ and $y$, and sketch the curve.

10 (a)  Show that if $(a, b)$ lies on the curve $x^2 + y^3 = 2$, then so does $(-a, b)$. What can you deduce from this about the shape of the curve?

   (b)  Differentiate $x^2 + y^3 = 2$ with respect to $x$, and deduce what you can about the gradient for negative and for positive values of $x$.

   (c)  Show that there is a stationary point at $\left(0, \sqrt[3]{2}\right)$, and deduce its nature.

   (d)  Sketch the curve.

**11** Find the coordinates of the points at which the curve $y^5 + y = x^3 + x^2$ meets the coordinate axes, and find the gradients of the curve at each of these points.

**12** Find the gradient of the curve $y^3 - 3y^2 + 2y = e^x + x - 1$ at the points where it crosses the $y$-axis.

### 11.3 An application to differential equations

All the differential equations in Chapter 9 had $\dfrac{dy}{dx}$ expressed as functions of either $x$ or $y$. Another common type of equation has the form

$$\frac{dy}{dx} = \frac{f(x)}{g(y)}.$$

This can be solved by reversing the process described in Section 11.2. Such an equation is said to have **separable variables**, because it can be rearranged to get just $y$ on the left side and just $x$ on the right.

Multiplying by $g(y)$ gives

$$g(y)\frac{dy}{dx} = f(x),$$

and this is the kind of equation you get when you differentiate an implicit equation. If you can find functions $G(y)$ and $F(x)$ such that $G'(y) = g(y)$ and $F'(x) = f(x)$, then the equation can be written as

$$G'(y)\frac{dy}{dx} = F'(x).$$

The term on the left is $\dfrac{d}{dx}G(y)$, so you can integrate with respect to $x$ to obtain the implicit equation

$$G(y) = F(x) + k.$$

This last step is based on $\displaystyle\int G'(y)\frac{dy}{dx}\,dx = \int G'(y)\,dy,$ which you use when doing integration by substitution.

### Example 11.3.1
The gradient of the tangent at each point $P$ of a curve is equal to the square of the gradient of $OP$. Find the equation of the curve.

If $(x, y)$ is a point on the curve, the gradient of $OP$ is $\dfrac{y}{x}$, so the gradient of the tangent at $P$ will be $\left(\dfrac{y}{x}\right)^2$. Therefore $y$ and $x$ satisfy the differential equation

$$\frac{dy}{dx} = \frac{y^2}{x^2}.$$

The variables can be separated by dividing by $y^2$, which gives $\dfrac{1}{y^2}\dfrac{dy}{dx} = \dfrac{1}{x^2}.$

Integrating with respect to $x$ gives the general solution $-\dfrac{1}{y} = -\dfrac{1}{x} + k.$

This can be written as

$$-\frac{1}{y} = -\frac{1-kx}{x}, \quad \text{so} \quad y = \frac{x}{1-kx}.$$

It is interesting to see what happens when you take different values of $k$. All the curves in Fig. 11.3 have the property described above. But you have to exclude the origin, since the property has no meaning if $P$ coincides with $O$.

Notice that all the curves have positive gradients at all points. This is expected, since at each point $P$ the gradient is the square of the gradient of $OP$.

Notice also that if you draw a line $y = mx$ through the origin ($m \neq 0$ or $1$), it will cut a lot of the curves. At every point $P$ of intersection the gradient of $OP$ is $m$, so the gradient of the curve will be $m^2$. So the tangents to the curves at the points where the line cuts them are all parallel.

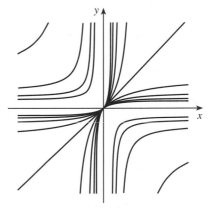

Fig. 11.3

## Example 11.3.2

For the differential equation $\dfrac{dy}{dx} = \dfrac{xy}{x^2+1}$, find

(a)  the equation of the solution curve which passes through $(1,2)$,

(b)  the general solution.

You can separate the variables by dividing by $y$, giving $\dfrac{1}{y}\dfrac{dy}{dx} = \dfrac{x}{x^2+1}.$

Integrating with respect to $x$ gives $\displaystyle\int \frac{1}{y}\frac{dy}{dx}dx = \int \frac{x}{x^2+1}dx.$

The left side can be expressed as $\displaystyle\int \frac{1}{y}dy$, and the right side has the form

$\dfrac{1}{2}\displaystyle\int \frac{f'(x)}{f(x)}dx$ with $f(x) = x^2+1$ (see Section 10.3). So

$$\ln|y| = \tfrac{1}{2}\ln(x^2+1) + k.$$

(a) Substituting $x = 1$, $y = 2$ in this equation gives $\ln 2 = \frac{1}{2}\ln 2 + k$, so the required solution has $k = \frac{1}{2}\ln 2$, and is

$$\ln|y| = \frac{1}{2}\ln(x^2 + 1) + \frac{1}{2}\ln 2.$$

This equation can be written without logarithms, as

$$|y| = \sqrt{2(x^2 + 1)}.$$

In this form the equation represents not one, but two solution curves, with equations $y = \pm\sqrt{2(x^2 + 1)}$. Since the square root on the right is positive, the curve which passes through $(1, 2)$ has the equation with the positive sign,

$$y = \sqrt{2(x^2 + 1)}.$$

(b) You already have one form of the general solution in the equation found above, but you should try to rearrange it in a simpler form. Notice that, for the particular solution through $(1, 2)$, the constant $k$ came out as a logarithm. Similarly, in the general solution it helps to write the arbitrary constant $k$ as $\ln A$, where $A$ is a positive number. Then

$$\ln|y| = \frac{1}{2}\ln(x^2 + 1) + \ln A,$$

which can be written without logarithms as

$$|y| = A\sqrt{x^2 + 1}.$$

Now $|y|$ is positive, and so is $A\sqrt{x^2 + 1}$. But $y$ might be negative, so

$$y = \pm A\sqrt{x^2 + 1}.$$

Finally, instead of writing the constant as $\pm A$, where $A$ is positive, it is simpler to write it as $c$, where $c$ can be positive or negative. The solution can then be expressed as

$$y = c\sqrt{x^2 + 1}.$$

There are a number of points to notice about the solution to the last example.

- Although when integrating you need to put the modulus sign in $\ln|y|$, it is not needed in $\ln(x^2 + 1)$, because $x^2 + 1$ is always positive.
- When integration introduces logarithms into the equation for the general solution, it is often worth adding the arbitrary constant in the form $+\ln A$, rather than $+k$.
- What about the value $c = 0$? You can't include $A = 0$ in the solution because $\ln 0$ has no meaning. But obviously $y = 0$ (the $x$-axis) is a solution of the original differential equation, since $\dfrac{dy}{dx} = 0$ at every point. This solution in fact got lost at the

very first step, dividing by $y$ to separate the variables; you can't do this if $y = 0$. But now that this special case has been checked, you can say that the general solution of the differential equation is $y = c\sqrt{x^2 + 1}$, where the constant $c$ can be any number, positive, negative or zero.

*Check this solution for yourself by finding $\dfrac{dy}{dx}$ and showing that it does satisfy the differential equation for any value of $c$.*

### Example 11.3.3

For a certain period of about 12 years, the rate of growth of a country's gross national product (GNP) is predicted to vary between $+5\%$ and $-1\%$. This variation is modelled by the formula $\left(2 + 3\cos\frac{1}{2}t\right)\%$, where $t$ is the time in years. Find a formula for the GNP during the cycle.

Denote the GNP after $t$ years by $P$. The rate of growth $\dfrac{dP}{dt}$ is given as a percentage of its current value, so

$$\frac{dP}{dt} = \frac{2 + 3\cos\frac{1}{2}t}{100}P.$$

The variables can be separated by dividing by $P$:

$$\frac{1}{P}\frac{dP}{dt} = \frac{2 + 3\cos\frac{1}{2}t}{100}.$$

Integrating,

$$\ln P = \frac{2t + 6\sin\frac{1}{2}t}{100} + k.$$

(Note that the GNP is always positive, so by definition $P > 0$.)

If $P$ has the value $P_0$ when $t = 0$, then

$$\ln P_0 = 0 + k,$$

and the equation can be written

$$\ln P = \frac{2t + 6\sin\frac{1}{2}t}{100} + \ln P_0, \quad \text{or} \quad P = P_0 e^{\frac{1}{100}\left(2t + 6\sin\frac{1}{2}t\right)}.$$

## Exercise 11B

1   Find the general solution of each of the following differential equations.

   (a) $\dfrac{dy}{dx} = \dfrac{x^2}{y^2}$       (b) $\dfrac{dy}{dx} = \dfrac{x}{y}$       (c) $\dfrac{dy}{dx} = xy$       (d) $\dfrac{dy}{dx} = \dfrac{1}{xy}$

**2**   Find the equation of the curve which satisfies the differential equation $\dfrac{dy}{dx} = \dfrac{y}{x(x+1)}$ and passes through the point $(1,2)$.

**3**   Find the general solution of the differential equation $\dfrac{dy}{dx} = -\dfrac{x}{y}$. Describe the solution curves, and find the equation of the curve which passes through $(-4,3)$.

**4**   Solve the differential equation $\dfrac{dy}{dx} = \dfrac{x+1}{2-y}$, and describe the solution curves.

**5**   Find the equations of the curves which satisfy the given differential equations, and pass through the given points.

   (a)   $\dfrac{dy}{dx} = \dfrac{3y}{2x}$      $(2,4)$          (b)   $\dfrac{dy}{dx} = -\dfrac{3y}{2x}$      $(2,4)$

   (c)   $\dfrac{dy}{dx} = \dfrac{\sin x}{\cos y}$      $\left(\tfrac{1}{3}\pi, 0\right)$        (d)   $\dfrac{dy}{dx} = \dfrac{\tan x}{\tan y}$      $\left(\tfrac{1}{3}\pi, 0\right)$

**6**   Solve the equation $v\dfrac{dv}{dx} = -\omega^2 x$, where $\omega$ is a constant. Find the particular solution for which $v = 0$ when $x = a$.

**7**   Find the general solution of the equations

   (a)   $\dfrac{dy}{dx} = \dfrac{2x(y^2 + 1)}{y(x^2 + 1)}$,        (b)   $\dfrac{dy}{dx} = \tan x \cot y$.

**8**   Find the equations of the curves which satisfy the following differential equations and pass through the given points.

   (a)   $\dfrac{dy}{dx} = \dfrac{y(y-1)}{x}$      $(1,2)$         (b)   $\dfrac{dy}{dx} = \cot x \cot y$      $\left(\tfrac{1}{6}\pi, 0\right)$

   (c)   $\dfrac{dy}{dx} = \dfrac{1+y^2}{y(1-x^2)}$      $\left(\tfrac{3}{2}, 2\right)$        (d)   $\dfrac{dy}{dx} = y \tan x$      $(0,2)$

**9**   Find the general solution of the differential equations

   (a)   $4 + x\dfrac{dy}{dx} = y^2$,      (b)   $e^y \dfrac{dy}{dx} - 1 = \ln x$,      (c)   $y\cos x\dfrac{dy}{dx} = 2 - y\dfrac{dy}{dx}$.

**10**   The gradient at each point of a curve is $n$ times the gradient of the line joining the origin to that point. Find the general equation of the curve.

**11**   The size of an insect population $n$, which fluctuates during the year, is modelled by the equation $\dfrac{dn}{dt} = 0.01n(0.05 - \cos 0.02t)$, where $t$ is the number of days from the start of observations. The initial number of insects is 5000.

   (a)   Solve the differential equation to find $n$ in terms of $t$.

   (b)   Show that the model predicts that the number of insects will fall to a minimum after about 76 days, and find this minimum value.

**12** The velocity $v$ m s$^{-1}$ of a spacecraft moving vertically $x$ metres above the centre of the earth can be modelled by the equation $v\dfrac{dv}{dx} = -\dfrac{10R^2}{x^2}$, where $R$ metres is the radius of the earth. The inital velocity at blast-off, when $x = R$, is $V$ m s$^{-1}$.

Find an expression for $v^2$ in terms of $V$, $x$ and $R$, and show that, according to this model, if the spacecraft is to be able to escape from the earth, then $V^2 \geqslant 20R$.

## 11.4 Implicit equations including products

The implicit equations in Section 11.2 contained terms in $x$ and terms in $y$, but there were no terms which involved both $x$ and $y$. Equations with more complicated terms can be differentiated using the product or quotient rule, sometimes in conjunction with the chain rule.

**Example 11.4.1**
Find the derivatives with respect to $x$ of

(a) $y\sin x$,    (b) $y^3 \ln x$,    (c) $e^{x^2 y}$,    (d) $\cos\dfrac{x}{y}$.

(a) By the product rule,

$$\frac{d}{dx} y\sin x = \frac{d}{dx} y \times \sin x + y \times \frac{d}{dx}\sin x = \frac{dy}{dx}\sin x + y\cos x.$$

(b) $\dfrac{d}{dx} y^3 \ln x = \dfrac{d}{dx} y^3 \times \ln x + y^3 \times \dfrac{d}{dx}\ln x = 3y^2 \dfrac{dy}{dx}\ln x + \dfrac{y^3}{x}.$

(c) Use the chain rule followed by the product rule.

$$\frac{d}{dx} e^{x^2 y} = e^{x^2 y} \times \frac{d}{dx} x^2 y = e^{x^2 y}\left(2xy + x^2 \frac{dy}{dx}\right).$$

(d) $\dfrac{d}{dx}\cos\dfrac{x}{y} = -\sin\dfrac{x}{y} \times \dfrac{1 \times y - x \times \dfrac{dy}{dx}}{y^2} = \dfrac{x\dfrac{dy}{dx} - y}{y^2}\sin\dfrac{x}{y}.$

**Example 11.4.2**
Find the gradient of $x^2 y^3 = 72$ at the point $(3,2)$.

Two methods are given: the first is direct; the second begins by taking logarithms. This makes expressions involving products of powers easier to handle.

**Method 1**   Differentiating with respect to $x$,

$$2xy^3 + x^2\left(3y^2 \frac{dy}{dx}\right) = 0.$$

At $(3,2)$, $2 \times 3 \times 8 + 9 \times 3 \times 4\dfrac{dy}{dx} = 0$, so $\dfrac{dy}{dx} = -\dfrac{4}{9}$.

**Method 2**    Write the equation as $\ln\left(x^2y^3\right)=\ln 72$. By the laws of logarithms, $\ln\left(x^2y^3\right)=\ln x^2+\ln y^3=2\ln x+3\ln y$, so the equation is $2\ln x+3\ln y=\ln 72$.

Differentiating, $\dfrac{2}{x}+\dfrac{3}{y}\dfrac{dy}{dx}=0$, so $\dfrac{dy}{dx}=-\dfrac{2y}{3x}$. At $(3,2)$, $\dfrac{dy}{dx}=-\dfrac{4}{9}$.

Method 2 is sometimes called 'logarithmic differentiation'.

### Example 11.4.3
The equation $x^2-6xy+25y^2=16$ represents an ellipse with its centre at the origin. What ranges of values of $x$ and $y$ would you need in order to plot the whole of the curve on a computer screen?

**Method 1**    The problem is equivalent to finding the points where the tangent to the curve is parallel to one of the axes.

Differentiating,

$$2x-6\left(1\times y+x\times\frac{dy}{dx}\right)+50y\frac{dy}{dx}=0,\quad\text{that is,}\quad (x-3y)+(25y-3x)\frac{dy}{dx}=0.$$

The tangent is parallel to the $x$-axis when $\dfrac{dy}{dx}=0$, which is when $x=3y$.

Substituting this into the equation of the ellipse gives

$$(3y)^2-6(3y)y+25y^2=16,\quad 16y^2=16,\quad y=-1\text{ or }1.$$

The tangents are therefore parallel to the $x$-axis at $(-3,-1)$ and $(3,1)$.

The tangent is parallel to the $y$-axis when $\dfrac{dx}{dy}=0$. Since $\dfrac{dx}{dy}=\dfrac{1}{\frac{dy}{dx}}$, this occurs

when $25y=3x$. Substituting $y=\frac{3}{25}x$ gives

$$x^2-6x\left(\tfrac{3}{25}x\right)+25\left(\tfrac{3}{25}x\right)^2=16,\quad \tfrac{16}{25}x^2=16,\quad x=-5\text{ or }5.$$

The points of contact are $\left(-5,-\tfrac{3}{5}\right)$ and $\left(5,\tfrac{3}{5}\right)$.

To fit the curve on the screen you need $-5\leqslant x\leqslant 5$ and $-1\leqslant y\leqslant 1$. This is illustrated in Fig. 11.4.

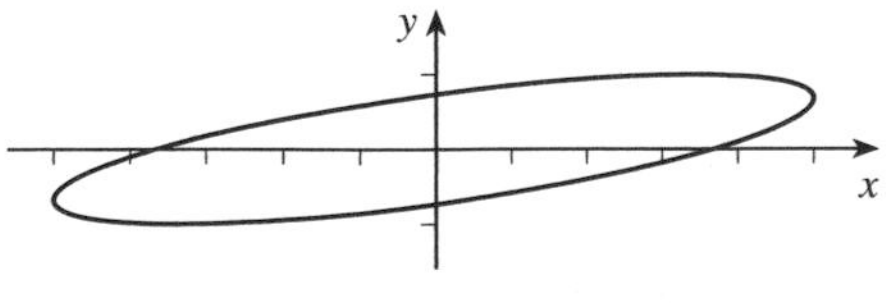

**Method 2**    The equation can be written as a quadratic in $x$:

$$x^2-6yx+\left(25y^2-16\right)=0.$$

The condition for this to give real values of $x$ is

Fig. 11.4

$$(6y)^2 - 4\left(25y^2 - 16\right) \geqslant 0, \quad \text{that is,} \quad 64 - 64y^2 = 0, \quad -1 \leqslant y \leqslant 1.$$

Similarly, from the quadratic in $y$, which is $25y^2 - 6xy + \left(x^2 - 16\right) = 0$, you get the condition

$$(6x)^2 - 4 \times 25\left(x^2 - 16\right) \geqslant 0, \quad \text{that is,} \quad 1600 - 64x^2 = 0, \quad -5 \leqslant x \leqslant 5.$$

## Exercise 11C

1  Find the derivatives with respect to $x$ of

   (a) $xy$,          (b) $xy^2$,          (c) $x^2y^2$,          (d) $\dfrac{x^2}{y}$.

2  Find the derivatives with respect to $x$ of

   (a) $\sqrt{xy}$,          (b) $\sin\left(x^2y\right)$,          (c) $\ln(xy)$,          (d) $e^{xy+y}$.

3  Differentiate the implicit equations of the following curves to find the gradients at the point $(3,4)$.

   (a) $xy = 12$          (b) $4x^2 - xy - y^2 = 8$

4  Find the gradient of each of the following curves at the point given.

   (a) $x \sin y = \frac{1}{2}$ $\left(1, \frac{1}{6}\pi\right)$          (b) $ye^x = xy + y^2$ $(0,1)$

   (c) $\ln(x + y) = -x$ $(0,1)$          (d) $\cos(xy) = \frac{1}{2}$ $\left(1, \frac{1}{3}\pi\right)$

5  Find the equation of the tangent to the curve $x^2 - 2xy + 2y^2 = 5$ at the point $(1,2)$.

6  Find the equation of the normal to the curve $2xy^2 - x^2y^3 = 1$ at the point $(1,1)$.

7  Find the points on the curve $4x^2 + 2xy - 3y^2 = 39$ at which the tangent is parallel to one of the axes.

8  (a) Show that the curve $x^3 + y^3 = 3xy$ is symmetrical about the line $y = x$, and find the gradient of the curve at the point other than the origin for which $y = x$.

   (b) Show that, close to the origin, if $y$ is very small compared with $x$, then the curve is approximately given by the equation $y = kx^2$. Give the value of $k$.

   (c) Find the coordinates of the points on the graph of $x^3 + y^3 = 3xy$ at which the tangent is parallel to one or other of the axes.

   (d) Suppose now that $|x|$ and $|y|$ are both very large. Explain why $x + y \approx k$, where $k$ is a constant, and substitute $y = k - x$ into the equation of the curve. Show that, if this equation is to be approximately satisfied by a large value of $|x|$, then $k = -1$.

   (e) Draw a sketch of the curve.

9  (a)  Explain why all the points on the curve $\left(x^2 + y^2\right)^2 = x^2 - y^2$ lie in the region
        $x^2 \geqslant y^2$.

   (b)  Find the coordinates of the points at which the tangent is either parallel to the
        $x$-axis or parallel to the $y$-axis.

   (c)  By considering where the curve meets the circle $x^2 + y^2 = r^2$, show that $r^2 \leqslant 1$, so
        the curve is bounded.

   (d)  Sketch the curve, which is called the *lemniscate of Bernoulli*.

## Miscellaneous exercise 11

1  (a)  Two quantities $x$ and $y$ are related to each other by the differential equation
        $y \dfrac{dy}{dx} = -16x$. Solve this equation to get an implicit equation of the solution curve
        for which $y = 0$ when $x = 0.1$.

   (b)  Sketch your solution curve from part (a), showing the values of $x$ and $y$ at which
        the curve cuts the coordinate axes.                                          (OCR)

2  Find the equation of the normal at the point $(2,1)$ on the curve $x^3 + xy + y^3 = 11$, giving
   your answer in the form $ax + by + c = 0$.                                        (OCR)

3  A curve has implicit equation $x^2 - 2xy + 4y^2 = 12$.

   (a)  Find an expression for $\dfrac{dy}{dx}$ in terms of $y$ and $x$. Hence determine the coordinates
        of the points where the tangents to the curve are parallel to the $x$-axis.

   (b)  Find the equation of the normal to the curve at the point $\left(2\sqrt{3}, \sqrt{3}\right)$.          (OCR)

4  Find the general solution of the differential equation $\dfrac{dy}{dx} = \dfrac{x\left(y^2 + 1\right)}{(x-1)y}$, expressing $y$ in terms
   of $x$.                                                                           (OCR, adapted)

5  Solve the differential equation $\dfrac{dy}{dx} = xye^{2x}$, given that $y = 1$ when $x = 0$.

6  A curve has equation $y^3 + 3xy + 2x^3 = 9$. Obtain the equation of the normal at the point
   $(2,-1)$.                                                                         (OCR)

7  Obtain the general solution of the differential equation $y \dfrac{dy}{dx} \tan 2x = 1 - y^2$.

                                                                                     (OCR, adapted)

8  Find the general solution of the differential equation $\dfrac{dy}{dx} = \dfrac{y^2}{x^2 - x - 2}$ in the region $x > 2$.
   Find also the particular solution which satisfies $y = 1$ when $x = 5$.           (OCR)

**9** Find the solution of the differential equation $\dfrac{dy}{dx} = \dfrac{\sin^2 x}{y^2}$ which also satisfies $y = 1$ when $x = 0$. (OCR)

**10** Solve the differential equation $\dfrac{dy}{dx} = \dfrac{x}{y} e^{x+y}$, in the form $f(y) = g(x)$, given that $y = 0$ when $x = 0$.

**11** A curve is defined implicitly by the equation $4y - x^2 + 2x^2 y = 4x$.

(a) Use implicit differentiation to find $\dfrac{dy}{dx}$.

(b) Find the coordinates of the turning points on the curve. (OCR, adapted)

**12** Show that the tangent to the ellipse $\dfrac{x^2}{a^2} + \dfrac{y^2}{b^2} = 1$ at the point $P(a\cos\theta, b\sin\theta)$ has equation $bx\cos\theta + ay\sin\theta = ab$.

(a) The tangent to the ellipse at $P$ meets the $x$-axis at $Q$ and the $y$-axis at $R$. The mid-point of $QR$ is $M$. Find a cartesian equation for the locus of $M$ as $\theta$ varies.

(b) The tangent to the ellipse at $P$ meets the line $x = a$ at $T$. The origin is at $O$ and $A$ is the point $(-a, 0)$. Prove that $OT$ is parallel to $AP$. (OCR)

**13** To control the pests inside a large greenhouse, 600 ladybirds were introduced. After $t$ days there are $P$ ladybirds in the greenhouse. In a simple model, $P$ is assumed to be a continuous variable satisfying the differential equation $\dfrac{dP}{dt} = kP$, where $k$ is a constant.

Solve the differential equation, with initial condition $P = 600$ when $t = 0$, to express $P$ in terms of $k$ and $t$.

Observations of the number of ladybirds (estimated to the nearest hundred) were made as follows:

| $t$ | 0 | 150 | 250 |
|-----|-----|------|------|
| $P$ | 600 | 1200 | 3100 |

Show that $P = 1200$ when $t = 150$ implies that $k \approx 0.00462$. Show that this is not consistent with the observed value when $t = 250$.

In a refined model, allowing for seasonal variations, it is assumed that $P$ satisfies the differential equation $\dfrac{dP}{dt} = P(0.005 - 0.008\cos 0.02t)$ with initial condition $P = 600$ when $t = 0$. Solve this differential equation to express $P$ in terms of $t$, and comment on how well this fits with the data given above.

Show that, according to the refined model, the number of ladybirds will decrease initially, and find the smallest number of ladybirds in the greenhouse. (MEI)

**14** The equation of a curve is $x^2 + 4xy + 5y^2 = 9$. Show by differentiation that the maximum and minimum values of $y$ occur at the intersections of $x + 2y = 0$ with the curve. Find the maximum and minimum values of $y$. (OCR)

**15** A biologist studying fluctuations in the size of a particular population decides to investigate a model for which $\dfrac{dP}{dt} = kP \cos kt$, where $P$ is the size of the population at time $t$ days and $k$ is a positive constant.

(a) Given that $P = P_0$ when $t = 0$, express $P$ in terms of $k$, $t$ and $P_0$.

(b) Find the ratio of the maximum size of the population to the minimum size.     (OCR)

**16** The organiser of a sale, which lasted for 3 hours and raised a total of £1000, attempted to create a model to represent the relationship between $s$ and $t$, where £$s$ is the amount which had been raised at time $t$ hours after the start of the sale. In the model $s$ and $t$ were taken to be continuous variables. The organiser assumed that the rate of raising money varied directly as the time remaining and inversely as the amount already raised. Show that, for this model, $\dfrac{ds}{dt} = k\dfrac{3-t}{s}$, where $k$ is a constant. Solve the differential equation, and show that the solution can be written in the form $\dfrac{s^2}{1000^2} + \dfrac{(3-t)^2}{3^2} = 1$. Hence

(a) find the amount raised during the first hour of the sale,

(b) find the rate of raising money one hour after the start of the sale.     (OCR)

**17** A curve $C$ has equation $y = x + 2y^4$.

(a) Find $\dfrac{dy}{dx}$ in terms of $y$.

(b) Show that $\dfrac{d^2y}{dx^2} = \dfrac{24y^2}{\left(1 - 8y^3\right)^3}$.

(c) Write down the value of $\dfrac{dy}{dx}$ at the origin. Hence, by considering the sign of $\dfrac{d^2y}{dx^2}$, draw a diagram to show the shape of $C$ in the neighbourhood of the origin.     (OCR)

**18** The curve $C$, whose equation is $x^2 + y^2 = e^{x+y} - 1$, passes through the origin $O$. Show that $\dfrac{dy}{dx} = -1$ at $O$. Find the value of $\dfrac{d^2y}{dx^2}$ at $O$.     (OCR)

**19** For $x > 0$ and $0 < y < \frac{1}{2}\pi$, the variables $y$ and $x$ are connected by the differential equation $\dfrac{dy}{dx} = \dfrac{\ln x}{\cot y}$, and $y = \frac{1}{6}\pi$ when $x = e$.

Find the value of $y$ when $x = 1$, giving your answer to 3 significant figures. Use the differential equation to show that this value of $y$ is a stationary value, and determine its nature.     (MEI)

# 12 Scalar products of vectors

This chapter shows how vectors can be used to find results about lengths and angles. When you have completed it, you should

- know the definition of the scalar product, and its expression in components
- be able to use the rules of vector algebra which involve scalar products
- be able to use scalar products to solve geometrical problems in two and three dimensions, using general vector algebra or components.

## 12.1 The magnitude of a vector

Any translation can be described by giving its magnitude and direction. The notation used for the magnitude of a vector $\mathbf{p}$, ignoring its direction, is $|\mathbf{p}|$.

If you have two vectors $\mathbf{p}$ and $\mathbf{q}$ which are not equal, but which have equal magnitudes, then you can write $|\mathbf{p}| = |\mathbf{q}|$.

If $s$ is a scalar multiple of $\mathbf{p}$, then it follows from the definition of $s\mathbf{p}$ (see Section 5.2) that $|s\mathbf{p}| = |s||\mathbf{p}|$. This is true whether $s$ is positive or negative (or zero).

The symbol for the magnitude of a vector is the same as the one for the modulus of a real number, but this does not present a problem. In fact, a real number $x$ behaves just like the vector $x\mathbf{i}$ in one dimension, where $\mathbf{i}$ is a basic unit vector. This can be used to represent a displacement on the number line, and the modulus $|x|$ then measures the magnitude of the displacement, whether it is in the positive or the negative direction.

A vector of magnitude 1 is called a **unit vector**. The basic unit vectors $\mathbf{i}$, $\mathbf{j}$, $\mathbf{k}$ defined in Chapter 5 are examples of unit vectors, but they are not the only ones: there is a unit vector in every direction.

Unit vectors are sometimes distinguished by a circumflex accent ^ over the letter. For example, a unit vector in the direction of $\mathbf{r}$ may be denoted by $\hat{\mathbf{r}}$. You can state that '$\mathbf{r}$ is a vector of magnitude $|\mathbf{r}|$ in the direction of the unit vector $\hat{\mathbf{r}}$' by writing $\mathbf{r} = |\mathbf{r}|\hat{\mathbf{r}}$. (Notice that $|\mathbf{r}|$ is a scalar which multiplies the vector $\hat{\mathbf{r}}$.) This notation is especially common in mechanics, but it will not generally be used in this chapter.

## 12.2 Scalar products

In Chapter 5 vectors were added, subtracted and multiplied by scalars, but they were not multiplied together. The next step is to define the product of two vectors:

> The **scalar product**, or **dot product** of vectors $\mathbf{p}$ and $\mathbf{q}$ is the number (or scalar) $|\mathbf{p}||\mathbf{q}|\cos\theta$, where $\theta$ is the angle between the directions of $\mathbf{p}$ and $\mathbf{q}$. It is written $\mathbf{p}\cdot\mathbf{q}$ and pronounced 'p dot q'.

The angle $\theta$ may be acute or obtuse, but it is important that it is the angle between $\mathbf{p}$ and $\mathbf{q}$, and not (for example) the angle between $\mathbf{p}$ and $-\mathbf{q}$. It is best to show $\theta$ in a diagram in which the vectors are represented by arrows with their tails at the same point, as in Fig. 12.1.

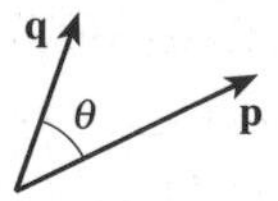

Fig. 12.1

The reason for calling this the 'scalar product', rather than simply the product, is that mathematicians also use another product, called the 'vector product'. But it is important to distinguish the scalar product from 'multiplication by a scalar', which you met in Chapter 5. To avoid confusion, many people prefer to use the alternative name 'dot product'.

For the same reason, you must always insert the 'dot' between $\mathbf{p}$ and $\mathbf{q}$ for the scalar product, but you must *not* insert a dot between $s$ and $\mathbf{p}$ when multiplying a vector by a scalar.

For example, you can never have a scalar product of three vectors, $\mathbf{p} \cdot \mathbf{q} \cdot \mathbf{r}$. You will remember from Section 5.2 that the sum of these three vectors can be regarded as $(\mathbf{p} + \mathbf{q}) + \mathbf{r}$ or as $\mathbf{p} + (\mathbf{q} + \mathbf{r})$, and that these expressions are equal. But $(\mathbf{p} \cdot \mathbf{q}) \cdot \mathbf{r}$ has no meaning: $\mathbf{p} \cdot \mathbf{q}$ is a scalar, and you cannot form a dot product of this scalar with the vector $\mathbf{r}$. Similarly, $\mathbf{p} \cdot (\mathbf{q} \cdot \mathbf{r})$ has no meaning.

However, $s(\mathbf{p} \cdot \mathbf{q})$, where $s$ is scalar, does have a meaning; as you would expect, $s(\mathbf{p} \cdot \mathbf{q})$ is equal to $(s\mathbf{p}) \cdot \mathbf{q}$. The proof depends on whether $s$ is positive (see Fig. 12.2) or negative (see Fig. 12.3).

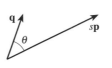

Fig. 12.2

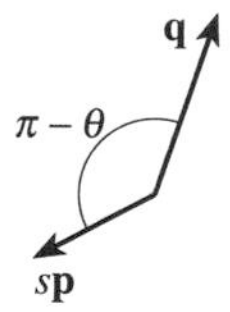

Fig. 12.3

If $s > 0$, then the angle between $s\mathbf{p}$ and $\mathbf{q}$ is $\theta$, so

$$(s\mathbf{p}) \cdot \mathbf{q} = |s\mathbf{p}||\mathbf{q}|\cos\theta = |s||\mathbf{p}||\mathbf{q}|\cos\theta = |s|(|\mathbf{p}||\mathbf{q}|\cos\theta) = s(\mathbf{p} \cdot \mathbf{q}).$$

If $s < 0$, then the angle between $s\mathbf{p}$ and $\mathbf{q}$ is $\pi - \theta$, and $s = -|s|$, so

$$(s\mathbf{p}) \cdot \mathbf{q} = |s\mathbf{p}||\mathbf{q}|\cos(\pi - \theta) = |s||\mathbf{p}||\mathbf{q}|(-\cos\theta) = -|s|(|\mathbf{p}||\mathbf{q}|\cos\theta) = s(\mathbf{p} \cdot \mathbf{q}).$$

Another property of the scalar product is that $\mathbf{p} \cdot \mathbf{q} = \mathbf{q} \cdot \mathbf{p}$, which follows immediately from the definition. This is called the **commutative rule for scalar products**.

There are two very important special cases, which you get by taking $\theta = 0$ and putting $\mathbf{p} = \mathbf{q}$, and taking $\theta = \frac{1}{2}\pi$, in the definition of scalar product.

> $\mathbf{p} \cdot \mathbf{p} = |\mathbf{p}|^2$ ($\mathbf{p} \cdot \mathbf{p}$ is sometimes written as $\mathbf{p}^2$).
>
> If neither $\mathbf{p}$ nor $\mathbf{q}$ is the zero vector,
>
> $\mathbf{p} \cdot \mathbf{q} = 0 \iff \mathbf{p}$ and $\mathbf{q}$ are in perpendicular directions.

These properties provide ways of using vectors to find lengths and to identify right angles.

## 12.3*The distributive rule

The rules in the last section suggest that algebra with scalar products is much like ordinary algebra, except that some expressions (such as the scalar product of three vectors) have no meaning. You need one more rule to be able to use vectors to get geometrical results. This is the **distributive rule** for multiplying out brackets:

$$(\mathbf{p}+\mathbf{q})\cdot\mathbf{r}=\mathbf{p}\cdot\mathbf{r}+\mathbf{q}\cdot\mathbf{r}.$$

You may, if you wish, omit the proof on a first reading, and go on to Section 12.4.

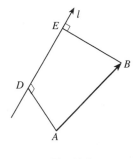

The proof of this needs a preliminary result. Fig. 12.4 shows a directed line $l$ and two points $A$ and $B$ (in three dimensions). If lines $AD$ and $BE$ are drawn perpendicular to $l$, then the directed length $DE$ is called the **projection** of the displacement vector $\overrightarrow{AB}$ on $l$.

Here the word 'directed' means that a positive direction is selected on $l$, and that (in this diagram) $DE$ is positive but $ED$ would be negative.

Fig. 12.4

**Theorem**    If $\mathbf{p}$ is the displacement vector $\overrightarrow{AB}$, and $\mathbf{u}$ is a unit vector in the direction of $l$, then the projection of $\overrightarrow{AB}$ on $l$ is $\mathbf{p}\cdot\mathbf{u}$.

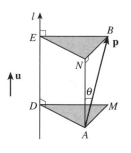

**Proof**    You will probably find the proof easiest to follow if $l$ is drawn as a vertical line, as in Fig. 12.5. Recall that $AD$ and $BE$ are perpendicular to $l$, and so are horizontal. The shaded triangles $ADM$ and $NEB$ lie in the horizontal planes through $D$ and $E$. The point $N$ is such that $AN$ is parallel to $l$ and perpendicular to $NB$.

Then $DE = AN$, and $\mathbf{u}$ is a unit vector in the direction of $AN$. If the angle $BAN$ is denoted by $\theta$, then

Fig. 12.5

$$\mathbf{p}\cdot\mathbf{u}=|\mathbf{p}|\times1\times\cos\theta = AB\cos\theta = AN = DE,$$

which is the projection of $\overrightarrow{AB}$ on $l$.

Notice that, if $B$ were below $A$, then the angle between $\mathbf{p}$ and $\mathbf{u}$ would be obtuse, so $\mathbf{p}\cdot\mathbf{u}$ would be negative. On $l$, $E$ would be below $D$, so the directed length $DE$ would also be negative.

When you have understood this proof with $l$ vertical, you can try re-drawing Fig. 12.5 with $l$ in some other direction, as in Fig. 12.4. If you then replace 'horizontal planes' by 'planes perpendicular to $l$', the proof will still hold.

**Theorem**    For any vectors $\mathbf{p}$, $\mathbf{q}$ and $\mathbf{r}$, $(\mathbf{p}+\mathbf{q})\cdot\mathbf{r}=\mathbf{p}\cdot\mathbf{r}+\mathbf{q}\cdot\mathbf{r}$.

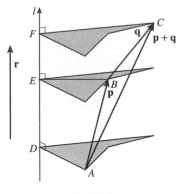

**Proof**    In Fig. 12.6 the displacement vectors $\overrightarrow{AB}$, $\overrightarrow{BC}$ and $\overrightarrow{AC}$ represent $\mathbf{p}$, $\mathbf{q}$ and $\mathbf{p}+\mathbf{q}$. The line $l$ is in the direction of $\mathbf{r}$; this is again shown as a vertical line. The horizontal planes through $A$, $B$ and $C$ cut $l$ at $D$, $E$ and $F$ respectively, so that $AD$, $BE$ and $CF$ are perpendicular to $l$. Let $\mathbf{u}$ be a unit vector in the direction of $\mathbf{r}$, and denote $|\mathbf{r}|$ by $s$, so that $\mathbf{r}=s\mathbf{u}$.

Fig. 12.6

Then

$$\mathbf{p}\cdot\mathbf{r}=\mathbf{p}\cdot(s\mathbf{u})=s(\mathbf{p}\cdot\mathbf{u})=s\times DE,$$

and similarly $\mathbf{q}\cdot\mathbf{r}=s\times EF$ and $(\mathbf{p}+\mathbf{q})\cdot\mathbf{r}=s\times DF$.

Since $DE$, $EF$ and $DF$ are directed lengths, it is always true that $DE+EF=DF$, whatever the order of the points $D$, $E$ and $F$ on $l$.

Therefore

$$(\mathbf{p}+\mathbf{q})\cdot\mathbf{r}=s\times DF=s\times(DE+EF)=s\times DE+s\times EF=\mathbf{p}\cdot\mathbf{r}+\mathbf{q}\cdot\mathbf{r}.$$

As before, when you have understood this proof with $l$ vertical, you can adapt it for any other direction of $l$.

## 12.4 Scalar products in component form

In the special cases at the end of Section 12.2, take $\mathbf{p}$ and $\mathbf{q}$ to be basic unit vectors. You then get:

> For the basic unit vectors $\mathbf{i}$, $\mathbf{j}$, $\mathbf{k}$,
>
> $$\mathbf{i}\cdot\mathbf{i}=\mathbf{j}\cdot\mathbf{j}=\mathbf{k}\cdot\mathbf{k}=1,$$
>
> and    $\mathbf{j}\cdot\mathbf{k}=\mathbf{k}\cdot\mathbf{i}=\mathbf{i}\cdot\mathbf{j}=0$.

It follows that, if vectors $\mathbf{p}$ and $\mathbf{q}$ are written in component form as $\mathbf{p}=l\mathbf{i}+m\mathbf{j}+n\mathbf{k}$ and $\mathbf{q}=u\mathbf{i}+v\mathbf{j}+w\mathbf{k}$, then

$$\begin{aligned}
\mathbf{p}\cdot\mathbf{q}&=(l\mathbf{i}+m\mathbf{j}+n\mathbf{k})\cdot(u\mathbf{i}+v\mathbf{j}+w\mathbf{k})\\
&=lu\,\mathbf{i}\cdot\mathbf{i}+lv\,\mathbf{i}\cdot\mathbf{j}+lw\,\mathbf{i}\cdot\mathbf{k}+mu\,\mathbf{j}\cdot\mathbf{i}+mv\,\mathbf{j}\cdot\mathbf{j}+mw\,\mathbf{j}\cdot\mathbf{k}\\
&\qquad+nu\,\mathbf{k}\cdot\mathbf{i}+nv\,\mathbf{k}\cdot\mathbf{j}+nw\,\mathbf{k}\cdot\mathbf{k}\\
&=lu\times1+lv\times0+lw\times0+mu\times0+mv\times1+mw\times0\\
&\qquad+nu\times0+nv\times0+nw\times1\\
&=lu+mv+nw.
\end{aligned}$$

In component form, the scalar product is

$$\begin{pmatrix} l \\ m \\ n \end{pmatrix} \cdot \begin{pmatrix} u \\ v \\ w \end{pmatrix} = (l\mathbf{i} + m\mathbf{j} + n\mathbf{k}) \cdot (u\mathbf{i} + v\mathbf{j} + w\mathbf{k}) = lu + mv + nw.$$

This result has many applications. In particular, $\mathbf{p} \cdot \mathbf{p} = l^2 + m^2 + n^2$, giving the length of $\mathbf{p}$:

$$|\mathbf{p}| = \sqrt{l^2 + m^2 + n^2}.$$

**Example 12.4.1**

A line has vector equation $\mathbf{r} = \begin{pmatrix} 0 \\ -4 \\ -5 \end{pmatrix} + t \begin{pmatrix} -2 \\ -3 \\ 6 \end{pmatrix}$. The point $A$ has coordinates $(5, -10, 10)$. Find

(a) the angle between $OA$ and the line,
(b) the projection of $OA$ on the line,
(c) the distance from $A$ to the line.

It will help you to draw a sketch and to mark the data on it.

(a) The line has direction vector $\mathbf{p} = \begin{pmatrix} -2 \\ -3 \\ 6 \end{pmatrix}$; the position vector of $A$ is $\mathbf{a} = \begin{pmatrix} 5 \\ -10 \\ 10 \end{pmatrix}$.

If the angle between the vectors is $\theta°$, $\mathbf{p} \cdot \mathbf{a} = |\mathbf{p}||\mathbf{a}|\cos\theta°$. So calculate

$$\mathbf{p} \cdot \mathbf{a} = (-2) \times 5 + (-3) \times (-10) + 6 \times 10 = 80,$$

$$|\mathbf{p}| = \sqrt{(-2)^2 + (-3)^2 + 6^2} = 7, \text{ and } |\mathbf{a}| = \sqrt{5^2 + (-10)^2 + 10^2} = 15.$$

Then $\cos\theta° = \dfrac{80}{7 \times 15}$ giving $\theta \approx 40.4$.

The angle between $OA$ and the line is $40.4°$, correct to the nearest $0.1°$.

(b) Since $|\mathbf{p}| = 7$, a unit vector $\mathbf{u}$ in the direction of the line is $\frac{1}{7}\mathbf{p}$. The

projection of $\overrightarrow{OA}$ on the line is $\mathbf{a} \cdot \mathbf{u} = \frac{1}{7}\mathbf{a} \cdot \mathbf{p} = \frac{80}{7}$.

(c) Any point $R$ on the line has position vector $\mathbf{r} = \begin{pmatrix} -2t \\ -4 - 3t \\ -5 + 6t \end{pmatrix}$, and the

displacement vector $\overrightarrow{AR}$ is

$$\mathbf{r} - \mathbf{a} = \begin{pmatrix} -2t - 5 \\ -4 - 3t - (-10) \\ -5 + 6t - 10 \end{pmatrix} = \begin{pmatrix} -2t - 5 \\ 6 - 3t \\ -15 + 6t \end{pmatrix}.$$

If $R$ is the foot of the perpendicular from $A$ to the line, $\overrightarrow{AR}$ is perpendicular to the line, so $\mathbf{p} \cdot \overrightarrow{AR} = 0$. This gives

$$(-2) \times (-2t - 5) + (-3) \times (6 - 3t) + 6 \times (-15 + 6t) = 0,$$

so $\quad 49t - 98 = 0, \quad$ that is $\quad t = 2.$

When $t = 2$, $\overrightarrow{AR} = \begin{pmatrix} -9 \\ 0 \\ -3 \end{pmatrix}$, and $|\overrightarrow{AR}| = \sqrt{(-9)^2 + 0^2 + (-3)^2} = \sqrt{90} = 3\sqrt{10}.$

## Example 12.4.2

Use vectors to prove the addition formula for $\cos(A - B)$.

Fig. 12.7 is a vector version of Fig. 1.4 in Chapter 1. The position vectors of $P$ and $Q$ are the unit vectors $\mathbf{p} = \cos A \, \mathbf{i} + \sin A \, \mathbf{j}$ and $\mathbf{q} = \cos B \, \mathbf{i} + \sin B \, \mathbf{j}$. So

$$\mathbf{p} \cdot \mathbf{q} = \cos A \cos B + \sin A \sin B.$$

The angle between $\mathbf{p}$ and $\mathbf{q}$ is $A - B$, so
$$\mathbf{p} \cdot \mathbf{q} = 1 \times 1 \times \cos(A - B).$$

Equating the two expressions for $\mathbf{p} \cdot \mathbf{q}$,

$$\cos(A - B) = \cos A \cos B + \sin A \sin B.$$

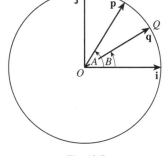

Fig. 12.7

## Example 12.4.3

An aircraft flies from London Gatwick (51°N, 0°E) to Uganda Entebbe (0°N, 31°E). Taking the radius of the earth as $6370 \text{ km}$, find the great-circle distance between the airports.

A great circle has its centre at the centre of the earth, and radius $R$ km. If the angle between the position vectors of Gatwick and Entebbe is $\theta$ radians, then the great-circle distance is $R\theta$.

Take the origin at the centre of the earth, the $z$-axis up the earth's axis, and the $x$-axis through the point where the Greenwich meridian meets the equator (Fig. 12.8). Taking the earth to be a sphere of radius $R$ km, the coordinates of Gatwick are $(R\cos 51°, 0, R\sin 51°)$ and the coordinates of Entebbe are $(R\cos 31°, R\sin 31°, 0)$.

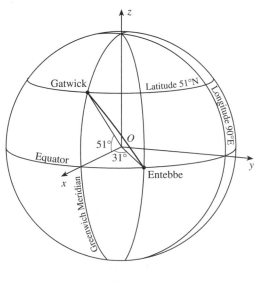

Fig. 12.8

The scalar product of the position vectors of Gatwick and Entebbe is

$$R\cos 51° \times R\cos 31° + 0 \times R\sin 31° + R\sin 51° \times 0,$$

and it is also equal to $R^2 \cos\theta$. So $\cos\theta = \cos 51° \cos 31°$, giving $\theta = 1.00\ldots$ radians. Taking $R = 6370$ gives $R\theta = 6370 \times 1.00\ldots$, which is a great circle distance of slightly under $6400$ km.

## Exercise 12A

1 Let $\mathbf{a} = \begin{pmatrix} 3 \\ 2 \end{pmatrix}$, $\mathbf{b} = \begin{pmatrix} -4 \\ 2 \end{pmatrix}$ and $\mathbf{c} = \begin{pmatrix} 1 \\ 4 \end{pmatrix}$. Calculate $\mathbf{a}\cdot\mathbf{b}$, $\mathbf{a}\cdot\mathbf{c}$ and $\mathbf{a}\cdot(\mathbf{b}+\mathbf{c})$, and verify that $\mathbf{a}\cdot(\mathbf{b}+\mathbf{c}) = \mathbf{a}\cdot\mathbf{b} + \mathbf{a}\cdot\mathbf{c}$.

2 Let $\mathbf{a} = 2\mathbf{i} - \mathbf{j}$, $\mathbf{b} = 4\mathbf{i} - 3\mathbf{j}$ and $\mathbf{c} = -2\mathbf{i} - \mathbf{j}$. Calculate $\mathbf{a}\cdot\mathbf{b}$, $\mathbf{a}\cdot\mathbf{c}$ and $\mathbf{a}\cdot(\mathbf{b}+\mathbf{c})$, and verify that $\mathbf{a}\cdot(\mathbf{b}+\mathbf{c}) = \mathbf{a}\cdot\mathbf{b} + \mathbf{a}\cdot\mathbf{c}$.

3 Let $\mathbf{p} = \begin{pmatrix} 3 \\ -1 \\ 4 \end{pmatrix}$, $\mathbf{q} = \begin{pmatrix} -1 \\ -9 \\ 3 \end{pmatrix}$ and $\mathbf{r} = \begin{pmatrix} 33 \\ -13 \\ -28 \end{pmatrix}$. Calculate $\mathbf{p}\cdot\mathbf{q}$, $\mathbf{p}\cdot\mathbf{r}$ and $\mathbf{q}\cdot\mathbf{r}$. What can you deduce about the vectors $\mathbf{p}$, $\mathbf{q}$ and $\mathbf{r}$?

4 Which of the following vectors are perpendicular to each other?

    (a) $2\mathbf{i} - 3\mathbf{j} + 6\mathbf{k}$     (b) $2\mathbf{i} - 3\mathbf{j} - 6\mathbf{k}$     (c) $-3\mathbf{i} - 6\mathbf{j} + 2\mathbf{k}$     (d) $6\mathbf{i} - 2\mathbf{j} - 3\mathbf{k}$

5 Let $\mathbf{p} = \mathbf{i} - 2\mathbf{k}$, $\mathbf{q} = 3\mathbf{j} + 2\mathbf{k}$ and $\mathbf{r} = 2\mathbf{i} - \mathbf{j} + 5\mathbf{k}$. Calculate $\mathbf{p}\cdot\mathbf{q}$, $\mathbf{p}\cdot\mathbf{r}$ and $\mathbf{p}\cdot(\mathbf{q}+\mathbf{r})$ and verify that $\mathbf{p}\cdot(\mathbf{q}+\mathbf{r}) = \mathbf{p}\cdot\mathbf{q} + \mathbf{p}\cdot\mathbf{r}$.

6 Find the magnitude of each of the following vectors.

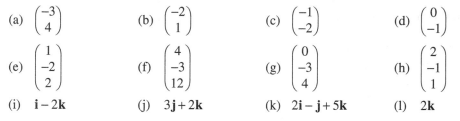

    (a) $\begin{pmatrix} -3 \\ 4 \end{pmatrix}$     (b) $\begin{pmatrix} -2 \\ 1 \end{pmatrix}$     (c) $\begin{pmatrix} -1 \\ -2 \end{pmatrix}$     (d) $\begin{pmatrix} 0 \\ -1 \end{pmatrix}$

    (e) $\begin{pmatrix} 1 \\ -2 \\ 2 \end{pmatrix}$     (f) $\begin{pmatrix} 4 \\ -3 \\ 12 \end{pmatrix}$     (g) $\begin{pmatrix} 0 \\ -3 \\ 4 \end{pmatrix}$     (h) $\begin{pmatrix} 2 \\ -1 \\ 1 \end{pmatrix}$

    (i) $\mathbf{i} - 2\mathbf{k}$     (j) $3\mathbf{j} + 2\mathbf{k}$     (k) $2\mathbf{i} - \mathbf{j} + 5\mathbf{k}$     (l) $2\mathbf{k}$

7 Let $\mathbf{a} = \begin{pmatrix} 4 \\ -3 \end{pmatrix}$. Find the magnitude of $\mathbf{a}$, and find a unit vector in the same direction as $\mathbf{a}$.

8 Find unit vectors in the same directions as $\begin{pmatrix} 1 \\ -2 \\ 2 \end{pmatrix}$ and $2\mathbf{i} - \mathbf{j} + 2\mathbf{k}$.

9 Let $A$ and $B$ be points with position vectors $\mathbf{a} = \begin{pmatrix} 3 \\ 1 \end{pmatrix}$ and $\mathbf{b} = \begin{pmatrix} 3 \\ 2 \end{pmatrix}$ respectively. Draw a diagram showing the points $O$, $A$ and $B$. Calculate the angle $AOB$

    (a) by finding the tangents of the angles $\alpha$ and $\beta$ between $\mathbf{a}$ and the $x$-axis, and $\mathbf{b}$ and the $x$-axis, and using the formula for $\tan(\alpha - \beta)$,

    (b) by using a method based on scalar products.

**10** Use a vector method to calculate the angles between the following pairs of vectors, giving your answers in degrees to one place of decimals, where appropriate.

(a) $\begin{pmatrix} 2 \\ 1 \end{pmatrix}$ and $\begin{pmatrix} 1 \\ 3 \end{pmatrix}$　　　　　(b) $\begin{pmatrix} 4 \\ -5 \end{pmatrix}$ and $\begin{pmatrix} -5 \\ 4 \end{pmatrix}$　　　　　(c) $\begin{pmatrix} 4 \\ -6 \end{pmatrix}$ and $\begin{pmatrix} -6 \\ 9 \end{pmatrix}$

(d) $\begin{pmatrix} -1 \\ 4 \\ 5 \end{pmatrix}$ and $\begin{pmatrix} 2 \\ 0 \\ -3 \end{pmatrix}$　　　　(e) $\begin{pmatrix} 1 \\ 2 \\ -3 \end{pmatrix}$ and $\begin{pmatrix} 2 \\ 3 \\ -4 \end{pmatrix}$　　　　(f) $\begin{pmatrix} 2 \\ -1 \\ 3 \end{pmatrix}$ and $\begin{pmatrix} 5 \\ -2 \\ -4 \end{pmatrix}$

**11** Let $\mathbf{r}_1 = \begin{pmatrix} x_1 \\ y_1 \end{pmatrix}$ and $\mathbf{r}_2 = \begin{pmatrix} x_2 \\ y_2 \end{pmatrix}$. Calculate $|\mathbf{r}_2 - \mathbf{r}_1|$ and interpret your result geometrically.

**12** Find the cosine of the angle between the lines $\mathbf{r} = \begin{pmatrix} 4 \\ 2 \end{pmatrix} + s\begin{pmatrix} -2 \\ 3 \end{pmatrix}$ and $\mathbf{r} = \begin{pmatrix} 2 \\ -3 \end{pmatrix} + t\begin{pmatrix} 1 \\ 2 \end{pmatrix}$.

**13** Find the cosine of the angle between the lines $\mathbf{r} = \begin{pmatrix} -1 \\ 2 \\ 3 \end{pmatrix} + s\begin{pmatrix} 4 \\ 1 \\ -1 \end{pmatrix}$ and $\mathbf{r} = \begin{pmatrix} 2 \\ -3 \\ 4 \end{pmatrix} + t\begin{pmatrix} -1 \\ 6 \\ 2 \end{pmatrix}$.

**14** Find the angle between the line joining $(1, 2)$ and $(3, -5)$ and the line joining $(2, -3)$ to $(1, 4)$.

**15** Find the angle between the line joining $(1, 3, -2)$ and $(2, 5, -1)$ and the line joining $(-1, 4, 3)$ to $(3, 2, 1)$.

**16** Find the angle between the diagonals of a cube.

**17** *ABCD* is the base of a square pyramid of side 2 units, and *V* is the vertex. The pyramid is symmetrical, and of height 4 units. Calculate the acute angle between *AV* and *BC*, giving your answer in degrees correct to one decimal place.

**18** Two aeroplanes are flying in directions given by the vectors $300\mathbf{i} + 400\mathbf{j} + 2\mathbf{k}$ and $-100\mathbf{i} + 500\mathbf{j} - \mathbf{k}$. A person from the flight control centre is plotting their paths on a map. Find the acute angle between their paths on the map.

**19** The roof of a house has a rectangular base of side 4 metres by 8 metres. The ridge line of the roof is 6 metres long, and 1 metre above the base of the roof. Calculate the acute angle between two opposite slanting edges of the roof.

**20** Let *P* be the point $(p, q)$ and let *l* be the straight line $ax + by + c = 0$.

(a) Find a vector in the direction of *l*.

(b) Find a unit vector $\mathbf{v}$ which is perpendicular to *l*.

(c) Write down in the form $\mathbf{r} = \mathbf{u} + t\mathbf{v}$ the equation of the line from *P* perpendicular to *l*.

(d) Calculate the value of the parameter *t* for the point where this perpendicular meets *l*, and hence find a formula for the perpendicular distance of *P* from *l*.

## 12.5 Some geometrical proofs

The algebra of vectors provides an effective and economical method for proving geometrical results. There were a few examples in Chapter 5, but with scalar products you can prove many more results, involving lengths and angles.

### Example 12.5.1

Prove that the angle in a semicircle is a right angle.

This means: if $AB$ is the diameter of a circle, and $C$ is any other point on the circle, then angle $ACB$ is a right angle (see Fig. 12.9).

Take an origin at the centre of the circle (radius $r$). If the position vector of $A$ is $\mathbf{a}$, then the position vector $\mathbf{b}$ of $B$ is $-\mathbf{a}$. If $\overrightarrow{OC} = \mathbf{c}$, then both $\mathbf{a} \cdot \mathbf{a}$ and $\mathbf{c} \cdot \mathbf{c}$ are equal to $r^2$. Therefore $\mathbf{c}^2 - \mathbf{a}^2 = 0$.

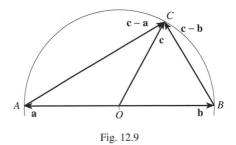

Fig. 12.9

This is the difference of two squares in vector form, and it can be factorised exactly as in ordinary algebra to give

$$(\mathbf{c} - \mathbf{a}) \cdot (\mathbf{c} + \mathbf{a}) = 0, \text{ which is } (\mathbf{c} - \mathbf{a}) \cdot (\mathbf{c} - \mathbf{b}) = 0, \text{ or } \overrightarrow{AC} \cdot \overrightarrow{BC} = 0.$$

At this point vector algebra differs from ordinary algebra. Since $C$ is not at $A$ or $B$, neither $\overrightarrow{AC}$ nor $\overrightarrow{BC}$ is zero. So $\overrightarrow{AC}$ and $\overrightarrow{BC}$ are perpendicular to each other; that is, $ACB$ is a right angle.

### Example 12.5.2 (the cosine formula)

Prove that, in a triangle $ABC$, $a^2 = b^2 + c^2 - 2bc \cos A$.

Denote the displacement vectors $\overrightarrow{AB}$ and $\overrightarrow{AC}$ by $\mathbf{p}$ and $\mathbf{q}$ (see Fig. 12.10).

Then $\overrightarrow{BC} = \mathbf{q} - \mathbf{p}$.

$$\begin{aligned}
a^2 = \overrightarrow{BC} \cdot \overrightarrow{BC} &= (\mathbf{q} - \mathbf{p})^2 \\
&= \mathbf{q}^2 + \mathbf{p}^2 - 2\mathbf{q} \cdot \mathbf{p} \\
&= \overrightarrow{AC} \cdot \overrightarrow{AC} + \overrightarrow{AB} \cdot \overrightarrow{AB} \\
&\quad - 2|\mathbf{q}||\mathbf{p}|\cos A \\
&= b^2 + c^2 - 2bc \cos A.
\end{aligned}$$

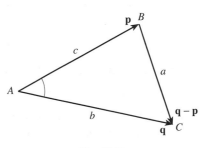

Fig. 12.10

### Example 12.5.3

Prove that, in a triangle, the lines through the vertices perpendicular to the opposite sides (called the **altitudes**) meet at a point.

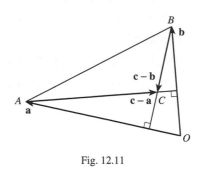

In Fig. 12.11, one vertex is taken as the origin, the other two vertices are $A$ and $B$, and the altitudes through $A$ and $B$ meet at $C$. The displacement vector $\overrightarrow{AC} = \mathbf{c} - \mathbf{a}$ is perpendicular to $\overrightarrow{OB} = \mathbf{b}$, and similarly $\mathbf{c} - \mathbf{b}$ is perpendicular to $\mathbf{a}$. So $(\mathbf{c} - \mathbf{a}) \cdot \mathbf{b} = 0$ and $(\mathbf{c} - \mathbf{b}) \cdot \mathbf{a} = 0$, which means that $\mathbf{c} \cdot \mathbf{b} = \mathbf{a} \cdot \mathbf{b}$ and $\mathbf{c} \cdot \mathbf{a} = \mathbf{b} \cdot \mathbf{a}$.

Since $\mathbf{a} \cdot \mathbf{b} = \mathbf{b} \cdot \mathbf{a}$, it follows from these two equations that $\mathbf{c} \cdot \mathbf{b} = \mathbf{c} \cdot \mathbf{a}$, so that $\mathbf{c} \cdot (\mathbf{b} - \mathbf{a}) = 0$. The geometrical interpretation of this is that $\overrightarrow{OC}$

Fig. 12.11

is perpendicular to $\overrightarrow{AB}$. So $OC$ is the third altitude. Therefore the three altitudes meet at the point $C$. This point is called the **orthocentre** of the triangle.

### Example 12.5.4

A tetrahedron $OABC$ has two pairs of perpendicular opposite edges. Prove that
(a) the third pair of opposite edges is perpendicular,
(b) the sums of the squares of the lengths of the three pairs of opposite edges are equal.

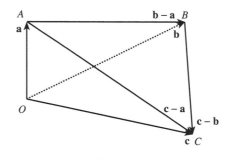

Fig. 12.12 shows the tetrahedron, with one vertex at the origin.

(a) What is required is to prove that, if $OA$ is perpendicular to $BC$, and $OB$ is perpendicular to $AC$, then $OC$ is perpendicular to $AB$. In the conventional notation for position vectors, what you have to prove is that, if $\mathbf{a} \cdot (\mathbf{c} - \mathbf{b}) = 0$ and $\mathbf{b} \cdot (\mathbf{c} - \mathbf{a}) = 0$, then $\mathbf{c} \cdot (\mathbf{b} - \mathbf{a}) = 0$.

Fig. 12.12

This is algebraically identical to the proof in the previous example! The algebra has one interpretation in two dimensions, and another in three dimensions.

(b) $OA^2 + BC^2 = \mathbf{a}^2 + (\mathbf{c} - \mathbf{b})^2 = \mathbf{a}^2 + \mathbf{b}^2 + \mathbf{c}^2 - 2\mathbf{c} \cdot \mathbf{b}$.

Similarly,

$$OB^2 + CA^2 = \mathbf{a}^2 + \mathbf{b}^2 + \mathbf{c}^2 - 2\mathbf{a} \cdot \mathbf{c} \text{ and } OC^2 + AB^2 = \mathbf{a}^2 + \mathbf{b}^2 + \mathbf{c}^2 - 2\mathbf{b} \cdot \mathbf{a}.$$

From the equations in (a),

$$\mathbf{c} \cdot \mathbf{b} = \mathbf{a} \cdot \mathbf{c} = \mathbf{b} \cdot \mathbf{a}.$$

Therefore

$$OA^2 + BC^2 = OB^2 + CA^2 = OC^2 + AB^2.$$

Where appropriate, the alphabet convention (page 60) has been used.

1  Draw two vectors **a** and **b** such that $|\mathbf{a}| = |\mathbf{b}|$, and complete the parallelogram $OACB$.
   Mark on your diagram the vectors $\mathbf{a} - \mathbf{b}$ and $\mathbf{a} + \mathbf{b}$. By considering the scalar product
   $(\mathbf{a} + \mathbf{b}) \cdot (\mathbf{a} - \mathbf{b})$, prove that the diagonals of a rhombus are at right angles.

2  $OACB$ is a parallelogram. Write down the vectors $\overrightarrow{OC}$ and $\overrightarrow{AB}$ in terms of **a** and **b**. Use
   scalar products to prove that, if the parallelogram has equal diagonals, then it is a rectangle.

3  Let $OAB$ be a triangle with $AB^2 = OA^2 + OB^2$. By considering the equation
   $(\mathbf{a} - \mathbf{b}) \cdot (\mathbf{a} - \mathbf{b}) = \mathbf{a} \cdot \mathbf{a} + \mathbf{b} \cdot \mathbf{b}$, prove that the triangle $OAB$ is right-angled at $O$.

4  Let $OABC$ be a kite, with $OB$ as its line of symmetry. Write down the vectors $\overrightarrow{AB}$ and
   $\overrightarrow{CB}$ in terms of **a**, **b** and **c**, and use the fact that the lengths of $AB$ and $CB$ are equal to
   write an equation involving scalar products. Use this equation, together with another
   equation, to prove that the diagonals of a kite are perpendicular.

5  Let $OAB$ be a triangle. Let $\hat{\mathbf{a}}$ be a unit vector in the direction of **a** and $\hat{\mathbf{b}}$ be a unit vector
   in the direction of **b**, and denote $|\mathbf{a}|$ and $|\mathbf{b}|$ by $a$ and $b$.

   (a)  What can you say about the direction of $\hat{\mathbf{a}} + \hat{\mathbf{b}}$ and the directions of $\hat{\mathbf{a}}$ and $\hat{\mathbf{b}}$?

   (b)  Write an expression for $\hat{\mathbf{a}}$ in terms of **a** and $a$, and a similar one for $\hat{\mathbf{b}}$.

   (c)  Use the vector equation of the line $AB$ in the form $\mathbf{r} = \mathbf{a} + t(\mathbf{b} - \mathbf{a})$ to find where
        the line $AB$ intersects the line drawn from $O$ in the direction $\hat{\mathbf{a}} + \hat{\mathbf{b}}$.

   (d)  Prove the angle bisector theorem, namely, that if the bisector of the angle $AOB$ of a
        triangle meets the opposite side in $D$, then $OA : OB = AD : DB$.

6  (a)  Show that, if a vector **p** is perpendicular to two vectors **a** and **b**, it is also
        perpendicular to $s\mathbf{a} + t\mathbf{b}$ for any values of $s$ and $t$ which are not both zero.

   (b)  Show that, if a line is perpendicular to two non-parallel lines in a plane, it is
        perpendicular to every line in the plane.

   (c)  In a tetrahedron $OABC$, the line from $C$ perpendicular to the plane $OAB$ and the line
        from $B$ perpendicular to the plane $OAC$ meet at a point $H$. Show that $\mathbf{h} \cdot \mathbf{a} = \mathbf{c} \cdot \mathbf{a}$,
        and find three more equations like this connecting **h** with **a**, **b** and **c**. Deduce that
        $\mathbf{a} \cdot (\mathbf{b} - \mathbf{c}) = 0$, and interpret this equation geometrically.

   (d)  Prove also that, for this tetrahedron, $OB^2 + AC^2 = OC^2 + AB^2$.

1  Point $A$ has coordinates $(2, -1, 3)$ and point $B$ has coordinates $(1, 0, 5)$.

   (a)  Write down the equation of the line $AB$ in the form $\mathbf{r} = \mathbf{a} + t\mathbf{u}$.

   (b)  Find the angle between the line $AB$ and the line $\begin{pmatrix} x \\ y \\ z \end{pmatrix} = \begin{pmatrix} 1 \\ 3 \\ 4 \end{pmatrix} + \lambda \begin{pmatrix} -4 \\ 7 \\ 6 \end{pmatrix}$, giving your

   answer to the nearest degree.

   (MEI, adapted)

2  Find which pairs of the following vectors are perpendicular to each other.

   $\mathbf{a} = 2\mathbf{i} + \mathbf{j} - 2\mathbf{k}$          $\mathbf{b} = 2\mathbf{i} - 2\mathbf{j} + \mathbf{k}$          $\mathbf{c} = \mathbf{i} + 2\mathbf{j} + 2\mathbf{k}$          $\mathbf{d} = 3\mathbf{i} + 2\mathbf{j} - 2\mathbf{k}$

3  The vectors $\overrightarrow{AB}$ and $\overrightarrow{AC}$ are $\begin{pmatrix} -1 \\ 0 \\ 3 \end{pmatrix}$ and $\begin{pmatrix} 2 \\ 4 \\ 3 \end{pmatrix}$ respectively. The vector $\overrightarrow{AD}$ is the sum of

$\overrightarrow{AB}$ and $\overrightarrow{AC}$. Determine the acute angle, in degrees correct to one decimal place, between the diagonals of the parallelogram defined by the points $A$, $B$, $C$ and $D$.     (OCR)

4  The points $A$, $B$ and $C$ have position vectors $\mathbf{a} = \begin{pmatrix} 2 \\ 1 \\ 2 \end{pmatrix}$, $\mathbf{b} = \begin{pmatrix} -3 \\ 2 \\ 5 \end{pmatrix}$ and $\mathbf{c} = \begin{pmatrix} 4 \\ 5 \\ -2 \end{pmatrix}$

respectively, with respect to a fixed origin. The point $D$ is such that $ABCD$, in that order, is a parallelogram.

(a)  Find the position vector of $D$.

(b)  Find the position vector of the point at which the diagonals of the parallelogram intersect.

(c)  Calculate the angle $BAC$, giving your answer to the nearest tenth of a degree.    (OCR)

5  A vertical aerial is supported by three straight cables, each attached to the aerial at a point $P$, 30 metres up the aerial. The cables are attached to the horizontal ground at points $A$, $B$ and $C$, each $x$ metres from the foot $O$ of the aerial , and situated symmetrically around it (see the diagrams).

Suppose that $\mathbf{i}$ is the unit vector in the direction $\overrightarrow{OA}$, $\mathbf{j}$ is the unit vector perpendicular to $\mathbf{i}$ in the plane of the ground, as shown in the Plan view, and $\mathbf{k}$ is the unit vector in the direction $\overrightarrow{OP}$.

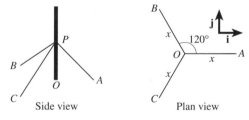

(a)  Write down expressions for the vectors $\overrightarrow{OA}$, $\overrightarrow{OB}$ and $\overrightarrow{OC}$ in terms of $x$, $\mathbf{i}$, $\mathbf{j}$ and $\mathbf{k}$.

(b)  (i)  Write down an expression for the vector $\overrightarrow{AP}$ in terms of vectors $\overrightarrow{OA}$ and $\overrightarrow{OP}$.

    (ii)  Hence find expressions for the vectors $\overrightarrow{AP}$ and $\overrightarrow{BP}$ in terms of $x$, $\mathbf{i}$, $\mathbf{j}$ and $\mathbf{k}$.

(c)  Given that $\overrightarrow{AP}$ and $\overrightarrow{BP}$ are perpendicular to each other, find the value of $x$.    (OCR)

6  The vectors $\mathbf{AB}$ and $\mathbf{AC}$ are $\begin{pmatrix} -2 \\ 6 \\ -3 \end{pmatrix}$ and $\begin{pmatrix} -2 \\ -3 \\ 6 \end{pmatrix}$ respectively.

(a)  Determine the lengths of the vectors.

(b)  Find the scalar product $\mathbf{AB} \cdot \mathbf{AC}$.

(c)  Use your result from part (b) to calculate the acute angle between the vectors. Give the angle in degrees correct to one decimal place.    (OCR)

7  The position vectors of three points $A$, $B$ and $C$ with respect to a fixed origin $O$ are $2\mathbf{i} - 2\mathbf{j} + \mathbf{k}$, $4\mathbf{i} + 2\mathbf{j} + \mathbf{k}$ and $\mathbf{i} + \mathbf{j} + 3\mathbf{k}$ respectively. Find unit vectors in the directions of $\overrightarrow{CA}$ and $\overrightarrow{CB}$. Calculate angle $ACB$ in degrees, correct to 1 decimal place.    (OCR)

8  (a)  Find the angle between the vectors $2\mathbf{i} + 3\mathbf{j} + 6\mathbf{k}$ and $3\mathbf{i} + 4\mathbf{j} + 12\mathbf{k}$, giving your answer in radians.

   (b)  The vectors $\mathbf{a}$ and $\mathbf{b}$ are non-zero.

       (i)  Given that $\mathbf{a} + \mathbf{b}$ is perpendicular to $\mathbf{a} - \mathbf{b}$, prove that $|\mathbf{a}| = |\mathbf{b}|$.

       (ii)  Given instead that $|\mathbf{a} + \mathbf{b}| = |\mathbf{a} - \mathbf{b}|$, prove that $\mathbf{a}$ and $\mathbf{b}$ are perpendicular.  (OCR)

9  *OABCDEFG*, shown in the figure, is a cuboid. The position vectors of $A$, $C$ and $D$ are $4\mathbf{i}$, $2\mathbf{j}$ and $3\mathbf{k}$ respectively. Calculate

   (a)  $|AG|$,

   (b)  the angle between $AG$ and $OB$.

       (OCR)

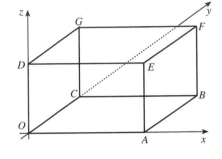

10  $\mathbf{i}$, $\mathbf{j}$ and $\mathbf{k}$ are unit vectors in the $x$-, $y$- and $z$-directions respectively.

   The three-dimensional vector $\mathbf{r}$ has magnitude 5, and makes angles of $\frac{1}{4}\pi$ radians with each of $\mathbf{i}$ and $\mathbf{k}$.

   (a)  Write $\mathbf{r}$ as a column vector, leaving any square roots in your answer.

   (b)  State the angle between $\mathbf{r}$ and the unit vector $\mathbf{j}$.       (OCR)

11  The points $A$, $B$ and $C$ have position vectors given respectively by $\mathbf{a} = 7\mathbf{i} + 4\mathbf{j} - 2\mathbf{k}$, $\mathbf{b} = 5\mathbf{i} + 3\mathbf{j} - 3\mathbf{k}$, $\mathbf{c} = 6\mathbf{i} + 5\mathbf{j} - 4\mathbf{k}$.

   (a)  Find the angle $BAC$.

   (b)  Find the area of the triangle $ABC$.       (OCR)

12  The points $A$, $B$ and $C$ have position vectors $\mathbf{a}$, $\mathbf{b}$ and $\mathbf{c}$ respectively relative to the origin $O$. $P$ is the point on $BC$ such that $\overrightarrow{PC} = \frac{1}{10}\overrightarrow{BC}$.

   (a)  Show that the position vector of $P$ is $\frac{1}{10}(9\mathbf{c} + \mathbf{b})$.

   (b)  Given that the line $AP$ is perpendicular to the line $BC$, show that
        $(9\mathbf{c} + \mathbf{b}) \cdot (\mathbf{c} - \mathbf{b}) = 10\mathbf{a} \cdot (\mathbf{c} - \mathbf{b})$.

   (c)  Given also that $OA$, $OB$ and $OC$ are mutually perpendicular, prove that $OC = \frac{1}{3}OB$.
        (OCR)

13  Let $\mathbf{r} \cdot \mathbf{r} = a^2$ be the equation of a sphere, centre the origin and radius $a$, and let $C$, with position vector $\mathbf{c}$, be any other point. Let $\mathbf{u}$ be a unit vector.

   (a)  Write down the vector equation of the line through $C$ in the direction $\mathbf{u}$ and write down a quadratic equation whose roots are the parameters of the points where this line meets the sphere.

   (b)  Find the condition that the line through $C$ in the direction $\mathbf{u}$ is a tangent to the sphere.

   (c)  Deduce that, if $\mathbf{R}$ is the position vector of $\mathbf{r}$ when the line of part (a) is a tangent to the sphere, then $\mathbf{R} \cdot \mathbf{u} = 0$. Interpret this geometrically.

# Revision exercise 2

1  (a)  Find the area of the region enclosed between $y = \tan x$ and the $x$-axis from $x = 0$ to $x = \frac{1}{3}\pi$.

(b)  Find the volume generated when this area is rotated about the $x$-axis.

2  The diagram shows a fixed semicircle, with centre $O$ and radius $r$, and an inscribed rectangle $ABCD$. The vertices $A$ and $B$ of the rectangle lie on the circumference of the semicircle, and $C$ and $D$ lie on the diameter. The size of angle $BOC$ is $\theta$ radians.

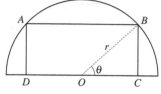

(a)  Express the perimeter, $p$, of the rectangle in terms of $r$ and $\theta$, and show that the area, $a$, may be expressed as $a = r^2 \sin 2\theta$.

(b)  Find the maximum value of $a$ as $\theta$ varies, and show that when $a$ has its maximum value, $p = 3r\sqrt{2}$.

(c)  Find, in terms of $r$, the area of the rectangle which has maximum perimeter.

(OCR, adapted)

3  A curve is defined parametrically by $x = \sqrt{3}\tan\theta$, $y = \sqrt{3}\cos\theta$, $\qquad 0 \le \theta \le \pi$.

(a)  Find $\dfrac{dy}{dx}$ in terms of $\theta$.

(b)  Find the equation of the tangent to the curve at the point where $\theta = \frac{1}{6}\pi$.  (OCR)

4  Express $\dfrac{1}{(1+x)(3-x)}$ as the sum of partial fractions. Hence express $\dfrac{1}{(1+x)^2(3-x)^2}$ as the sum of partial fractions.

A region is bounded by parts of the $x$- and $y$-axes, the curve $y = \dfrac{1}{(1+x)(3-x)}$ and the line $x = 2$. Find the area of the region, and the volume of the solid of revolution formed by rotating it about the $x$-axis.  (OCR)

5  The vectors $\mathbf{a}$ and $\mathbf{b}$ are shown on the grid of unit squares.

(a)  Calculate $|\mathbf{a} + \mathbf{b}|$.

(b)  Calculate $\mathbf{a} \cdot \mathbf{b}$.

(c)  Calculate the angle between $\mathbf{a}$ and $\mathbf{b}$.  (OCR)

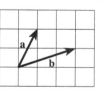

6  (a)  Use the substitution $y = \frac{1}{2}\pi - x$ to show that $\displaystyle\int_0^{\frac{1}{2}\pi} \sin^2 x \, dx = \int_0^{\frac{1}{2}\pi} \cos^2 y \, dy$.

(b)  Show that $\displaystyle\int_0^{\frac{1}{2}\pi} \cos^2 y \, dy = \int_0^{\frac{1}{2}\pi} \cos^2 x \, dx$, and $\displaystyle\int_0^{\frac{1}{2}\pi} \sin^2 x \, dx = \int_0^{\frac{1}{2}\pi} \cos^2 x \, dx$.

(c)  Find $\displaystyle\int_0^{\frac{1}{2}\pi} \left(\sin^2 x + \cos^2 x\right) dx$ and hence show that $\displaystyle\int_0^{\frac{1}{2}\pi} \sin^2 x \, dx = \frac{1}{4}\pi$.

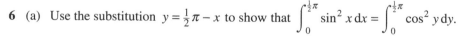

7 An anthropologist is modelling the population of the island of A. In the model, the population at the start of the year $t$ is $P$. The birth rate is 10 births per 1000 population per year. The death rate is $m$ deaths per 1000 population per year.

(a) Show that $\dfrac{\mathrm{d}P}{\mathrm{d}t} = \dfrac{(10-m)P}{1000}$.

(b) At the start of year 0 the population was 108 000. Find an expression for $P$ in terms of $t$.

(c) State one assumption about the population of A that is required for this model to be valid.

(d) If the population is to double in 100 years, find the value of $m$.

(e) Explain why the population cannot double in less than 69 years.     (OCR)

8 A model for the way in which a population of animals in a closed environment varies with time is given, for $P > \frac{1}{3}$, by $\dfrac{\mathrm{d}P}{\mathrm{d}t} = \frac{1}{2}\left(3P^2 - P\right)\sin t$, where $P$ is the size of the population in thousands at time $t$. Given that $P = \frac{1}{2}$ when $t = 0$, show that

$\ln \dfrac{3P-1}{P} = \frac{1}{2}(1 - \cos t)$. Rearrange this equation to show that $P = \dfrac{1}{3 - e^{\frac{1}{2}(1-\cos t)}}$.

Calculate the smallest positive value of $t$ for which $P = 1$, and find the two values between which the number of animals in the population oscillates.     (MEI, adapted)

9 Two small insects $A$ and $B$ are crawling on the walls of a room, with $A$ starting from the ceiling. The floor is horizontal and forms the $xy$-plane, and the $z$-axis is vertically upwards. Relative to the origin $O$, the position vectors of the insects at time $t$ seconds $(0 \le t \le 10)$ are $\overrightarrow{OA} = \mathbf{i} + 3\mathbf{j} + \left(4 - \frac{1}{10}t\right)\mathbf{k}$, $\overrightarrow{OB} = \left(\frac{1}{5}t + 1\right)\mathbf{i} - 3\mathbf{j} + 2\mathbf{k}$, where the unit of distance is the metre.

(a) Write down the height of the room.

(b) Show that the insects move in such a way that angle $BOA = 90°$.

(c) For each insect, write down a vector to represent its displacement between $t = 0$ and $t = 10$, and show that these displacements are perpendicular to each other.

(d) Write down expressions for the vector $\overrightarrow{AB}$ and for $\left|\overrightarrow{AB}\right|^2$, and hence find the minimum distance between the insects, correct to 3 significant figures.     (OCR)

10 (a) Differentiate $x\sqrt{2-x}$ with respect to $x$.

(b) Find $\displaystyle\int x\sqrt{2-x}\,\mathrm{d}x$

(i) by using the substitution $2 - x = u$, (ii) by integration by parts.

11 Find the coordinates of the points at which the tangent to the curve with equation $x^2 + 4xy + 5y^2 = 4$ is parallel to one of the axes.

12 A curve is given parametrically by the equations $x = \sin t$, $y = t\cos t$ for $0 \le t \le \frac{1}{2}\pi$. Find an expression for $\dfrac{\mathrm{d}y}{\mathrm{d}x}$ terms of $t$, and find the cartesian equation of the curve. Check your answer by drawing the curve on your calculator from the parametric equations and from your cartesian equation, and comparing the results.

# Mock examination 1

**Time** 1 hour 20 minutes

Answer all the questions.
Only scientific calculators are allowed.

1. Solve the differential equation $\dfrac{dy}{dx} = e^y \sin 2x$, given that when $x = \frac{1}{4}\pi$, $y = 0$. [4]

2. Use the substitution $u = 2x - 1$ to find $\displaystyle\int x(2x - 1)^5 \, dx$. [4]

3. Differentiate $x^2(1 - 2x)^{-\frac{1}{2}}$ with respect to $x$. [2]

   Find the binomial expansion of $(1 - 2x)^{-\frac{1}{2}}$ in ascending powers of $x$, up to and including the term in $x^3$. [3]

4. The value of $\sec\theta$ is given to be $-3$, where $\pi < \theta < 2\pi$.
   (i) Find the exact value of $\tan\theta$, showing your reasoning clearly. [3]
   (ii) Let $\alpha = \cos^{-1}\left(-\frac{1}{3}\right)$. Write down the value of $\theta$ in terms of $\alpha$. [2]

5. Let $C$ be the circle with equation $x^2 + y^2 - 2x + 4y - 11 = 0$.
   (i) Find whether the origin lies inside or outside $C$, explaining your reasoning carefully. [3]
   (ii) Find the equation of the chord which is bisected by the point $(2, -1)$. [3]

6. Split $\dfrac{2x + 11}{(x - 2)(2x + 1)}$ into partial fractions, and use your result to find the exact value of

   $\displaystyle\int_4^7 \dfrac{2x + 11}{(x - 2)(2x + 1)} \, dx$, giving your answer as a single logarithm. [7]

7. A curve is defined parametrically by the equations $x = t + \dfrac{1}{t}$, $y = t - \dfrac{1}{t}$, where $t \neq 0$.

   Find the values of the parameter for which $x = 4\frac{1}{4}$, and hence find the corresponding values of $y$. [3]

   (i) Find the gradient of the tangent of the point in the fourth quadrant for which $x = 4\frac{1}{4}$, and hence find the equation of the tangent at this point. [3]
   (ii) Find the cartesian equation of the curve. [2]

**8** An ellipse with its centre at the origin $O$ has equation $41x^2 + 24xy + 34y^2 = 1250$.

   (i)   Find an expression in terms of $x$ and $y$ for $\dfrac{dy}{dx}$.                    [3]

   (ii)  Show that, if the tangent to the ellipse at a point $P$ is perpendicular to the line $OP$, then $12x^2 - 7xy - 12y^2 = 0$.                    [3]

   (iii) By first factorising $12x^2 - 7xy - 12y^2$, show that the ends of the axes of the ellipse are at the points $(\pm 4, \pm 3)$, $\left(\pm 3\sqrt{2}, \mp 4\sqrt{2}\right)$.                    [4]

**9** (i)   Show that the straight lines with equations $\mathbf{r} = 2\mathbf{i} - \mathbf{j} + 3\mathbf{k} + s(\mathbf{j} - \mathbf{k})$ and $\mathbf{r} = -2\mathbf{i} + 7\mathbf{j} + 3\mathbf{k} + t(2\mathbf{i} - 3\mathbf{j} - \mathbf{k})$ intersect, and find the coordinates of their point of intersection.                    [4]

   (ii)  Find the angle between the lines in part (i), giving your answer in radians correct to one place of decimals.                    [4]

   (iii) Find the coordinates of the foot of the perpendicular from the point $(-2, 7, 3)$ on to the line $\mathbf{r} = 2\mathbf{i} - \mathbf{j} + 3\mathbf{k} + s(\mathbf{j} - \mathbf{k})$.                    [3]

# Mock examination 2

**Time** 1 hour 20 minutes

Answer all the questions.
Only scientific calculators are allowed.

1 Show that the point $(-1,1)$ lies on the curve with equation $y - x^2 = 2(1 - x^2 y)$. Find the gradient of the tangent to the curve at $(-1,1)$. [4]

2 Express $\dfrac{1}{x(4-x)}$ in partial fractions, and hence find $\displaystyle\int_1^3 \dfrac{1}{x(4-x)}\, dx$, giving your answer in an exact form. [4]

3 (i) Differentiate $x^2 e^{2x}$ with respect to $x$. [2]

(ii) Use integration by parts to find $\displaystyle\int xe^{2x}\, dx$. [4]

4 (i) Find the expansions of $(1+8x)^{\frac{1}{2}}$ and $(1-4x)^{-\frac{1}{2}}$ in ascending powers of $x$ up to and including the term in $x^2$. [4]

(ii) Hence find the expansion of $\sqrt{\dfrac{1+8x}{1-4x}}$ in ascending powers of $x$ up to and including the term in $x^2$, stating the values of $x$ for which the approximation is valid. [3]

5 The population of a community with finite resources has been modelled by the equation $\dfrac{dn}{dt} = 0.01ne^{-0.01t}$, where $n$ is the population at time $t$. Find the solution of this equation in the form $\ln n = f(t)$, given that the population at $t = 0$ is 5000. [5]

What happens to the population in the long term? [2]

6 (i) Decide whether or not the point $(1,3,-1)$ lies on the line with the vector equation
$$\mathbf{r} = \begin{pmatrix} 1 \\ 2 \\ -3 \end{pmatrix} + t \begin{pmatrix} 1 \\ 3 \\ 7 \end{pmatrix}, \text{ showing your reasoning.}$$ [2]

(ii) Find a vector in the direction of the line which passes through the points $(1,2,-3)$ and $(-4,-1,-1)$, and show that this vector is perpendicular to the direction vector of the line $\mathbf{r} = \begin{pmatrix} 2 \\ 5 \\ 4 \end{pmatrix} + t \begin{pmatrix} 1 \\ 3 \\ 7 \end{pmatrix}$. [3]

(iii) Find whether or not the line which passes through the points $(1,2,-3)$ and $(-4,-1,-1)$ meets the line with the vector equation $\mathbf{r} = \begin{pmatrix} 2 \\ 5 \\ 4 \end{pmatrix} + t \begin{pmatrix} 1 \\ 3 \\ 7 \end{pmatrix}$. [5]

**7**  *OAB* is a stiff bent rod, consisting of two straight parts *OA* and *OB* of length 6 and 4 respectively, with a right-angle bend at *A*, as shown in the figure. The rod can rotate freely about *O*, and the angle that *OA* makes with the *x*-axis is $\theta$. The projections of *B* on the *x*- and *y*-axes are *P* and *Q* respectively.

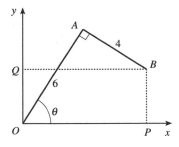

(i)  Show that $OP = 6\cos\theta + 4\sin\theta$, and find a similar expression for *OQ*.  [3]

(ii)  Prove that the area of the rectangle *OPBQ* is $10\sin 2\theta - 24\cos 2\theta$.  [3]

(iii)  Find the maximum value of this area, and the corresponding value of $\theta$, in degrees correct to one decimal place.  [4]

**8**  A curve is given parametrically by the equations
$$x = 1 + \cos\theta + \sin\theta, \quad y = 2 + \cos\theta - \sin\theta \text{ for } 0 \leqslant \theta < 2\pi.$$

Find the gradient of the curve at the point with parameter $\theta$, and show that the equation of the normal at the same point is
$$(\sin\theta + \cos\theta)y + (\sin\theta - \cos\theta)x = 3\sin\theta + \cos\theta.$$  [5]

By first writing the parametric equations in the form
$$\left.\begin{aligned} \cos\theta + \sin\theta &= x - 1 \\ \cos\theta - \sin\theta &= y - 2 \end{aligned}\right\},$$

solve the equations for $\cos\theta$ and $\sin\theta$ in terms of $x$ and $y$.  [2]

Find the cartesian equation of the curve and show that the curve is a circle. Give its centre and radius.  [5]

# Answers

## 1 Trigonometry

### Exercise 1A (page 4)

1. (a) $-0.675$  (b) $1.494$  (c) $1.133$

2. (a) $\operatorname{cosec} x$  (b) $\cot x$  (c) $\sec x$
   (d) $\sec^2 x$  (e) $\cot x$  (f) $-\operatorname{cosec} x$

3. (a) $\sqrt{2}$  (b) $1$  (c) $-\sqrt{3}$
   (d) $-\sqrt{2}$  (e) $-\frac{1}{3}\sqrt{3}$  (f) $\frac{2}{3}\sqrt{3}$
   (g) $0$  (h) $-\frac{2}{3}\sqrt{3}$

4. (a) $0.951$  (b) $1.05$  (c) $3.73$
   (d) $2$  (e) $-0.924$  (f) $3.73$
   (g) $-1.04$  (h) $-1.73$

5. (a) $\frac{5}{4}$  (b) $\frac{4}{3}$  (c) $-\frac{1}{3}\sqrt{3}$
   (d) $\frac{2}{3}\sqrt{3}$

6. $\pm 4\sqrt{3}$, $\pm\sqrt{2}$, $\pm\frac{1}{2}\sqrt{5}$

7. (a) $|\tan\phi|$  (b) $\sin\phi\cos\phi$  (c) $\cot\phi$
   (d) $|\sin\phi|$  (e) $|\tan\phi|$  (f) $\cot^2\phi$

8. (a) $3\sec^2\phi - \sec\phi - 3$  (b) $0.72$, $\pi$, $5.56$

9. $1.11$, $2.82$, $4.25$, $5.96$

10. $\frac{1}{4}\pi, \frac{1}{2}\pi, \frac{3}{4}\pi, \frac{5}{4}\pi, \frac{3}{2}\pi, \frac{7}{4}\pi$

### Exercise 1B (page 9)

1. $\frac{1}{4}\left(\sqrt{6}+\sqrt{2}\right)$, $2+\sqrt{3}$

2. (a) $\frac{1}{4}\left(\sqrt{2}-\sqrt{6}\right)$  (b) $\frac{1}{4}\left(\sqrt{6}+\sqrt{2}\right)$
   (c) $-2-\sqrt{3}$

3. $\frac{1}{2}\cos x - \frac{1}{2}\sqrt{3}\sin x$

4. $-\cos\phi$, $-\sin\phi$

5. $\dfrac{\sqrt{3}+\tan x}{1-\sqrt{3}\tan x}$, $\dfrac{1+\sqrt{3}\tan x}{\tan x - \sqrt{3}}$

7. (a) $\frac{4}{3}$  (b) $\frac{7}{25}$  (c) $\frac{4}{5}$  (d) $\frac{117}{44}$

8. $-\frac{63}{65}$, $-\frac{33}{56}$

### Exercise 1C (page 11)

1. $-\frac{1}{3}\sqrt{5}$, $-\frac{4}{9}\sqrt{5}$, $-4\sqrt{5}$

2. $\frac{1}{8}$, $\pm\frac{1}{4}\sqrt{14}$

3. $\sin 3A = 3\sin A - 4\sin^3 A$

4. $\cos 3A = 4\cos^3 A - 3\cos A$

5. $\tan^2\frac{1}{2}x$

7. $\pm\frac{5}{6}$, $\pm\frac{1}{6}\sqrt{11}$

8. $\frac{2}{3}$, $-\frac{3}{2}$

9. $\pm\sqrt{2}-1$, $\sqrt{2}-1$

10. (a) $\pi$  (b) $\frac{1}{2}\pi$, $3.99$, $5.44$
    (c) $0$, $0.87$, $2.27$, $\pi$, $4.01$, $5.41$, $2\pi$

### Exercise 1D (page 14)

1. $33.7$

2. $53.1$

3. $\sqrt{34}$

4. $\sqrt{37}$, $0.166$

5. (a) $\sqrt{5}$, $1.11$  (b) $\sqrt{5}$, $0.464$
   (c) $\sqrt{5}$, $1.11$  (d) $\sqrt{5}$, $0.464$

6. $\sqrt{61}\cos(\theta - 0.876)$  (a) $\sqrt{61}$ when $\theta = 0.876$
   (b) $-\sqrt{61}$ when $\theta = 4.018$

7. Translation of $\frac{1}{3}\pi$ in the positive $x$-direction and a one-way stretch parallel to the $y$-axis with scale factor 6.

8. $\sqrt{52}\cos(x+0.588)$; translation of $0.588$ in the negative $x$-direction and a one-way stretch parallel to the $y$-axis with scale factor $\sqrt{52}$.

9. $10\sin(x+36.9)°$  (a) $1$  (b) $0$

10. $0.87$ or $3.45$, correct to 2 decimal places

### Exercise 1E (page 16)

1. (a) $\frac{1}{6}\pi$  (b) $\frac{1}{4}\pi$  (c) $\frac{1}{2}\pi$  (d) $\frac{1}{3}\pi$
   (e) $-\frac{1}{3}\pi$  (f) $-\frac{1}{2}\pi$  (g) $\frac{1}{2}\pi$  (h) $\pi$

2. (a) $\frac{1}{4}\pi$  (b) $-\frac{1}{6}\pi$  (c) $\frac{2}{3}\pi$  (d) $\frac{1}{6}\pi$

3. (a) $0.5$  (b) $-1$  (c) $\sqrt{3}$  (d) $0$

4. (a) $\frac{1}{2}\pi$  (b) $\frac{1}{6}\pi$  (c) $\frac{1}{6}\pi$  (d) $0$

5. (a) $\frac{1}{2}$  (b) $\frac{1}{2}$  (c) $\frac{1}{2}\sqrt{3}$  (d) $1$

6. $0.739$; $\cos x = x$

### Miscellaneous exercise 1 (page 16)

1. (b) $-\frac{25}{24}$

2. $60, 120, 240, 300$

3. (a) $1$  (b) $\frac{4}{5}$

4. (b) $60, 300$

5. $\frac{1}{4}\left(\sqrt{6}-\sqrt{2}\right)$

7. (a) $-\frac{4}{5}$  (b) $-\frac{24}{25}$, $\frac{7}{25}$

8. $73.9$

9. $26.6, 90, 206.6, 270$

12. $2\sin(\theta+60)°$; $90, 330$

13. (a) $2\cos(x+60)°$  (b) $0, 60, 180, 240, 360$

14. (a) $15\cos(x-0.644)$  (b) $0.276$

**15** $\sqrt{5}\cos(x-26.6)^\circ$    (a)   $90, 323.1$
    (b)   $-\sqrt{5} \leqslant k \leqslant \sqrt{5}$

**16** (a)   $13\cos(x+67.4)^\circ$
    (b)   $7.5$ when $x = 202.6$, $1$ when $x = 22.6$

**17** $5\cos(x+53.1)^\circ$    (a)   $13.3, 240.4$
    (b)   $\frac{1}{3}$, $\frac{1}{13}$

**18** (a)   $\frac{1}{6}\pi$    (b)   $\dfrac{x+y}{1-xy}$

**19**   $-0.5$

**20** (b)   $\dfrac{1}{x}$, $1-2x^2$

**21** (a)   $x+2y=3$
    (b)   $r = \sqrt{5}$, $\alpha = \tan^{-1} 2 = 63.4\ldots$
    (c)   $(2\sin\theta^\circ, 2\cos\theta^\circ)$, $74.4$

**22** (a)   $(56.8, 0)$, $(123.2, 0)$
    (b)   $53.1$, $120$; $(53.1, 0.6)$, $(120, -0.5)$

# 2 Differentiating trigonometric functions

## Exercise 2A (page 25)

**2** (a)   $-\cos x$       (b)   $\sin x$
   (c)   $4\cos 4x$      (d)   $-6\sin 3x$
   (e)   $\frac{1}{2}\pi\cos\frac{1}{2}\pi x$    (f)   $-3\pi\sin 3\pi x$
   (g)   $-2\sin(2x-1)$    (h)   $15\cos\left(3x+\frac{1}{4}\pi\right)$
   (i)   $5\cos 5x$      (j)   $2\cos\left(\frac{1}{4}\pi-2x\right)$
   (k)   $2\cos 2x$      (l)   $-\pi\sin\pi x$

**3** (a)   $2\sin x\cos x$      (b)   $-2\cos x\sin x$
   (c)   $-3\cos^2 x\sin x$     (d)   $5\sin\frac{1}{2}x\cos\frac{1}{2}x$
   (e)   $-8\cos^3 2x\sin 2x$    (f)   $2x\cos x^2$
   (g)   $-42x^2\sin 2x^3$
   (h)   $\sin\left(\frac{1}{2}x-\frac{1}{3}\pi\right)\cos\left(\frac{1}{2}x-\frac{1}{3}\pi\right)$
   (i)   $-6\pi\cos^2 2\pi x\sin 2\pi x$
   (j)   $6x\sin^2 x^2\cos x^2$
   (k)   $0$       (l)   $-\cos\frac{1}{2}x\sin\frac{1}{2}x$

**4** (a)   $2\sec 2x\tan 2x$    (b)   $-3\operatorname{cosec} 3x\cot 3x$
   (c)   $-3\operatorname{cosec}\left(3x+\frac{1}{5}\pi\right)\cot\left(3x+\frac{1}{5}\pi\right)$
   (d)   $\sec\left(x-\frac{1}{3}\pi\right)\tan\left(x-\frac{1}{3}\pi\right)$
   (e)   $8\sec^2 x\tan x$    (f)   $-3\operatorname{cosec}^3 x\cot x$
   (g)   $-12\operatorname{cosec}^4 3x\cot 3x$
   (h)   $10\sec^2\left(5x-\frac{1}{4}\pi\right)\tan\left(5x-\frac{1}{4}\pi\right)$

**5** (a)   $2\cot 2x$      (b)   $-3\tan 3x$
   (c)   $-\cot x$       (d)   $4\tan 4x$
   (e)   $2\cot x$       (f)   $-6\tan 2x$

**6** (a)   $\cos x\, e^{\sin x}$      (b)   $-3\sin 3x\, e^{\cos 3x}$
   (c)   $10\sin x\cos x\, e^{\sin^2 x}$

**8** (a)   $2y-x = \sqrt{3}-\frac{1}{3}\pi$
   (b)   $3y = \sqrt{2}\left(x-\frac{3}{2}-\frac{1}{4}\pi\right)$
   (c)   $\sqrt{2}y+x = 2+\frac{1}{4}\pi$
   (d)   $y = x+\frac{1}{2}\ln 2-\frac{1}{4}\pi$
   (e)   $y = 3$

**9** (a)   $\left(\frac{1}{4}\pi, \sqrt{2}\right)$, max.; $\left(\frac{5}{4}\pi, -\sqrt{2}\right)$, min.
   (b)   $(\pi, \pi)$, neither max. nor min.
   (c)   $(0, 2)$, max.; $(\pi, -2)$, min.
   (d)   $\left(\frac{1}{12}\pi, \frac{1}{2}\sqrt{3}+\frac{1}{12}\pi\right)$, max.;
       $\left(\frac{5}{12}\pi, -\frac{1}{2}\sqrt{3}+\frac{5}{12}\pi\right)$, min.;
       $\left(\frac{13}{12}\pi, \frac{1}{2}\sqrt{3}+\frac{13}{12}\pi\right)$, max.;
       $\left(\frac{17}{12}\pi, -\frac{1}{2}\sqrt{3}+\frac{17}{12}\pi\right)$, min.
   (e)   $\left(\frac{1}{4}\pi, 2\sqrt{2}\right)$, min.; $\left(\frac{5}{4}\pi, -2\sqrt{2}\right)$, max.
   (f)   $\left(\frac{1}{2}\pi, -3\right)$, min.; $\left(\frac{7}{6}\pi, \frac{3}{2}\right)$, max.; $\left(\frac{3}{2}\pi, 1\right)$, min.;
       $\left(\frac{13}{6}\pi, \frac{3}{2}\right)$, max.

**10**   $\cos(a+x)$,   $-\sin a\sin x+\cos a\cos x$

**11**   $\sin\left(\frac{3}{2}\pi-x\right)$;   $-\sin x$,   $-\cos x$

**12**   As $2\cos^2 x-1 = 1-2\sin^2 x = \cos 2x$, they all differ by only a constant, and therefore have the same derivative.

**13**   $\cos 2x$

**14**   above, at $y = \cos\frac{5}{6}\pi+\frac{5}{12}\pi \approx 0.443$

**15** (a)   $\dfrac{\cos\sqrt{x}}{2\sqrt{x}}$    (b)   $\dfrac{-\sin x}{2\sqrt{\cos x}}$    (c)   $-\dfrac{1}{x^2}\cos\dfrac{1}{x}$

**16**   The curve bends downwards when $y > 0$, and upwards when $y < 0$; $y = \sin(nx+\alpha)$.

**17**   $\dfrac{1+\sin^2 x}{\cos^3 x} = \sec^3 x+\tan^2 x\sec x$

**19** (a)   growing at 50 million dollars per year
   (b)   falling at 9.7 million dollars per year

**20** (a)   $55.2$ mm s$^{-1}$    (b)   $152$ m s$^{-2}$

## Exercise 2B (page 29)

**1** (a)   $\frac{1}{2}\sin 2x+k$      (b)   $-\frac{1}{3}\cos 3x+k$
   (c)   $\frac{1}{2}\sin(2x+1)+k$    (d)   $-\frac{1}{3}\cos(3x-1)+k$
   (e)   $\cos(1-x)+k$    (f)   $-2\sin\left(4-\frac{1}{2}x\right)+k$
   (g)   $-2\cos\left(\frac{1}{2}x+\frac{1}{3}\pi\right)+k$
   (h)   $\frac{1}{3}\sin\left(3x-\frac{1}{4}\pi\right)+k$    (i)   $2\cos\frac{1}{2}x+k$

**2** (a) 1 (b) $\frac{1}{2}\sqrt{2}$ (c) $\frac{1}{2}$

(d) $-\frac{1}{6}\sqrt{2}$ (e) $\frac{1}{6}(\sqrt{3}-1)$ (f) 0

(g) $\sin 1$ (h) $2\cos 1 - 2\cos\frac{5}{4}$ (i) 4

**3** (a) $\frac{1}{2}\ln\sec 2x + k$ (b) $\frac{1}{5}\ln\sin 5x + k$

(c) $\frac{1}{3}\sec 3x + k$ (d) $-\frac{1}{4}\operatorname{cosec} 4x + k$

(e) $\ln\cos\left(\frac{1}{4}\pi - x\right) + k$

(f) $-\frac{1}{2}\ln\sin\left(\frac{1}{3}\pi - 2x\right) + k$

(g) $2\sec\left(\frac{1}{2}x + 1\right) + k$ (h) $\frac{1}{2}\operatorname{cosec}(1 - 2x) + k$

(i) $\frac{1}{2}\sec 2x + k$

**4** (a) $\frac{1}{2}\ln 2$ (b) $\frac{1}{6}\ln 2$

(c) $\frac{1}{3}(1 - \sqrt{2})$ (d) $\ln 2$

(e) $\frac{1}{2}\left(\operatorname{cosec}\frac{1}{2} - \operatorname{cosec} 1\right)$

(f) $4(\sec 0.075 - \sec 0.025)$

**5** (a) $\frac{1}{2}\left(x + \frac{1}{2}\sin 2x\right) + k$ (b) $\frac{1}{2}(x + \sin x) + k$

(c) $\frac{1}{2}\left(x - \frac{1}{4}\sin 4x\right) + k$ (d) $\frac{1}{4}\sin^4 x + k$

(e) $\frac{1}{3}\sec^3 x + k$ (f) $-\frac{1}{10}\operatorname{cosec}^5 2x + k$

(g) $\frac{1}{2}\cos x - \frac{1}{14}\cos 7x + k$

(h) $\frac{1}{3}\cos^3 x - \cos x + k$

(i) $-\cos x + \frac{2}{3}\cos^3 x - \frac{1}{5}\cos^5 x + k$

(j) $\frac{1}{8}\sin 4x - \frac{1}{16}\sin 8x + k$

**6** (a) $2\sec^2 x \tan x$ (b) $\sec^2 x$
(c) $\tan x + k$, $\tan x - x + k$
(d) $-\cot x + k$, $x - \operatorname{cosec} x + k$

**7** $1, \frac{1}{4}\pi^2$

**8** $\pi + 2, \frac{1}{2}\pi(8 + 3\pi)$

**9** (a) $2 - \sqrt{2}$ (b) $\frac{1}{4}\pi(\pi - 2)$

**10** $(0,1), \left(\frac{3}{4}\pi, 0\right); 1 + \sqrt{2}; \frac{1}{4}\pi(3\pi + 2)$

### Miscellaneous exercise 2 (page 31)

**1** (a) $2\cot 2x$

(b) $-\frac{1}{2}(\cos 2x + \cos x) + k$

(c) $-2\cos x \sin x$

(d) $3t^2\cos(t^3 + 4)$

(e) $\frac{1}{2}x + \frac{1}{12}\sin 6x + k$

(f) $-\dfrac{1}{2\sqrt{x}}\sin\sqrt{x}$

(g) $\frac{1}{2}x - \frac{3}{4}\sin\frac{2}{3}x + k$

**2** (a) $\frac{1}{2}(1 - \cos 2x)$

**3** (a) $\frac{1}{4}\sqrt{2}(\sqrt{3} - 1), \dfrac{\sqrt{3} - 1}{\sqrt{3} + 1}$

(c) $3.106, 3.215$

**4** $\dfrac{\sec^2 x \tan x}{\sqrt{\sec^2 x - 1}} = \sec^2 x$, $\sec^2 x$

**5** $(0, -0.404); 1.404, 1.360, 1.622$

**6** $\frac{1}{6}$; better, values are 0.5236 and 0.4997 approximating to 0.5.

**7** 4.4934

**8** (a) $x = 11\left(1 - \cos\left(\dfrac{\pi}{45}t\right)\right)$, 90 seconds

(b) 990 metres, $11 \text{ m s}^{-1}$

(c) $0.665 \text{ m s}^{-2}$

**9** (b) $\frac{1}{2}\pi, \frac{5}{6}\pi$

(c) The model suggests that the motion will continue indefinitely, but in practice it will gradually die out because of friction. In the new model the motion will die out.

**11** (a) $\frac{2}{3}\pi, \pi, \frac{4}{3}\pi, 2\pi$

**12** (a) $\frac{1}{2}\cos\frac{1}{2}x - \frac{1}{3}\sin\frac{1}{3}x$ (b) $1, \frac{1}{2}$
(c) $4\pi, 6\pi$
(d) any integer multiple of $12\pi$

## 3 Circles

### Exercise 3 (page 39)
**1** (a) $x^2 + y^2 = 9$
(b) $(x - 2)^2 + y^2 = 25$
(c) $(x - 1)^2 + (y - 4)^2 = 4$
(d) $(x + 5)^2 + (y - 7)^2 = 1$
(e) $(x - 6)^2 + (y + 2)^2 = 100$
(f) $(x + 7)^2 + (y + 3)^2 = 100$

**2** (a) $(3,2), 5$ (b) $(-4, -1), 3$
(c) $(6,0), 2\sqrt{5}$ (d) $(2,5), 7$
(e) $(-4,1), 3\sqrt{2}$ (f) $\left(1, -\frac{1}{2}\right), \frac{1}{2}$

**3** $x^2 + y^2 - 4x + 10y + 9 = 0$

**4** $x^2 + y^2 - 10x - 10y = 0$

**5** $x + 3y = 0$

**6** $3x - 5y - 6 = 0$

**7** $3x - y + 10 = 0$

**8** $x + y - 3 = 0$

**9** $4x - y = 0$

**10** $2x + 3y = 0$

11  (b)  $\left(-\frac{5}{2},\frac{3}{2}\right), \frac{7}{2}\sqrt{2}$

    (c)  $\left(-\frac{2}{3},\frac{4}{3}\right), \frac{4}{3}$

    (f)  $(-1,-1), 32$

12  $(6,1), (8,1)$

13  $(-10,-32), (-10,16)$

14  $(-3,-3), (-1,3)$

15  $(3,1), (5,-1)$

17  $(5,-3)$

18  $2\sqrt{5}$

20  (a)  $3a$    (b)  $2a$    (c)  $y=-a$

21  $-3, 17$

22  $\frac{4}{3} \pm \frac{1}{3}\sqrt{7}$

## Miscellaneous exercise 3 (page 41)

1  $\left(\frac{7}{2},-\frac{1}{2}\right), \frac{3}{2}\sqrt{2}$

2  88

3  on, inside, outside, on, inside

4  $\left(\frac{3}{2},-\frac{5}{2}\right), \frac{1}{6}\sqrt{30}$

5  $x^2+y^2-6x+4y-39=0$

6  $(0,3), 3; \left(-\frac{9}{5},\frac{3}{5}\right), (3,3)$

7  $3x+2y+3=0$

9  $x^2+y^2-2x-12y+27=0$

11  $4\sqrt{10}$

14  $x^2+y^2-6x+18y-10=0$,
    $x^2+y^2-6x-14y-42=0$

15  (a)  3 units in the negative $x$-direction and
        1 unit in the positive $y$-direction
    (b)  $x^2+y^2-17x+3y+59=0$
    (c)  $x^2+y^2+2x+2y-14=0$

16  $10, 26$

17  $\pm 10$

18  $-9 < k < 1$

19  $x^2+y^2-26x-8y+181=0$

20  $3x+4y+11=0$

21  (a)  $B(1,3), D(-7,-1)$
    (b)  $x^2+y^2+6x-2y=0$

22  (a)  $-23$    (b)  $-7$

23  $x^2+y^2-10x-10y+25=0$,
    $x^2+y^2-34x-34y+289=0$
    (a)  $(2,9)$    (b)  $x+y=11$

24  $3x+4y-35=0$,  $4x-3y-30=0$,
    $4x-3y+20=0$

25  $x^2+y^2-14x+16y+28=0$

26  $-7 < a < 5$

27  $\frac{52}{3}\pi$

28  $\frac{32}{3}\pi$

29  $3x-4y+60=0$

# 4  Parametric equations

## Exercise 4A (page 47)

1  (a)  $(180,60)$    (b)  $(5,-10)$

2  (a)  $\left(\frac{2}{3},\frac{4}{3}\right)$    (b)  $(2,0)$

3  $\frac{1}{2}\pi$

4  $\frac{2}{3}\pi$

9  (a)  $y^2 = \dfrac{1}{x}$    (b)  $y^2 = 12x$

    (c)  $x^2+y^2=4$

10  (a)  $x+y=1$, for $0 \leqslant x \leqslant 1$
    (b)  $x^{\frac{2}{3}}+y^{\frac{2}{3}}=1$
    (c)  $x+y=2$, excluding $(1,1)$
    (d)  $4x^3 = 27y^2$

## Exercise 4B (page 50)

1  (a)  $\dfrac{2}{3t^2}$    (b)  $-\tan t$

    (c)  $-\frac{3}{2}\cot t$    (d)  $\dfrac{2t-1}{3t^2+1}$

2  (a)  $2$    (b)  $\frac{1}{3}$    (c)  $-1$    (d)  $-\frac{1}{54}$

3  (a)  $-3$    (b)  $1$    (c)  $\sqrt{3}$    (d)  $-8$

5  (a)  $\frac{1}{3}$    (b)  $3y=x-1$

6  $x+y=1+\pi$

7  (a)  $3y=x+9$    (b)  $5y=3\sqrt{3}x-30$

8  (a)  $3x+y=165$    (b)  $y=-\sqrt{3}x$

9  (a)  $y=4x-30$    (b)  $\left(-\frac{1}{2},-32\right)$

10  (a)  $y=2x-36$    (b)  $(27,18)$

## Exercise 4C (page 52)

7  (b)  The point $N$ always lies on the circle with
        centre at the origin and radius $\sqrt{2}$.

## Miscellaneous exercise 4  (page 53)

1  (a)  $\frac{1}{4}\pi$    (b)  $2x+y=2\sqrt{2}$

2  $6\cos t$

3  (a)  $\dfrac{t^2-1}{t^2+1}$    (c)  $y^2-x^2=4$

4  (a)  $\dfrac{2t}{3t^2+1}$    (b)  $2x+y=6$

5  (a)  $-\sqrt{3}\tan t$    (b)  $x+y=2$

6  $\dfrac{1}{e^t-1}$,  $\ln 2$

7 (b) $y = 2x - 2$   (c)   $(0, -2)$

8 (a) $2x + y = 9$   (b)   $y = 4x - x^2$

10 (a) the half-line of gradient 1 through $(0,0)$ for which $x \geqslant 0$

   (b) $y = x$; the straight line of gradient 1 through $(0,0)$

   (c) Each point of the curve given by the parametric equations lies on the curve given by the cartesian equation, but the reverse is not necessarily true, as this example shows.

# 5 Vectors

## Exercise 5A (page 59)

2 (a) $(4\mathbf{i} + \mathbf{j}) + (-3\mathbf{i} + 2\mathbf{j}) = \mathbf{i} + 3\mathbf{j}$
  (b) $3(\mathbf{i} - 2\mathbf{j}) = 3\mathbf{i} - 6\mathbf{j}$
  (c) $4\mathbf{j} + 2(\mathbf{i} - 2\mathbf{j}) = 2\mathbf{i}$
  (d) $(3\mathbf{i} + \mathbf{j}) - (5\mathbf{i} + \mathbf{j}) = -2\mathbf{i}$
  (e) $3(-\mathbf{i} + 2\mathbf{j}) - (-4\mathbf{i} + 3\mathbf{j}) = \mathbf{i} + 3\mathbf{j}$
  (f) $4(2\mathbf{i} + 3\mathbf{j}) - 3(3\mathbf{i} + 2\mathbf{j}) = -\mathbf{i} + 6\mathbf{j}$
  (g) $(2\mathbf{i} - 3\mathbf{j}) + (4\mathbf{i} + 5\mathbf{j}) + (-6\mathbf{i} - 2\mathbf{j}) = \mathbf{0}$
  (h) $2(3\mathbf{i} - \mathbf{j}) + 3(-2\mathbf{i} + 3\mathbf{j}) + (-7\mathbf{j}) = \mathbf{0}$

3 (a) $\begin{pmatrix} 1 \\ 2 \end{pmatrix}$   (b) $\begin{pmatrix} 3 \\ 0 \end{pmatrix}$   (c) $\begin{pmatrix} -1 \\ 1 \end{pmatrix}$   (d) $\begin{pmatrix} 4 \\ -3 \end{pmatrix}$

4   $s = 2$

5   $s = 4$; $\mathbf{q} = \frac{1}{4}(\mathbf{r} - \mathbf{p})$

6   2, 3

7   $1\frac{1}{2}, -\frac{1}{2}$

8   $\begin{pmatrix} 4 \\ -2 \end{pmatrix}$ and $\begin{pmatrix} -6 \\ 3 \end{pmatrix}$ are parallel, $\begin{pmatrix} 3 \\ 1 \end{pmatrix}$ is in a different direction;

   $\begin{pmatrix} -1 \\ 2 \end{pmatrix}$ is not parallel to $\begin{pmatrix} 1 \\ 1 \end{pmatrix} - \begin{pmatrix} 3 \\ 4 \end{pmatrix}$

9   any multiple of $1, -1, 2$

10 (a) no   (b) $-2, 0$;
   $\mathbf{p}$ is parallel to $\mathbf{r}$, but $\mathbf{q}$ is in a different direction

## Exercise 5B (page 62)

1 (a) $(9,3)$    (b) $(-1,-2)$    (c) $(2,-1)$
  (d) $(-8,-1)$    (e) $(10,5)$    (f) $\left(5, 2\frac{1}{2}\right)$

2 (a) $(-13,-23)$   (b) $(-1,1)$

3   $\mathbf{c} = 2\mathbf{b} - \mathbf{a}$

4   $\frac{3}{7}\mathbf{a} + \frac{4}{7}\mathbf{b}$

6   $\mathbf{b} - \mathbf{a} = \mathbf{c} - \mathbf{d}$

7   $\frac{1}{2}(\mathbf{b} + \mathbf{c} - 2\mathbf{a}), \frac{1}{4}(\mathbf{b} + \mathbf{c} - 2\mathbf{a})$;   $G$ is the mid-point of $AD$

8   $\mathbf{b} = \mathbf{a} + \mathbf{c}$,   $\mathbf{m} = \frac{1}{2}(\mathbf{a} + 2\mathbf{c})$,   $\mathbf{p} = \frac{1}{3}(\mathbf{a} + 2\mathbf{c})$;   $O$, $P$ and $M$ are collinear, and $OP = \frac{2}{3}OM$

9   $\mathbf{d} = \frac{1}{2}(\mathbf{b} + \mathbf{c})$,   $\mathbf{e} = \frac{1}{4}(2\mathbf{a} + \mathbf{b} + \mathbf{c})$,   $\mathbf{f} = \frac{1}{3}(2\mathbf{a} + \mathbf{c})$,   $\mathbf{g} = \frac{1}{4}(\mathbf{b} + 2\mathbf{a} + \mathbf{c})$

10   $\frac{4}{15}\mathbf{b} - \frac{13}{15}\mathbf{a}$,   $k = \frac{15}{13}$,   $\mathbf{r} = \frac{4}{13}\mathbf{b}$;   $R$ is on $OB$, with $OR:RB = 4:9$   $S$ is on $OA$, with $OS:SA = 2:9$

## Exercise 5C (page 66)

Note that, since vector equations are not unique, other correct answers are sometimes possible.

1 (a) $\mathbf{r} = \begin{pmatrix} 2 \\ -3 \end{pmatrix} + t\begin{pmatrix} 1 \\ 2 \end{pmatrix}$, $y = 2x - 7$

  (b) $\mathbf{r} = \begin{pmatrix} 4 \\ 1 \end{pmatrix} + t\begin{pmatrix} -3 \\ 2 \end{pmatrix}$, $2x + 3y = 11$

  (c) $\mathbf{r} = \begin{pmatrix} 5 \\ 7 \end{pmatrix} + t\begin{pmatrix} 1 \\ 0 \end{pmatrix}$, $y = 7$

  (d) $\mathbf{r} = t\begin{pmatrix} 2 \\ -1 \end{pmatrix}$, $x + 2y = 0$

  (e) $\mathbf{r} = \begin{pmatrix} a \\ b \end{pmatrix} + t\begin{pmatrix} 0 \\ 1 \end{pmatrix}$, $x = a$

  (f) $\mathbf{r} = \begin{pmatrix} \cos\alpha \\ \sin\alpha \end{pmatrix} + t\begin{pmatrix} -\sin\alpha \\ \cos\alpha \end{pmatrix}$, $x\cos\alpha + y\sin\alpha = 1$

2 (a) $\mathbf{r} = \begin{pmatrix} 2 \\ 0 \end{pmatrix} + t\begin{pmatrix} 0 \\ 1 \end{pmatrix}$    (b) $\mathbf{r} = \begin{pmatrix} 1 \\ 2 \end{pmatrix} + t\begin{pmatrix} 3 \\ -1 \end{pmatrix}$

  (c) $\mathbf{r} = \begin{pmatrix} -1 \\ -1 \end{pmatrix} + t\begin{pmatrix} 5 \\ 2 \end{pmatrix}$

3 (a) $(7,3)$   (b) $(8,-5)$   (c) no common points
  (d) $(4.76, 3.68)$
  (e) the lines coincide, $2x + 3y = 17$
  (f) $(-1,1)$

4   $x = 2 + t$, $y = -1 + 3t$; $(4,5)$

5   $(3,1)$

6   (a), (d), (e)

7 (a) $\mathbf{r} = \begin{pmatrix} 3 \\ 7 \end{pmatrix} + t\begin{pmatrix} 2 \\ -3 \end{pmatrix}$    (b) $\mathbf{r} = \begin{pmatrix} 2 \\ 3 \end{pmatrix} + t\begin{pmatrix} 0 \\ 1 \end{pmatrix}$

  (c) $\mathbf{r} = \begin{pmatrix} -1 \\ 2 \end{pmatrix} + t\begin{pmatrix} 2 \\ -1 \end{pmatrix}$    (d) $\mathbf{r} = \begin{pmatrix} -3 \\ -4 \end{pmatrix} + t\begin{pmatrix} 2 \\ 3 \end{pmatrix}$

  (e) $\mathbf{r} = \begin{pmatrix} -2 \\ 7 \end{pmatrix} + t\begin{pmatrix} 1 \\ 0 \end{pmatrix}$    (f) $\mathbf{r} = \begin{pmatrix} 1 \\ 3 \end{pmatrix} + t\begin{pmatrix} 1 \\ 1 \end{pmatrix}$

**8** (a) $\mathbf{r} = \begin{pmatrix} 4 \\ -1 \end{pmatrix} + s\begin{pmatrix} 3 \\ 1 \end{pmatrix}, \mathbf{r} = \begin{pmatrix} -3 \\ 2 \end{pmatrix} + t\begin{pmatrix} 1 \\ -1 \end{pmatrix}; (1,-2)$

   (b) $\left(13\tfrac{1}{3}, -5\right), \left(4, 11\tfrac{4}{5}\right)$

**9** (a), (b) yes

   (c) meaningless, since **0** has no direction;

   $\mathbf{r} = \begin{pmatrix} 1 \\ 2 \end{pmatrix} + t\begin{pmatrix} -4 \\ 3 \end{pmatrix}$

**10** $\begin{pmatrix} 1 \\ 3 \end{pmatrix}$, $\mathbf{r} = \begin{pmatrix} 1 \\ 5 \end{pmatrix} + t\begin{pmatrix} -3 \\ 1 \end{pmatrix}$; $(4,4)$

**11** $(2,0)$

**12** $\mathbf{r} = \begin{pmatrix} -1 \\ 1 \end{pmatrix} + t\begin{pmatrix} 1 \\ 2 \end{pmatrix}$; $x = -1+t, y = 1+2t$;

   $(-1,1)$, $(3,9)$

**13** $(1,8), (-7,-4)$

### Exercise 5D (page 69)

**1** (a) $2, -3$  (b) $3, 1$    (c) no solution

**2** Any multiple of $1, 2, -3$; the translations are all parallel to the same plane.

**3** $(4, -3, 0)$

**4** All $\tfrac{1}{4}(\mathbf{a}+\mathbf{b}+\mathbf{c}+\mathbf{d})$; the lines joining the mid-points of opposite edges of a tetrahedron meet and bisect one another.

**5** $\tfrac{1}{4}\mathbf{e} + \tfrac{3}{4}\mathbf{f}$; $\tfrac{1}{3}(\mathbf{a}+\mathbf{b}+\mathbf{c})$, $\tfrac{1}{4}(\mathbf{a}+\mathbf{b}+\mathbf{c}+\mathbf{d})$

**6** (a) intersect at $(1, -1, 0)$

   (b) parallel    (c) skew   (d) skew

**7** $\mathbf{r} = \begin{pmatrix} 3 \\ 2 \\ 6 \end{pmatrix} + t\begin{pmatrix} -3 \\ 1 \\ 2 \end{pmatrix}$; $(12,-1,0)$, $(9,0,2)$

**8** $(-9, 10, 0)$

**9** $0.4$ m

### Miscellaneous exercise 5 (page 70)

**1** $\begin{pmatrix} 9 \\ -1 \\ 4 \end{pmatrix}$

**2** (a) $y = 4x - 14$    (b) $\mathbf{r} = \begin{pmatrix} 0 \\ 1 \end{pmatrix} + t\begin{pmatrix} 3 \\ 2 \end{pmatrix}$

   (c) $2x - 3y + 17 = 0$, or $\mathbf{r} = \begin{pmatrix} -1 \\ 5 \end{pmatrix} + t\begin{pmatrix} 3 \\ 2 \end{pmatrix}$

**3** (a) no intersection  (b) $(-3,-1)$

   (c) same line

**4** (a) $\mathbf{r} = \begin{pmatrix} 2 \\ 1 \end{pmatrix} + t\begin{pmatrix} 3 \\ -2 \end{pmatrix}$    (b) $y = 3x - 5$

   (c) $(2,1)$

**5** (a) $\begin{pmatrix} 14 \\ 2 \\ 5 \end{pmatrix}, \begin{pmatrix} -5 \\ 10 \\ 10 \end{pmatrix}$; $(13,14,18)$

   (b) $\tfrac{1}{3}, \tfrac{2}{15}$; the origin lies in the plane of the parallelogram.

**6** $\mathbf{r} = \begin{pmatrix} 2 \\ 3 \\ 5 \end{pmatrix} + \lambda\begin{pmatrix} 1 \\ 1 \\ -0.5 \end{pmatrix}$   (b) $25$ m

**7** $\mathbf{r} = \begin{pmatrix} f(\theta) \\ g(\theta) \end{pmatrix} + t\begin{pmatrix} f'(\theta) \\ g'(\theta) \end{pmatrix}$;

   (a) $\mathbf{r} = \begin{pmatrix} \theta^2 \\ \theta^3 \end{pmatrix} + t\begin{pmatrix} 2\theta \\ 3\theta^2 \end{pmatrix}$, $2y = 3\theta x - \theta^3$

   (b) $\mathbf{r} = \begin{pmatrix} 3\cos\theta \\ 2\sin\theta \end{pmatrix} + t\begin{pmatrix} -3\sin\theta \\ 2\cos\theta \end{pmatrix}$,

   $2\cos\theta\, x + 3\sin\theta\, y = 6$

**8** $\tfrac{4}{5}, \tfrac{9}{5}$; break up 4 Individual bags and 9 Jumbo bags, and use the fruit to make 5 King-size bags.

**9** $(\cos 2\alpha, \sin 2\alpha)$; for all $\alpha$, the intersection lies on the circle with $(-1,0)$ and $(1,0)$ at ends of a diameter.

**10** $(11.4, 3, 0)$ at 8.04 a.m.

**11** (a) above $(61, 77)$ on the ground    (b) $4200$ m

   (c) $384$ km h$^{-1}$, $38.7°$

   (d) $386$ km h$^{-1}$, $5.35°$

**12** $(85, -10)$; $2200$ m, 2 minutes

**13** $u < -1$ or $u > 0.5$; $0.5 < u < 0.753$

## 6 The binomial expansion

### Exercise 6 (page 78)

**1** (a) $1 - 3x + 6x^2$   (b) $1 - 5x + 15x^2$

   (c) $1 + 4x + 10x^2$   (d) $1 + 6x + 21x^2$

**2** (a) $1 - 4x + 16x^2$   (b) $1 + 6x + 24x^2$

   (c) $1 + 12x + 90x^2$  (d) $1 - x + \tfrac{3}{4}x^2$

**3** (a) $84$   (b) $-8$   (c) $-270$  (d) $256$

   (e) $\tfrac{56}{27}$   (f) $-20a^3$  (g) $20b^3$

   (h) $\tfrac{1}{6}n(n+1)(n+2)c^3$

**4** (a) $1 + \tfrac{1}{3}x - \tfrac{1}{9}x^2$   (b) $1 + \tfrac{3}{4}x - \tfrac{3}{32}x^2$

   (c) $1 - \tfrac{3}{2}x + \tfrac{3}{8}x^2$  (d) $1 + \tfrac{1}{2}x + \tfrac{3}{8}x^2$

**5** (a) $1 + 2x - 2x^2$   (b) $1 - x + 2x^2$

   (c) $1 - 8x + 8x^2$  (d) $1 + \tfrac{1}{8}x + \tfrac{5}{128}x^2$

**6** (a) $-\tfrac{1}{2}$  (b) $\tfrac{625}{16}$  (c) $\tfrac{5}{24}$  (d) $-\tfrac{5}{2}$

   (e) $20$   (f) $\tfrac{1}{8}\sqrt{2}$  (g) $-\tfrac{1}{16}a^3$

   (h) $\tfrac{1}{48}n(n+2)(n+4)b^3$

**7** (a) $1 - \tfrac{1}{8}x - \tfrac{1}{128}x^2$  (b) $1 + \tfrac{1}{8}x^2 - \tfrac{1}{128}x^4$

   (c) $2 + \tfrac{1}{4}x - \tfrac{1}{64}x^2$  (d) $6 + \tfrac{3}{4}x - \tfrac{3}{64}x^2$

**8** $|x| < \frac{2}{3}$

   (a) $4 + 12x + 27x^2 + 54x^3$

   (b) $\frac{1}{4} + \frac{3}{4}x + \frac{27}{16}x^2 + \frac{27}{8}x^3$

**9** (a) $1 - 3x - \frac{9}{2}x^2 - \frac{27}{2}x^3, |x| < \frac{1}{6}$

   (b) $1 - 5x + 25x^2 - 125x^3, |x| < \frac{1}{5}$

   (c) $1 - 3x + 18x^2 - 126x^3, |x| < \frac{1}{9}$

   (d) $1 + 8x + 40x^2 + 160x^3, |x| < \frac{1}{2}$

   (e) $1 + x^2 - \frac{1}{2}x^4 + \frac{1}{2}x^4, |x| < \frac{1}{2}\sqrt{2}$

   (f) $2 - \frac{4}{3}x - \frac{8}{9}x^2 - \frac{80}{81}x^3, |x| < \frac{1}{2}$

   (g) $10 - 4x + \frac{6}{5}x^2 - \frac{8}{25}x^3, |x| < 5$

   (h) $1 + \frac{1}{2}x + \frac{1}{4}x^2 + \frac{1}{8}x^3, |x| < 2$

   (i) $\frac{1}{8} - \frac{3}{16}x + \frac{3}{16}x^2 - \frac{5}{32}x^3, |x| < 2$

   (j) $2x - \frac{1}{4}x^4 + \frac{3}{64}x^7 - \frac{5}{512}x^{10}, |x| < \sqrt[3]{4}$

   (k) $1 + 2x - 6x^2 + 28x^3, |x| < \frac{1}{8}$

   (l) $\frac{4}{3} - \frac{16}{9}\sqrt{3}x + \frac{40}{9}x^2 + \frac{80}{27}\sqrt{3}x^3, |x| < \sqrt{3}$

**10** $1 + 4x - 8x^2 + 32x^3, 1.039\,232$

   (a) $10.392\,32$   (b) $1.732\,05$

**11** $1 + \frac{4}{3}x - \frac{16}{9}x^2$   (a) $5.065\,78$   (b) $9.996\,67$

**12** $6$

**13** $15$

**14** $1 + 3x + \frac{15}{2}x^2, |x| < \frac{1}{4}, 4.123$

**15** $4, 6, -100$

**16** $1 + x + 2x^2 + 3x + 5x^4, 1.001\,002\,003\,005$

**17** (a) $2 - 2x + \frac{7}{2}x^2$   (b) $1 + 5x + 6x^2$

**18** $-\frac{56}{27}$

## Miscellaneous exercise 6 (page 80)

**1** $1 + 5x + \frac{15}{2}x^2 + \frac{5}{2}x^3$

**2** $1 - 2x - 2x^2 - 4x^3$

**3** $1 - 6x + 24x^2 - 80x^3$

**4** $1 - 4x^2 + 12x^4 - 32x^6$

**5** $2 + \frac{1}{4}x - \frac{1}{64}x^2, |x| < 4$

**6** $1 - \frac{3x^2}{2a^2} + \frac{15x^4}{8a^4}$

**7** $1 + \frac{1}{2}x - \frac{1}{8}x^2, a = 2, b = -\frac{3}{4}$

**8** $1 + 2x + 3x^2 + 4x^3, a = 5, b = 7$

**9** $4 + x - \frac{1}{16}x^2, |x| < \frac{8}{3}$

**10** $1 - \frac{1}{3}x - \frac{1}{9}x^2 - \frac{5}{81}x^3$

**11** $1 + \frac{1}{4}x - \frac{3}{32}x^2$

**12** $n = 15, 1 - \frac{1}{2}x - \frac{1}{8}x^2, \frac{1351}{780}$

**13** $\frac{3}{2} - \frac{3}{4}x + 3x^2$

**15** $|x| < \frac{1}{4}$

**16** (a) $1 - 2x + 3x^2 - 4x^3$

   (b) $1 + 2x^2 + 3x^4 + 4x^6$

   (c) $1 - 4x^2 + 12x^4 - 32x^6$

**17** $A = 1, B = -1, C = 0, D = 1, E = -1$

   (a) $0.999\,700\,000\,026\,991\,9$

**18** $1 + 2x + 3x^2 + 4x^3, 1.000\,200\,030\,004$

**19** $1 - \frac{1}{4}x + \frac{5}{32}x^2, 1.495\,35$

**20** $1 - \frac{1}{2}x + \frac{3}{8}x^2 + \frac{5}{16}x^3$

**23** $1 + \frac{3}{2}x + \frac{3}{8}x^2, 3.605\,525$

**24** $1 - 2x + 4x^2 - 8x^3 + 16x^4, 0.346\,056, 0.692\,112$

**25** $3 + \frac{7}{2}x + \frac{1}{2}x^2, 3\frac{1}{24}$

**26** $1 - 2x^2 + 15x^4, 0.531$

# Revision exercise 1

**(page 83)**

**2** (b) $\sin\alpha$   (c) $\left(\alpha, \frac{1}{2}\sin\alpha\right)$

**3** (a) $\dfrac{300}{\pi}, 240\cos600t$   (a) $0$   (b) $\pm0.4$

**4** $-3, y^2 = 9x(2 - x)$

**5** $1 + \frac{1}{2}x - \frac{1}{2}x^2 + \frac{1}{2}x^3 - \frac{5}{8}x^4$

**6** $5$

**7** $\sqrt{37}\cos(x + 0.165\ldots); 0.441, -0.771$

**8** The point does lie on the line.

**9** (a) $-\frac{1}{2}\cos\left(2x + \frac{1}{6}\pi\right) + k$

   (b) $\frac{1}{2}x - \frac{1}{12}\sin6x + k$

   (c) $\frac{1}{6}\sin^3 2x + k$

**10** $\mathbf{r} = \begin{pmatrix} 1 \\ 4 \\ 2 \end{pmatrix} + t\begin{pmatrix} -3 \\ -1 \\ 1 \end{pmatrix}, (-5, 2, 4)$

**11** $(33, 27)$

**12** $2\pi$

**13** $1 - \frac{1}{2}x + \frac{5}{8}x^2 - \frac{5}{16}x^3$

**14** $\sqrt{\frac{2}{3}}$

**15** $\mathbf{r} = \begin{pmatrix} 2 \\ -1 \\ 4 \end{pmatrix} + s\begin{pmatrix} -3 \\ -1 \\ 1 \end{pmatrix}$

**16** $(7.8, 1.6)$

**17** $1.04, 3.03, 4.18, 6.17$

**18** $t^2 y + x = 2ct$

**19** $3y = 4x + 2$

**20** (a) $\sqrt{52}$   (b) $0.6$

**21** (a) $\pi - 2\theta, 2r^2 + 2r^2\cos2\theta$

   (b) $2r\cos\theta$

**22**   $a = nc$,   $b = \frac{1}{2}n(n-1)c^2$;

$$c = \frac{a^2 - 2b}{a}, \quad n = \frac{a^2}{a^2 - 2b}$$

**23**   $y - 1 = m(x - 2)$; $m$ is the gradient of the line.

**25**   (a)   $\tan\theta$, $|t|$ is the distance of a point on $l$ from $A$.

     (b)   $x^2 + y^2 = R^2$

     (c)   $t^2 + 2(a\cos\theta + b\sin\theta)t$
            $+ (a^2 + b^2 - R^2) = 0$

     (e)   The point $A$ must be outside or on the circle $C$ for it to be possible to draw tangents from $A$ to $C$.

# 7 Rational functions

## Exercise 7A (page 89)

**1**   (a)   $2x - 4$        (b)   $3x + 2$

    (c)   $x^2 - 3x + 6$      (d)   $\dfrac{1}{3x + 2}$

    (e)   $(x + 3)(x - 2)$    (f)   $\dfrac{1}{x^2 + x + 1}$

**2**   (a)   5     (b)   $\frac{1}{4}$     (c)   1

    (d)   $-1$     (e)   1     (f)   $\frac{2}{3}$

**3**   (a)   $x + 4$   (b)   $\dfrac{1}{x + 7}$   (c)   $\dfrac{3x + 2}{2x + 1}$

    (d)   $\dfrac{x + 6}{x - 3}$   (e)   $\dfrac{x + 4}{x - 4}$   (f)   $\dfrac{-2(4x + 5)}{3x + 1}$

**4**   (a)   $\dfrac{5x}{12}$   (b)   $\dfrac{25x}{12}$   (c)   $\dfrac{7x + 11}{12}$

    (d)   $\dfrac{x - 7}{15}$   (e)   $\dfrac{x^2 + 4x + 2}{4}$   (f)   $\dfrac{13x + 14}{5}$

**5**   (a)   $\dfrac{8 + 3x}{4x}$        (b)   $\dfrac{5}{2x}$

    (c)   $\dfrac{7}{12x}$        (d)   $\dfrac{3x - 5}{2x}$

    (e)   $\dfrac{5x - 2 - x^2}{2x}$    (f)   $\dfrac{x^2 + 2x + 1}{x^2}$

**6**   (a)   $\dfrac{6x + 10}{(x + 1)(x + 3)}$    (b)   $\dfrac{13x - 1}{(x - 2)(2x + 1)}$

    (c)   $\dfrac{2x + 10}{(x + 3)(x + 4)}$    (d)   $\dfrac{5x + 13}{(x - 3)(x + 1)}$

    (e)   $\dfrac{22x + 19}{(2x + 3)(3x + 1)}$   (f)   $\dfrac{26x - 20}{(2x + 1)(5x - 3)}$

**7**   (a)   $\dfrac{4x + 7}{(3x - 1)(2x + 1)}$   (b)   $\dfrac{-3}{2x(4x + 1)}$

    (c)   $\dfrac{8x^2 + 13x}{(x + 2)(x + 1)}$   (d)   $\dfrac{6x^2 + 17x}{(2x - 1)(x + 2)}$

    (e)   $\dfrac{2x^2 + 6x + 5}{(x + 1)(x + 2)}$   (f)   $\dfrac{x^2 - 2x + 18}{(x + 4)(x - 2)}$

**8**   (a)   $\dfrac{4x + 5}{(x + 1)(x + 3)}$   (b)   $\dfrac{6x - 1}{(x + 2)(x - 1)}$

    (c)   $\dfrac{6x + 2}{x(x - 3)}$   (d)   $\dfrac{-4x}{(x + 2)(x - 2)}$

    (e)   $\dfrac{1}{x - 3}$   (f)   $\dfrac{5}{2x - 1}$

**9**   (a)   6        (b)   $3x$

    (c)   $\dfrac{3x + 15}{x + 3}$   (d)   $\dfrac{x + 3}{x + 1}$

    (e)   $\dfrac{2x + 2}{x + 3}$   (f)   $\dfrac{(2x + 3)(3x - 2)}{(2x - 3)(3x + 2)}$

**10**   (a)   2        (b)   $-\frac{1}{3}$

    (c)   $\dfrac{x + 4}{x + 2}$   (d)   $\dfrac{(5x - 1)(x + 2)}{x - 1}$

    (e)   1        (f)   $-1$

**11**   $a = 5, b = 10, c = 4$

**12**   $x^2 - 9$

**13**   (a)   $\dfrac{16x - 6}{(x + 4)(x - 3)}$   (b)   $\dfrac{7x - 77}{(x + 4)(x - 3)}$

**14**   (a)   $\dfrac{3}{x(x - 1)(x - 3)}$   (b)   $\dfrac{1}{(2x + 1)(3x - 1)}$

## Exercise 7B (page 94)

**1**   (a)   $\dfrac{1}{x + 5} + \dfrac{1}{x + 3}$   (b)   $\dfrac{3}{x - 1} + \dfrac{7}{x + 5}$

    (c)   $\dfrac{-4}{x - 4} + \dfrac{5}{x - 5}$   (d)   $\dfrac{8}{2x - 1} - \dfrac{4}{x + 3}$

**2**   (a)   $\dfrac{5}{x + 2} + \dfrac{3}{x - 1}$   (b)   $\dfrac{5}{x - 4} - \dfrac{5}{x + 1}$

    (c)   $\dfrac{4}{x - 3} + \dfrac{6}{x + 3}$   (d)   $\dfrac{3}{x} - \dfrac{6}{2x + 1}$

**3**   (a)   $\dfrac{3}{x + 2} - \dfrac{5}{x - 1} + \dfrac{2}{x - 3}$

    (b)   $\dfrac{9}{x + 3} - \dfrac{2}{x + 1} + \dfrac{1}{x - 1}$

    (c)   $\dfrac{3}{x} + \dfrac{5}{x - 6} + \dfrac{7}{x + 4}$

**4**   (a)   $10\ln|x - 3| - 3\ln|x - 1| + k$

    (b)   $\ln|x - 2| - \ln|x + 2| + k$

    (c)   $7\ln|x| + \frac{1}{2}\ln|2x + 5| + k$

    (d)   $\frac{5}{3}\ln|3x + 1| - \frac{3}{2}\ln|2x - 1| + k$

**5**   (a)   $\ln 18$   (b)   $\ln 40$   (c)   $3\ln\frac{16}{7}$   (d)   $\ln\frac{54}{125}$

**6**   $\dfrac{1}{1 + x} + \dfrac{1}{1 - 2x}$;   $2 + x + 5x^2 + 7x^3$

**7** $\dfrac{6}{1+4x}-\dfrac{3}{1+2x}$; $3-18x+84x^2-360x^3$, $|x|<\frac{1}{4}$

**8** $\dfrac{3a}{x+2a}+\dfrac{a}{x-a}$

**9** $2\ln\frac{3}{2}$

## Exercise 7C (page 99)

**1** (a) $\dfrac{1}{x-1}-\dfrac{1}{x-3}+\dfrac{2}{(x-3)^2}$

(b) $\dfrac{5}{x+2}+\dfrac{2}{(x+2)^2}+\dfrac{1}{x-1}$

(c) $\dfrac{3}{2x}-\dfrac{3}{2(x-2)}+\dfrac{3}{(x-2)^2}$

(d) $\dfrac{2}{2x-1}-\dfrac{1}{x+1}-\dfrac{5}{(x+1)^2}$

**2** (a) $4\ln|x+1|+2\ln|x+2|-\dfrac{5}{x+2}+k$

(b) $\ln|2x-3|-\ln|5x+2|-\dfrac{1}{5(5x+2)}+k$

**4** $\frac{5}{2}+2\ln 2-\frac{3}{2}\ln\frac{7}{5}$

**5** $1-3x+9x^2$

## Miscellaneous exercise 7 (page 99)

**1** $\dfrac{1}{x-3}-\dfrac{1}{x+1}$

**2** $-\dfrac{2}{x}+\dfrac{1}{x+1}+\dfrac{1}{x-1}$

**3** $\dfrac{1}{x}+\dfrac{1}{x-1}+\dfrac{3}{(x-1)^2}$

**4** $\dfrac{1}{x+2}+\dfrac{1}{(x+2)^2}-\dfrac{2}{3x-1}$

**5** $\ln|x|-\ln|x+1|+k$

**6** $-\ln|x+1|+2\ln|x+2|+k$

**7** $-\dfrac{1}{x}-\dfrac{1}{x^2}+\dfrac{1}{x-1}$, $-\ln|x|+\dfrac{1}{x}+\ln|x-1|+k$

**8** $\dfrac{x(2x+1)}{2(x-1)(2x+3)}$

**9** $\left|\dfrac{3x-1}{4x-3}\right|$

**10** $\dfrac{2x}{(x-3)(x+3)}$

**11** $-\dfrac{2}{2x+1}+\dfrac{1}{x-1}$, $\ln\frac{10}{7}$

**12** $\dfrac{1}{7(x+3)}+\dfrac{1}{7(4-x)}$, $\frac{1}{7}\ln\frac{10}{3}$

**13** $\dfrac{2}{1-x}-\dfrac{2}{2-x}$, $1+\frac{3}{2}x+\frac{7}{4}x^2+\frac{15}{8}x^3$, $|x|<1$

**14** $\dfrac{1}{2+x}+\dfrac{1}{1-2x}$, $\frac{3}{2}+\frac{7}{4}x+\frac{33}{8}x^2$, $|x|<\frac{1}{2}$

**15** $B=1, C=3$

**16** $A=2, B=2, C=-1$, $2+\frac{1}{2}x-\frac{3}{4}x^2+\frac{17}{8}x^3$, $\frac{1}{2}$

**17** $\dfrac{1}{1-x}+\dfrac{2}{(1-x)^2}+\dfrac{3}{4-x}$, $2\ln 2+1$

**18** $-\dfrac{1}{1+x}-\dfrac{2}{1-x}+\dfrac{3}{(1-x)^2}$, $c_0=0, c_1=5, c_2=6$,

$3r+1-(-1)^r$

**19** (a) $2x^3-3x^2-11x+6$

(b) $-14$

(c) $\dfrac{2}{5(2x-1)}-\dfrac{1}{5(x+2)}$

**20** $\dfrac{x^2-3x+4}{x(x+2)(x+4)}$

**21** $\pi(2-\ln 2)$

**22** $-\dfrac{1}{30(x+3)}+\dfrac{1}{30(x-3)}-\dfrac{1}{20(x-2)}+\dfrac{1}{20(x+2)}$

**23** $\dfrac{1}{x-1}+\dfrac{2}{x+2}$, $y=x+3$, $3$

**24** $\dfrac{1}{n}-\dfrac{1}{n+1}$

**25** $\dfrac{1}{n}-\dfrac{2}{n+1}+\dfrac{1}{n+2}$

# 8 Differentiating products

## Exercise 8A (page 104)

**1** (a) $2x$    (b) $3x^2+4x$

(c) $5x^4+9x^2+8x$    (d) $63x^2+100x+39$

(e) $3x^2$    (f) $(m+n)x^{m+n-1}$

**2** (a) $(x+1)e^x$    (b) $x(2\ln x+1)$

(c) $3x^2(\sin x+1)+x^3\cos x$

(d) $\cos^2 x-\sin^2 x$    (e) $\cos x-x\sin x$

(f) $e^{-x}(\cos x-\sin x)$

**3** (a) $(x^2+2x+3)e^x$

(b) $2x(\sin x+\cos x)+x^2(\cos x-\sin x)$

(c) $\sin^2 x+2x\sin x\cos x$

**4** (a) $4x+(2x+x^2)e^x$    (b) $x^2(3+2x)e^{2x}$

(c) $6x\ln x+\dfrac{4}{x}+3x$

**5** (a) $-3e^{-4}$  (b) $e^2(\sin 2+\cos 2)$

(c) $1+\ln 6$

**6** (a) $y = -\pi x + \pi^2$    (b) $y = x - 1$
   (c) $8y = 47x - 75$    (d) $y = 0$

**7** $(2, 4e^{-2})$, $(0,0)$

**8** (a) $2x\sin^3 2x + 6x^2 \sin^2 2x \cos 2x$

   (b) $\dfrac{(5x^2 + 5x + 2)e^x}{\sqrt{5x^2 + 2}}$

   (c) $8\sin^3 2x \cos 2x \cos^3 5x$
       $- 15\sin^4 2x \cos^2 5x \sin 5x$

   (d) $12(4x+1)^2 \ln 3x + \dfrac{(4x+1)^3}{x}$

   (e) $\dfrac{\ln 2x + 2}{2\sqrt{x}}$    (f) $-e^{ax}(a\sin bx + b\cos bx)$

**9** $\sin 2 + 2\cos 2$

**10** $x + 2y = 1$

**11** $(1, -3\sqrt{3})$

**12** $V \approx 51.8$, $x = 6.4$

**13** When $n$ is even, there is maximum at $x = n$, and a minimum at $x = 0$. When $n$ is odd, there is a maximum at $x = n$; if $n > 1$, there is also a point of inflexion at $x = 0$.

**14** (a) $(\sin x + x\sin x + x\cos x)e^x$

   (b) $(2x\cos 4x - 3x^2 \cos 4x - 4x^2 \sin 4x)e^{-3x}$

## Exercise 8B (page 109)

**1** (a) $\sin x - x\cos x + k$    (b) $3(x-1)e^x + k$
   (c) $(x+3)e^x + k$

**2** (a) $\frac{1}{4}(2x-1)e^{2x} + k$

   (b) $\frac{1}{4}x\sin 4x + \frac{1}{16}\cos 4x + k$

   (c) $\frac{1}{4}x^2(2\ln 2x - 1) + k$

**3** (a) $\frac{1}{36}x^6(6\ln 3x - 1) + k$

   (b) $\frac{1}{4}(2x-1)e^{2x+1} + k$

   (c) $x(\ln 2x - 1) + k$

**4** (a) $\frac{1}{4}(e^2 + 1)$    (b) $\frac{1}{2}\sqrt{2}(4 - \pi)$

   (c) $\dfrac{ne^{n+1} + 1}{(n+1)^2}$

**5** (a) $\frac{1}{7}x(1+x)^7 - \frac{1}{56}(1+x)^8 + k$

   (b) $\frac{1}{15}x(3x-1)^5 - \frac{1}{270}(3x-1)^6 + k$

   (c) $\frac{1}{13}\dfrac{x(ax+b)^{13}}{a} - \frac{1}{182}\dfrac{(ax+b)^{14}}{a^2} + k$

**6** $(2 - x^2)\cos x + 2x\sin x + k$

   (a) $\frac{1}{4}(2x^2 - 2x + 1)e^{2x} + k$

   (b) $2(x^2 - 8)\sin\frac{1}{2}x + 8x\cos\frac{1}{2}x + k$

**7** (a) $\frac{1}{6}x(4x-1)^{\frac{3}{2}} - \frac{1}{60}(4x-1)^{\frac{5}{2}} + k$

   (b) $-\frac{2}{3}x(2-x)^{\frac{3}{2}} - \frac{4}{15}(2-x)^{\frac{5}{2}} + k$

   (c) $\frac{1}{3}x(2x+3)^{\frac{3}{2}} - \frac{1}{15}(2x+3)^{\frac{5}{2}} + k$

**8** $1 - 3e^{-2}$, $\frac{1}{4}\pi(1 - 13e^{-4})$

**9** $\frac{1}{9}\pi$, $\frac{1}{324}\pi^2(2\pi^2 - 3)$

**10** (a) $-\frac{1}{2}(1 + e^\pi)$

   (b) $\frac{1}{10}e^{4\pi} - \frac{1}{10}e^{-4\pi}$

   (c) $\dfrac{a - e^{-2a\pi}(a\cos 2b\pi - b\sin 2b\pi)}{a^2 + b^2}$

**11** (a) $\frac{1}{2}$    (b) $\frac{4}{3}$

## Exercise 8C (page 112)

**1** (a) $\dfrac{1}{(1+5x)^2}$    (b) $\dfrac{3x^2 - 4x}{(3x-2)^2}$

   (c) $\dfrac{2x}{(1+2x^2)^2}$    (d) $\dfrac{(12x-13)e^{3x}}{(4x-3)^2}$

   (e) $\dfrac{1-2x^3}{(1+x^3)^2}$    (f) $\dfrac{(x-1)^2 e^x}{(x^2+1)^2}$

**2** $-\text{cosec}^2 x$

**3** (a) $\dfrac{x\cos x - \sin x}{x^2}$    (b) $\dfrac{\sin x - x\cos x}{\sin^2 x}$

   (c) $\dfrac{2x(\sin x - x\cos x)}{\sin^3 x}$

**4** (a) $\dfrac{x+2}{2(x+1)^{\frac{3}{2}}}$    (b) $\dfrac{10-x}{2x^2\sqrt{x-5}}$

   (c) $-\dfrac{3x+4}{4x^2\sqrt{3x+2}}$

**5** (a) $-\dfrac{2x\sin x + \cos x}{2x\sqrt{x}}$    (b) $\dfrac{3e^x - 10 - 5xe^x}{(e^x - 2)^2}$

   (c) $\dfrac{-1}{(1+x)^{\frac{3}{2}}(1-x)^{\frac{1}{2}}}$

**6** (a) $\dfrac{1 - \ln x}{x^2}$    (b) $\dfrac{2}{x^2 + 4} - \dfrac{\ln(x^2 + 4)}{x^2}$

   (c) $\dfrac{3}{(3x+2)(2x-1)} - \dfrac{2\ln(3x+2)}{(2x-1)^2}$

**7** $4y = x + 3$

**8** (a) $\dfrac{(2x-1)e^x}{(2x+1)^2}$    (b) $\left(\frac{1}{2}, \frac{1}{2}e^{\frac{1}{2}}\right)$

**9** $14y = 8x - 37$

**10** $\left(\frac{1}{2}(\sqrt{2}-1), 2(1+\sqrt{2})\right)$, $\left(-\frac{1}{2}(1+\sqrt{2}), -2(\sqrt{2}-1)\right)$

**11** (a) $\dfrac{x^2+2x-3}{(x+1)^2}$

   (b) $-3 \leqslant x < -1,\ -1 < x \leqslant 1$

## Miscellaneous exercise 8 (page 113)

**1** (a) $3x^2\sin x + x^3\cos x$  (b) $\dfrac{x+6}{2(x+3)^{\frac{3}{2}}}$

**2** $(1-3x)\mathrm{e}^{-3x},\ \left(\tfrac{1}{3},\tfrac{1}{3}\mathrm{e}^{-1}\right)$

**3** (a) $\mathrm{e}^x(\cos x - \sin x)$  (b) $\tfrac{1}{4}\pi < x < \tfrac{5}{4}\pi$

   (c) The gradient is negative for these values of $x$.

**4** (a) $2\cos 2x\cos 4x - 4\sin 2x\sin 4x$

   (b) $\dfrac{3x(2\ln x - 1)}{(\ln x)^2}$  (c) $-2\left(1-\dfrac{x}{5}\right)^9$

**5** $-\dfrac{1}{\pi^2}$

**6** $\left(\tfrac{1}{2},4\sqrt{2}\right)$

**7** $\dfrac{\mathrm{d}y}{\mathrm{d}x} = \dfrac{x\cos x - \sin x}{x^2}$

**9** $2\ln 2 - \tfrac{3}{4}$

**10** $\tfrac{1}{4} - \tfrac{1}{12}\mathrm{e}^{\frac{2}{3}}$

**11** $1 - 2\mathrm{e}^{-1}$

**12** $2x(x-1)^{\frac{3}{2}} - \tfrac{4}{5}(x-1)^{\frac{5}{2}} + k$

**13** $\tfrac{3}{4}\pi$

**14** 16

**15** (a) $(-3,0),\ x=1$  (b) $8y = 3(x+3)$

   (c) $\left(3,4\tfrac{1}{2}\right)$

# 9 Differential equations

## Exercise 9A (page 117)

**1** (a) $y = x^3 - 5x^2 + 3x + k$

   (b) $x = \tfrac{1}{2}t - \tfrac{1}{12}\sin 6t + k$

   (c) $P = 500\mathrm{e}^{0.01t} + k$

   (d) $u = k - 50\mathrm{e}^{-2t}$

   (e) $y = \tfrac{2}{3}\sqrt{x}(x+3) + k$

   (f) $x = \ln\sin t + 2\sin t + k$

**2** (a) $x = 5\mathrm{e}^{0.4t} - 4$

   (b) $v = 3 - 3\cos 2t - 2\sin 3t$

   (c) $y = -\ln\!\left(1-t^2\right)$

**3** (a) $y = \ln x + \dfrac{1}{x} - 1$

   (b) $y = 2\sqrt{x} - 4$

   (c) $y = x - 2\ln(x+1)$

**4** $14.1\,\mathrm{s}$

**5** $2$

**6** $-6 - \tfrac{5}{2}\pi,\ 2.237$

**7** $y = k - \tfrac{1}{2}x^2$

**8** $0.483\,\mathrm{m};\ -0.1h + 0.0483$

**9** (a) $A + kt$  (b) $A + k\!\left(t - \dfrac{1}{4\pi}\sin 2\pi t\right)$

   (c) $A + k\!\left(t + \dfrac{5}{4\pi}\sin\tfrac{1}{5}\pi t\right)$

   (d)
   $$A + k\!\left(\begin{array}{l} t - \dfrac{1}{4\pi}\sin 2\pi t + \dfrac{5}{4\pi}\sin\tfrac{1}{5}\pi t \\[2mm] -\dfrac{5}{176\pi}\sin\tfrac{11}{5}\pi t - \dfrac{5}{144\pi}\sin\tfrac{9}{5}\pi t \end{array}\right);$$

   all give $A + 10k$

## Exercise 9B (page 124)

**1** (a) $y = \dfrac{1}{k-x}$  (b) $y = \sin^{-1}\mathrm{e}^{x-k}$

   (c) $x = A\mathrm{e}^{4t}$  (d) $z = \sqrt{2t+c}$

   (e) $x = \cos^{-1}(k-t)$  (f) $u = \sqrt[3]{3ax+c}$

**2** (a) $x = 3\mathrm{e}^{-2t}$  (b) $u = \dfrac{1}{\sqrt{1-2t}}$

**3** (a) $y = \dfrac{\mathrm{e}^x}{2-\mathrm{e}^x},\ x < \ln 2$

   (b) $y = -\ln(3-x),\ x < 3$

**4** about $6\tfrac{1}{2}$ minutes

**5** $3.6$ minutes

**6** $443\,\mathrm{s}$

**7** (a) $\dfrac{\mathrm{d}h}{\mathrm{d}t} = 0$ when $h = 25$, so the tree stops growing.

   (b) $\dfrac{\mathrm{d}h}{\mathrm{d}t} = 0.2\sqrt{25-h},\ t = -10\sqrt{25-h} + 50$

   (c) (i) $1.0$ years  (ii) $10$ years

   (d) $h = t - 0.01t^2$ for $0 \leqslant t \leqslant 50$

**8** $m = \tfrac{1}{3}$; enlargement factors over the 4 months for $m = \tfrac{1}{3}$ and $m = \tfrac{1}{2}$ are $25.6$ and $35.3$ respectively.

## Miscellaneous exercise 9 (page 125)

**1** $y = x^2 + 7x + 3\ln x + 2$

**2**  $t = \dfrac{10z}{20-z}$

**3**  $y = x^3 - 4x^2 + 5x + 3$;
  $(1,5)$ maximum, $\left(\frac{5}{3}, 4\frac{23}{27}\right)$ minimum

**4**  (a)  $2\pi r, \dfrac{1}{2\pi r}$   (b)  $\dfrac{1}{\pi r(t+1)^3}$

  (c)  $A = 1 - \dfrac{1}{(t+1)^2}$

**5**  $\dfrac{dx}{dt} = -kx$

**6**  (a)  the number of people served in each minute,
  $x = 0.7t^2 - 4t + 8$

**7**  $N = 3000e^{0.02t} + 5000$, 35 days; $\dfrac{dN}{dt} = \dfrac{1}{50}N - F$;
  since $N$ decreases, $\dfrac{dN}{dt} < 0$ but $\left|\dfrac{dN}{dt}\right|$ gets larger,
  so $N$ decreases with increasing rapidity.

**8**  (a)  $T = 470 - 6x$, $360\,°C$
  (b)  $\dfrac{dT}{dx} = -kx$, $T = 380 - \frac{1}{10}x^2$

**9**  (a)  $q = Q\left(1 - (1-\lambda)e^{-kt}\right)$

**10**  2 minutes; $\frac{1}{4}\pi$

**11**  (a)  12, $4\frac{1}{2}$, rate of increase $\to 0$, $N$ will
  never exceed 500
  (c)  $t = 10\ln\dfrac{N}{500-N} + k$, $t = 10\ln\dfrac{4N}{500-N}$,
  18 years

**12**  $p = \dfrac{mAe^{kt}}{1 + Ae^{kt}}$; 54 000;
  $\displaystyle\int_{30\,000}^{54\,000} \dfrac{5}{p\left(1 - \left(\frac{1}{100\,000}p\right)^5\right)}\,dp$, 3.0 years

## 10  Integration by substitution

### Exercise 10A (page 132)

**1**  (a)  $2\ln\left|\sqrt{x}-2\right| + k$   (b)  $-\dfrac{1}{3(3x+4)} + k$
  (c)  $2\cos\left(\frac{1}{3}\pi - \frac{1}{2}x\right) + k$
  (d)  $\frac{1}{6}(x-1)^6 + \frac{1}{7}(x-1)^7 + k$
    $\equiv \frac{1}{42}(6x+1)(x-1)^6 + k$

  (e)  $\ln(1+e^x) + k$   (f)  $\frac{1}{2}\ln(3+4\sqrt{x}) + k$
  (g)  $\frac{6}{5}(x+2)^{\frac{5}{2}} - 4(x+2)^{\frac{3}{2}} + k$
    $\equiv \frac{2}{5}(3x+4)(x+2)^{\frac{3}{2}} + k$
  (h)  $6(x-3)^{\frac{1}{2}} + \frac{2}{3}(x-3)^{\frac{3}{2}} + k$
    $\equiv \frac{2}{3}(x+6)\sqrt{x-3} + k$
  (i)  $\ln(\ln x) + k$   (j)  $\sin^{-1}\left(\frac{1}{2}x\right) + k$

**2**  (a)  $\frac{1}{20}(2x+1)^5 - \frac{1}{16}(2x+1)^4 + k$
    $\equiv \frac{1}{80}(8x-1)(2x+1)^4 + k$
  (b)  $\frac{1}{28}(2x-3)^7 + \frac{7}{24}(2x-3)^6 + k$
    $\equiv \frac{1}{168}(12x+31)(2x-3)^6 + k$
  (c)  $\frac{1}{6}(2x-1)^{\frac{3}{2}} + \frac{1}{10}(2x-1)^{\frac{5}{2}} + k$
    $\equiv \frac{1}{15}(3x+1)(2x-1)^{\frac{3}{2}} + k$
  (d)  $4(x-4)^{\frac{1}{2}} + \frac{2}{3}(x-4)^{\frac{3}{2}} + k$
    $\equiv \frac{2}{3}(x+2)\sqrt{x-4} + k$
  (e)  $\ln|x+1| + \dfrac{1}{x+1} + k$
  (f)  $\frac{1}{2}x - \frac{3}{4}\ln|2x+3| + k$
  (g)  $\frac{1}{3}\sin^{-1}3x + k$
  (h)  $\frac{8}{3}\sin^{-1}\frac{3}{4}x + \frac{1}{2}x\sqrt{16-9x^2} + k$
  (i)  $\frac{1}{2}\ln(2e^x + 1) + k$
  (j)  $\frac{3}{5}(x+1)^{\frac{5}{3}} - \frac{3}{2}(x+1)^{\frac{2}{3}} + k$
    $\equiv \frac{3}{10}(2x-3)(x+1)^{\frac{2}{3}} + k$
  (k)  $\dfrac{x}{\sqrt{1-x^2}} + k$
  (l)  $-2\sqrt{x} - 4\ln\left|2-\sqrt{x}\right| + k$

**3**  (b)  $\tan^{-1}e^x + k$

**4**  (a)  $\frac{1}{2}\ln\left|\dfrac{e^x+1}{e^x-1}\right| + k$   (b)  $2\ln\dfrac{\sqrt{x}}{\sqrt{x}+1} + k$

**5**  (a)  $x\cos^{-1}x - \sqrt{1-x^2} + k$
  (b)  $x\tan^{-1}x - \frac{1}{2}\ln(1+x^2) + k$
  (c)  $x\left((\ln x)^2 - 2\ln x + 2\right) + k$

### Exercise 10B (page 134)

**1**  (a)  $\ln\left(\frac{1}{2}(1+e)\right)$   (b)  $2\ln 2$   (c)  $\frac{13}{42}$
  (d)  $1\frac{1}{15}$   (e)  $\frac{1}{6}\pi$   (f)  $109\frac{1}{15}$
  (g)  $8\pi$   (h)  $\frac{1}{2}\left(\tan^{-1}3 - \tan^{-1}\frac{1}{2}\right) = \frac{1}{8}\pi$
  (i)  $\frac{1}{2}$   (j)  $\frac{1}{3}\sqrt{3}$   (k)  $3\ln\frac{4}{3}$   (l)  $\frac{1}{2}\pi - 1$

**2** $\frac{1}{4}\pi - \frac{1}{2}$

**3** (a) $\frac{1}{4}\pi$    (b) $\frac{1}{2}\pi$    (c) $\frac{1}{6}\pi$

    (d) $\pi$    (e) $1 - \frac{1}{2}\sqrt{2}$    (f) $\frac{1}{2}\pi$

**4** (a) $\dfrac{1}{2(\ln 2)^2}$    (b) $\ln 2$

    (c) $2(1 - \ln 2)$    (d) $1$

**7** $\pi$

## Exercise 10C (page 137)

**1** (a) $\frac{1}{4}(x^2 + 1)^4 + k$   (b) $\frac{1}{3}(4 + x^2)^{\frac{3}{2}} + k$

    (c) $\frac{1}{6}\sin^6 x + k$    (d) $\frac{1}{4}\tan^4 x + k$

    (e) $-\sqrt{1 - x^4} + k$    (f) $-\frac{1}{8}\cos^4 2x + k$

**2** (a) $-\frac{1}{12}(1 - x^2)^6 + k$    (b) $-\frac{1}{6}(3 - 2x^2)^{\frac{3}{2}} + k$

    (c) $-\frac{1}{63}(5 - 3x^3)^7 + k$    (d) $\frac{2}{3}\sqrt{1 + x^3} + k$

    (e) $\frac{1}{4}\sec^4 x + k$    (f) $\frac{1}{16}\sin^4 4x + k$

**3** (a) $\ln(1 + \sin x) + k$    (b) $\frac{1}{3}\ln\left|1 + x^3\right| + k$

    (c) $\ln|\sin x| + k$    (d) $\ln(4 + e^x) + k$

    (e) $-\frac{2}{3}\ln\left|5 - e^{3x}\right| + k$    (f) $\frac{1}{3}\ln|\sec 3x| + k$

**4** (a) $\frac{2}{3}$    (b) $78$

    (c) $\frac{1}{12}(4 - \sqrt{2})$    (d) $\ln(e + 1)$

    (e) $\frac{860}{3}\sqrt{2}$    (f) $\frac{1}{6}$

    (g) $\frac{2}{3}(10\sqrt{10} - 1)$    (h) $\frac{1}{2}\ln 2$

    (i) $\frac{1}{2}\ln\frac{4}{3}$    (j) $\frac{1}{3}$

    (k) $\dfrac{1}{n + 1}$    (l) $\frac{7}{3}$

**5** $\dfrac{1}{2(n - 1)}\left(1 - \dfrac{1}{(1 + a^2)^{n-1}}\right)$ if $n \neq 1$,

    $\frac{1}{2}\ln(1 + a^2)$ if $n = 1$; $n > 1$, $\dfrac{1}{2(n - 1)}$

## Miscellaneous exercise 10 (page 138)

**1** $\frac{1}{2}\ln|2x - 1| - \dfrac{1}{2(2x - 1)} + k$

**2** $\frac{1}{6}\tan^{-1}\frac{2}{3}x + k$

**3** $\frac{1}{110}$

**4** $\frac{1}{2}\tan^{-1}\frac{1}{2}e^x + k$

**5** $\ln(1 + 3x^2) + k$

**6** $\frac{1}{2}\ln 10$

**7** $\frac{2}{5}\sin^5 x + k$

**8** $2\sqrt{x} - 2\ln(1 + \sqrt{x}) + k$

**11** $\frac{1}{54}(3x - 1)^6 + \frac{1}{45}(3x - 1)^5 + k$

**12** $\frac{1}{8}\pi + \frac{1}{4}$

**13** $\pi(8\ln 2 - 3)$

**14** (a) $0.70$    (c) $1.69$

    (d) $\pi\left(\frac{1}{4} + \frac{3}{32}\pi\right) \approx 1.71$

**15** $1.701$; $\frac{1}{4}\ln 1201$

**16** (a) $0.792$    (c) $0.748$

**17** $3\pi a^2$, $5\pi^2 a^3$

**18** $\frac{1}{4}\pi c^2$, $\frac{1}{3}\pi c^3$

**19** $\frac{3}{8}\pi a^2$

# 11 Curves defined implicitly

## Exercise 11A (page 146)

**1** (a) $\frac{3}{4}$   (b) $6$   (c) $\frac{3}{4}$   (d) $-\frac{1}{2}$

**2** (a) $(\pm 1, 0), \left(0, \pm\frac{1}{2}\right)$   (c) $y = \pm\left(\frac{1}{2} - \frac{1}{4}x^2\right)$

    (e) $x = \pm(1 - 2y^2)$

**3** (a) $(\pm 1, 0)$

    (c) There are no values of $y$ for small values of $x$.

    (e) $x = \pm\left(1 + \frac{1}{2}y^2\right)$

**4** (a) $(1, 0)$, $(0, 1)$    (b) $y < 0$

    (c) $\dfrac{2(x - 1)}{3y^2}$, $-\frac{2}{3}$

    (d) The modulus of the gradient becomes very large.

**5** $-\frac{1}{3}$

**6** $3x - 2y = 8$

**7** $x - 2y = 7$, $-\frac{86}{13}$

**9** (b) $\dfrac{dy}{dx} = -e^{x-y}$

    (c) Both $x$ and $y$ are less than $\ln 2$.

**10** (a) The curve is symmetrical about the $y$-axis.

    (b) $\dfrac{dy}{dx} = -\dfrac{2x}{3y^2}$; when $x$ is positive $\dfrac{dy}{dx}$ is negative, and vice versa.

    (c) maximum

**11** $(0, 0)$, $(-1, 0)$; $0$, $1$

**12** 1, −2 and 1 at $(0,0)$, $(0,1)$ and $(0,2)$ respectively

## Exercise 11B (page 151)

**1** (a) $y^3 = x^3 + k$    (b) $y^2 = x^2 + k$

   (c) $y = c e^{\frac{1}{2}x^2}$    (d) $y^2 = \sqrt{2\ln|x| + k}$

**2** $y = \dfrac{4x}{x+1}$

**3** $x^2 + y^2 = k$; a set of circles, centre $(0,0)$, $x^2 + y^2 = 25$

**4** $(x+1)^2 + (y-2)^2 = k$, circles, centre $(-1,2)$

**5** (a) $y = \sqrt{2} x^{\frac{3}{2}}$    (b) $y = 8\sqrt{2} x^{-\frac{3}{2}}$

   (c) $\sin y = \frac{1}{2} - \cos x$    (d) $\cos y = 2\cos x$

**6** $v^2 = k - \omega^2 x^2$, $v^2 = \omega^2\left(a^2 - x^2\right)$

**7** (a) $y^2 + 1 = k\left(x^2 + 1\right)^2$, $k > 0$

   (b) $\sec y = c\sec x, c \neq 0$

**8** (a) $y = \dfrac{2}{2-x}$    (b) $2\sin x \cos y = 1$

   (c) $y = \sqrt{\dfrac{2}{x-1}}$    (d) $y = 2\sec x$

**9** (a) $y = \dfrac{2\left(1 - kx^4\right)}{1 + kx^4}$    (b) $y = \ln(k + x\ln x)$

   (c) $y^2 = 4\left(k + \tan\frac{1}{2}x\right)$

**10** $y = kx^n$

**11** (a) $n = 5000 e^{0.01(0.05t - 50\sin 0.02t)}$

   (b) 3150

**12** $v^2 = \dfrac{20R^2}{x} + V^2 - 20R$

## Exercise 11C (page 155)

**1** (a) $y + x\dfrac{dy}{dx}$    (b) $y^2 + 2xy\dfrac{dy}{dx}$

   (c) $2xy^2 + 2x^2 y\dfrac{dy}{dx}$    (d) $\dfrac{2xy - x^2\dfrac{dy}{dx}}{y^2}$

**2** (a) $\dfrac{y + x\dfrac{dy}{dx}}{2\sqrt{xy}}$    (b) $\left(2xy + x^2\dfrac{dy}{dx}\right)\cos\left(x^2 y\right)$

   (c) $\dfrac{1}{x} + \dfrac{1}{y}\dfrac{dy}{dx}$    (d) $\left(y + x\dfrac{dy}{dx} + \dfrac{dy}{dx}\right)e^{xy+y}$

**3** (a) $-\frac{4}{3}$    (b) $\frac{20}{11}$

**4** (a) $-\frac{1}{3}\sqrt{3}$   (b) 0   (c) −2    (d) $-\frac{1}{3}\pi$

**5** $3y = x + 5$

**6** $x = 1$

**7** $(3,1)$, $(-3,-1)$

**8** (a) −1    (b) $\frac{1}{3}$

   (c) $(0,0)$, there are two branches there, one parallel to each axis; $\left(2^{\frac{1}{3}}, 2^{\frac{2}{3}}\right)$, $\left(2^{\frac{2}{3}}, 2^{\frac{1}{3}}\right)$

**9** (a) $\left(x^2 + y^2\right)^2 \geqslant 0$ so $x^2 - y^2 \geqslant 0$

   (b) $\left(\pm\frac{1}{4}\sqrt{6}, \pm\frac{1}{4}\sqrt{2}\right)$, $(\pm 1, 0)$

## Miscellaneous exercise 11 (page 156)

**1** (a) $400x^2 + 25y^2 = 4$

   (b) $(\pm 0.1, 0)$, $(0, \pm 0.4)$

**2** $5x - 13y + 3 = 0$

**3** (a) $\dfrac{x-y}{x-4y}$, $(2,2)$, $(-2,-2)$

   (b) $2x - y = 3\sqrt{3}$

**4** $y = \pm\sqrt{k(x-1)^2 e^{2x} + 1}$

**5** $\ln y = \frac{1}{4} + \left(-\frac{1}{4} + \frac{1}{2}x\right)e^{2x}$

**6** $3x - 7y = 13$

**7** $y^2 = 1 + c\operatorname{cosec} 2x$

**8** $y = \dfrac{3}{\ln\dfrac{x+1}{x-2} - k}$, $y = \dfrac{3}{\ln\dfrac{e^3(x+1)}{2(x-2)}}$

**9** $y = \sqrt[3]{\frac{1}{4}(4 + 6x - 3\sin 2x)}$

**10** $(1+y)e^{-y} = (1-x)e^x$

**11** (a) $\dfrac{2 + x - 2xy}{2 + x^2}$    (b) $(2,1)$, $\left(-1, \frac{1}{2}\right)$

**12** (a) $\dfrac{a^2}{x^2} + \dfrac{b^2}{y^2} = 4$

**13** $P = 600 e^{kt}$, $P = 600 e^{0.005t - 0.4\sin 0.02t}$; the model $P = 600 e^{kt}$ is not consistent with the data; the model $P = 600 e^{0.005t - 0.4\sin 0.02t}$ is consistent with the data, given to the nearest 100. Smallest number is 549.

**14** 3, maximum; −3, minimum

**15** (a) $P = P_0 e^{\sin kt}$    (b) $e^2$

16  (a)  According to the model, £745.

(b)  £$\frac{400}{3}\sqrt{5}$ per hour, which is approximately £298 per hour.

17  (a)  $\dfrac{1}{1-8y^3}$

(c)  1; since $\dfrac{d^2y}{dx^2}$ is zero at the origin, but positive close to the origin, the curve has a point of inflexion there of the same orientation as $y=x^3$.

18  4

19  0.185; minimum

# 12 Scalar products of vectors

## Exercise 12A (page 165)

1  $-8$, 11, 3

2  11, $-3$, 8

3  18, 0, 0; **r** is perpendicular to both **p** and **q**.

4  (a) and (d) are perpendicular; so are (b) and (c).

5  $-4$, $-8$, $-12$

6  (a)  5       (b)  $\sqrt{5}$       (c)  $\sqrt{5}$       (d)  1
    (e)  3       (f)  13       (g)  5       (h)  $\sqrt{6}$
    (i)  $\sqrt{5}$       (j)  $\sqrt{13}$       (k)  $\sqrt{30}$       (l)  2

7  5, $\begin{pmatrix}\frac{4}{5}\\-\frac{3}{5}\end{pmatrix}$

8  $\begin{pmatrix}\frac{1}{3}\\-\frac{2}{3}\\\frac{2}{3}\end{pmatrix}$, $\frac{2}{3}\mathbf{i}-\frac{1}{3}\mathbf{j}+\frac{2}{3}\mathbf{k}$

9  15.3°

10  (a)  45°       (b)  167.3°       (c)  180°
    (d)  136.7°       (e)  7.0°       (f)  90°

11  $\sqrt{(x_2-x_1)^2+(y_2-y_1)^2}$ ; the distance between the points with position vectors $\mathbf{r}_1$ and $\mathbf{r}_2$.

12  $\frac{4}{65}\sqrt{65}$

13  0

14  172.2° (or 7.8°)

15  99.6° (or 80.4°)

16  70.5°

17  76.4°

18  48.2°

19  48.2°

20  (a)  $\begin{pmatrix}-b\\a\end{pmatrix}$ or $\begin{pmatrix}b\\-a\end{pmatrix}$       (b)  $\begin{pmatrix}\dfrac{a}{\sqrt{a^2+b^2}}\\\dfrac{b}{\sqrt{a^2+b^2}}\end{pmatrix}$

(c)  $\mathbf{r}=\begin{pmatrix}p\\q\end{pmatrix}+t\begin{pmatrix}\dfrac{a}{\sqrt{a^2+b^2}}\\\dfrac{b}{\sqrt{a^2+b^2}}\end{pmatrix}$

(d)  $-\dfrac{ap+bq+c}{\sqrt{a^2+b^2}}$ , $\left|\dfrac{ap+bq+c}{\sqrt{a^2+b^2}}\right|$

## Exercise 12B (page 169)

4  $\mathbf{b}-\mathbf{a}$, $\mathbf{b}-\mathbf{c}$; $(\mathbf{b}-\mathbf{a})\cdot(\mathbf{b}-\mathbf{a})=(\mathbf{b}-\mathbf{c})\cdot(\mathbf{b}-\mathbf{c})$

5  (a)  $\hat{\mathbf{a}}+\hat{\mathbf{b}}$ is in the direction of the bisector of the angle between the directions of $\hat{\mathbf{a}}$ and $\hat{\mathbf{b}}$.

(b)  $\dfrac{1}{a}\mathbf{a}$, $\dfrac{1}{b}\mathbf{b}$

(c)  $\dfrac{b}{a+b}\mathbf{a}+\dfrac{a}{a+b}\mathbf{b}$

6  (c)  $\mathbf{h}\cdot\mathbf{b}=\mathbf{c}\cdot\mathbf{b}$, $\mathbf{h}\cdot\mathbf{a}=\mathbf{b}\cdot\mathbf{a}$, $\mathbf{h}\cdot\mathbf{c}=\mathbf{b}\cdot\mathbf{c}$; the edges $OA$ and $BC$ are perpendicular to each other.

## Miscellaneous exercise 12 (page 169)

1  (a)  $\mathbf{r}=\begin{pmatrix}2\\-1\\3\end{pmatrix}+t\begin{pmatrix}-1\\1\\2\end{pmatrix}$       (b)  21°

2  **a** and **b**, **a** and **c**, **b** and **c**, **b** and **d**

3  58.5°

4  (a)  $\mathbf{d}=\begin{pmatrix}9\\4\\-5\end{pmatrix}$       (b)  $\begin{pmatrix}3\\3\\0\end{pmatrix}$       (c)  120.5°

5  (a)  $x\mathbf{i}$, $-\frac{1}{2}x\mathbf{i}+\frac{1}{2}\sqrt{3}x\mathbf{j}$, $-\frac{1}{2}x\mathbf{i}-\frac{1}{2}\sqrt{3}x\mathbf{j}$

(b)  (i)  $\overrightarrow{AP}=\overrightarrow{OP}-\overrightarrow{OA}$
     (ii)  $-x\mathbf{i}+30\mathbf{k}$, $\frac{1}{2}x\mathbf{i}-\frac{1}{2}\sqrt{3}x\mathbf{j}+30\mathbf{k}$

(c)  $30\sqrt{2}$

6  (a)  7, 7       (b)  $-32$       (c)  130.8°

**7**   $\dfrac{\mathbf{i}-3\mathbf{j}-2\mathbf{k}}{\sqrt{14}}$, $\dfrac{3\mathbf{i}+\mathbf{j}-2\mathbf{k}}{\sqrt{14}}$, $73.4°$

**8**   (a)   $0.148$

**9**   (a)   $\sqrt{29}$    (b)   $119.9°$ ( or $60.1°$)

**10**   (a)   (i)   $\begin{pmatrix} \frac{5}{2}\sqrt{2} \\ 0 \\ \frac{5}{2}\sqrt{2} \end{pmatrix}$    (b)   $90°$

**11**   (a)   $60°$    (b)   $\frac{3}{2}\sqrt{3}$

**13**   (a)   $\mathbf{r}=\mathbf{c}+t\mathbf{u}$,   $t^2+2\mathbf{c}\cdot\mathbf{u}t+\left(\mathbf{c}\cdot\mathbf{c}-a^2\right)=0$

     (b)   $\left(\mathbf{c}\cdot\mathbf{u}\right)^2=\mathbf{c}\cdot\mathbf{c}-a^2$

     (c)   The radius to a sphere at the point of contact of a tangent is perpendicular to the tangent.

## Revision exercise 2

**(page 172)**

**1**   (a)   $\ln 2$       (b)   $\sqrt{3}\pi-\frac{1}{3}\pi^2$

**2**   (a)   $p=2r(2\cos\theta+\sin\theta)$

     (b)   $r^2$

     (c)   $0.8r^2$

**3**   (a)   $-\sin\theta\cos^2\theta$    (b)   $3x+8y=15$

**4**   $\dfrac{\frac{1}{4}}{1+x}+\dfrac{\frac{1}{4}}{3-x}$, $\dfrac{\frac{1}{16}}{(1+x)^2}+\dfrac{\frac{1}{16}}{(3-x)^2}+\dfrac{\frac{1}{32}}{1+x}+\dfrac{\frac{1}{32}}{3-x}$;

     $\frac{1}{2}\ln 3$, $\left(\frac{1}{12}+\frac{1}{16}\ln 3\right)\pi$

**5**   (a)   $5$    (b)   $5$    (c)   $\frac{1}{4}\pi$

**7**   (b)   $P=108\,000e^{0.001(10-m)t}$

     (c)   For example, no immigration or emigration.

     (d)   $m=10(1-\ln 2)$

     (e)   If the death rate were zero, that is, the lowest possible, the population would take $100\ln 2\approx 69$ to double.

**8**   $1.97$;   $500$, $3550$

**9**   (a)   4 metres    (c)   $-\mathbf{k}$, $2\mathbf{i}$

     (d)   $\left(\frac{1}{5}t\right)\mathbf{i}-6\mathbf{j}+\left(\frac{1}{10}t-2\right)\mathbf{k}$, $\frac{1}{20}t^2-\frac{2}{5}t+40$, $6.26$ m

**10**   (a)   $\dfrac{4-3x}{2\sqrt{2-x}}$    (b)   $-\frac{2}{15}(4+3x)(2-x)^{\frac{3}{2}}+k$

**11**   $(4,-2)$, $(-4,2)$; $\left(2\sqrt{5},-\frac{4}{5}\sqrt{5}\right)$, $\left(-2\sqrt{5},\frac{4}{5}\sqrt{5}\right)$

**12**   $1-t\tan t$,   $y=\sqrt{1-x^2}\,\sin^{-1}x$

## Mock examinations

### Mock examination 1 (page 174)

**1**   $y=-\ln\left(1+\frac{1}{2}\cos 2x\right)$

**2**   $\frac{1}{168}(12x+1)(2x-1)^6+k$

**3**   $\dfrac{2x-3x^2}{(1-2x)^{\frac{3}{2}}}$,   $1+x+\frac{3}{2}x^2+\frac{5}{2}x^3$

**4**   (i)   $2\sqrt{2}$

     (ii)   $\theta=2\pi-\alpha$

**5**   (i)   inside

     (ii)   $x+y=1$

**6**   $\dfrac{3}{x-2}-\dfrac{4}{2x+1}$,   $\ln\frac{45}{8}$

**7**   $4,\frac{1}{4}$; $3\frac{3}{4},-3\frac{3}{4}$

     (i)   $-\frac{17}{15}$,   $17x+15y=16$

     (ii)   $x^2-y^2=4$

**8**   (i)   $\dfrac{dy}{dx}=-\dfrac{41x+12y}{12x+34y}$

**9**   (i)   $(2,1,1)$

     (ii)   $1.2$

     (iii)   $(2,3,-1)$

### Mock examination 2 (page 176)

**1**   $\frac{2}{3}$

**2**   $\dfrac{\frac{1}{4}}{x}+\dfrac{\frac{1}{4}}{4-x}$,   $\frac{1}{2}\ln 3$

**3**   (i)   $2xe^{2x}+2x^2e^{2x}$    (ii)   $\frac{1}{2}xe^{2x}-\frac{1}{4}e^{2x}+k$

**4**   (i)   $1+4x-8x^2$,   $1+2x+6x^2$

     (ii)   $1+6x+6x^2$,   $-\frac{1}{8}<x<\frac{1}{8}$

**5**   $\ln n=1-e^{-0.01t}+\ln 5000$, it approaches $5000e\approx 13\,600$

**6**   (i)   The point does not lie on the line.

     (ii)   $\begin{pmatrix} -5 \\ -3 \\ 2 \end{pmatrix}$

     (iii)   The lines do not meet.

**7**   (i)   $OQ=6\sin\theta-4\cos\theta$

     (iii)   $26$, $78.7°$

**8**   $\dfrac{\sin\theta+\cos\theta}{\sin\theta-\cos\theta}$,

     $\cos\theta=\frac{1}{2}(x+y-3)$,   $\sin\theta=\frac{1}{2}(x-y+1)$

     $(x-1)^2+(y-2)^2=2$,   $(1,2)$, $\sqrt{2}$

# Index

The page numbers refer to the first mention of each term, or the shaded box if there is one.